Class, Culture and Social Change

A New View of the 1930s

Class, Culture and Social Change

A New View of the 1930s

Edited by

FRANK GLOVERSMITH
School of English and American Studies,
University of Sussex

With a Foreword by
ASA BRIGGS

THE HARVESTER PRESS · SUSSEX
HUMANITIES PRESS · NEW JERSEY

First published in England in 1980 by
THE HARVESTER PRESS LIMITED
Publishers: John Spiers and Margaret A. Boden
16 Ship Street, Brighton, Sussex

and in the USA by
HUMANITIES PRESS INC.,
Atlantic Highlands, New Jersey 07716

British Library Cataloguing in Publication Data
Class, culture and social change.
1. Great Britain – History – George V, 1910-1936 – Addresses, essays, lectures 2. Great Britain – History – Edward VIII, 1936 – Addresses, essays, lectures 3. Great Britain – History – George VI, 1936-1952 – Addresses, essays, lectures
941.083'08 DA578

ISBN 0-85527-938-9

Humanities Press Inc.
ISBN 0-391-01739-X

Printed in Great Britain by
St. Edmundsbury Press, Bury St. Edmunds

This book is dedicated, affectionately, to the memory of Tom Harrisson: world-traveller, anthropologist, founder of Mass Observation. Unstinting in giving time and friendly encouragement, in talking to and with us. From the several generations of students and tutors on the Sussex 1930s courses: Thank you.

Contents

Contributors

Asa Briggs (Baron Briggs) is the Provost of Worcester College, Oxford, and was formerly Professor of History and Vice-Chancellor of the University of Sussex. His publications include *Victorian People, The Age of Improvement, 1783-1867, The History of Broadcasting in the United Kingdom* (4 vols.), *Victorian Cities* and *Governing the BBC*. He is editor of Chartist Studies.

Martin Ceadel is Fellow and Tutor in Politics at New College, Oxford, and was formerly Lecturer in History at the University of Sussex and at Imperial College, London. He is author of *Pacifism in Britain 1914-45: The Defining of a Faith.*

John Coombes is Lecturer in Literature at the University of Essex, where he is Director the MA course in the Sociology of Literature. In 1980 he will be Visiting Lecturer at the University of Algeria. He has published articles on Marx's 18th Brumaire, George Orwell, Foucault, Edgell Rickword and Charles Péguy. He is at present engaged in research and writing on literature and the Left in France and England in the 1930s.

Valentine Cunningham is Fellow and Tutor in English Literature at Corpus Christi College, Oxford, and Visiting Professor at Amherst College, USA. He is author of *Everywhere Spoken Against: Dissent in the Victorian Novel*, and editor of *The Penguin Book of Spanish Civil War Verse*. His latest book, a study of literature and society in the 1930s, will be published in 1980.

Frank Gloversmith was part-time Tutor at Queens' College, Cambridge from 1962 to 1964. He is now Lecturer in English and American Studies at the University of Sussex, and Visiting Professor at the University of California at Berkeley, the University of Pittsburgh, and at the University of Munich. He is author of *D.H. Lawrence: The Rainbow,* and editor of *Wives and Daughters* by Elizabeth Gaskell. In February 1972 he organized a '1930s' colloquium at the University of Sussex. He is advisory editor of a new series of bibliographies of British, American and European writers, to be published by the Harvester Press.

Alun Howkins is Lecturer in Modern History at the School of Cultural and Community Studies, University of Sussex, and a member of the editorial collective of 'History Workshop Journal'.

He has published articles on agricultural history, the rural labour movement, the decline of Liberalism and the rise of Labour movements. He is co-author of *Trends in Leisure, 1919-39*.

Stuart Laing is Lecturer in English at the School of Cultural and Community Studies, University of Sussex, and author of a study of Walter Greenwood's *Love on the Dole*.

Jane Lewis is Lecturer in the Social Administration Department at the London School of Economics. She is author of 'The English Birth-Control Movement in the Interwar Period' and 'The English Movement for Family Allowance', and her first book, *The Politics of Motherhood: The Child and Maternal Welfare Movement, 1900-39*, will soon be published.

John Lowerson is Lecturer in History at the Centre for Continuing Education, University of Sussex. He is editor of *Southern History*, and author of *A Short History of Sussex* and *Victorian Sussex*, and co-author of *Time to Spare in Victorian England* and *Trends in Leisure 1919-39*.

David Mellor is Lecturer in the History of Art at the School of English and American Studies, University of Sussex. He has written essays and monographs on twentieth-century painters and photographers for the Arts Council, and has organized several exhibitions: 'The Real Thing' and 'Cityscapes' (for the Arts Council) and an exhibition of Mass Observation photographs by Humphrey Spender.

Foreword

We were already separated from the 1930s by more than a generation, not to speak of a whole World War, when I discussed with Tom Harrisson the possibility of creating a Mass Observation Archive at the University of Sussex. The discussions were stimulating and fruitful, and they properly ended with a great party. The thousands of items in the new Archive began to look neat and tidy for the first time in their brief history. Alas, when history begins to look neat and tidy, the life may be going out of it. This book proves that for its authors, at least, there is still life in the issues of the 1930s. Yet within a few months of the meeting Tom, who loved life, was dead.

The Archive is an invaluable collection of primary source material, unique in this country. Yet even before it was assembled and catalogued at the University of Sussex—and much still remains to be done—the young university, child of a very different decade from the 1930s, was keenly interested in what Frank Gloversmith, editor of this collection of essays, calls a 'key decade'.

There were four reasons for the interest. First, and simplest, many of the characters most associated with the 1930s lived in Sussex — or had lived there for part of their lives. Kingsley Martin was one of them, and he frequently lectured at the University. Of course, such people usually represented only one element of the experience of the 1930s. Brighton was not Jarrow, nor was Lewes Bolton. Yet the Sussex 'men of the 1930s' were articulate, and they wanted to communicate, not to escape. Second, and equally simple, it was my personal ambition to make the University of Sussex a centre of 'contemporary' historical studies, to attract to it papers as well as people, to develop the resources of oral and visual history, to encourage not only research but argument. There were other universities in the country suited to the development of quite different fields of study. Sussex should be distinctive. Third, our related stress on inter-disciplinary work made the 1930s a tempting territory to explore. The economic history of the period was under review. The social history fascinated undergraduates. The political history carried messages. The cultural history was ripe for fresh examination. How British history — still the history of sub-cultures — was related to European history or to world history was still very little appreciated, except perhaps in relation to the experience of the Spanish Civil War. Interdisciplinary work is not the same as multi-disciplinary work, putting different disciplines and their contributions to knowledge side by side: it means a search through divergent methodologies and converging insights for interconnections. The complexity of this task contrasts with the simplicity of the first two drives behind Sussex's interest in the 1930s.

The fourth reason was related very closely to the other three. Just because we were a generation away from the 1930s — and by 'we' I mean undergraduates more than academic colleagues — our curiosity was stirred. G.M. Young seems to me to have got nearer than any other historian to understanding the intricate interplay of different generations. There was no interest in the 1950s and not much in the 1940s during the early 1960s. At the end of the decade Vietnam mattered, not Korea. Baldwin was beginning to interest more than Attlee and unemployment more than full employment. The decade of the 1960s had begun with the publication of Julian Symons' *The Thirties: A Dream Revolved* in which the author, born in 1912, introduced himself as 'a standard Thirties model ... sharing deep admiration of Auden's poetry and to a less extent of Auden–Isherwood plays, and the typical Thirties tendency to insist that works of art must be seen first of all as events in society and yet to say that form and style were vitally important to an artist'.

By the end of the 1960s, Symons' testimony did not stand alone. There had been a burst of new writing, proliferating, asserting and counter-asserting, qualifying. There was no longer — if there ever had been — one single image of a lost decade. There were almost as many images as there were of Edwardian England, another favourite decade for study. And the images reflected contrasting experience as well as, or more than, contrasting ideology. The contrasts in the experience of the 1930s had been a major topic while the decade lasted. Statistics had focused on them just as much as the camera did. As for the contrasts in ideology, they had led to genuine confrontation. There is rather more on ideology in the essays in this volume than on experience, although the relationship between the two is frequently considered. Storm Jameson's perceptive article on 'Documentary', published in *Fact* in 1937, is rightly singled out by Stuart Laing as a key document for a key decade.

How the historiography of the period has changed and is changing can be explained only in terms of both the background and habits of historians and the new twists and turns in history itself. A simplified version of the process is set out in Frank Gloversmith's account of Auden's revisions of his own pre-war poems. In Auden's case, however, he wanted to eliminate much of the topical entanglement, and the victim was history, not the History with a capital H, which he systematically changed throughout into a small h. There have been Marxists, too, who have tried to blot out characters and themes from re-written official history, and it is all too easy to produce a version of the 1930s that leaves out the fact — dare I add 'for example'? — that it ended in 1939 with a German–Soviet Pact. It is for these and other reasons that there is much to be said for going back to the original source, or rather sources — tinged though they may sometimes be by sentimentality, as David Mellor shows — or by nostalgia, sometimes more difficult to pin down. As Mellor recalls, when a popular newspaper ran a competition in 1935 for photographs of Britain there were two categories — 'the picturesque old Britain' with its 'traditional pastimes and toil', and 'the new Britain embodying all that is best in twentieth-century work, life and social custom. I myself turn back most naturally to J.B. Priestley when I want to place all this in perspective, for he had been brought up, as I was, in industrial Britain, which then came somewhere in between, neither 'traditional' nor 'new'. It is only recently that the nostalgia has begun to gather around that.

David Mellor's essay is illuminating because it brings art — and architecture — into the picture as well as literature, and this is a welcome development in recent historiography. Yet there is more to be said about the architecture, and more has already been said on the film, the Press and radio. These essays from inside and outside the University of Sussex do not aim at completeness. Clearly, not all the preoccupations of a decade can be discussed; many other 1930s voices are to be heard; as an historian, I would want to indicate other places on the map, to foreground economic and political analyses. But economic and political conformations can also be discerned in the shapes of experiences and attitudes – social, cultural, ideological, imaginative – often misleadingly displaced to subordinate or to peripheral areas. (e.g. women's experience – see chapter 8; or living in, or thinking about, the countryside – see chapter 10.) The writers here bring together social history, the sociology of art and literature, political and ideological debate, cultural theory and socio-cultural practice, to suggest some of the ways they interpenetrate in our understanding the living moments. The terrain is complex, the experiences are multiple, intriguing, significant. The contours of the 1930s are still to be fully charted: there can be no finality in the historiography. Louis MacNeice's *Autumn Journal* concludes too firmly:

> 'There will be time to audit
> The accounts later, there will be sunlight later
> And the equation will come out at last.'

I should add that MacNeice was writing with the University of Oxford in the background:

I hasten to explain
That having once been to the University of Oxford
You can never really again
Believe anything that anyone says and that of course is an asset
In a world like ours.'

That was not the mood of the University of Sussex in 1961 nor in 1968. Professor C.L. Mowat might well have been writing an inaugural for the University in 1961 in his article on 'The Mood of the Thirties' which appeared in *The Critical Quarterly* in the autumn of that year, when the first fifty-one under-graduates were admitted: 'Raymond Williams' *Long Revolution*, despite certain shortcomings, reopens for writers and artists the question of the relationship between culture and society. In very different ways this was what the writers of the Thirties were concerned with. We may well find a new interest in their ideas and their work today.' Those are *our* contours.

ASA BRIGGS

Worcester College, Oxford, 1979

1 DEFINING CULTURE: J.C. POWYS, CLIVE BELL, R.H. TAWNEY & T.S. ELIOT

Frank Gloversmith

For the man of culture, philosophy is a means to cope with the chaos of reality, to facilitate the selecting, refining, sifting and analysing of conscious impressions, to discover and to create that 'secondary world' which is 'life in itself'. This indispensable removedness is a major, reiterated principle in John Cowper Powys' confident definitions of the meaning of culture.[1] Some constitutive element of the intransitive, the contemplative, is vital to the multiple aspects of his 'Analysis' and 'Application' of the complex, major term. The consciously developed 'awareness of existence' leads to 'an intensification of the cosmic-sense' — of things 'planetary or particular' — which now replaces the inevitably lost ecstacies of religious faith. The 'innermost thrill' out of all things comes from response to Nature and 'to whatever it may be that lies behind Nature'. Acquiring culture is then acquiring the art to gather these responses, impressions, and sensations into imaginative structures that 'give the seal of the eternal and the significant' to the 'impression-waves and thought-waves of the transitory and the meaningless'.

According to Powys, what is acquired to stimulate and to control this life-defining process is, ideally, the sum-total of great art — comprehending the works of writers, thinkers, artists and religious leaders. Their images and their passionate responses impregnate the cultured mind, tinting its roots, so that perceptivity itself is transmuted: 'What it sees is a fragment of Nature double-dyed', the imagination being 'already charged', reinforced, pre-focused. For the spiritual force of this universal cultural heritage is in its peculiar mode of being: not as artefacts, material objects, institutions, systems, but as 'worlds', 'ideas', which are 'spread out, like a Platonic over-world of ideal forms, just a little above the "real world" in which we spend our material being'. The authentically cultured mind is one that perceives, then, the equipoise of all these ideal forms, the spiritual and philosophical parity of their content when reduced to ideas: 'Truth lies . . . in the bringing close together, in full illuminating contrast, of the most opposite interpretations'. Vital to this pursuit of truth is abstention from reconciling, relating, or co-ordinating of these 'psychic contraries of history'. This openness and multiplexity — mis-described as 'dualism' by its proponent — creates the paradox of a familiarity with all creative visions, concomitant with adhesion to none. The fundamentally cultured mind can live here and now, for instance, 'according to Homer', who guides the choice of 'first and last things'; while avoiding all controversy and commitment: 'He will know that there is much good to be got out of every single heart-felt way of life'. The privilege of the cultured person is access to a free-standing position, a vantage-point from which to survey, dispassionately, all human involvements from the rigid and reactionary to the new-fashioned and fanatical.

This polarization of the general and the particular, an assumption of near-universal comprehensiveness, is the firmly designated philosophical fulcrum of Powys' autobiographical treatise. Much re-printed throughout the 1930s, widely read, translated, and winning 'an astonishing number of impassioned adherents', the proud author looking back finds its honesty sprang from its dealing with 'one's own culture'. After a decade, historical research and social observation are increasingly tempered by self-observation: 'My introspection seems to reveal a stronger belief than I used to have in the right of my own mind and in the power of my own mind *to re-create itself on lines selected by itself*'.[2] Yet this individualistic and idealistic preoccupation marked each and every specific conclusion inside the ambitiously generalized thematic rubrics: Culture and Philosophy, Culture and Human Relations, Culture and Destiny, etc. Powys early and revealingly adverts to the 'self's secret dialogue' — solitary and one-sided! — and its 'own secret orientation of life' (to which religion is a parallel and 'sister-cult'). A cultured nature is egocentric, and must achieve (as Pater recommends) a 'beautiful crystalline integrity, delicate and evasive, infinitely reserved, courteous and detached'. This becomes Powys' slogan, 'Sink into your own soul'. By such silence, and such a cultivation of interiority, 'the great and sacred is protected'. This is the mysterious reservoir of cosmic sensations, of ideal visions, images, 'moods' and 'worlds', fashioning and enhancing the individual's spiritual culture.

The mystification and the abstractness of these bizarrely cosmic speculations and philosophically pretentious formulations reduce themselves to the mean-spirited advice of 'Keep your culture to yourself . . . keep it for ever to yourself'. The gestures of generality fall away into a bleak and priggish advocacy of privatism. Gregariousness is an obstacle to intellectual or imaginative life: 'social pressure' wrecks the 'innate flavour' of intimate treasured reactions to life. The appended (1939) Conclusion asseverates in pietistic phrasing: 'True culture was, is and ever will be personal, individual, anarchistic'. Invoking 'all the high traditions of our race', Powys evangelically pronounces, of Culture: 'One thing it can do, and one thing alone: it can save the individual'. Of the insistent, irreconcilable claims of Self and of Others, the call for self-realization obliterates those for service to others, social kindness and 'brotherhood warmth'. (Punctuation authorially stresses the irreality of the concept.) 'Active goodness' is depicted as deleterious to 'the integrity of one's being'; and sociability is regressive, sustaining interests long outgrown by the refined selfhood. Culture here resists these popular preferences, being the source of energies 'to protect you from those arid and sterile moments when you find yourself forced to live in a group of people'.

The declared intention is pluralistic, comprehensive in scope, a consideration of every possible angle, and a tolerance of ideas and approaches that precludes rigidity of definition or dogmatism in conclusions. The achievement is singularly restrictive, though the tone and pitch of the rhetoric work mostly to suggest the desiderated fluidity and inclusiveness. The elisions of meaning inside Powys' reiterated key-term, 'culture', are multiple and obvious, and the cloudy phrasing hardly masks the sharp, ungenerous antipathies. The claims to philosophical detachment, rational argument, and scholarly critique are just not tenable. The thinness of texture, the paucity of arguments, and the illiberality of feelings betray unexamined nihilism (behind its 'mysticism') and a cynicism about human relationships (behind its defence of the 'cultured self'). The moods of rapture, exaltation, and of sudden access to the cosmic 'overworlds' are transparently linked to Powys' sense of a primordial, meaningless flux, the monstrosity of unmediated nature. However, there are homologous responses to raw exposure to social experience: the considered, rational tone, and the grandiloquent abstractions make even more transparent the profound distaste, which proffers itself as intellectual sympathy and social pity. In his section on 'Culture and Human Relations', indeed, Powys confesses that restraint of our genuine feelings about people (assumed to be negative) is deplorable self-deception, 'perhaps the only kind that is intrinsically bad'. A régime of regulated hatred is prescribed: behind gentle manners and amiability, the cultured mind can 'indulge in savage mental caricatures . . . or demonic malice-dances'. Nothing here to be ashamed of in licensing 'some deep atavistic craving', for it recompenses for the hurt, the thwarting of that intense longing for solitude, the vital nourishment of the cultured self.

Powys, beyond his appeals to sentiment and romance, beyond the air of inspired enthusiasm, gives play to feelings of frustration, sourness and disdain. There is, certainly, a desperate effort to be positive, sincere and convincing: but the undertone of social cynicism, inside a larger nihilistic drift, is often clearly discernible. It gives the reductive, defensive cast to each and every function of culture that Powys touches on — random, erratic and imprecise as these are. The recurrent principle is that of privatization, appropriation by the individual of denoted culture-objects; the common function is to guard the cultured mind from social pressures and from the vortex of contemporary chaos. There is an unexamined assumption that 'commercially orientated life' — 'What people want is money' — automatically produces the 'disintegrating tendencies of our day'. The disquisition on the life of a city (in 'Obstacles to Culture') as 'the vortex of vulgar sensationalism', rapidly sketches in, as needing no supporting discussion, the spiritual brutalization of modern man. Contempt streams out for the 'debauched wits' of average people beyond the reach of culture. For this 'bustling ineptitude of the unenlightened' is the major hindrance: fiercely, unremittingly aggressive, they are 'enemies of tolerance, enemies of light, enemies of pity, enemies of imagination'. The 'stark and austere' means of resistance to this onslaught, however, are the supreme gift of culture:

> How are we to stiffen ourselves against all this external hideousness, these poisonous effluviae, this brazen clamour? . . . . The art of forgetting is indeed culture, her very self, practising her own peculiar magic. The grand device is to see these horrors without seeing them, to hear them without hearing them; to smell them without smelling them, to taste them without tasting them . . . to reduce the whole crowd before you to invisibility; which can be done by thinking it away.

A sour, bitter and blind confusion about the aim of cultivating personal sensitivity; but madly logical, since the whole structure of feeling is built from negative responses to forms of contemporary living. Powys unhesitatingly assumes the validity of modern myths of the nature and purport of mass culture. The talk is of art, philosophy, education, literature; the concern is with the advent of vast industralized democracies, rapid technological advance, and 'admass' civilization. 'More means worse': Powys unhesitatingly assumes the validity of all the clichés and the stock responses about 'the revolt of the masses'. 'All honour to social progress, to social emancipation', writes Powys perfunctorily; 'even though paid for by so terrific a price'. The cost is glibly assumed to be the debasement of all standards, the disintegration of everything that has been packed into the universal portmanteau terminology of 'culture'. Industry, technology, science, education, the press, the pulpit: 'all pandering to that universal taste which is the opposite of all taste'. The original concluding section, 'Culture and Destiny', allegorizes a death-struggle between the two principles or forces, 'Destiny' being equated with 'the great standardized torrent of megalopolitan pleasures, sports, and values', and 'Culture' incarnating 'the eternal elements of Nature and human nature'.

This last ascription grandiosely annexes for Culture the basic, incontestable virtues which Clive Bell begins by sardonically eliminating from the definition he concurrently proffered in *Civilization*.[3] His inventory of 'primitive virtues' — said to be discoverable in one or other of early peoples — rehearses the *petit bourgeois* fundamental concerns as follows: 'I think we must take it as settled that neither a sense of the rights of property, nor candour, nor cleanliness, nor belief in God, the future life and eternal justice, nor chivalry, nor chastity, nor patriotism even are among the distinguishing characteristics of civilization.' All these features are compatible with barbarism; even equal treatment for women may be so, alleges Bell: conversely, 'In those notoriously civilized ages of Tang and Sung the Chinese have regarded [women] as little better than livestock'.

So by his mental audacity, his agility of argument, and his paradoxical inversions, Bell raises the discussion well above the level of Powys' irate, grandiloquent moral melodrama. *Civlization* has the control, the precision, the articulate deployment of learning which appears to enact the desiderated qualities of the cultured mind. The clipped, ironic tones, the fluency, and the rich allusiveness give sharp, suggestive power to the notion of 'Civlization', where the uneven rhetoric, the diffuse generalizations, and the pedagogic illustrations empty the content from Powys' 'Culture'. Eventually, the positions and the purposes of the essays can be seen as closely comparable; and they certainly betray identical strategies of evasion, suppression, and omission. Initially, however, they bifurcate, following antipodal routes to their declared goals, as they redefine and reaffirm Arnold's 'inward condition of the mind and spirit' as the essence of culture. Powys celebrates the sensitive individual's power, with 'some immortal book', to withdraw from living into 'his secret psychic watch-tower'. Bell, stressing the source of all values in the minds of individuals, nevertheless centres discussion on discriminations between societies.

This orientation seems to give Bell's treatise the right to its larger title, to deal with the universal issues of civilization itself, to thrust far beyond questions of the individual sensibility. 'Culture and History' is not one of Powys' headings; nor, of course, does any form of historical specificity fill out the contours of his concept of 'Destiny' or of 'Culture' itself. Bell's primary concern is declaredly just that impletion: from critical scrutiny of a handful of great societies, to distinguish the few authentically civilized ones that remain as the paragons. These initially comprise the Athenian (sc.

Ionian) 480–323 BC; the Roman Empire's first and second centuries; Italy in the fifteenth and early sixteenth centuries; and France from 1653 to 1789, from Fronde to Revolution. The Tang and the Sung dynasties are (reluctantly) discarded, like the Persian periods, through paucity of historical information; the Greek fourth century is kept in 'with some demur'; and the Roman periods are dropped entirely, being cultural carbon-copies of Greek culture, and on many counts so inadequate: 'For anything I can see the Romans were incapable of passionate love, profound aesthetic emotion, subtle thought, charming conversation, or attractive vices'. The epigrammatic essayist has taken over from the scholarly historical researcher; and facts seem to count for little in the opposite instance of Bell's enthusiastic apologia for the French eighteenth-century *noblesse*, against whose excessive powers, unearned privileges and romanticized bloody mindedness the Revolution was aimed, more than against the principle of monarchy as such.

The partiality and the incompleteness of the historical representation are not the main point; nor the constrictedly exclusive principle of selecting the favoured periods. Central to Bell's use of history is the constructing of cultural paradigms, reconstituting the quintessential elements of the triad of civilized moments, abstracted as moral and psychological qualities. These are inter-related and interactive: 'The one is Reason, sweetened by a Sense of Values, the other a Sense of Values, hardened and pointed by Reason'. They are fundamentally, permanently defined in Athenian aestheticism and intellectuality; reincarnated with equal force in Renaissance art and thought; and last displayed in the 'generous heart' of eighteenth-century *beau monde*, with its love of speculative knowledge, its elegant *ton*, and its rigorous sense of values. So the historical scrutiny extrapolates from specific contexts these 'twin characteristics' to hypostatize and to absolutize them as the atemporal, transcendent form or ideal, 'Civilization'.

The dual key terms do not, however, have either the historical-philosophical objectivity nor the exploratory, critical function that the argument assumes. Perhaps strangest of all is the way these hypostatized terms gather a moral resonance, a modernized Arnoldian collocation of the aesthetic and the ethical. Yet they are applied to societies in which the majority comprises slaves, serving the civilized minority — one said to excuse cruelty if it fostered art; or societies in which women are seen in innately inferior, merely decorative possessions, or as livestock; or in which duelling and war are glorified, and peasants, workers, and soldiers are degraded and bestial. More generally, when the moral resonance seems clearest, it proves to be a peculiar ethic of intransitivity. The sense of values discounts moral earnestness, strenuous idealism, dedication to social action, just as Powys affirmed; but Bell theorizes the principle: 'What is peculiar to civilized people is, in the first place, that they are capable of recognizing the value of knowledge as a means to exquisite spiritual states, and, in the second, that they esteem this value above any remote, utilitarian virtue'. Knowledge — medical or mechanical, for instance — obviously has practical importance; but it is to be most esteemed for its 'nourishing quality', feeding the intellect and the imagination, so that, once assimilated, it becomes 'a direct means to good states of mind'.

Bell's formulations crystallize a distinctive moral psychology and philosophy in which his concept of art is foregrounded and centralized.[4] [5] This mode of thought makes his study of civilizations into a form of aestheticized sociology. The emphases in the historical researches are major displacements, even considering them as outlines of cultural history or sketches of the sociology of knowledge. The seventeenth century is left out of the chosen paragons of civilization, though it was 'greatly creative', because the preferred eighteenth century, a selected paragon, was supremely concerned with speculation and contemplation: 'So here again is evidence that the essential characteristic of a highly civilized society is not that it is creative, but that it is appreciative: savages create furiously'. The artist is accorded no priority or responsibility: the final phrase is even tinged with amused condescension. So a society qualifies as civilized when its sense of values focuses and cherishes the powers of disinterested speculation and the arts of appreciation.

The promotion of art as central to culture, and the assumption that the issues focused inside such perimeters will necessarily comprehend the fundamental concerns of a society, are signals of radical displacements and transfers. For the terms are totalizing, comprehensive, and established as the crucial measure of the kind and the quality of a society's achievement. Politics, for instance, is demoted to the manipulating and distribution of the good things produced by others; and the relation to great events of famous politicians is merely one of association. Domination, diplomacy, warmongering: all have their sources in modes of self-assertion, and smack of the compensation for inadequacy that characterizes all forms of action. Altruism, social controls, and the gospel of work are products of such perverted envy. People of action are deformed or deficient artists, frustrated of true expressiveness: 'They cannot find satisfaction in love, friendship, conversation, the creation or contemplation of beauty, the pursuit of truth and knowledge, the gratification of their senses: they must have power, they must impose themselves'. All action is downgraded, whatever its scale, and is equated with barbarism. Its innate tendency is to destroy the conditions of civility and the possibility of culture. As protest is incipient action, it must annul creativity in art; so 'no genuine artist is a protestant by nature', for 'civilization makes protestation unnecessary'.

Bell's key terms, the 'twin-characteristics' of Reason and a Sense of Values, are inextricable since they are rooted in the fundamental self-validating concept of the 'Critical Spirit', or the principle of self-consciousness. This is enmeshed in some characteristic contradictions: it is the specific moment of humanization, of man's rising — by thought, by self-reflection — above the beasts; and it is the artificial product, as 'reason', of education, of man's understanding that everything requires explanation and justification. It is species-specific, constitutive of rationality itself; yet it distinguishes (and then only partially) a very restricted number of historical societies. As reason, and as a sense of values, the critical spirit creates man's subtle intuitions of how to live; yet it raises him above the constricting power of natural instincts (witnessed in self- and family-preservation) whose scope is to fashion the immediate, practical goods necessary for survival. The vital, interlocking principles are aligned, in this version of the allegory of culture, with the virtues of self-consciousness, art and thought — all that is artificial and rare. They oppose all that is natural and habitual: instincts, traditional beliefs and tastes, the physical, and the practical. Reason and the critical sense triumph by non-utility, by transcending the useful and the instrumental.

These hypostatized entities — Reason, Sense of Values, Self-consciousness — objectified and Platonized, are retroactively attributed to historical contexts, and by circular argument, reinferred, assessed almost quantitatively, and ascribed as the supreme goals of sophisticated, complex attainments in the process of human civilization. They acquire the status of historical entities as well as that of philosophical concepts; they fuse the quality and prestige of absolutes with the function of relative, analytical terms. These, like the other contradictions, converge in the essay's god-term, 'states of mind': for this ultimate value represents a commitment with ramifications, personal and social, that envelops every other term in the total argument. The semantic and rhetorical ambiguities of all the major terms and concepts would exemplify a superb case of ideological mystification, of passing off as generally valid propositions the peculiar and personal interests of a special group — were it not that, amost bathetically, Bell's summary spells out the implications, naively proffering as wisdom on 'How to Make a Civilization' the offensively condescending special pleading of his own exclusive social circle.

Civilization, as the Dedication to Virginia Woolf explains, was the final refurbishing of material prepared for Bell's proposed *The New Renaissance*, 'my *magnum opus*, a book to deal with nothing less than every significant aspect of our age'. A 200-page essay distills the matter prepared for that encyclopaedic tome — meant to cover contemporary art, thought and social organization — but the ambitious scope remains. It was an enterprise springing from Bell's undertaking to apply to his historical research the master-findings of G.E. Moore's *Principia Ethica*.[6] This highly restricted, narrowly angled philosophical discussion nucleated itself on propositions about 'intrinsic value' and 'goodness' — taken as simple, unanalysable properties, and interlocked with appreciation of beauty, defined as 'that of which the admiring contemplation is good in itself'. Moore sums up the central tenets:

> By far the most valuable things, which we know or can imagine, are certain states of consciousness, which may be roughly described as the pleasures of human intercourse and the enjoyment of beautiful objects . . . . It is the ultimate and fundamental truth of Moral Philosophy that it is only for the sake of these things — in order that as much of them as possible may at some time exist — that anyone can be justified in performing any public or private duty; that the are the *raison d'̃etre* of virtue; that it is these complex wholes *themselves* . . . that form the rational ultimate end of human action and the sole criterion of social progress.

With witty aplomb and with breath-taking literalness, Bell illustrates this 'ultimate, fundamental truth' of Moore's. In extending it, adopting its values and its measures, he magnifies its fissures, and converts its silences and its omissions into terrifyingly irresponsible rejections. The 'significant aspects of the age' cannot include the application of knowledge, men's practical work, the public sphere, political activity, nor, indeed, anything 'utilitarian' or instrumental.

For the historical paragons turn out to be synchronically displayed patterns of social arrangement. The selected society is seen in arrest, caught, frozen as a cultural paradigm: Greek, Renaissance Italian, or eighteen-century French aristocratic — they display each the valorized equipoise. The social complementaries are not represented in tension, conflict, or indeed in any specific form of process or interchange. Each civilization in the triad is evoked as exemplifying a philosophic duality: one group has a culture of the critical spirit, a refinement of reason and a sense of values; the other has a practical, instrumental existence, which precludes the alternative commitment. This interweaving of the historical and the philosophical systems of description has the function of raising to an imaginary (aesthetic) plane the specificities of material, social, historical realities.

The whole discussion of what qualities condition a civilized culture is, by these strategies and forms of mystification, detemporalized and staticized. Inside all the transpositions and displacements is the theory of élites, far from academic or disinterested in its claims, and of immediate (instrumental) consequence for groups like Bell's own social circle. The accounts of the cultural paragons rehearse the arguments for contemporary dispositions and social choices; they work as theatrical metaphors for insistent, pragmatic recommendations. These are spelt out in the egregious special pleading of the last chapter, which (especially in its tone) undoes all the earlier scholarly claims and lays bare its prejudices:

> Civlization requires the existence of a leisured class ... that nucleus that gives it civility ... and a leisured class requires the existence of slaves — of people, I mean, who give some part of their surplus time and energy to the support of others ... willing servants ... people content to make sacrifices for an ideal .... Few are born with ability to discover for themselves that world of thought and feeling whence come our choicest pleasures .... This civilizing élite ... will merely live their lives; and living will be seen to have pleasures and desires, standards and values, an attitude to life, a point of view, different from those of the busy multitude. By living passively they become the active promoters of good .... You will keep the number as low as you can without jeopardizing the essential, which is that there should be a class of men and women of whom nothing is required — not even to justify their existence.

The practical claims — £800 per year, the State to provide for the group's children — are trivial, amusingly arrogant alongside the attitudes to social and political power. Rejecting Renan's argument for the political responsibilities of such groups or élites, Bell finds no incompatibility between despotism — Russian and Italian, 1927 — and civilization: 'If despotism and its correlative slavery are the means to the greatest good — to the maximum of the good states of mind — I should suppose only bad men would be averse from employing them'. All civilizations, he concludes, have been 'imposed by the will of a tyrant or maintained by an oligarchy'.

The pejorative comments on the public sphere, and the dismissal of politicians as insignificant intermediaries, are licensed, then, by these encompassing securities. The groups sustaining civility and cultural standards are best able to function within an authoritarian political system. Since their attitudes, interests, and activities are self-referential, inner-directed, the low assessment of action itself as a moment or principle of civilized society is inherently definitive of their position. The contradiction is only a witty pseudo-paradox: the forms and practices of power must have maximum implementation, before the free exercise of the 'Critical Spirit' of the non-participant élite relegates such practice to the inferior realm of action.

For the privileged few, then, a freedom from answerability: the collocated 'Reason' and 'Sense of Values' entail no ethic of social responsibility. All the supreme qualities are definitively intransitive; their own personal existence is quintessentially one of refined appreciativeness, receptivity, promoting good by living passively:

> The mind receives a myriad impressions — trivial, fantastic, evanescent, or engraved with the sharpness of steel. From all sides they come, an incessant shower of innumerable atoms; and as they fall . . . they shape themselves into the life of Monday or Tuesday . . . . Life is a luminous halo, a semi-transparent envelope surrounding us from the beginning of consciousness to the end.

Virginia Woolf's words, purporting to describe the inflections of the modern novel, more aptly evoke that sensitivity of reception, that rapt, aesthetic intransitivity which alone creates the states of mind composing the 'good', in Moore's and Bell's formulations. The passage simultaneously defines, provides symbols for, and enacts the mode of assimilative sensitivity which is alone identified as refined consciousness. Any of its modulations or transpositions will have this highly distinctive non-transitive, self-reflective form: it is a theory of the nature of consciousness which determines fundamental concepts of personal identity, relationships, social communities, and can have (however seemingly fugitive at first) the most direct affiliations with the authoritarian doctrine of political power. This odd consorting of apparent incompatibilities — detached, cultural élites, and stark, disciplinary central government — follows on the vountary powerlessness (and specialized pre-occupations) of the first relying upon the unquestioning support of the second.

The key concept, telescoping all these differentiated notions together, is that of autonomy. All the major selected modes of consciousness — the operations of the critical sense and of reason, the activity of the sense of values — are self-contained, self-validating, non-instrumental. Consciousness is an end in itself, not a means; its nature and function are perfectly realized in the hypostatized 'states of mind'. These are non-purposive, where purpose involves consequence in the practical activities of the world. Even the purposeful knowledge that theorizes practice can be abstracted, essentialized as stimulant to the valorized states of mind and feeling. From this, it is translucently clear why all the discussions, whatever their social and political implications, centre upon the exemplary definitions of the nature and function of art. The aesthetic realm is seen as indubitably autonomous: the aesthetic response to great artworks is supremely the instance of pure consciousness, the ascesis or the rapt, intransitive attention which creates the ecstasy of awareness which is fullness of living. This is Moore's 'rational ultimate end of human action, and the sole criterion of social progress'. So the modes of art and of human consciousness are not merely parallels, but exact homologues, interlocked and, ideally, interchangeable.

This extrapolating from one activity of the sensibility, defined as hermetically autonomous, to the total, complex activity of consciousness itself — reified as a self-ordering entity — is central to the philosophical validation of the theory of cultural élites. Bell insists on how few are authentically qualified for access to 'that world of thought and feeling' which he adumbrates, and how restricted the numbers are — and enforcedly so, if necessary — of the guardians of civilized standards who compose the élite. By this displacement into a separated reserve area (de-nominated as 'culture' or 'civilization') the material realities of socio-political dispositions which secure the élite's situation are obscured. Bell, of course, makes no concessions at all to any form of democracy, which he finds inimical to culture and to civility; and the political asides are pointed and brusque. The more insidiously pervasive strategy of evasion is this transposition itself of intrinsically socio-economic and political considerations into the irreducibly aestheticized terms of autonomous art, which control and give pattern to all cultural activity. (Each of the paragons of civilization represents an historical incarnation of 'Significant Form'.) By linking the concept of the élite with the definition of civilized values and cultural standards, the interrelations of élite and social class are suppressed. (Since the élite defines the standards, and the values of the élite qualify the members for that task, the definitions are circular and the group is impenetrable.) Notably omitted are the fundamentally economic supporting systems for élites or for highly placed social groups; at least, in Forster's *Howards End*, there is an admission of how, quite directly, this kind of specialized high culture depends on wealth, unearned income, dividends, stocks and shares. Bell, by simply ignoring these connections, masks the irresistible pressure on every single point of his argument of a comprehensive vision of social structuration. The indifference to the public sphere, the dismissal of politicians, the stance of neutrality about sociological issues, reveals — not just acceptance or conformity — but a passionately patrician, hierarchical cluster of commitments.

In the 1929 Halley Stewart lectures, composed as Bell's book reached its third impression, the historian R.H. Tawney tackled its conclusions and implications, under the heading '*Equality and Culture*'. (The lectures were printed in 1931 as *Equality*.)[7] His characteristically good-tempered, tolerant summary immediately pinpoints the fundamental assumptions vital to the argument:

> An élite . . . was released for the life of the spirit by the patient labour of slaves and peasants. If [a mature society] is to possess, not merely the comforts, but the graces, of existence, it must be enamoured of excellence. It must erect a standard of perfection, and preserve it inviolate against the clamour for the commonplace which is the appetite of the natural man, and of his eager hierophant, the practical reformer. But a standard of perfection is the achievement of a minority, and inequality is the hedge which protects it . . . . It perpetuates a tradition of culture, by ensuring the survival of a class which is its visible embodiment, and which maintains that tradition in maintaining itself.

A theory of society is contingent upon any of the multiple definitions of what culture comprises: whether it, traditionally, centres upon the arts, religion, philosophy or learning, and a focus upon the individual sensitivity or group-civility that these foster; or whether it centres upon the behaviour, interests, attitudes and values — the 'life-style' — of a group, an élite, or a class assumed to be disrelated from the alternative practices of the majority. All the versions have as a fulcrum the dichotomy of society: Patricians/Plebeians; Court/People; Aristocrats/Citizens; Noble/Vulgar; Civilized/Barbarians; Educated/Uneducated. The structure of the society is always a form of dividing the Many — unrefined, undistinguished — from the Few — civilized, eminent. Whether the measure is one of birth and breeding, of rank, of function, or of civility — manners, taste, interests — the markers are between the vast body of ordinary persons and the select 'happy few'. Whatever is chosen as the nature and validating function of the élite, its general ratification is ineluctably founded on rigid stratification of the levels of society. What Tawney demonstrates is both the artificiality and the arbitrariness of this collocation of élites and inequalities, and its anti-humanism, its ungenerosity of spirit.

'Clever men are impressed by their difference from their fellows; wise men are conscious of their resemblance to them.' From this centrally humane position, Tawney demonstrates how the cult of inequality works to maintain, even inside a political democracy, the lineaments of a social oligarchy; and he proceeds to show how this restrains, and even subverts, the movement of a society towards attainment of its preferred civilizing values, when he writes that 'Violent contrasts of wealth and power, and an indiscriminating devotion to institutions by which such contrasts are maintained and heightened, do not promote the attainment of [civilized and spiritual] ends, but thwart it.' He describes as barbarous and odious all maintenance of systems and institutions which stunt the faculties of most in the supposed interests of the minority. The sectarian exclusivity of the eminent cliques who control or benefit from privileges and power is itself fundamentally inhibitory of cultural refinement. The élite tends to be self-appointed — birth, rank, talent, knowledge — and to define its standards appropriately; then shrugging off criticism as the politics of envy, as the hatred of the inferior. 'But the condition of recognizing genuine superiority is a contempt for unfounded pretensions to it.' Where recognition and social deference — institutionalized as systematic inequality in all areas — are to be automatically accorded — to rank, wealth, or 'culture' — then the unavoidable outcome, for Tawney, is the diffusion of 'sham criteria of excellence'. This is as harmful and as erroneous as the élites' universally shared execration of the supposed prevalence (among the Many) of materialistic and basely utilitarian values.

Tawney's analysis of the false linkages between civilization and the maintenance of élites includes his deconstruction of the historical paragons proposed by Clive Bell's writings. Comparing Athens at its cultural apogee with Florence in the fourteenth and fifteenth centuries, Tawney depicts communities of interacting, multiplex groupings: Athens itself was a bustling, commercial city, arrogant in its patriotism, with sharp political enthusiasms provoking crude and violent outbreaks. Artists and philosophers were involved in public affairs, readily contributing to current major debates, expounding their fundamental commitments. The intelligentsia provoked controversy, and disseminated ideas; and the general discussion of art was most often in terms of issues, meanings and moral principles. The same comprehensiveness, practicality, and involvement were displayed in eighteenth-century France: thought was no specialized, disinterested concern of a detached group. Men of letters and men of action were then most closely related, and their mutual interchange fostered speculation that impinged upon practice and policy. For one essential principle distinguishing these major moments of civilization is that of humanism, the expectation that knowledge would infinitely improve the life of all men; and the estimation of reason as that faculty evincing the dignity and uniqueness of man, not as the select mark of an elect minority.

Tawney's historical scrutiny of earlier societies renders Bell's account of them invalid. (Though *Civilization* makes a great rhetorical flourish with its cultural paragons, its fundamental motives and concerns are probably ultimately separable from that representation.) The vertical model is that of pyramidal society with select, superior minorities interlocking at the peak. Tawney shows a horizontal interplay of variegated groups, where mutuality, amicable or hostile, expresses the living tensions suppressed by hypotheses of group-insulation and functional separateness. Whatever kind of distinction, quality or eminent skill set men or groups apart, in Athens, Florence, or Paris, their otherness and their social performance thrived on the recognition, support and enthusiasm of larger groups, of other classes, and even of the whole population. Strictly élitist theories, quite apart from ignoring the contributions of single individuals, postulate a scarcely practicable monadic, atomistic distinctiveness of innovatory groups. The creation of civilized practices and cultural values, by artists, patrons, connoisseurs, disseminators of ideas, leaders, innovators and men of action, has (by definition) to impinge on existing forms, to impact, convert, to change behaviour and beliefs. To single out aesthetic receptivity is incredibly reductive; to displace creative practice by appreciativeness is presumptive; to arrange history and sociological hypotheses around these prejudices is intellectually irresponsible.

Tawney, though prone to softening his critique by an unremitting amiability and reasonableness of tone, still dismantles the assumptions, theoretical and practical, of élitism. For historical facticity and theoretical feasibility converge: the processes of developing civilization cannot be privatized, externally or internally. No agents — as individuals, groups, or class-élites — can arrogate to themselves, as innovators or as receptors, any authentically civilizing practices, objects or institutions, without reversing or stultifying the appropriations. Historically, civilizing forces can only achieve cultural substance by receptivity inside significantly large social areas. As part of social tradition and of practical inheritance, their substantiality depends on renewal, revitalization, and so general (theoretically total, socially universal) accessibility. Cultural élitism, as expounded by Bell, is the defensiveness of 'a cloistered and secluded refinement'; its intolerant separatist insistence is repellent in its fastidiousness, which, along with gentility and compacency, Tawney highlights as characteristics more inimical to cultural health than the vulgarity they seek to annul. Such attitudes and values condone 'the harshness and brutality of traditional systems of social petrification'; they sterilize, instead of enriching civility by its diffusion. But exclusivity is not excusable as pettiness or self-regard: it necessarily coarsens the excluded, and becomes an instrumentality of a spiritually most offensive kind, since others are seen as a means, not as ends-in-themselves. Human identity, integrity, and personal dignity are dispensed with in the actual, tangible conditions of social arrangements and practices; and this consequence can consort with any degree of an élite's philosophical recognition of human worth as an axiomatic principle.

Tawney's theme, equality, in its relations to culture and to civilization, confronts and controverts every basic assumption in the books by Powys and Clive Bell — positions resumed later by T.S. Eliot's *The Idea of a Christian Society*[8] (and further developed in the post-war *Notes Towards the Definition of Culture*).[9] From this last book, Tawny's 151 postscript to his revised treatise picked up a phrase of Eliot's that Powys and Bell would certainly have endorsed: 'Equality is the poison to culture'. With varying degrees of explicitness, Powys, Bell and Eliot are utterly convinced of the anti-egalitarian case: so unqualifiedly so, that each indulges the mystification of attributing this extreme *parti-pris* to the 'natural' determinations visible both in the differing endowments of individuals and the constitutive discriminations of societal formation. The first of these natural determinations starts from direct observation of the myriad differences between individuals, an infinite range of temperaments, skills, abilities, receptivities and kinds of intelligence. This, as Tawney promptly stresses, may contain elements of incontrovertible truth: but egalitarianism is not founded on obtuseness to this perception. What Tawney vigorously denies is that the second perception is logically consequent upon this first: the differences between individuals do not 'naturally' predetermine the differences on which, historically, societies have established themselves. There is no simple equation between the individual's qualities and potentialities, and his allotted place in society, since the former have most often been inferred from the latter. Tawney refuses direct equations which deterministically work from the observed individual differences to the socially sanctioned discriminations between larger groupings and total classes. There is no demonstrable causal connection between the individual 'given' and the socially 'given' — though to elide and to so identify the two is the universally observable ratification of any status quo.

Tawney acutely singles out the kinds of feeling that compulsively drive through the logic of the inegalitarian theorem. They comprise a variety of fears and apprehensions: of social standardization, of imposed cultural uniformity, of the inculcation of homogenized emotions. Any full-scale conversion to the principle of equality would be a surrender to mediocrity, to the institutionalizing of the attitudes, the values, and the interests of the spiritually impoverished. This anticipation of the cultural tyranny which must follow the triumph of one-dimensional man assumes a mere reversal of the dominative patterning usually in force. It barely conceals the dread that equality, economical and social, must involve political domination, by the Many, and so the demolition of privileged minorities, the civilized Few. But the argument edges around these considerations by its emphasis on the need to maintain cultural standards — the major function of élites — and to staunchly resist the 'levelling-down' process. This, Tawney points out, is a pejorative term, begging all the questions, foreclosing the issue, which he refers back to what is essentially an open situation. For whether culture would be debased or enriched by its extension in an egalitarian society depends on complex series of fundamental changes which cannot be trivialized by the reductive terminology of 'levelling'.

Tawney's redistribution of emphases is not evasive: his concern to deal with the vital issue of how to maintain levels of excellence while maximally extending cultural values is persistent and precise, inside his characteristic rhetoric:

> The aim [of the humanist spirit] is to liberate and cultivate the powers which make for energy and refinement; and it is critical, therefore, of all forms of organization . . . which seek to reduce the variety of individual character and genius to a drab and monotonous uniformity. But it desires to cultivate these powers in all men, not only in a few; . . . it is the enemy of arbitrary and capricious divisions which are based not upon what men, given suitable conditions, are capable of becoming, but on external distinctions between them.

There is a remorseless exposure of the inextricable connections between élites and the stratification of social classes, seen as a mechanistic enforcement of 'external distinctions'. Insofar as levels of excellence are defined as coincident with levels of social discrimination, then Tawney is right to call for demonstrable proof, and to insist on disparities between intelligence and social 'placing', on the unpredictable manifestation of genius, sensitivity, and powers of imagination. Neither aristocracy, plutocracy nor the ruling classes have a monopoly of civilizing qualities; and Tawney's irony is a rebuttal of the contemptible condescension which attributes dull and degraded taste specifically to groups placed (by the same methods of observation) in low social categories. The strongest, most impassioned impulse behind Tawney's project to preserve while diffusing standards of cultural excellence, not easily expressible in the current terms of the debate, is his insight into the stunting of men's capacities, and his acceptance of their rich potentiality. He respects any historical manifestation of:

> an outlook on society which sympathized with the attempt to bring the means of a good life within the reach of all, and regarded the subordination of class to class, and the arrogance and servility which such subordination naturally produces, as barbarian or gothic, as the mark of peoples which were incompletely civilized . . . . Herodotus remarks that 'It is evident, not in one thing alone, but on all sides of life, how excellent a thing is equality among men.'

To bring about a society which would deserve Herodotus' commendation is Tawney's priority: it puts into proper perspective the question of élites' guaranteeing standards; and, keeping his persuasive rationality — part of his generous, compassionate fellow-feeling — he yet looks for a fundamental restructuring of every aspect of social practice. Only massive, total changes in social systems and practice would show the pathetic inadequacy of the two opposite and equal errors: to maintain cultural excellence (through élites) while implementing general changes; and to diffuse (through education) the values of civilization, while promoting social reforms within the given system.

T.S. Eliot's notes to *The Idea of a Christian Society* confess his deep indebtedness to other writers, 'notably to R.H. Tawney'. This admission — there being no textual discussion to support it — is quite startling, since Eliot's assumptions, arguments, and conclusions are the exact reverse of Tawney's; but his positions are simply ignored. Eliot endorses a stringently defined system of classes, whose cultural aims are taken up into the standards of a unified religious-social code of behaviour. The discussion insists that, though they are elusive of definition, the affiliations of a common culture and a common faith must have theoretical and practical priority. Behaviour, of private persons as of public figures, must be 'correctible by the Church'. Social customs in general must 'take on' religious sanctions. For Eliot claims that, historically, no culture has appeared without a religion; any dichotomizing must consequently be rectified. They are — though Eliot is here apologetically very uncertain in exposition — aspects of the same thing; they are, however, neither to be confused as identical, nor polarized as entities to be related. Eliot struggles to articulate his convictions about these complicated interlockings, since he works from an all-encompassing (but unquestioned and unargued) identification of the development of all European culture and the coetaneous history of (Western) Christendom.

At first, it can seem that Tawney has been left aside because the issues involve principles of faith, and their practice in a living Church. However, Eliot is as much involved in the immediacies of socio-political dispositions, questions of the class-system, state controls, and the place within all these of the general intellectual and artistic life of the times. The concepts of faith, the practices of a belief, the nature of the Church (in the 1930s) are wholly undefined, mere gestures in the argument; the definitions are sharper, the inflections of concern are stronger, in just those areas that concern Powys, Bell and Tawney. The principles enunciated ring with fully honourable intention, the definitions are commendably comprehensive. Culture is whatever makes life worth living (as Powys often says); and it is so hard to conceptualize because it must articulate 'the substratum of collective temperament, ways of behaviour and unconscious values'. Culture, religion, political philosophy, social practice: none can be reduced to the total sum of forms of activities. There must be due weighting of ways of thinking, feeling, behaving, of attitudes and qualities not readily visible or assessable, nor producible for discussion.

Eliot's broadening of the definition — at specific points, not sustainedly — is both ambiguous and rather misleading. It has to be seen that cultural concepts and practices are, in some way, socially universal, since it is Eliot's central axiom that a culture is an incarnation of a people's religion. (Most of his difficulty and persistent vagueness surely stem from using this anthropological model of early societies for contemporary social formations.) It is misleading, historically, in that Eliot ignores (as Niebuhr, for example, does not) the many ways that the Christian church has often exemplified hostility and hatred for Western European civilized values and cultural practices. It is misleading, sociologically, in that Eliot's descriptions and recommendations are marked by forms of illiberal élitism, cultural separatism and anti-egalitarianism. The fundamental ambiguity is that the humanistic generalities about the whole way of life are sharply undercut by the restrictive, dominative patterns that weight the whole essay. A major instance is the way that Eliot slides, unconcernedly, from insistence on 'continuity and coherence' in national life, politics and the arts, from 'a certain uniformity of culture' — suggesting, that is, its non-exclusivity — to establishing guarantees for all these through a 'Community of Christians', identified as an élite, selected men 'of intellectual and spiritual superiority'. This fits exactly the plangent regret for 'the disappearance of any class of people who recognise public and private responsibility of patronage of the best that is made and written'. The conscious and dominative patterning implicit in all this denies, of course, the validity of the neutral, comprehensive notions of cultural values as those ways of living, valueing, thinking and feeling shared by a whole people. The post-war essay on culture was to deplore the catastrophe that always must follow when a dominant or an upper class is removed, however badly it has neglected its responsible functions. The 'Community of Christians' is to replace such a class: its anachronistic flavour perhaps conceals the proposal's narrow, reactionary implications.

The contradictions initially masked by vagueness acquire a more distinct form, with sharper inflections from Eliot's emotional involvement, when he delineates the contemporary moment of cultural transition. The 'Idea' of modern (English) society, that is, the ends for which it is arranged, is the Idea of a Neutral Society, which, in this context, means that it is a Pagan Society. (The charge against the Third Reich, that it is a viciously brutalized totalitarian régime is not, for Eliot — in the closing months of 1939 — a more pressing one, than the charge that it is a Pagan Society.) The prevailing tone of studied impartial description breaks repeatedly into fierce moralistic strictures on the composition and characterizing processes of such a society — expressing, in Eliot's view, a negative moment of civilization. Neutral or Pagan, the society produces a deformation of humanity, a spiritual stunting directly consequent upon the rule of 'unlimited industrialism'. The sole conscious aim is then prosperity, a disintegrating philosophy of liberalism promoting profitability as a central principle, and 'getting on' as its social ethic. The only form of modern belief, ratifying the exploitation of Nature and of men's labour alike, is in the strange gods of 'Compound Interest and Maintenance of Dividends'. The gravamen of the case against the commercialized, anarchic society — with its furtive admiration for the efficiency of totalitarian régimes — is that it fosters, in its own interests, an alienated, susceptible mob-mentality. Eliot sketches the execrable depression of standards that commercialized manipulation ensures: the prevalence of advertizing, popular writing, and all forms of propaganda. The world's first industrialized society having produced an urban massification — Eliot's reiterated term being simply 'mob' — it forwards its degenerated liberal democratic purposes by maintaining 'an illiterate and uncritical mob'. The intellectuals are irresponsibly over-specialized, the political leaders similarly blinkered. So the Neutral/Pagan Society perpetuates its anarchic non-culture: 'A state secularized, a community turned into a mob, and a clerisy disintegrated'. The next, apparently immediately imminent, social transition must be to a regimented society: propaganda will have homogenized attitudes and opinions, produced uniformity, and helped to repress all individuality. There will be 'hygienic' morality only, a clinically-controlled uniformity of sexual practice, this possibly involving periods of enforced breeding. Art will have totally degenerated into the sycophantic exposition of officially approved ideas and doctrines.

The fundamental cultural pessimism marking Eliot's discussion is that of a commentator finding that all the forebodings of a decade before — voiced in Powys' and Bell's essays — were now traumatically, maximally realized in everyday life. Huxley's satiric inflations — in *Brave New World* in 1932 — are the soberly observed outlines of daily life: Orwell's hysterical evocations of a drab and vicious totalitarian society are anticipated, attributed to

Britain at the close of the 1930s. So much of the text is either vague or bewilderingly anachronistic, irrelevant or contradictory when measured by signals of his obsessive, topical concerns. Yet it is disturbing to find that these emergent major principles have only the base of an irrational, naive 'Admass' society position. All the proffered speculation, the convergence of philosophy, sociology, theology, work from a cluster of assumptions which have no more intellectual force or observational grounding than similar ones in the Powys book. The wholesale simplifications are only made possible by the acrobatic, rhetorical strategies of representing the Many — Eliot's 'mob' — as agent-victims. They seek prosperity, they wish to 'get on', they neglect customary (Christian) values; they are contented to exist in a vulgar world, uncritical or what surrounds them. Simultaneously, the Many are manipulated, compelled by exploitative systems (run by profiteers and financiers) which create alienation, an emotional stultification, and so a susceptibility to all the debased attitudes, behaviour and values foisted upon them. An essential mystification vital to the perpetuation of this allegory of cultural decadence is the non-specifying of the superior power-groups, of their dominative systems which ensure total manipulation; and the absence of particular analyses of the situations, behaviour and practices of actual persons, groups and classes which tolerate and support such a glaringly obvious unilateral system.

The different formulations of the post-war reflections, *Notes Towards the Definition of Culture*, and the surer control of their tone, may seem to modify considerably the unacceptable tendencies of the earlier treatise. There are fewer negative notes, less overtly hostile reference to the principles of democracy, and some clearer definitions of what Eliot desiderates in a civilized ordering of society. However, in the central, more considered sections, the more clearly articulated arguments still enclose the contradictions displayed earlier. One major instance can represent the elisions prompted by these contradictions, an example that betrays the merely nominal form of Eliot's gestures about 'democracy'. We must not, he warns, be 'hypnotized' into believing that the principles of *aristocracy* and of *democracy* are irreconcileable, and in 'The Class and the Elite' he asserts their compatability:

> The whole problem is falsified if we use these terms antithetically . . . . [This] is a plea on behalf of a form of society in which an aristocracy should have a peculiar and essential function . . . . What is important is a structure of society in which there will be, from 'top' to 'bottom', a continuous gradation of cultural levels . . . the upper levels representing a more conscious culture and a greater specialisation of culture . . . . No true democracy can maintain itself unless it contains these different levels of culture]which] may also be seen as levels of power. A smaller group at a higher level will have equal power with a larger group at a lower level . . . .

The implications are stark, despite the assumption of a 'reasonable' tone, and the disclaimers throughout of not wishing to impose, or even to argue for the implementation of, the prescribed 'conditions of culture'. The 'continuous gradation' implies strict stratification; '"top" to "bottom" ' is pseudo-apologetic terminology for a hierarchal society with distinctly marked ranks; 'upper levels'/'aristocracy'/'élites' are imprecisely interchangeable concepts. The reservations about Mannheim's notions of the constituting and functioning of élites — superfluous reservations, since Mannheim makes them himself — are not in a liberalizing direction. They express Eliot's alarm that, having to recruit from outside — some tilting towards a 'meritocracy' — the civilizing élites will lack the force that only continuity, social stability, and fixity of membership can ensure. Like Mannheim, Eliot wants to reinstate an hereditary, genuinely powerful, extremely select group: an aristocracy, in fact. The socio-cultural changes — seen, in the responses of Powys, Bell and Eliot, as contributory to crisis and disintegration — had, half-a-century earlier, been marked by the dissociation of social class and socio-political function. Yet this process — seen as a 'problem' — is assumed to be resolvable by reversion, essentially a restoration vital to the growth and the survival of culture: 'If the reader finds it shocking that culture and equalitarianism should conflict, if it seems monstrous to him that anyone should have "advantages of birth" — I do not ask him to change his faith, I merely ask him to stop paying lip-service to culture'.

The breakdown of reasoned objectivity, of the scholarly detachment, into irrational assertion and (as Raymond Williams points out)[10] into a dogmatism that betrays not only prejudice but insolence — these are a *volte-face* that reveals how begrudgingly the references to 'democracy' are made at all. *The Idea of a Christian Society* has unguarded dismissals of the 'mob', as uncritical, illiterate, vulgar; the position is identical in *Notes Towards the Definition of Culture*, though a cursory attempt at periphrases is made. 'A larger group at a lower (social) level' is to compose the ' "bottom" cultural level'. But in a non-dominative society, such a larger group would necessarily be 'licentious', an insupportable situation for the conscientious few: 'Complete equality means universal irresponsibility' — where, in such a context, 'universal' must apply only beyond the province of the élites. The 'conscientious few' who would find it totally oppressive to allow egalitarian principles any increased practical expression must act to prevent such 'further deterioration of culture'.

Linking the two treatments of culture and civilization by the same author — arguments gaining enormously in influence because of his major creative work — shows how the inter-war positions on central contemporary issues have been re-presented with on-going force.[11] [12] The irrational undercurrent, the near-hysterical apprehensions that surfaces so often, in all these like-minded discussions, signal the intellectual/emotional loops and linkages between 'aristocratic' (hierarchical) social theorizing and the conviction that contemporary situations are anarchic, degenerate, aggressive expressions of a mass-society. The dichotomized society assumed, reinforced, or proposed in all these (and many similar) arguments, the multiple versions of the Many/Few division, are formalizations, structures claiming rational force in their ensuring cultural continuities; while they persistently ground themselves in arbitrary collocations of cultural with social standards. Eliot's identification of the two is typical, and displays the fundamental prejudice which is the source of this irresponsible confusion: 'Each individual would inherit greater or less responsibility towards the commonwealth, according to the position in society which he inherited'. The fear of the spread of mediocrity, the fear of inevitable destruction of all standards of excellence, the conviction that the qualities of civilization are continuously eroded: these are all rationalized as concern with social order, with the protection and the transmission of traditional values. As even a single term like 'inherit' exemplifies, there is a wish to fix, to make absolute, the positions reached in the past; and to naturalize, to present as 'given', to stabilize social situations which are obviously in flux. This strategy of imposition — presented as observation and inference — is compelled by an assumption that arrested, set disciplines of order among social classes are the fundamental guarantees of civilized values and attainments.

That the antitheses and polarizations of the Many and the Few occur throughout historical societies is no warranty of their truth; philosophies and theories assuming such validity can be seen as post-factum rationalizations, or ideological expositions which seek to naturalize the existing dispositions of property and power. Disturbing contradictions have inevitably crowded into all forms of dichotomy theory, since the élites have so customarily subscribed to notions of man's innate dignity while enjoying privileges dependent on men's indignities. Later versions of cultural separatism developed inside the increasingly powerful middle-ranking classes — who, as a total force tended to move against established higher classes — as sub-groups became disaffected from the values and purposes of their own class. One major strand in the versions current in nineteenth-century industrialized societies was prompted by disenchantment with the ideals of Progress, associated with technological modernization and its accompanying urbanization. The simpler arguments used cultural values as intellectual sticks to beat money-grubbing philistines; the sophisticated discussions used Arnold's principle of erecting culture into a salvationary creed to restore general social health to a community fragmented by the pressures of materialism. The compounding of confusion here is a result of transposing the dichotomy — the Many/the Few — into a trichotomy: Arnold's prototypical scheme, comprising Barbarians (upper classes), Philistines (middle classes), and Populace (the lower classes).[13] But apparent ironic distancing is Arnold's means of goading into action those who must assume their responsibilities — social, political, cultural — by taking over from the traditional ruling classes, and by reorganizing in these major areas, must revivify communal life. The Populace are still the Many: illiterate, brutalized, and (at best) infected by the Philistine values of degrading commercialism. (The repeated synonym for the Populace in Arnold's writings is, inevitably, 'the masses'.) Essentially, Arnold works from the dichotomy, cultured/uncultured.

The central and most damaging misconstruction inside this influential tradition of cultural interpretation stems from its modes of incorporating its socio-political evaluations. Arnold's work signifies the rhetorical transposition into the terminology of culture — the arts, learning, education — of a theorizing vitally concerned with social discipline, government, the ratification of the hegemonic values of the controlling middle-classes. From this position, apologists have felt it a matter of social conscience to document the case against the anarchy intrinsic to processes of massification. 'Anarchy' is a neatly ambivalent term, comprehending intimations of public disorder and political disruptiveness, while providing the complementary, antithetical principle to 'Culture'. There are subtle transvaluations and inversions inside this whole process: so that the social-political (and, necessarily, economic) depression of the majority of people — blocking their acquisition of any forms of 'Culture' — can be stood on its head: the uncultured Many must be depressing the civilized standards of the (superior) minorities. The symptoms, which in reality signal the material deprivations of great numbers of the working population, are treated as causes, as signs of rejection, as hostility to values central to the observers' way of life.

The persistent terminology, the unvarying circumscription of the areas for discussion, the consent to neutralizing issues comprised in the categories of 'Culture': these have affected the freedom in argument of radical critics, from Tawney[14] to Raymond Williams; and have weighted discussions in the later commentaries on the nature of Mass Society. (That Eliot noticed, approvingly, the connections between the earlier 'Culture' and later 'Mass Society' arguments is evident in his singling-out Dwight Macdonald's seminal 1944 essay in the Preface to *Notes Towards the Definition of Culture*.) However, in positive and in negative ways, the political principles make their pressures felt, and betray the ideological weighting of all the variegated versions of what culture comprehends. Arnold's trichotomy only apparently, by its satiric, metaphoric group-personification, transposes its assessments into 'literary', cultural taxonomics. It effectively recuperates, through the defensive irony, traditional rankings, socio-political levels, with their concomitant cultural attainders. So with Clive Bell's and with Eliot's deployment of such groupings as traditional, autonomously defined levels of cultural activity, specifically related to restricted groups ensuring the essentials of civilization. There is the identical transposition: a pyramidal arrangement, of distinctly monadic groups, adumbrating a ranking and a firm stratification made acceptable by its cultural (apolitical) modes. Its patrician forms are made to seem metaphoric, since qualities long associated with court and nobility are displaced into the realm of taste. 'Nobility' and 'grandeur' are metamorphosed, taken into the aesthetic realm; and the élites are a privileged caste in possessing refined sensibility. The ineluctable connections between such élites and the socio-economic, political realities of existing classes are tactically blurred. But none of the commentators supposes, or wishes for, the disappearance of distinctions between social classes. Bell assumes that power vested in the foremost groups helps sustain the civilized élites; Eliot proposes that the smaller, superior groups — seen as interacting élites — should have greater powers than the massive but lower-placed social groups.

To bring together the commentaries of Powys, Bell and Eliot is not to ignore differences: the levels of sensitivity, intellectual insight, and philosophical coherence are varied between the three critics. However, these expositions do share their fundamental modes, patterns and purposes. Probably most distinctive of all is their synchronic mode: with whatever content the term 'culture' is impleted, it is free of diachronic entailments. Bell's culture-paragons, a selected triad of perfected moments of civilization, as Tawney penetratingly shows, are completely mis-described, and of no historical validity. Their inaccuracies are consistent in that they allow Bell to display a culture free from social tensions, conflicts and practical (uncivilized) activities. Bell's rhetorical purpose is to fashion models for the 'new Renaissance' which the Bloomsbury Group is initiating: but they are spatialized, hermetic, socially sealed. (As Keynes was to point out, this falsely idealized the nature and actual history of their group.) Again, Bell and Eliot use a concept of 'class' which is philosophically and logically consistent with their synchronic models of history and tradition. As the associated use of 'élites' and the supporting description of 'levels' suggest, the implications of 'class' are those of rank, of (inherited) place, as 'élite' itself retains the associations of 'caste'. There is in all these writers, in contradistinction to Tawney, no appreciation of social class as inherently a relational reality, as a process of self-identification in conflictual interaction with other such groups.

In the circumscribed areas and modes of this debate — of which Tawney, in struggling to respect them, showed the devastating limitations — history, civilization, society, culture are spatialized, dehistoricized concepts. All the component elements are rendered as free, autonomous entities, with no dynamic features. So the major defining principle of culture itself is an intransitive sensibility, aspiring to the 'good' which consists of self-validating states of mind. Outside the sensibility, the visible constituents of culture are *objets d'art*, possessable items; or practices — knowledge, learning, arts — which can be appropriated in terms of their defining essence. All the approved 'good' of culture can be internalized, nourishing the increasingly refined consciousness, itself an entity, not here definable as 'consciousness of', as a form of objective-subjective interaction or consequential process. All activities are reduced to a defining essence, which is responded to by the cultured sensibility; and these complementary essences and personal qualities facilitate the determining of the civilized standards of excellence. The individual capable of recognition and response of this nature can attain complete self-fulfilment, an attainment which justifies his membership of the élite, and serves to define, by practice, the qualities that shape the culture and the civility treasured by the élite. T.S. Eliot's first essay transposes similar conditions and practices into the realm of Christian faith and the control of its Church. The later essay more straightforwardly attempts to legitimate the class, élites, and public order, abstracted and arrested from the past, and seen as desirable, stable and absolute.

The implications of Powys' popularizing reflections, and the stricter theorizing offered by Bell and Eliot, convert social processes and historically definable practices into structures, into spatial relations. This is largely determined by their understanding of 'culture' as an hierarchical concept; the arguments then consequently assume a monolinear, atemporal form. Process and tradition tend to be translated into matters of transmission, of modes which preserve (selected) standards and attributes. The construing in these terms of society — as an ordered, inherited system, a culture, or a civilization — has already foreclosed the major issues. All forms of hierarchy-theory (including the Mass Society sociologies like Macdonald's), are intrinsically class-committed, and determinately bound to class-ideology. They necessarily entail prescriptions for the maintaining of élites, claiming unquestionably high social positions besides public esteem; and they assume (like Eliot's) the validity of the anti-egalitarian case. Though Bell and Eliot implicitly claim descriptive objectivity and scholarly-critical impartiality, each is readily prescriptive and each carries strongly authoritarian implications.

The definitive fixities of order, traditions, social stratifications, encapsulating ideal standards, essential qualities, the absolutes of cultural excellence: these seem part of an anachronistic hypostatizing of past achievements. To theorize culture as *praxis*, as multiplex process, is to see qualities and standards as tactical abstractions, and to restore social patterning to its complicated dynamics of behaviour, tension, conflict and change. Any social moment or structuration is a vortex, an interaction moving from past crises and purposes, to an immanent new moment, then on. The refusal of social theorizing, which (without predicting the future patterning) takes conflicts, process and change into proper account, means such motion insisently signals crisis, breakdown, disorder, anarchy. There is a fundamental resistance, conscious or unconscious, to the on-going social change, giving all these conventional commentaries their inverted, atemporal form. In seeking versions of Ortega y Gasset's 'Culture without Yesterday', they deny the notion of society as *praxis*, and seek to make permanent an illusionary stability. Insofar as they describe the formative activities and initiatory processes, they have to transpose them into fragmentations, fissures, a one-way slippage which is only correctible by authoritarian control. (Early Mass Society theorizing based its black prognostications on the vision of social catastrophe, of cataclysmic breakdown.)

Such forms of cultural pessimism as the inter-war critics display stop short of these ultimates. They are, however, not only invalid theoretically, in annulling all notions of *praxis*, but obtuse to empirically observable phenomena which might question their basic assumptions, prejudices and apprehensions. Whatever area of social activity is focused — political, industrial, educational, cultural — the focus is monocular, the observation is unilinear. None of the conservative accounts evokes the simultaneity of opposite phenomena and forces. In the inter-war society they observe, conditions producing alienation and anonymity were at the same historical moment favourable to forms of freedom and to pluralism.

Social processes are always many-sided (something Mill and De Tocqueville always emphasized); and the living of society (as Durkheim insists) is a constant process of union and division. The idealizing of notions of community (based on past models, popularizing the concept of *Gemeinschaft*) ignores the cruelty, conflict, intolerance and authoritarianism that went with its forms of morality, social place and function, its modes of identification. The opposite trend (in popularizations of the *Gesellschaft* concept) remorselessly exposes the glaring faults of the over-commercialized world that *laissez-faire* ideologies have produced: Powys, Bell and (especially) Eliot isolate these results; but none sees that this world of 'association' (replacing 'community') produces enriching results. Amongst all the private and public blights, the post-*laissez-faire* world ensured increasingly free behaviour, the possibility of choosing one's own aims and objects, with moral values and the criteria of discrimination undergoing, not dissolution, but positive transpositions and socially valid reconstitution. The social construction of meaning, however uneven its processes and achievements, is positive, complex, but discernible.

The tradition that Eliot writes in is one that has driven itself into a rhetorical cul-de-sac, its radical cultural pessimism strongly inverting the early optimism of 'Progress' theories. The historicism involves prophecy of social anarchy, with emphasis now on signs of its imminence. The deadlock is also a time-lock: social phenomena not consistent with the idealized model are deplored; as Eliot sharply attacks modern education: 'The chaos of ideals and confusion of thought in our large-scale mass education is against [standards of art and culture]'. This would have, at least, surprised Arnold, that for modern anarchy (the inter-war years) education bears 'the capital responsibility'. Even the local facts are against this dog-in-the-manger illiberalism: empirical studies show that attention, interest and participation in what was denoted as 'high' art have grown at the same rate as the opposite, much-deplored lower tastes. The élites whose existence seemed threatened by such diffusion have, in practice, been strengthened, and (in Europe) increasingly interconnected. That education, on the widest scale — which, of course, is yet narrow, on the fuller view — should produce sensitivity, imagination, intelligence and skills among groups excluded before, this only goes with a sense of how incredibly restrictive were the treasured items, activities and specialized sensitivity earlier determinative of 'standards of excellence'. Again, none of these writers has any serious awareness of the achievements, varieties and potentialities of popular culture over so many areas. They consider cultural artefacts at a consistently high pitch, making of them a social preserve; while falsifying the very intricate interweaving of differing degrees and kinds of response that are essential to the aesthetic vitality of both the individual, the sub-group and the whole society.

The foundations of a common culture are economic, as Tawney's analyses show; and its general conditions are a large measure of equality. Though slow-paced, piecemeal, and so limited, instances of change recognising these goals show the prejudice and partiality of the commentators on culture considered here. One massive, damaging omission is any consideration to the economic bases of all social stratifications, and the failure to relate cultural questions to analysis of wealth, status and power among the classes and sub-groups. To have attempted such analysis would, of course, have inevitably involved considerations about ideology — including the writer's own. In the assumption that 'culture' is an area or activity free of such determinations, they necessarily convert it to a distinctively loaded ideological concept, its presentation mystified by claims to impartiality and to (neutral) critical description. Whether the term then comprises specific art objects, institutions, or practices; whether it is confined to élites, and to (class-based) sub-groups claiming certain qualities of sensibility; or whether it seems to cover a whole 'way of life' — hierarchically stratified — it is strategically arguing for a minority, and expresses fierce strictures upon the majority. These writers cannot be offered as representatives of some traditional, centralized view, some measure against which to test the practices and theories of later commentators. (Their partialities were transmitted into the early exaggerations of those who popularized the dubious generalizations of the Mass Society commentaries.) What they do seem to share, in their backward-looking apologias, and their strictures on cultural disintegration, is a grave fear of social change on a large scale. The least outdated elements can only serve as an apologia for the status quo. What they are blind to are the advances in the larger self-knowledge of mankind, the enlargement of consciousness and moral conscience that fundamentally strengthens civilization. Provincial and parochial definitions of both terms, 'culture' and 'civilization', are actual hindrances to the practising and the valuing of the full, free human interchange between individuals and groups whose potentialities are unconstrained, the dichotomies destroyed.

Notes

1 J.C. Powys (1930), *The Meaning of Culture*, Cape, London. New edition published 1939.

2 *Ibid.* 1939 edition, Introduction, original italics.
3 C. Bell (1928), *Civilization*, Chatto, London. New edition (1938) Penguin, Harmondsworth.
4 C. Bell (1922), *Since Cézanne*, Chatto, London.
5 C. Bell (1915), *Art*, Chatto, London.
6 G.E. Moore (1903), *Principia Ethica*, Cambridge University Press.
7 R.H. Tawney (1931), *Equality*, Allen & Unwin, London. Republished with additions 1952 and 1964.
8 T.S. Eliot (1938), *The Idea of a Christian Society*, Faber & Faber, London.
9 T.S. Eliot (1948), *Notes Towards the Definition of Culture*, Faber & Faber, London.
10 R. Williams (1958), *Culture and Society 1780–1950*, Chatto, London.
11 F.R. Leavis (1930), *Mass Civilization and Minority Culture*, Minority Press, Cambridge.
12 F.R. Leavis (1933), *For Continuity*, Minority Press, Cambridge.
13 M. Arnold (1869), *Culture and Anarchy*, Murray, London. New edition (1938) Macmillan, Basingstoke.
14 R.H. Tawney (1964), in R. Hinden (ed.) *The Radical Tradition*, Allen & Unwin, London.

2 NEUTRAL?: 1930s WRITERS AND TAKING SIDES

Valentine Cunningham

The pressure to 'take sides' in the 1930s was evidently terrific. Discussing the newly created *New Writing* in the *Criterion* Frank Chapman, for one, talks plaintively of the 'increasing anxiety among writers . . . to find something firm to cling to in the chaos of contemporary life; the determination to be on one side or other of the fence, not sitting on it as a mark for both parties. To join no party seems, now, a sign of weakmindedness . . .'.[1] And nowhere are the pressure and the determination more sharply focused than in the pamphlet *Authors Take Sides on the Spanish War*, published by *Left Review* from the offices of its publishers Lawrence & Wishart Ltd, at 2 Parton Street, London WC1. ('May I say how much I like your postal address?' jeered Sean O'Faolain: for Parton Street wasn't just the home of Wishart and *Left Review*; next door was the Parton Street Bookshop started by David Archer in 1932, and notorious mecca of juvenile 'revolutionaries' like Esmond Romilly, Philip Toynbee, John Cornford, George Barker, David Gascoyne, Dylan Thomas and the like).[2]

Instigated, apparently, by Nancy Cunard, a letter dated June 1937 had been sent from Paris 'To the Writers and Poets of England, Scotland, Ireland and Wales' in the names of Aragon, Auden, Bergamin, Bloch, Ms Cunard, Brian Howard, Heinrich Mann, Ivor Montagu, Pablo Neruda, Ramon Sender, Spender and Tristan Tzara. Revamping the memorable tones of Auden's recently published 'Spain' — 'Today, the struggle is in Spain. Tomorrow it may be in other countries — our own' — the letter urged writers to come clean about Fascism: '*Are you for, or against, the legal Government and the people of Republican Spain? Are you for, or against, Franco and Fascism*? For it is impossible any longer to take no side'. This absolutism was emphatically underscored: 'It is clear to many of us throughout the whole world that now, as certainly never before, we are determined or compelled, to take sides. The equivocal attitude, the Ivory Tower, the paradoxical, the ironic detachment, will no longer do'.

The replies published by *Left Review* — 149 of them in all, comprising 127 'FOR the Government', only 5 'AGAINST the Government', a mere sixteen less transigent customers ('NEUTRAL?'), with one late 'STOP PRESS: UNCLASSIFIED' response from George Bernard Shaw — look tellingly unequivocal too. They appear to indicate a massive vote of sympathy by British authors for the Spanish Republic, a mass willingness to endorse the United Front against Fascism. Here, if anywhere, is evidence of the 1930s writer's readiness to take sides, and to take the Red or reddish side at that. Here, it would undeniably seem, is the Red Decade, formed up and on parade, ready to be counted. And this is, of course, precisely the reading of the case that the Communist core of the literary United Front wished at this point in the Spanish War to promote. 'As the reader will see at the first glance, the overwhelming majority of authors are "FOR THE GOVERNMENT" . . . . This publication is . . . both representative and important, since it reflects faithfully the frame of mind of British authors today'. So runs the Publisher's Note. The pamphlet reflected *Left Review*'s orthodoxy. And it has become ours to such an extent that when 1930s orthodoxies get reinspected this one is usually exempted from scrutiny. Disappointly, for instance, the recent volume edited by John Lucas, *The 1930s: A Challenge to Orthodoxy* (1978), though squaring up admirably to 'an increasingly narrow orthodoxy about the decade', and seeking rightly to look beyond Auden, Spender, Isherwood and company, continued in a sense to narrow and specialize literary history by sticking for its part to Party men, to *Left Review* cadres — Rickword, Caudwell, Randall Swingler, Montagu Slater, James Boswell, Grassic Gibbon. Challenging *The Auden Generation* myth, the challengers have only endorsed the Red Decade assumption. And like all orthodoxies this assumption does need scrutinizing, and nowhere more appropriately than at one of its key fountainheads, at a point of emergence, of manufacture even: in a publicity venture such as *Authors Take Sides*.

'Manufacture' may be too harsh a term. No one would deny the broad picture the survey grants, of a lot of leftists ranked against many fewer non-leftists. But in some of its details, at least, *Authors Take Sides* looks as though its compilers weren't at all above a deal of rigging. How widely, one is driven to keep on wondering, was the original surveying net cast? The ranks of those 'Against the Government' do look so conveniently thin. Was Roy Campbell approached, for instance? Or Yeats, or Wyndham Lewis, or Robert Graves, or Henry Williamson, or Count Potocki de Montalk, the editor of the frantically Franco-ist *Right Review*? To be sure, Edmund Blunden, Arthur Machen and Evelyn Waugh are sufficient to make the Rightist ranks seem not wholly comical. But their modicum of credibility is made just absurd in company with Geoffrey Moss and Eleanor Smith who, considered as writers, are simply nonentities. Was this the intention? Were heavyweights like Yeats and Wyndham Lewis, not known for bashfulness, deliberately bypassed? Worse, were replies from their side of the fence silenced?

We know for certain that the survey's organizers were capable of acts of suppression that seem scarcely unpolitical. James Joyce replied by phone, but only to tell Nancy Cunard 'I am James Joyce. I have received your questionnaire': too unquotable an indifference it would seem. Orwell's response was angrier. In April 1938 he told Spender how he'd responded to 'that bloody rot which was afterwards published in book form (called *Authors Take Sides*)' and 'that damned rubbish of signing manifestos to say how wicked it all is': 'I sent back a very angry reply in which I'm afraid I mentioned you uncomplimentarily, not knowing you personally at that time'.[3] The sort of rough handling *Homage to Catalonia* was to receive from the Communists and their publishing and reviewing sympathizers within the British Left is a measure of how dangerous Orwell's disillusioned Republicanism was felt to be. And the *Left Review* clique was evidently not going to allow Orwell to upset the pamphlet's orthodox pretences about seamless unity to its cause, to expose rifts within socialism. That the Spanish situation might be complicated and that honourably wounded Republican sympathizers like Orwell might have developed unsimple opinions unsettled the desired myth. If only in the case of Orwell the pamphlet's Publisher's Note was misleadingly reassuring: 'It has proved impossible to include all the answers received . . . in no instance has an Answer been omitted on grounds of "policy" . . . all the answers omitted fell under the . . . head of "FOR"'.

It was all very well to have the expectable droves of sympathizers, the people in and about the Party, and in and out of the offices of *Left Review* or the *New Statesman* rallying round. People like Valentine Ackland, Mulk Raj Anand, Pearl Binder, Auden, Calder-Marshall, Connolly, Day Lewis, Willie Gallacher MP, David Gascoyne, Victor Gollancz, James Hanley, Lancelot Hogben, Storm Jameson, Koestler, John Langdon-Davies, John Lehmann, H. Laski, Jack Lindsay, Hugh MacDiarmid, MacNeice, Madge, Tom Mann, Ivor Montagu, Naomi Mitchison, Harry Pollit, Raymond Postgate, D.N. Pritt KC, MP, V.S. Pritchett, Rickword, Paul Rotha, Spender, Hannen Swaffer, Randall Swingler, Sylvia Townsend Warner, Rex Warner, Rebecca West, and Amabel and Clough Williams-Ellis. It was cheering enough to the cause's case that these all found assent so natural. 'Of course', replied Gollancz and Aldous Huxley and John Lehmann; 'No question', said Naomi Mitchison. But all these were the old reliables. 'A prize-fighter's view on ballet, or on Bach, could not be solicited to better purpose, or to conclusions more foregone', thought Hugh Gordon Porteous, noting 'all the dozen examples of "of course" (an expression which Mr Stephen Spender has characterised as symptomatic of Fascist English)'.[4] Better still, then, to have the rather less expectable names, like Samuel Beckett, Havelock Ellis, Ford Madox Ford, David Garnett, C.E.M. Joad, Rosamund Lehmann, John Middleton Murray, Llewellyn Powys, or Leonard Woolf: people who, even if they were not exactly strangers to readers of *Left Review* or to the whereabouts of the *New Statesman* offices (or at least to people who themselves starred in those circles), did help give the Popular Front idea some credence. A credence undermined most of all, of course, by the antagonism or reluctance of people broadly within the 1930s leftish affiliation — men like Orwell, or like Michael Roberts, editor of the *New Country* and *New Signatures* anthologies and *The Faber Book of Modern Verse*. It's unclear whether Michael Roberts actually replied to the questionnaire. But his attitude is clear from his reply to Laura Riding's own survey about writers and international affairs:

> I was in the French Alps for a month, and was followed round by circulars asking for six lines saying that Franco is a devil and Caballero a gentleman (or words to that effect). I don't think that the outwide world is as simple as that. I suspect that kind of symposium: it is an easy way out for people who think that they ought to do something at this moment and ease their minds by signing a manifesto.[5]

Authors Take Sides takes care not to name those who did not even choose to reply: their silence damaged the orthodoxy it promotes as much as hostility like Orwell's did.

If only by silence, then, the pamphlet tampers with the full picture of the period's political feelings. But tampering does not stop there. There is the occasionally rough and ready way its editors have of sorting the replies they actually print. On the one hand, the careful, the hedged, the lukewarm in the anti-Fascist stable are all briskly bundled into capacious 'For the Government' bag. Orthodoxy did not want to linger overlong about possible ironies in George Barker's 'I am for the people of Republican Spain, for the people of China, for the people of England, for the people of Germany, etc.', nor dwell on the reservations of a Geoffrey Grigson ('I am equivocal enough to be *against* politically, and not *for*, to fear and distrust any mass in its own control'), or a Tom Harrisson ('The equivocal attitude, the Ivory Tower, the ironic detachment, are words your letter uses to sway with superstitious feeling our immediate judgement. But even without them we must feel horror and terror and hate at that Franco . . .').

Pink doubters like that were smoothly bustled into line on the Left side. Conversely, considerable latitude of opinion was allowed in order to keep the Right side looking grotesquely under-populated. Sean O'Faolain ('For the love of mike . . .'); Vita Sackville-West ('What you really mean is that you want to see Communism established in Spain'); and Robert Byron ('Had I been a Spaniard when the rebellion broke out, I cannot say for certain that I would not have favoured it') sound scarcely neutral, nor even 'Neutral?'. Certainly they're no more neutral than was Evelyn Waugh's reply ('As an Englishman I am not in the predicament of choosing between two evils'), that got itself classified as 'Against'. No cosmetic, I suppose, could mitigate Waugh's well-publicized Christian Rightism: *Waugh in Abyssinia* (1936) had made his Fascist leanings unequivocally clear. But if right-wingers could be at all disguised they would be, so that even Ezra Pound, almost as well known a Mussolini-fancier as Waugh — as least to the readers of the *Criterion* — was smuggled over into 'neutrality?'. Clearly, Social Credit could be given credit for not being directly Fascist: certainly Pound was not confusable with a capitalist ('Questionnaire an escape mechanism for young fools who are too cowardly to think, too lazy to investigate the nature of money, its mode of issue, the control of such issue by the Banque de France and the stank of England'). Nevertheless, he was toughly hostile to the survey's sponsors: 'You are all had. Spain is an emotional luxury to a gang of sap-headed dilettantes'. If this were neutrality, it was neutrality dubiously bestowed and precariously held.

But having, in aid of making the Right look ludicrously skinny, prevented Pound and O'Faolain and Vita Sackville-West from swelling the Francoist party where they evidently belong, the survey's compilers then proceed to belittle the notion of the neutrality they've allowed such people. For what else is that question-mark doing? 'Neutral?' could, of course, be taken neutrally, as indicating merely genuine difficulty in weighing the blurred position taken by the uncommitted, although, as we've seen, there's scarcely any problem about detecting that Pound and company should be categorized as 'Against'. A more likely explanation is that the compilers wanted to reinforce their declared belief that neutrality was impossible in this crisis hour ('The equivocal attitude . . . will no longer do'). Better, naturally, to be made to look 'Neutral?' than to be allowed publicly to vote for Franco. But dare actually to declare neutrality — and there's little doubt that that's what Norman Douglas, for example ('To hell with sides'), or Vera Brittain (who was pacifistically against any kind of fighting) were purporting to be — and the *Left Review* crowd would disinfect your declaration with the impugning suspicion of a question mark. And, here again, silence about who was or was not approached detracts from the statistical value of *Authors Take Sides*. Many possible neutrals not reported in the survey spring quickly to mind — like Virginia Woolf (capable of endless equivocation in such matters as her *Three Guineas* of 1938 shows), or Elizabeth Bowen, or William Empson, or Ivy Compton-Burnett and Anthony Powell. One would like very much to know whether Graham Greene, a leftish Catholic who wrote the not unsympathetic *The Confidential Agent* (1939) about Spain, was asked, and refused to respond, or responded too cagily for the compilers' pleasure.

It is clear, though, whatever the silences and equivocations of *Authors Take Sides*, that indifference to Leftism, the most emphatic kind of neutrality, could be more startingly widespread than the pamphlet's compilers were prepared for, or that we who have on the whole accepted their map of the decade's allegiances have been schooled to expect. Take, for instance, the magical iconography of redness. Our conventional 1930s acquires its quintessential colouring from publications like E.A. Osborne's compendium *In Letters of Red* (1938), an anti-fascist anthology (with, interestingly, its epigraph consisting of Sir Peter Chalmers Mitchell's response to *Authors Take Sides*: 'Fascism is a pathological condition . . .'). Or from magazines like *The Red Stage: Organ of the Workers' Theatre Movement*,[6] with its enthused reports of agitprop troupes with names like 'Red Pioneers', 'Red Front', 'Red Radio', 'Red Players', 'Red Flag', 'Red Anchor', 'Red Magnets', 'Red Blouses', and its provision of essential kit for the red actor, like *The Soviet Airman's Song*:

> Fly higher, higher, and higher;
> Our emblem the Soviet Star
> And ev'ry propellor is RED FRONT! [shouted]
> Defending the USSR.

But this kind of redness left some consciousnesses unmoved. For instance, D.C. Thomson & Co.'s *Red Letter* had been going since 1899 and was still pumping out its serials 'of love, mystery, pathos and stirring incidents', its short stories ('dramatic with strong love or domestic interest') and its articles 'on subjects of feminine interest'. *Red Star Weekly*, founded in 1929, also had nothing to do with the Soviet Union: it was just another Thomson paper purveying 'strong emotional interest'. *Red Magazine* (founded 1910), another general fiction paper, and even *Red Tape*, the Civil Service Magazine, started in 1911 ('Well-written articles and stories of a light character . . . . Also verse, photographs, and humorous drawings of interest to Civil Servants'), only underscore the point. These descriptions of the unpolitically red papers come from *The Writers' and Artists' Year Book* of 1937, the year of *Authors Take Sides*, the year following the one generally thought to compose the heart of the literary 1930s. But the *Writers' and Artists' Year Book* might be inhabiting another world from the Spanish War and Mass-Observation, *The Road to Wigan Pier*, *Fact*, *Forward from Liberalism* and *Illusion and Reality*, the events and the texts that preoccupy Samuel Hynes's chapter on '1937'.[7] It does not, for instance, list either the *Daily Worker* or *Left Review*, though it does mention *New Verse* ('Poems and critical articles on peotry — highest standard . . . . Georgian, and adolescent love poetry not required'). Another sort of clientèle keeps it going. Its most prominent, front end-papers advertisement ('Authors! Breezy Writing Pays') announces *Money-making Authorship* by R.A.H. Goodyear, a ten-part course now available in one volume. Goodyear comes heavily 'Endorsed by countless unsolicited testimonials', including one from a Reginald Glossop, author of *The Ghastly Dew* and *The Crystal Globe*. 'I have had your book bound', Glossop announces, evidently unaware which decade he is supposed to be in, 'in red Russian leather for my travelling library'.

Glossop, admittedly, packs only a tiny punch. But another witness from 1937 carries a much greater weight of testimony for something suspiciously like neutrality. What's striking about the weekly magazine *Night and Day* is not just its extemely short life (it ran only from 1 July 1937 until 23 December 1937 (No.26), when its publishers Chatto & Windus closed it down because of two libel actions, including a large one brought by Shirley Temple against its film critic and literary editor Graham Greene), but the way in which it managed to combine 'all the talents', left and right, into a lively and glossy stab at doing a British *New Yorker*.[8] Peter Fleming ran a gossip-column as 'Slingsby'. Felix Topolski ('a talented anthropologist') supplied sketched features on British social life. Graham Greene was the regular film critic, Elizabeth Bowen the regular theatre critic, Evelyn Waugh the main books reviewer, Herbert Read a frequent crime fiction reviewer, Osbert Lancaster the art critic. William Empsom and Anthony Powell sent in light personal pieces and letters from abroad (Alistair Cooke did a 'New York Letter'). Stevie Smith was there; so were Henry Miller and R.K. Narayan (Greene's protégé), Walter Allen and Malcolm Muggeridge, John Betjeman, Cyril Connolly and Michael Roberts. Christopher Isherwood contributed a notable, and too unregarded, 'extract' from an 'autobigraphical work in progress, *The North West Passage*', entitled 'The First Journey', about a school trip to France with Chalmers (the persona Isherwood later granted Edward Upward in *Lions and Shadows*).[9]

Not surprisingly, given this mix, the tones of left and right nudge along side by side in the pages of *Night and Day*. There is, of course, a level of unabashedly bourgeois chat about Oxford and the Ritz and such in Old Etonian Slingsby's column, and Topolski's sketch-pad has been sported at obviously unproletarian locations like the Eton–Harrow cricket match, the Henley Regatta, and the 'Débutantes' Last Round-Up'. A strongly satirical tone is frequently taken towards manifestations of literary leftism, especially in Waugh's books-pieces. *The Mind in Chains* gets put in its place as authoritarian schoolmasters' job (which it was, of course).[10] Making deft use of Wyndham Lewis's jeers at the period's juvenility, Waugh slights Arthur Calder-Marshall's novel *The Changing Scene* as adolescently Marxist ('political Peter Pans drifting wistfully through the woods').[11] Rex Warner's *The Wild Goose Chase* is badly political ('Kafka's allegory is religious and timeless: Mr. Warner's is political and as Victorian as Marx'). Equally expectably, Osbert Lancaster keeps up a polemic against politics in painting.[12] *Night and Day*, ever good at satire and parody (one of its aims was to outdo what its sponsors thought the wearisome *Punch*), is particularly sharp in burlesques of Magnetogorsk worship, the Left Book Club,[13] and the unhappily all too parodiable Spender:

> At a literary luncheon in the Holborn Restaurant yesterday, the guest of honour Mr. Stephen Spender, gave readings from poems written while on active service in Spain. Proposing a vote of thanks, Miss Maude Royden said that whatever their political views might be, they must all surely recognise in the poems they had just listened to, the most poignant expression since Rupert Brooke of youth going gallantly into battle. Certain lines of those they had just heard would, she knew, forever linger in her memory:
>
> If I die in Spain
> I do not die in Spain
> I die in the future
> And shall live again
> When the future has overtaken the past.[14]

On the other hand, contributors more leftwardly placed are equally welcomed. There's a notable run of documentary pieces cast, roughly, in the Mass-Observation mould: William Plomer on all-in wrestling,[15] Kenneth Allott on Oxford's St Giles' Fair,[16] Walter Allen on the origins of Aston Villa football club.[17] The three parts of Cyril Connolly's 'The House of Arquebus', about a Hampstead literary family with a black-sheep son at Cambridge and in the Party, who fails to run away to Spain, and who talks of 'red terror', and is eventually sent down from the university 'For canvassing for the C.P. and making communist speeches', is a bright pastiche full, to be sure, of snappily superior dialogue that didn't demand any particular political leanings to concoct, but whose Leftish affections nevertheless emerge very unambiguously.[18] A.S.J. Tessimond's *Song of the City* strikes the clear-cut anti-capitalist note characteristic of the period's insulters of the international arms-traffic (best example: Eric Ambler's 1930s novels):

> Oh, brighter than the starry firmament
> And fairer than my well-beloved's charms:
> A block of cumulative 5%
> Preferred Participatory Shares in Arms.[19]

And, of course, Graham Greene keeps up the grouching about the awful untruthfulness of the usual screen-images of the world, which he began as film-critic of the *Spectator*. 'No sign, of course, of the Karl Marx Hof', he notes of the Austrian-made *Tales from the Vienna Woods* (shot in 1934), 'only palaces and big Baroque dictatorial buildings.'[20] Greene not only writes debunkingly well ('she toted a breast like a man totes a gun').[21] He continues his strong advocacy for films out of the radical documentary-film school—like Basil Wright's *Children at School* (Realist Film Unit, 1937).[22] Greene was by no means incautiously simplistic in his admiration of documentaries. (His caveats as well as his enthusiasms are amply set out in his *Spectator* essay (26 May 1939) on GPO Film Unit offerings by Pat Jackson, Humphrey Jennings and Alberto Cavalcanti.) Nor was he a naive supporter of Soviet films. (He regarded *Lenin in October* (Mosfilm 1937) as not only stupidly Stalinist ('History . . . has to be rewritten . . . the elimination of Trotsky . . . Stalin slides into all the important close-ups'), but also so hero-worshipful as to be merely Fascist and wrote that 'We have reached the end of the Communist film. It is to be all "Heroes and Hero-Worship" now: the old films are to be remade for the new leaders: no more anonymous mothers will run in the van of the workers against the Winter Palace. The USSR is to produce Fascist films from now on.'[23] But his left-of-centre position, schooled, admittedly, by his obsession with Original Sin, his feel for the Dantesque in modern life, does emerge openly. Just so, the keenness of Elizabeth Bowen — quite a surprising enthusiasm in the light of her more detached 1930s fiction — for Unity Theatre ('important and vital'; 'a real purpose, so a real energy. This is a Workers' Theatre') is clearly expressed. Producers should, she avers, 'cross London to the Unity to see what can be what'. 'There still exists a strong feeling, that few of us are quite clear of, against "propagandistic art". Visit the Unity to see whether Art suffers'. *Waiting for Lefty* 'is impressive'. So too is Unity's production of Pogodin's *Aristocrats* ('has qualities in common with the great Russian films').[24]

Also, and expectably, there is about *Night and Day* a strong strain of mere indifferentism. A lot of the time it simply wants to get unpolitically on with its cultural soundings (John Summerson, it might be, or Hugh Casson, on architecture, for example). Empson's contributions aim for an extraordinarily flippant tone, a steady preoccupation with the frivolous (like his 'Notice this Gate' article on redundant signs) or the personal (like 'Learning Chinese': 'The character for the male organ is a combination of signs meaning the Imploring Corpse, or the Corpse in Pain', and so on).[25] And although the editor, John Marks, was half Spanish (he was *The Times* correspondent in Spain after World War II), the Spanish Civil War failed even to get itself mentioned in *Night and Day* until issue No.6 (5 August) when, at last, George Steer's 'The Fall of Bilbao: An Eye-witness's Account' appeared. For the whole of July 1937, then, straight after the *Authors Take Sides* letter of June had declared the unavoidable compulsion 'to take sides', there was silence on Spain. And there wasn't even any taking of sides when the silence was at last broken. Steer's article even-handedly describes the indiscriminate aerial assault by the Fascists and the incompetence of the Basque militia under Colonel Vidal ('. . . a rout, shameless and concerted. A real Italian rout, each man legging it across the open to beat his neighbour').[26] And this neutral note is sounded later in No.6 in Osbert Lancaster's art piece of the week, 'Kultur-Bolshevismus', which jibes both at Hitler and at 'the United Artists Front' for their misguided disgruntlement with 'those who give us green grass and blue skies', the old-fashioned representational painters.

A busy stir of left and right, then, of indifferents and neutrals: in condoning this mix, the editorial policy of *Night and Day* is visibly at odds with the 1930s commitment myth, with the *Authors Take Sides*, the *Left Review* resistance to politically compromised stances. Rightists and Leftists share the same bed; with a reddish literary editor as the genially presiding Madame. The economic pressures on young writers have, of course, not a little to do with it: V.S. Pritchett (who was 'For the Government') was surely not unique in being happy (as he tells me) to get paid for his stories even if they had perforce to be jostled in the publishing by more conservative contributions. Be that as it may, however, Greene's literary editorship is still noteworthy. And it is by no means unique. It's not altogether unlike T.S. Eliot's own tolerant opening of the *Criterion* to people and opinions adverse to his own position. To A.L. Morton, for example; to the young Marxist A.L. Rowse; to James Hanley, the radical story-teller whose apter-seeming beat was frequently the *Left Review*; and to Hugh MacDiarmid.[27]

Was T.S. Eliot, though — arguably the biggest literary fish trawled up by *Authors Take Sides* — seeking to be neutral in his reply: 'While I am naturally sympathetic, I still feel convinced that it is best that at least a few men of letters should remain isolated, and take no part in these collective activities'? Of all the replies published, his is in many respects the most ingriguing; certainly it's the one with most to offer on this problematic of 'neutrality'. Neither Eliot, nor the *Criterion* was, of course, indifferentist. But can Eliot's stance on Spain be categorized with that of the editors of *Night and Day* as a neutral one? It looks like a profession of neutrality — far more so than Pound's does. With how much of a pinch of salt, however, must we take it? For we all know what professions of neutrality tend to amount to. We know which side Yeats was actually on, despite the pretentions of 'Politics' (1938):

> How can I, that girl standing there,
> My attention fix
> On Roman or on Russian
> Or on Spanish politics?

We know, too, on the other side, what John Lehmann really intended for *New Writing* even though he declared it would be 'independent of any political party'. Indeed, he went on to prick this bubble of neutrality himself: *New Writing* did 'not intend to open its pages to writers of reactionary or Fascist sentiment'. In the light of these well known instances of non-neutral 'neutrals' one can perhaps sympathize with that suspicious 'neutral?'.

But what of Eliot's neutral-seeming reply? In the first place, it mustn't be looked at in isolation. From the start we must notice that the Paris letter seems to have been consciously taking up a rejection by T.S. Eliot of the very pressure to take sides that it was seeking to apply. The Spanish War, Eliot wrote in the *Criterion* of January 1937, had caused 'a deterioration of political thinking, with a pressure on everyone, which has to be stubbornly resisted, to accept one extreme philosophy or another'. Polarization he rejected as the mentally slothful response of the press — the *Tablet* on the one hand and the *New Statesman* on the other — whose intellectual laziness was likely to upset 'the precarious balance of ideas in our heads':

> Now an ideally unprejudiced person, with an intimate knowledge of Spain, its history, its racial characteristics, and its contemporary personalities, might be in a position to come to the conclusion that he should, in the longest view that could be seen, support one side rather than the other. But so long as we are not compelled in our own interest to take sides, I do not see why we should do so on insufficient knowledge. . . .[28]

So it was pretty sanguine to expect Eliot, only five months later, to feel 'compelled to take sides'. Sanguine, furthermore, to expect from him any enthusiastic joining in a manifesto of writers. For his reluctance to countenance collective activity at the instance of the *Left Review* was only the latest of the reservations about manifestoes that this period found him delivering himself of. In 1933, writing from America (where he'd gone to give the *After Strange Gods* lectures), Eliot had deplored the trend forcing editors to reveal their papers' ideological position; he wasn't even going, he said, to be drawn into a manifesto against this current enthusiasm for manifestoes:

> It seems to be the necessity of the moment — at least in America — for the editor of a literary periodical to explain exactly where that periodical stands on the great political and social issues of the day. I have no intention of doing that myself on this occasion; and I have not yet framed any manifesto against manifestoes.[29]

At the period of the Abyssinian crisis Eliot took time — the 'moment of crisis' compelled him to do so — to discuss the manifestoes of some French *clercs*. But, he insisted, this entailed a departure from normal *Criterion* practice: the paper ordinarily eschewed 'topical political issues', preferred 'political philosophy' to 'politics'. And Eliot appeared relieved that the English intellectuals' skin was generally healthier, less pustular than the French: 'The discharge of collective manifestoes is not such a regular part of the activity of intellectuals in this country, as it is in France.'[30] Soon enough, though, the English themselves took to discharging in the French fashion and the *Criterion*'s resistance to topicality wavered. In October 1936 Eliot was 'impelled, by the receipt of manifestoes to be signed by "artists and writers", as well as by scientists and other intellectual workers, to pursue reflection on the subject of peace and war'. But the old rhythmic grumbler was still swayed by the rhythm of his earlier anti-French grouse. In particular, he didn't want to be appealed to as a writer:

> The first difficulty that I experience with the leaflet that I have received from the 'International Peace Campaign' is that it makes a special appeal to members of my own profession: it is headed *War and Writers*. While I am not insensible to argument in favour of anything which will help me to ply my own trade to the best of my ability, the assertion that 'modern war and preparations for war are hostile to the arts, and most of all to writing' (I do not understand why most of all to writing), seems to be almost trifling when the issue is so serious.

He refused to allow that intellectuals have a special case:

> In any case I do not like to be appealed to as an 'intellectual', if it be implied that intellectuals, as a class, have any *special interest* in the maintenance of peace. It is for the whole human race, not for any particular elements, that I should consider peace worth maintaining.[31]

It was a point he would recur to after the *Authors Take Sides* invitation, when he had also received the catalogue of the 1937

Exhibition of 'Unity of Artists for Peace, Democracy and Cultural Development':

> No one can object to 'artists' banding themselves together for the purpose of advancing political tendencies with which they sympathise; but they can only legitimately do this as human beings, or at most as representatives of a particular movement in art: they have no claim to speak in the name of 'Art' in general.[32]

So, as the compilers of the Paris letter recognised when they took up his words about not being compelled to take sides, and as his kept-up distrust of manifestoes revealed, Eliot constituted an exceedingly unpromising source of the ready signature. Readers of even a little of his published writing would not have been surprised at his reluctance. His suspicion of *writers'* collectives was not unique either. It was rooted in hostility to any sort of collective apart from that of the Christian Church. That crowd flowing over London Bridge in *The Waste Land* is locked into an urban hell, and is in fact dead ('I had not thought death had undone so many'). And life, especially Christian life, consists for Eliot in aloofness from the ghostly, Dantesque mob of the lost:

> I am already oppressed, not so much by the theory which reacts violently against 'atomistic individualism', and with which, as a theory, I can feel from a Christian point of view a certain sympathy, as by the 'collectivism' which I see already in existence about me, and which makes a London crowd (the members of which perhaps take pride in their individualism and their love of liberty) the sheep-like suggestible entity that it is.[33]

He opposed mass education,[34] 'poetry for the million' (a notion that had the 'wrong smell' about it),[35] mass production,[36] mass meetings,[37] and mass conversions in any usual sense.[38] He talked glibly of 'mass-identity' as 'herd-feeling'.[39] His distaste for the cinema, or flickers (remember the 'flicker' over the tube-travellers' faces in *Burnt Norton*: people 'Distracted from distraction by distraction') seems closely related to its being a mass art ('a question of what happens to the minds of the thousands of people who feast their eyes every night . . .').[40] The words 'mass' and 'masses' and 'mob' ring pejoratively again and again throughout *The Idea of a Christian Society* — 'great mass of humanity', 'masses of the people' 'mass of the population', 'mass society organised for profit', 'mass education', 'the mass', 'mass civilization', 'mass suggestion: in other words, a mob', 'illiterate and uncritical mob', 'a state secularized, a community turned into a mob, and a clerisy disintegrated' — forming the tonal base for his development of the idea of a super-élite, the 'Community of Christians' within the already privileged élite of the Church.

Eliot was, of course, drawn towards élites. He sustains a notable rhetoric of fewness, of the few, the leading minds whose ideas are implicitly and explicitly, imposable on the mass. Unblushing, he says: 'It will not do merely to call for better individuals; the asceticism must first, certainly, be practised by the few, and it must be definite enough to be explained to, and ultimately imposed upon, the many'.[41] 'If the intellectual is a person of philosophical mind philosophically trained' — as T.S. Eliot (naturally) was — 'who thinks things out for himself, then there are very few intellectuals about'.[42] A priori, then, joining a collective — signing a manifesto, thinking about things with others — is a simple token you're no intellectual. It 'is best that at least a few men of letters should remain isolated': the aloofness over Spain was part of this continuing concern with fewness. There 'should always be', he pursued in 1955, 'a few writers preoccupied in penetrating to the core of the matter . . . without too much hope, without ambition to alter the immediate course of affairs.'[43] The fewer people who held to a position the better — and almost masochistically so. Eliot bleakly enjoys minorities, preferably 'hopeless' ones.[44] In his depressed 'Last Words' from the cross of the modern problem, he could see hope only in the smallest of groups: 'the continuity of culture may have to be maintained by a very small number of people indeed.'[45]

Aloofness had become a principle; but it evidently started in deeply rooted feelings. Eliot the élitist is also Eliot the congenital non-joiner. He hated allies. He found it difficult to stomach other supporters of his causes. 'I am afraid of exciting the approval', he told his radio audience in 1932, 'of people whose approval I do not especially want'.[46] 'I do not wish', he insisted again in this 'Modern Dilemma' series of broadcasts, 'to be named among the usual antagonists of communism'.[47] At the end of 1940 he was dismayed that the trend of opinion among young writers might actually be running his way:

> Mob rule is denounced — yet I feel like a Tory who becomes aware that he is also (having been born when he was and not several generations earlier) something of a Liberal . . . or a Frenchman attached to the *ancien régime*, who having come to accept the Marseillaise as the national anthem, might find himself jailed for singing it.[48]

Furthermore, in keeping apart, in maintaining the privateness of the self, in insisting on the impersonal recessiveness of the poet, he was (as usual) following the most pukka models. Like that of Thomas Middleton ('inscrutable, solitary, unadmired . . . dying no-one knows when and no one knows how; attracting, in three hundred years, no personal admiration');[49] or Keats:

[whose] sayings about poetry, thrown out in the course of private correspondence, keep pretty close to intuition; and they have no apparent bearing upon his own times, as he himself does not appear to have taken any absorbing interest in public affairs — though when he did turn to such matters, he brought to bear a shrewd and penetrating intellect . . . we cannot accuse Keats of any withdrawal, or refusal; he was merely about his business. He had no theories, yet in the sense appropriate to the poet, in the same sense, though to a lesser degree than Shakespeare, he had a 'philosophic' mind. He was occupied only with the highest use of poetry . . . .[50]

The paradox there — no 'absorbing interest in public affairs', but no 'withdrawal, or refusal either' — is typical, in one sense, of Eliot's confusion, the confusion and obscurity of thought to which he admitted his *Criterion* commentaries were prone.[51] In another, though, the profession of a Keatsian unconcern for public affairs, the separation, the refusal to allow the joining of the categories 'poetry' and 'public affairs', clearly relates to the effort at clearing up confusions that he felt being a post-Arnoldian Christian imposed on him. If Eliot was a non-joiner, he was so because there was too much joining going on — for his liking, and to the detriment of the religious sense. Arnold had led men of letters dangerously into a 'cloud cuckoo land' where poetry was blurred into — made to join in with — religion.[52] But poetry was not religion, as Eliot repeatedly insisted. Literature was not religion. Nor was drama.[52] Religion must be kept separate from science,[53] from economics,[54] from psychology,[55] and above all from politics. Eliot is ever hostile to muddled terms — to 'loose talk', and the 'vague jargon of our time'[56] — but politics is the greatest muddler of all, incompatible, he suggests, with exact meanings. And Communism, like Fascism in being a religion falsely so-called and inciting 'misplaced religious fanaticism', inspires in Eliot as the 1930s go on the deepest mistrust as a confuser, a joiner of the unjoinable.[57]

In an impressive and extended rebuttal of Middleton Murry's and John Macmurray's 'monism' — what Eliot calls their 'sort of dissolving trick', their dissolving of religion into Marxism — he argues that Christianity remains forever dualistic, the transcendent properly unconfusable with the earthly.[58] As the poet serves 'the highest use of poetry' by steering clear of politics, so Christianity must represent a dissociated position. Though the Christian social philosopher, for instance, may draw on 'associated ideas', he 'can only follow such a course safely if he is equally prepared for a *dis*sociation of ideas. He must be able to consider the ideas of class, of property, of nationality not according to current or local prejudices, but according to permanent principles'.[59] Ideas are best, in fact, when they clash antagonistically. Only woolly liberals, in politics as in theology, want to build bridges, to make words and positions collaborate in a kind of semantic United Front.[60]

What though, one is compelled by this analysis to enquire, of the much flaunted *middle way*? Does not Eliot's Christianity represent the *via media*, the third way between Communist and Fascism — a position that might be regarded as truly neutral? Eliot, of course, professes to desire the *via media* — doubly desirable because it's not only Anglican, it's also English.[61] Does not heresy consist, as he sees it, in extremism, the over-emphasis of one part of the truth. Is not orthodoxy precisely the holding of the middle, and difficult because it is a middle position.[62] Indeed, it's 'almost impossible to the frail human being at every moment of his life'.[63] Like the 'uneasy bed' of the Church of England, the quest for this orthodoxy of the middle commits you to 'mortification' and 'sacrifice'. It is also, though, the way of 'thought' and 'study'.[64] And extremism, according to Eliot, is not just too old-fashioned for thinking people (he talks of the either/or 'methods with which the nineteenth century consoled itself'),[65] it is unthinkingly easy,[66] a relaxation into 'facile' alternatives.[67] 'To surrender individual judgement to a Church is a hard thing', he wrote in 1934; but 'to surrender individual responsibility to a party is, for many men, a pleasant stimulant and sedative. And those who have once experienced this sweet intoxication are not easily brought back to the difficult path of thinking for themselves'.[68]

Taking the middle way neatly combines Eliot's twin needs for self-mortifying and high moral satisfaction:

> . . . the *via media* is of all ways the most difficult to follow. It requires discipline and self-control, it requires both imagination and hold on reality. In a period of debility like our own, few men have the energy to follow the middle way in government; for lazy or tired minds there is only extremity or apathy: dictatorship or communism, with enthusiasm or with indifference.[69]

And in tune with this advocacy Eliot keeps pressing for some other way than the 'brainless' alternative of Labour and Tory in 1929,[70] of Fascism and Communism, of Italy and Russia,[71] of nationalism and imperialism ('the problems of our time . . . more serious than such as can be eased by national or imperial nostrums'),[72] of Berlin and Moscow.[73] He is never, alas, very specific about what exactly this middle consists in; perhaps because he is not too clear himself. (In his fourth radio talk on 'The Modern Dilemma' he was deliberately vague, resisting any spelling out about kingship, aristocracy, democratism, money, scouting or folk-dancing: 'My whole purpose has been to stimulate the belief that a Christian organisation of society is possible, that it is perhaps now more that at any previous time possible; to encourage the search for it and the testing of all offers of reform and revolution by its standards'; but into specificity he will not venture.[74]) Certainly, over Spain, Eliot is clearer in his rejection of the offered extremes than at any more positive analysis. The clash of extremist alternatives is what he finds nightmarish (so much for the excitement of antagonism that he elsewhere admires):

> The situation in Spain has provided the perfect opportunity for extremists of both extremes. To turn from the shrill manifestoes of the Extreme Left, and the indiscretions of the Dean of Canterbury, to the affirmations of Mr. Jerrold and Mr. Lunn, is only to intensify the nightmare. On the First of May *The Tablet* provided its explanation of the destruction of Guernica: the most likely culprits, according to *The Tablet*, were the Basques' own allies, their shady friends in Catalonia.[75]

But what did happen in Guernica? And is it proper to keep on suspending judgement in the fashion blessed by Eliot in 1935, when he praised Aldous Huxley for not taking either the 'red ticket' or the 'blue':

> It is better to suspend decision than to surrender oneself to a belief merely for the sake of believing something. There is a kind of scepticism which is caused merely by the refusal to think things out; and there is a kind of belief springing from the same cause: both are illustrations of the sin of mental sloth.[76]

It is evident that Spain became for Eliot not only the apotheosis of all he'd ever preached about extremism, but also the battle-ground over which he worked most strenuously to establish the honourableness of taking no side. Viewing a victory in Spain for the (secular) Right as dyspeptically as he regards a victory for the (non-humanitarian) Left, he feels, as one who has 'at heart the interests of Christianity in the long run', that he has 'especial reason for suspending judgement'. He shrinks from partisanship because 'That balance of mind which a few highly-civilized individuals, such as Arjuna, the hero of the *Bhagavad-Gita*, can maintain in action, is difficult for most of us even as observers, and . . . is not encouraged by the greater part of the Press.'[77] 'Balance of mind': it was to be stressed again in World War II in the exhortation in *The Dry Salvages* to 'consider the future/And the past with an equal mind': a little reflection, this, about action, conducted in a suspended, middle position, 'At the moment which is not of action or inaction'. And at face value it does look like a not dishonourable striving for poise between opposites, for yoga, in fact — the 'even, or equal, mind'.[78] It looks, it must be admitted, very like neutrality: neither 'Attachment' nor 'detachment', as Eliot puts it in *Little Gidding*, but 'growing/ Between them, indifference'.

But is Eliot's middle way really neutral? In fact, on inspection, the rhetoric of the mind balanced between extremes, of the middle way, turns out in no sense to cancel the rhetoric of antagonism, of dualism. One quickly spots that the two models of Eliot's self-realization run side by side and in and out of each other. His Christianity remains intransigently the opponent of Communism: toying with the arduousnesses of the third, the middle way has not shifted him from his fundamentally polarized station. 'There can only be the two, Christianity and Communism: and there, if you like, is your dilemma'.[79] 'There are two and only two finally tenable hypotheses about life: the Catholic and the materialistic'.[80] What's more, 'I and any who agree with me . . . loathe communism'.[81] The religion of Communism is 'ludicrous and repulsive'.[82] Communism is 'the devil'.[83] Marxism 'is equally repugnant whether it fails or succeeds' economically. 'The Bolsheviks at any rate believe in something which has what is equivalent for them to a supernatural sanction', and they must be opposed 'with a genuine supernatural sanction'. Only Christian Toryism will make 'a worthy adversary for Communism'.[84]

In other words, the middle way, the 'indifferent' or 'even' mind, can be dissolved, and keeps on being dissolved, at will, at Eliot's arbitrary and privileged whim, into a much more aggressively dualistic or 'attached' position. Neutrality is repeatedly just overwhelmed by rightist aggression. Eliot had, of course, built a ready excuse for this frequent collapse, into his accounts of the difficulties of sticking to the middle way, to orthodoxy, to Anglicanism. But there's little doubt that we must add his middle way — and his repeated murmurs about the problematic of the yoga position — to the instances of 'feeble velleity' that Raymond Williams talks of.[85]

There is in Eliot's writing a rhetoric of 'natural sympathy' with democratic and leftist causes. ('While I am naturally sympathetic', as he put it in *Authors Take Sides*; 'Sympathy with Communism seems to me . . .'; 'No one who is seriously concerned can fail to be impressed by the work of Karl Marx . . . his power is so great, and his analysis so profound . . .'[86]; and so on.) Eliot's attraction towards Social Credit — and the *Criterion*'s pages are thrown wide open to Social Creditors — is mildly cheering. So are his rebuttals of profit, Empire exploitation and capitalism, his disgruntlement with 'the present system' which 'does not work properly',[87] and his concern about 'the ancient prejudice that Christianity is, or has become merely the parasitic supporter of things as they are'.[88]

So are the sympathies with the plight of the poor that he keeps evincing in *The Rock* (1934) and *Murder in the Cathedral* (1935). But all this looks only like the gent's occasional night out, slumming it with Marie Lloyd or with Bill, Lou and May in some 'public bar in

Lower Thames Street', a suspectingly distant peering into the fearful murks of the urbanized wasteland hell, when it is set against the more continuing strain. For though he continually hedged, waiving his more embarrassingly clear enthusiasms — like his Preface to *For Lancelot Andrewes*, his liking for Matthew Arnold's nostrums and for the Action Française and Italian Fascism, the distaste of *After Strange Gods* for 'foreign populations', 'foreign races', 'free-thinking Jews', and the Nonconformity that bred D.H. Lawrence — he had a way of nonetheless continuing to stick just where the embarrassing declarations appeared to have landed him in the first place. It's the continuity and coherence of Eliot's thought that is remarkable, not the occasional wobbles and deviations.[89]

Preaching 'continuity and coherence'[90]; equating the literary tradition with the orthodoxy of High Anglicanism; defending *reaction* as an honorific, indeed 'revolutionary' concept[91]; presenting education as a device that 'should help to preserve the class and to select the élite' (he mooned with Dr Joad over Winchester, just as Professor Arnold fawned over Oxford — places not created by 'equality of opportunity . . . but by a happy combination of privilege and opportunity');[92] continuously suspicious of internationalist politics, of cosmopolitans like the 'Jewish economist' Karl Marx,[93] of *cosmopolis*, even of the *polis* (agriculture, he insisted, was 'the normal life';[94] 'What is fundamentally wrong is the *urbanization of mind*');[95] continually hankering, despite the Edward VIII débâcle, after the divine right of the kingship; snugly set in the bourgeois Christian status quo ('I should prefer to employ a large staff of servants, each doing much lighter work but profiting by the benefits of the cultured and devout atmosphere of the home in which they lived');[96] what are all these but, clearly defined, a strongly held religious Conservatism. It is the ground marked out for Eliot by Lancelot Andrewes, by Maurras and Maritain, by Hulme and Hesse, by the agrarians of the southern United States; and held fast more or less to the end of the poet's life.

The *Left Review* compilers of *Authors Take Sides* should not have hesitated. 'Neutral?' Eliot was not. Even if his talk of 'a few men of letters' and his resistance to 'collective activities' were not enough sufficiently to help them place his response — though they should have been enough — his *Criterion* 'Commentary' of October 1937 (the pamphlet came out in November) would have served promptly to scatter any lingering doubts. In it, Eliot strongly refutes the notion that 'all good (or as the author [of the Unity of Artists Catalogue] might say "sane") men are liberal-minded'. He questions the assumption that Art and democracy do, or must, go together. He does not know, he says, what 'cultural progress' is. What's more, Art is not 'international', it is 'racial and local'. And he ends swingeingly by rebuking the Poet Laureate, John Masefield, for his idea of taking poetry into pubs: the audience for poetry 'should be sensitive, critical and educated — conditions only possible for a small public'.[97]

A year later, readers of the *Criterion* who remembered Arjuna of the 'even mind' might have wondered about the nature of 'indifference', as evenness of tone got sucked once again down the plughole of waspish partisanship. To be sure, Eliot endorses Jacques Maritain's refusal to label Franco's struggle a 'holy war', and calls this 'the just impartiality of a Christian philosopher'. But, interestingly speedily, he starts in on the other lot: 'Our concern should be . . . with that part of the public which is inclined to attribute all the "holiness" of this war to the party of Valencia and Barcelona'. The Left's error looms larger with him than Franco's; and its intellectuals come in for far more of the sharp end of the going scorn:

> Meanwhile the supposed progressive and enlightened 'intellectuals' shout themselves hoarse in denunciations of foreign systems of life which they have not taken the trouble to comprehend; having never considered that the preliminary to criticizing anything must be an attempt to understand how it came about, and that criticism involves discerning the good from which we might profit, as a qualification for condemning the evil which we wish to avoid.[98]

A richly sweeping disposal, that, of the English and French critics of Franco, Mussolini and Hitler. But, of course, if Eliot's readers had known the *Bhagavad-Gita* as well as he did they would have straightaway seen what was really being implied when Eliot invoked Arjuna. As Helen Gardner explains, the *Gita* begins at the point where one of the Pandava brothers, Arjuna, refuses to fight, even at the instance of Krishna, because the war about to begin is against his cousins the Kauravas: 'At the last moment, with battle imminent, Arjuna cannot bring himself to fight, knowing the appalling slaughter that will follow and that he will be fighting his own kith and kin, among whom are his benefactors'. Dame Helen is anxious to apply this sense of the 'enemy' being one's kin to the 'fratricidal war' in Europe in 1941 (the time of *The Dry Salvages*). She is perhaps too unperturbed that Eliot should allow his sense of European kinship to lead him into implying that Hitler is 'kith and kin'. Be that as it may, the application of Arjuna's reluctance, as Eliot first applied it, to the Spanish War cannot be allowed not to perturb.[99] What is implied, altogether consciously or not, is that Eliot won't oppose Franco because the European Fascists are cousins and benefactors. Utilizing Arjuna as the model of a 'highly civilized' disinterest cannot be other than an admission not merely that Maurras and his ilk are

Eliot's intellectual benefactors, but that for all its wire-drawing and intellectual demarcation disputes his Lancelot Andrewesism, his merry Andrewesism, is first cousin to the Fascism the *Left Review* wanted him to denounce. Taking sides against Franco would be to smite his friends. In implying so, Eliot was *de facto* depositing himself on the same side as the *Daily Mail* and the *Tablet* and all the other crude anti-Communists whose pronouncements he kept on professing himself disconcerted by. It was the side where he was always suspected of belonging.

Manifestoes are blunt expressions. *Authors Take Sides* is blunter than usual. Busily mongering an orthodoxy, its compilers fell noisily into a trap of their own devising. There was, as we've seen, actual political indifference in the period, actual neutrality. But the pacificism of Vera Brittain, like the reluctance to reply (we'll charitably assume) of a Graham Greene, or the colour-blindness of the *Writers and Artists' Year Book*, are the sorts of neutral stance the pamphlet seeks to deny by the built-in scepticism of its 'Neutral?' category. And though Eliot wasn't, as every reader of the *Criterion* would know or suspect, neutral, he might, with Pound, just be credibly 'Neutral?'. And since the very big names like Eliot and Pound must at all costs be stopped from voting for Franco, and since the 'Neutral?' category had been created to enforce the doctrinal orthodoxy about taking sides, Pound and Eliot could at a pinch — must, in fact, even at a pinch — be crammed into it. And thus in one go the dangers of distorting things to make orthodoxies stood very starkly revealed. Real neutrals and indifferents were denied entry into the period's calculations: an absurd denial. And the position of a false neutral like Eliot, a richly devious and complex stance, was shielded from scrutiny, sheltered, in effect, both from the sympathy and the hostility its desperate trickiness deserved to excite. Ironically, *Authors Take Sides* left Eliot — in every sense — alone. He was rescued, in fact, was laughably saved by his political enemies from their friends' and his fans' properly nettled resentments. From the likes, no less, of W.T. Nettlefold and his 'Fan Mail for a Poet' ('To be read over a network of high-power Radio Stations by an American Hot-gospeller'):

HOW NICE for a man to be clever,
So famous, so true;
So sound an investment; how EVER
So nice to be YOU.

To peer into basements, up alleys,
A nose for the search.
To challenge with pertinent sallies,
And then JOIN the Church.

First comes Prufrock, then Sweeney, and then
Thomas à Becket.
How frightfully nice of the good men
In cloth to forget it.

The broad-backed Hippo so weak and frail
Succumbed to the shock.
But the TRUE Church now can never fail,
Based upon 'THE ROCK'.

As a POET you visit today
The NICE Portuguese.
You can help England SO in this way;
I DO hope you please.

You WILL watch Spain's terrible border;
Take care where you tread.
How AWFUL for England if you were
Shot down for a 'RED'.

I like you, and what's more I READ you;
There are such a few
Christian Poets so noble; indeed you
Must know it — YOU DO.

How nice for a man to be clever
So famous, so true;
So sound an investment; how EVER
So nice to be YOU.

Notes

1 The *Criterion* (cited hereafter as C), XVI, No. lxii (October 1936), 164.
2 See for example, P. Toynbee (1954), *Friends Apart*, MacGibbon & Kee and C. Fitzgibbon (1965), *The Life of Dylan Thomas*, Dent, London.
3 S. Orwell and I. Angus (ed.) (1968) *The Collected Essays, Journalism and Letters of George Orwell*, Secker & Warburg, London, & Penguin (1970).
4 C, XVII, No. lxviii (April 1938), 593–4.
5 L. Riding (1938), *The World and Ourselves*, 239 ('represents the fourth volume of the literary series' *Epilogue: A Critical Summary*, originally edited by L. Riding & R. Graves.
6 I've seen only *The Red Stage*, Nos. 1–5 (November 1931 – April–May 1932) and its continuation as *New Red Stage*, Nos. 6–7 (June–July–September 1932).
7 *The Auden Generation* (1976), Ch. VIII.
8 The only copy known to me is (minus Greene's Shirley Temple offence) in the British Library. I'm grateful to Sir Victor (V.S.) Pritchett (a contributor) and Ian Parsons, one of Chatto's directors in 1937 (as he is now), for supplying me with details about the paper.
9 'The First Journey', *Night and Day*, No. 12 (16 September 1937), 10ff.

10 'For Schoolboys Only', *ibid.* No. 2 (8 July 1937), 24–5.
11 'Peter Pan in Politics', *ibid.* No. 11 (9 September 1937), 25–6.
12 For example 'Holiday from Politics', *ibid.* No. 18 (28 October 1937), 26–7.
13 See, particularly, 'Night and Day Dope News (With Apologies to Left Book Club)', *ibid.* No. 22 (25 November 1937), 17–8.
14 H. Kingsmill and M. Muggeridge (1937), 'New Year's News: A Preview of 1938', *ibid.* No. 18 (28 October 1937), 14f.
15 'All-in Wrestling: Actors at Blackfriars', *ibid.* No.10 (2 September 1937), 32.
16 'The Autumn Fairs: Zero-Hour in Oxford', *ibid.* No. 13 (23 September 1937), 27f.
17 'High Seriousness and Aston Villa', *ibid.* No. 22 (25 November 1937), 32.
Both Allott and Allen were early Mass Observers, sending their reports dutifully in (their contributions can be seen in the Mass Observation archive at Sussex University).
18 *Ibid.* No. 7 (12 August 1937), 8ff; No.10 (2 September 1937), 8ff; No. 26 (23 December 1937), 12ff.
19 *Ibid.* No. 13 (23 September 1937), 31.
20 *Ibid.* No. 16 (14 October 1937), 39. All Greene's film reviews (except for the 'libellous' Shirley Temple piece) are reprinted in J. Russell Taylor (ed.) (1972), Graham Greene, *The Pleasure-Dome: The Collected Film Criticism 1935–40*.
21 *Night and Day*, No. 9 (26 August 1937), 30. 'She' is Jean Harlow.
22 *Ibid.* No. 16 (14 October 1937), 39. Cf. his piece on Edgar Anstey's *Nutrition, Spectator* (16 October 1936); *The Pleasure-Dome*, 108, 109.
23 *Spectator* (25 November 1938); *The Pleasure-Dome*, 206.
24 *Night and Day*, No. 23 (2 December 1937), 29–30; No. 25 (16 December 1937), 30.
25 *Ibid.* No. 1 (1 July 1937), 24; No.8 (19 August 1937), 19.
26 *Ibid.* No. 6 (5 August 1937), 17–19.
27 A.L. Morton was a fairly frequent reviewer. A.L. Rowse was evidently the *Criterion*'s Marxist correspondent. And Eliot didn't only favour the regionalist, Scottish Nationalist MacDiarmid ('English Ascendency in British Literature', *C*, X, No. xli (July 1931), 593–613); he also published the 'Second Hymn to Lenin', *C*, XI, No. xlv (July 1932), 593–8.
28 'A Commentary', *C*, XVI, No. lxiii (January 1937), 289–93.
29 'A Commentary', *C*, XII, No. xlix (July 1933), 642–7.
30 'A Commentary', *C*, XV, No. lix (January 1936), 265–9.
31 'A Commentary', *C*, XVI, No. lxii (October 1936), 63–9.
32 'A Commentary', *C*, XVII, No. lxvi (October 1937), 81–6.
33 'A Commentary', *C*, XV, No. lx (April 1936), 461–2.
34 For example 'A Commentary', *C*, XIII, No.l (October 1933), 117: 'We insist upon "educating" too many people . . . '.
35 'A Commentary', *C*, XVII, No. lxvi (October 1937), 84ff.

36 'A Commentary', *C*, X, No. xxxix (January 1931), 314.
37 'A Commentary', *C*, XVIII, No. lxx (October 1938), 59: 'The irresponsible "anti-fascist", the patron of mass-meetings and manifestoes . . .'.
38 'I conceive then, not of conversions one by one to the faith, but of a kind of mass-conversion — by which I mean just the opposite of what is meant by a revival or a mass-meeting'. 'Building up the Christian World', *The Listener*, VII (6 April 1932), 501.
39 'A Commentary', *C*, XI, No. xliv (April 1932), 470.
40 'A Commentary', *C*, VI, No. iv (October 1927), 290.
41 'A Commentary', *C*, X, No. xxxix (January 1931), 314.
42 'A Commentary', *C*, XVIII, No. lxx (October 1938), 59.
43 'The Literature of Politics', in *To Criticize the Critic and Other Writings* (1965), Faber & Faber, London, 144.
44 'Building up the Christian World', *Listener*, VII (6 April 1932), 502.
45 'Last Words', *C*, XVIII, No. lxxi (January 1939), 274.
46 'Christianity and Communism', *Listener*, VII (16 March 1932), 383.
47 'Building up the Christian World', *ibid.* VII (6 April 1932), 502.
48 *New English Weekly* (5 December 1940); quoted in Roger Kojecký (1971), *T.S. Eliot's Social Criticism*, Faber & Faber, London, 147–8.
49 'Thomas Middleton' (1927), in *Selected Essays* (3rd edn., 1951), Faber & Faber, London, 169–70.
50 'Shelley and Keats' (17 February 1933), in *The Use of Poetry and the Use of Criticism* (1933), Faber & Faber, London, 102.
51 'Last Words', *C*, XVIII, No. lxxi (January 1939), 272.
52 For example 'A Dialogue on Dramatic Poetry' (1928), in *Selected Essays*, 44, 48; see also *After Strange Gods* (1934), Faber & Faber, London, 44.
53 'The Pensées of Pascal', in *Selected Essays,* 414–5.
54 'A Commentary', *C*, XIV, No. lvi (April 1935), 432.
55 'The Search for Moral Sanction', *Listener*, VII (30 March 1932), 446.
56 See T.S. Eliot's review of Middleton Murry's *Son of Woman: The Story of D.H. Lawrence,* *C*, X, No. xli (July 1931), 772; and 'Lancelot Andrewes' (1926), in *Selected Essays*, 347.
57 'The Literature of Fascism', *C*, VIII, No. xxxi (December 1928), 282; 'A Commentary', *C*, XVIII, No. lxx (October 1938), 59.
58 'A Commentary', *C*, XIV, No. lvi (April 1935), 431–6.
59 'A Commentary', *C*, XIII, No. li (January 1934), 270–8.
60 *Ibid*, for example; 'A Commentary', *C*, XV, No. lix (January 1936), 269; and 'A Commentary', *C*, XVI, No. lxv (July 1937), 667.
61 'Lancelot Andrewes', in *Selected Essays*, 341.
62 See, for example, T.S. Eliot's review of Clive Bell's *Civilization*, *C*, VIII, No. xxx (September 1928), 164; 'Christianity and Communism', *Listener*, VII (16 March 1932), 382; and *After Strange Gods, passim.*
63 'Christianity and Communism', *loc. cit.*
64 'Thoughts After Lambeth', in *Selected Essays*, 373, 385.
65 'Review of Conservative Literature', *C*, VI, No. i (July 1927), 69.
66 'A Commentary', *C*, XII, No. xlvii (January 1933), 244.

67 'A Commentary', *C*, VIII, No. xxxii (April 1929), 380.
68 'A Commentary', *C*, XIII, No. lii (April 1934), 453.
69 'John Bramhall' (1927), in *Selected Essays*, 359.
70 'A Commentary', *C*, VIII, No. xxxiii (July 1929), 578–9.
71 For example 'A Commentary', *C*, XI, No. xlii (October 1931), 65ff.
72 'A Commentary', *C*, XII, No. xlvi (October 1932), 74.
73 'A Commentary', *C*, XVI, No. lxiii (January 1937), 290.
74 'Building up the Christian World', *Listener*, VII (6 April 1932), 502.
75 'A Commentary', *C*, XVI, No. lxv (July 1937), 670.
76 *Time and Tide*, (5 January 1935); quoted Kojecký, *op. cit.*, 90.
77 'A Commentary', *C*, XVI, No. lxiii (January 1937), 289–93.
78 H. Gardner (1978), *The Composition of Four Quartets*, Faber & Faber, London, 56–7.
79 'Christianity and Communism', *Listener*, VII (16 March 1932), 383.
80 'Modern Education and the Classics' (1932), in *Selected Essays*, 514.
81 'Building up the Christian World', *Listener*, VII (6 April 1932), 502.
82 'A Commentary', *C*, XI, No. xliv (April 1932), 468.
83 'A Commentary', *C*, XV, No. lix (January 1936), 269.
84 'A Commentary', *C*, XI, No. xlii (October 1931), 70, 71.
85 'Against the actual and powerful programme for the maintenance of social classes, against the industrial capitalism which actually maintains the human divisions that he endorses, the occasional observation, however deeply felt, on the immorality of exploitation or usury seems, indeed, a feeble velleity'. R. Williams (1961) *Culture and Society 1780–1950*, Penguin, 237–8.
86 'A Commentary', *C*, XI, No. xliv (April 1932), 467–8.
87 *Ibid*, 467.
88 'Building up the Christian World', *Listener*, VII (6 April 1932), 502.
89 See the powerful, late, and moved tribute to Maurras, in 'The Literature of Politics', in *To Criticize the Critic*, 142–3.
90 For example, *The Idea of a Christian Society* (1939), Faber & Faber, London, 40.
91 'A Commentary', *C*, XV, No. lxi (July 1936), 667.
92 *Notes Towards the Definition of Culture*, (1948), Faber & Faber, London, 101–3.
93 'A Commentary', *C*, XIV, No. lvi (April 1935), 433.
94 'A Commentary', *C*, XI, No. xlii (October 1931), 72.
95 'A Commentary', *C*, XVIII, No. lxx (October 1938), 60.
96 'A Commentary', *C*, XI, No. xliii (January 1932), 275.
97 *C*, XVII, No. lxvi (October 1937), 81–6.
98 'A Commentary', *C*, XVIII, No. lxx (October 1938), 58–62.
99 Christopher Ricks reminded Dame Helen of Arjuna's greater pertinence to the Spanish conflict: 'Intense Transparencies', *The Times Literary Supplement* (15 September 1978), 1006–8.
100 W.T. Nettlefold (1938) 'Fan Mail for a Poet', in *New Verse*, No. 30 (Summer 1938), 11–12.

3 BRITISH INTELLECTUALS AND THE POPULAR FRONT

John Coombes

Winstanley spoke for those workers who, if once the pall of ignorance which is imposed on them can be lifted, must be natural materialists. For they live by understanding and controlling the forces of nature. For them knowledge and practice can never be separated, for they do not live, as do the *savants* of all possessing classes, upon the labours of other men: they can never be what Winstanley gloriously called the clerical philosophers of his day, monsters who are all tongue and no hand.

(John Strachey, *The Theory and Practice of Socialism*, 1936).

In the narrative histories of the inter-war years, the motives, nature and ideological effectivity of British Popular Frontism do not, of course, figure largely. The political and intellectual situation of Britain in the mid-1930s differed materially from that of France, where the defensive/progressive reformist alliance of liberal intelligentsia and professional middle classes with the vast majority of the organised working class came briefly to office — though not to power — with the election of the *Front Populaire* government in May–June 1936. The alliance was eventually to enact in political practice a whole range of complex and inter-related problems, notably, those of State power and of the relations between leadership and base, intellectuals and proletariat[1] — which in the British context were to remain unrehearsed, largely untheorized and, indeed, unregistered at any general conscious level. Quite evidently, a People's Front movement on the French model — with its initial impetus from groups of intellectuals and (especially after the Seventh Congress of the Comintern in 1935) from a Communist Party giving every appearance of increasing dynamism; its aim of the preservation from fascism and war of 'European civilization' and liberal democracy, by an electoral strategy of left discipline and by a mass ideology of popular unity; its attempt at the regeneration of a national economy deep in crisis by extensive measures of economic reform — little of this could be reproduced directly in the British context. For one thing the traditions of the British intelligentsia — of insularity and empiricism — militated against the type of collective intervention in politics practised by their French counterparts, from the time of the high Enlightenment through the Dreyfus affair to the crisis of the 1930s (nor, reciprocally, could such intervention command the attention in Britain which it did among the French popular Left); for another, the developed structures and traditions of British politics, in terms both of electoral arrangements and of practical ideologies, had tended to the constitution of façade parties of Left and Right and the consequent inhibition of mass movements of a Communist or openly Fascist nature (these elements to a large extent being incorporated in the parties of the established spectrum); moreover, the successive accommodations amongst varying fractions of the British ruling class which had been practised ever since the seventeenth century had had the effect, largely, of inducing assent to established class-rule and dynastic continuity, and of submerging the British revolutionary tradition to the extent that — in marked contrast to the revived Jacobinism of 1936 in France — there was no longer available to the British Left an actively progressive rhetoric, capable of uniting tactically workers and liberal middle and lower-middle class elements by reference to past revolutionary aims and achievements. Finally, and perhaps decisively, the relative recovery of the British economy which occurred between 1934 and 1937 — however uneven its distribution throughout the nation — undoutedly had a certain neutralizing effect on considerable sectors of the population whose radical potential was not to make itself felt in electoral terms until 1945. In the event, Labour's parliamentary representation after the 1935 election was still no higher than it had been in the early 1920s, whereas the rise to parliamentary power of the *Front Populaire* has to be measured against the delayed impact of the world depression on the French economy, in terms of rising unemployment and declining living standards in the years between the rise of fascism in Germany and Austria, and 1936.[2]

In these circumstances, it was hardly surprising that Popular Frontism in Britain, rejected moreover by the leadership of the Labour party, should remain largely restricted as a political force to the membership of the Communist Party, Cripps's dissident Socialist league, artists and intellectuals associated with minority journals such as *Fact* and *The Left Review*, and, most significantly, the Left Book Club, whose 'self-imposed task', as the Club's official historian informs us, 'was to create the clear understanding out of which alone effective measures such as the formation of the Popular Front could come'.[3] Indeed, at its period of maximum influence, from the end of 1936 to the Nazi-Soviet pact, the Club's membership of over 50, 000 may reasonably be taken to include the vast majority of the members of those organizations already mentioned, together with some dissident Liberals, pacifists, and non-aligned socialists.

For British Marxist and non-Marxist alike, the immediate point of reference for the development of Popular Front ideology was, of course — in spite of discrepancies of scale and of political and intellectual relationships between the two countries — the French experience:

France has, indeed, for a long time now been an example and an inspiration . . . . From a spectacle so magnificent the transition to our own Left Book Club must seem a trifle grotesque. But . . . what the Left Book Club is intending to do is to provide the indispensable basis of *knowledge* without which a really effective United Front of all men and women of good will cannot be built.[4]

That the note of traditional liberal humanism which characterizes Gollancz' founding statement is by no means a personal idiosyncrasy but a significant ideological determinant of Popular Frontism, is evident in a review by Laski (like Gollancz a selector for the Left Book Club) of the autobiography of the French Communist leader Thorez. Here the incorporation of Communist politics into the mythology of the liberal bourgeoisie is accepted as axiomatic, as evidence of 'the infinite flexibility of Communist doctrine. The party appears less as a body of revolutionaries than as the inheritor of the central tradition of French policy; M. Thorez can even inscribe Joan of Arc and Richelieu on his banner . . .'; and Laski's conclusion — 'M. Thorez is an advocate of which any movement might be proud'[5] — encodes, without conscious irony, the transition from revolutionary socialism to functionalism. (It is perhaps worth noting here an earlier validation by Kingsley Martin of 'class jingoism' as 'the main driving force behind the formation of Popular Front Governments'[6] and its subsequent degeneration into a jingoism devoid of class content — the necessary outcome of the attempted appropriation of a bourgeois mystification as a proletarian weapon.)

Assent to such functional accommodations of revolutionary theory to the cultural politics of the liberal bourgeoisie may be seen as having close connections with the negotiations of Fabianism and Stalinism attempted by an earlier generation of British socialist thinkers — the common result, in many instances, being the dilution of collective revolutionary potential by the invocation of individuality and the maintenance of bourgeois cultural norms. Significantly, however, the reactions of the older generation to the rise of the Popular Front — in many ways the logical extension of their earlier espousal of Stalinism with its imposed moderation of revolutionary proletarian consciousness, and now its constitution of a 'popular' progressive class-coalition in each Western state as the internal paradigm of the anti-fascist alliance sought between the Soviet Union and the capitalist democracies[7] — would seem to have met with their scepticism if not outright rejection. Wells, commenting somewhat belatedly on the issue early in 1939, nevertheless displays a characteristic local prescience in foreseeing a new wave of 'probably a very patriotic Radicalism'[8] (a mood incidentally which George Orwell was later to adopt and publicize as a reaction to the Nazi–Soviet pact — ironically, a delayed Popular

Frontism which in 1940 could count neither on the internal support of the CPGB nor on external support of the Soviet Union!).[9] Yet, equally characteristically, Wells is not prepared to underpin his prediction with ideological assent, immediately taking refuge in the archaic liberal-positivist dream of 'a phase of education, clarification and explanation (with) . . . some such name as the New Liberalism, World Socialism, Scientific World Organisation or World Radicalism . . .'[10], reductively equating anti-Fascism ('an altogether barren thing') with anti-Communism and anti-Semitism, and concluding with an absurd defensive individualism: 'I do my best to keep Pro-World-Pax'.[11]

Of more substantive interest, perhaps, are the attitudes of Shaw and the Webbs. Shaw, with that continuing clarity of perception, and correspondingly intense distrust of the manoeuvres and motives of the bourgeoisie which were among the most positive elements of his political consciousness, was particularly well placed to estimate the nature of a *rapprochement* between the Soviet Union and the West, and the likely social stratagem behind a Stalinist/Popular Frontist foreign policy, partly engineered by the bourgeoisie of Western capitalism: '. . . our diplomatists, after having for years denounced the revolutionary leaders as the most abominable villains and tyrants, have to do a right turn and invite them to dinner. . . . This prodigious mass of humbug . . . [is] . . . meant to delude the enslaved masses . . .';[12] and though Shaw draws no clear conclusion, suggesting indeed that it is the ruling class who may eventually be the most deceived, his distaste for the convergence-strategy of the Popular Front — a strategy which blurred his by now manichean distinction between capitalist incompetence and model autocracy — is perhaps indicated by the absence of any direct reference to it in the chapters added to the new edition of the *Intelligent Woman's Guide to Socialism, Capitalism, Sovietism and Fascism* in 1937.

The Webbs, writing of 'the United Front from Above' at the end of *Soviet Communism*, whilst similarly critical, are clearer in import: '. . . such a defensive alliance among disparate and mutually antagonistic organisations, appealing for the allegiance of the masses of the people, serves rather to emphasize these difficulties, and may even make for the continuance of their common rivalry in pursuit of their several objects.'[13] The Webbs were, of course, untroubled by Shaw's occasional radical anarchist impulsions towards individual liberation — impulsions which could lead to genuine moments of identification with the working class as a whole, as a collective subject. As ever, decided advocates of authoritarian collectivism, they are evidently more concerned at the threat to oligarchic discipline and control from a movement constituted upon the basis of mass participation *as such* — however attenuated that participation might, under the 'United Front *from Above*', effectively be — rather than at any dilution of revolutionary potential which the Popular Front might be seen as representing to those who, like Shaw and the Webbs elsewhere, had advocated the alignment of British politics on the Soviet model.

The old Fabians, then, confronted with the novel complexities of Popular Frontism, remained true to type: responding, respectively, by reaffirmation of liberal-positivist idealism; sustained philippic against the idiocy of bourgeois politics; reassertion of the need for bureaucratic control of the mass movement. The cultural politics of younger left-wing intellectuals in Britain, notably those of members of the Communist Party such as Ralph Fox, exemplify the 'flexibility' which Laski noted in Thorez, the result of the change of policy following the rise of Hitler (both on the part of the Comintern and of national Communist parties) from an affirmation of the exclusive vanguard role of the Communist Party and consequent denunciation of socialist and social-democratic Parties as 'social fascist' (during the so-called 'Third period') to a policy of class conciliation and defence of capitalist democracy against Fascism. The change has conventionally been characterized as a transition from 'sectarianism' to 'realism'; there is no space here to debate the claim in general political terms.[14] As far as cultural politics in general, and the relationship of art to social practice, of writers and intellectuals to the political movement, and to political commitment in particular, are concerned, however, a comparison of Communist texts from the 'Third period' and the Popular Front era reveals that the abandonment of sectarianism (certainly a political gain) was accompanied by a loss of intellectual direction and cohesion which amounted in many instances to full-scale capitulation to the values and norms of bourgeois liberalism — in effect, the Fabian ideology of permeation would appear to some extent to have operated in reverse!

A comparison of texts by Ralph Fox from 1932 and 1935 gives some idea of the extent of the trajectory, though it must be said that Fox exemplifies it to an extreme degree: in 1932 the proletarian exclusivism of his writing is by any standard excessive — a colleague, T.A. Jackson, is accused of 'smuggling' 'anti-party, non-Leninist ideas' into *The Daily Worker*; non-Party members who sympathize with the Soviet Union, 'charlatans like Middleton Murry' are sneered at, their good faith denied: '. . . their aim is obvious, to put up again the old story that Bolshevism is wonderful for Russia, only for Britain it is not necessary'.[15]

By 1935, the tone is entirely different; yet arguably the dogmatism, transferred now from uncertain identification with the political mission of the proletariat to a restored confidence in the exclusive mission of liberal culture, is still present, its inconspicuousness merely confirming its conventionality:

Among the millions of workers who are *barred from real cultural activity* today, there is an immense thirst for knowledge, for health and for beauty, which only Socialism can satisfy. *The demand of these millions* for schools, laboratories, clinics, new modes of travel, art, literature and music *means a new and splendid future of creative work* for scientists, artists, doctors and teachers.

This is *the basis of the unity* between the intellectual and cultural workers and the working-class . . . .

A writer who can influence thousands through his work, *if he comes ever so little towards the working-class, even if only to understand that Fascism and war are evils*, is a valuable ally.[16]

The initial fetishizing delimitation of 'real' culture as activity in name only — in fact as a pre-constituted commodity to be distributed and absorbed, not as a process to be collectively enacted — has, as in conventional liberal cultural practice, the effect of relegating the working class to the status of, at best, passive recipients, who, moreover, are to ensure the 'spendid' 'creative' future of the cultural élite more effectively than is possible under crisis-ridden capitalism. Significantly this one-way cultural transaction, rather than the mutual extension of both intellectuals' and workers' experience through concerted political practice, is seen as the 'basis' of popular unity; in effect, a manifestation of middle-class cultural exclusivism that largely cancels Fox's proletarian exclusiveness of 1932. Moreover, consideration of the role of the committed intellectual — ever a thorny problem, admittedly — has been shelved; marginally 'politicized' by the minimal demands made of his political consciousness — demands lower, incidentally, than those made of the average worker — he can nonetheless remain centrally disengaged, the value of the culture he dispenses to the mass of the people at most talismanic.

A more coherent formulation of the intellectuals' role in the political struggle is provided by R. Palme Dutt's statement on 'Intellectuals and Communism' of 1932. Here the stress is laid, not on the specific and distinct function of the intellectual, but on the need for an inter-related cultural advance, 'a very great transformation on the part of these intellectuals, as well as skill and understanding on the side of the Party to draw them in and make the best use of their capacities'.[17]

The danger of token involvement in practical politics (such as that apparently envisaged later by Fox) is stressed as generative of a condescending élitism, as is the need for criticism of 'any signs of tendencies in [the intellectuals] to *limitation* of their interests to supposed "ideological" fields in place of the whole field of the revolutionary working-class fight'.[18] What is suggested, as opposed to the fragmented political culture of distribution and consumption (rather than of collective *production*) acceptable to Fox, is what may be characterized as a revolutionary organicism: 'It is for the intellectuals themselves to break their chains, to break their isolation and separate character as "intellectuals" '.[19]

Yet, in general, the dominant trend in Communist cultural politics was directed away from such demands, and towards the enthusiastic concessions to liberal cultural practice outlined by Fox. Furthermore, this separation of cultural activity from the class-struggle was developed in conjunction with a general political strategy which, under the guise of anti-fascist unity, consciously preferred the claims of middle-class ideology:

> When we speak of the People's Front . . . especially we have in mind those large sections of the middle classes who have been profoundly impressed by the effects of the recent crisis of capitalism . . . . Middle-class parents cannot look into the future without profound misgiving; they realise only too well what another war would mean for themselves and their children, and they have lost all sense of security . . . . The achievement of Socialism means not only the abolition of Fascism and of the causes of war, it also means the opening up of limitless opportunities for all the technicians, scientists, writers and artists for whom today Capitalism offers no scope.[20]

The attempted balance of such an appeal to middle-class professionalism — to middle-class privilege, even — against the continued claims of working-class organization and social transformation (rather than the integration of intellectuals and workers propounded by Dutt), could only be provisionally sustained by Pollitt through efforts at moral exhortation verging on the mystical:

> Once the fight for the united working-class movement has been carried through . . . then all the hesitations and vacillations now characterizing the progressive movement will begin to disappear and the final form to be taken by the People's Front movement will be determined by the concrete circumstances that exist at the moment.[21]

Such appeals to the subjective sense of status and the professional self-interest of the progressive intelligentsia are a centrally constitutive element of Popular Frontism. The Front's leading Liberal apologist saw their effect, indeed, as the displacement and suspension — if not the termination — of the class struggle: 'I tell you, and I believe it sincerely, that today with these dangers of fascism in front of us the fight is not between the slaves and the parasites. It is between the wise men and the fools of all classes'.[22] In such a context it is not surprising that such expressed commitment as the following, at pains to stress the *dual* function of the Popular Front in cultural affairs — not merely the defence of literature and culture, but also its extension through the transformation of cultural relations in society — should be comparatively rare: 'It is against Fascism and war that the People's Front is directed in defence of Peace, democracy and personal freedom. And by his support of it the artist is taking a logical step to defend his right and freedom to work, and to extend the public to whom his work can speak'.[23]

More characteristic of the period is the suggestion, made by a speaker at the 1935 London Congress of Peace and Friendship with the USSR, that it is Socialism which is the social system most capable, not merely of defending the artist's interest, but of satisfying his individual entrepeneurial drives: 'I had the good fortune to be treated by Russian authors in Paris and London. They just throw money about like water: they are so rich, it is simply horrible [Laughter]. . . . I consider Russia must be a great country, because the rich people there are authors and playwrights [Applause].'[24] Such a quintessentially capitalist attitude to the relations governing the production of culture in the Soviet Union (whose jocularity cannot obscure its serious point), must of course determine the view taken of the likely resultant product; thus, having surveyed recent Soviet literary innovations, the speaker concludes: 'You will notice a certain sense of strain about these books that I have spoken of. I am very much interested to see what the new, easier life will bring forth in literature . . . . I expect . . . a settling down to something more leisurely, more charming [Applause]'.[25]

The prophecy — of the development of Soviet literature into something passively reflective of the social formation and moreover parallel in function to bourgeois literature of escapism and consolation — was of course to prove a depressingly accurate one as, during the 1930s, Soviet cultural norms (in literature, cinema, morals etc.) increasingly declined to a virtual parallel with those obtaining in the capitalist democracies. As a result of these attitudes and tendencies, both the Marxist theory and practice of culture in the Popular Front period could, without difficulty, be assimilated into the norms of bourgeois cultural liberalism, as the following comments from a 'sympathetic' non-Marxist source make plain — here restriction of cultural production to the bourgeoisie is accepted as axiomatic: 'Art and culture are practically the monopoly of the bourgeois and, as we all admit, the art which most clearly reflects the crisis through which we are passing has been produced by this class — while the proletariat has ceased to produce anything at all.'(!)[26] Yet the 'wisdom of Marxists' is to accord a 'privileged position' to the artist; moreover: 'It is not surprising that Marxism should have appealed so strongly to many of our younger writers. It is clear from literary history that it is easier to write well in an age dominated by a common outlook than in an age in which there is none. . . .'[27]

The success — or failure? — of Popular Front ideological permeation was, then, such that Marxist cultural practice could be seen as reconcilable both with the organicism of Arnold and Leavis, and, by the same token, with the continued cultural domination of the bourgeoisie.

The very title of Stephen Spender's *Forward from Liberalism* published in 1937 — publication of which by the Left Book Club led to an invitation to join the Communist Party from Harry Pollitt[28] — suggests critical engagement with the process of the incorporation, into liberal modes, of revolutionary cultural activity. Indeed, at various points in his political and intellectual development in the 1930s Spender appears fully aware of the contradictions within which Popular Frontism tended to encapsulate the liberal intellectual; contradictions presciently summarized (admittedly in the context of a particularly static and reductionist validation of proletarian culture) by an English enthusiast for the Soviet Writers' Congress of 1934:

> There is a widespread belief that it is possible slightly to rearrange middle-class ideas on art and culture by the introduction of Marxist ideas, and thus to obtain a truer theoretical account. This is not so . . . the middle-class position . . . is both a partial, incomplete position and a class position . . . it falls back on individualism, on the fiction of an individual against a homogeneous, undifferentiated and irrelevant background, which he is sensitive to, but in which he plays no active part.[29]

Spender's acute grasp of the general point being made here about the necessary unity of theory and practice, and consequently about the probably abortive nature of intervention in the working-class struggle from a liberal-individualist standpoint, is aphoristically expressed in his early volume of literary criticism *The Destructive Element* — a work which it is, incidentally, instructive to compare with contemporary statements (such as Virginia Woolf's 1936 essay 'The Artist and Politics') from the Bloomsbury group with which Spender was tangentially connected. On the notion that a new politics can 'support' and 'inspire' the individual artist, he writes: 'It is not a question of sticks for dahlias. The answer to that remark is, "Don't be a dahlia, and you won't need a stick". It is a question of what *in the widest sense* is going to be the social or political subject of writing.'[30]

That Spender's preoccupations go beyond the notion of writing 'about' politics to an awareness of literary production as a form of political practice in itself, is demonstrated by his opposition to literary cliques as a 'literary fascism' inherently connected with its political counterpart — a critique as unpalatable to liberals as it was applicable to, say, an aesthete like Clive Bell.[31] The sophistication of the analysis seems all the more remarkable when we consider the extreme apolitical primitivism which characterised contemporary aesthetic circles and which alone can account for the desperate simplicity of Spender's appeal for commitment made to other writers elsewhere in the same text: 'If we hope to go on existing, if we want a dog's chance of a right to breathe, to go on being able to write, it seems that we have got to make some choice outside the private entanglements of our personal life.'[32]

Spender's thinking in the 1930s continued to veer between sophistication and simplicity, the variations themselves revelatory of a radical uncertainty as to the role of the writer in left-wing politics. In *Forward from Liberalism*, the problems of popular frontism are effectively presented from the starting-point of a critique of turn-of-the-century liberalism:

> Because the theological, political and psychological implications of liberalism could be ignored, it was possible for everyone with benevolent emotions to be, in the nineteenth century, a Liberal, just as today, the same person without at all inquiring into his beliefs, can call himself a Socialist. All distinctions melt down into the same democratic cauldron . . . in fact we have a mingling of every kind of contrary motive, religious and anti-religious, reformist and reactionary, traditional and revolutionary, which presents the spectacle of bourgeois capitalist society.'[33]

This radical questioning of progressive orthodoxy is sustained in Spender's critique of the liberal bourgeois individualist:

> . . . he suspects — and may suspect rightly — that this class to which he is confined and which possesses the treasury of all the world's greatness, is nevertheless dead and unproductive, partly no doubt because its members are spiritually dried up by their common isolation. The real life, the real historic struggle, may, in fact, be taking place outside this country of fantastic values . . . but . . . he must express himself in the symbolic language of the existing culture, which is bourgeois.'[34]

The approach, here, to a genuinely materialist account of language and culture in bourgeois society runs counter to the more conventional left-liberal statements which had initially set the tone of the work — the definition of civilization, for instance 'as an end, more important than the means by which it is achieved'[35] (in effect its designation as a commodity rather than a process); the concomitant idealist view of the purpose of politics in the preservation of culture as a given quantity, rather than the progressive production and transformation of that culture: 'Politics to me is the effort to "assimilate the treasures of knowledge accumulated by humanity as a whole"; to make this knowledge available to the greatest number of human beings, so that it may be the widely disseminated basis of a better society';[36] and the ultimate vision of the 'withering away' of politics itself, its eventual subjugation to aesthetics rather than the progressive integration of the two categories: 'The final aim of civilized man must be an unpolitical age, where conditions of peace and security are conducive to a classical art, rooted not in a small oligarchy but in the lives of the whole people.'[37]

The liberal humanist dream expressed here, of course, is ultimately irreconcilable with the materialist analysis of language and culture hinted at elsewhere — the weight of Spender's pronouncements as a whole, ironically, is towards confirmation of that very liberal inability to transcend the 'symbolic language of the bourgeoisie' which he had himself stigmatized, examplified by the following statement with its combination of manifest individualism (as opposed to any notion of redefinition of the subject through a collective project), latent condescension (the intellectual as acknowledged legislator for the masses), and perhaps most significant, the dislocation seen as eternally feasible between cultural pluralism and social unity (a covert plea for the perpetuation of a cultural élite?): 'To go forward, the masses must be given not merely political but also economic freedom, so that they may produce their own free individualists and their own culture. The future of individualism lies in the classless society.'[38]

The perpetuation of liberal élitism under the mask of 'humanist' Marxism in the Popular Front period was a process which Spender was subsequently, during the cold war, to analyse as follows: 'The 1930s, which seemed so revolutionary, were in reality the end of a Liberal phase in history. They offered Liberal individualists their last chance to attach Liberal democracy to a people's cause . . .'[39] This, in retrospect, seems true enough; yet the admission sets the quasi-hysterical denunciation of alleged *Communist* bad faith in cultural politics which precedes it,[40] to say the least, in a highly questionable context.

A somewhat similar move to the Right — from Communism in all but party affiliation to moderate social democracy — was made in the 1940s by John Strachey, as author and principal selector for the Left Book Club perhaps the most influential of all British apologists for the Popular Front, and a brilliant syncretistic popularizer of Marxism[41] — who was in 1960 to describe as 'preposterous' in its 'utter lack of any critical analysis of Russian society' (a polemical exaggeration to say the least) the Webbs' *Soviet Communism*, which in 1936 he had reviewed in *Left News* as 'the culminating achievement of the two greatest social investigators of the English-speaking world'.[42]

It would be too crude to view the politics of Strachey's declining years as a partial capitulation to his class-conditioning (an Etonian, he was also the son of the owner/editor of *The Spectator*). Admittedly, in one of the first of Strachey's political texts — a private letter written after his arrest for incitement during the General Strike — we find in his early motivation a confused expression of sudden political illumination, of what may be characterized as the unstable politics of patrician goodwill; the text veers rapidly from expression of the zeal of the convert through a sentimental workerism to its resolution in — or rather perhaps deflection into — the rhetoric of privileged aestheticism:

> . . . I thought very often of you and your wise and tender eyes. I thought that you would say I had done right in throwing myself wholly onto the workers' side — in going with them all the more in their foolishness and mistakes than in their victories and wisdom. Of course, the working people are always fundamentally right and it was — and is — great peace of mind to be wholly and irrevocably with them . . . It was, as you would say, *du cinéma*, pure and simple. Tom [i.e. — ironically — Oswald Mosley, then a Labour MP] was superb — half the hero of melodrama — half laughing at himself![43]

By the early 1930s, a reading of Marx had contributed to the elaboration of what is here a random selection of inchoate and discrepant personal drives, into a (for its time) remarkably sophisticated sense of historical process as a layered structure, a perspective which avoids both mechanism and total randomness:

> It has been well said that all distinctions in nature and society are unstable and to a certain extent arbitrary. Just as in the heyday of feudalism there was a good deal of buying and selling, so at the height of the era of the free market, there were many fixed human relationships . . . . For no type of social order has as yet completely monopolized human relationships . . .

Yet to concede this is not to capitulate to a totally pluralist view of social development: '. . . in spite of the undeniable fact that historical categories are never absolute, it should be possible for even an historian to detect a difference between the England of 1840 and the Rome of 1300, between the outlook on the world of St Thomas Aquinas and that of Mr Jeremy Bentham . . .' Moreover 'history' assumes different meanings when viewed from different angles, notably those of different social classes:

The perspective of history is long. But the angle of vision is very important. This, however, can be said confidently. The view of history here adopted is a hypothesis which gives sense and coherence to the human past.[44]

This is preferable, Strachey maintains, to both total eclecticism and to aestheticised biography and 'the art of story-telling'. The confusion evident in Strachey's early commitment has here been supplanted by a genuine sense of complexity which recognises the necessity, for an adequate revolutionary project, of the continuous inter-relation of perception and reality: a recognition in strong contrast with the more dogmatic statements of Marxism in the immediate pre-Popular Front period, which, with their monolinear insistence on the 'inevitability of working-class revolution', often contrived to be simultaneously triumphalist and mechanistic.

Strachey's perception of the inter-relation of intellectual and material forms is apparent in the following statement, from 1936, on the nature of the causation underlying the social change and complexity already noted:

Marxists do, it is true, consider that the economic event is primary in time . . . . But once the series has started off, political and social changes often react back powerfully upon the economic situation, again changing it radically . . . the materialist concept of history does not assert that history is a one-way street . . . It asserts, on the contrary, that history is a complex of reciprocations between technical, economic, social and political events.[45]

An awareness such as this of the multiplicity of social causation was capable of providing, when transposed into social terms, a more adequate foundation for the relationship between intelligentsia and proletariat, a more genuinely dynamic Popular Front, than did either Pollitt's opportunistic appeal to middle-class liberals, or Spender's exercise in the incorporation of Marxism into a form of liberal humanism. (In this respect, Strachey's thinking on the role of the intellectual may be seen as closely allied with that of Dutt to which reference has already been made.) The sense of a new identity for the intellectual, his feeling of achievement extended rather than limited by its incorporation in the revolutionary project, is expressed with an enthusiasm which is the reverse of condescension:

We shall say that their [i.e. the capitalists'] especial fury with those whose function is to enlighten that overwhelming majority of the population which consists in wage-workers, as to the cause, nature and objective of the struggle in which they find themselves engaged, is a supreme honour and reward.[46]

Not that the achievements of the relationship, characterized ideally in the marvellous representation of Winstanley which I have selected as an epigraph for this essay, is seen as unproblematic; Strachey's qualifications as to the material obstacles to such a project, set by the unavoidable use of hegemonic language itself, recall Spender's questioning at its most radical: 'Only too often we have stated our case in the worst possible way. Only too often we have been strident, abusive, dogmatic, supercilious — all the things which the shrewd, practical workers of the movement hate, and rightly hate, most.'[47]

The totality of commitment is nonetheless seen as necessarily based upon a clarity of vision, a rational detachment, which at times would appear to have more in common with the aristocratic scepticism of, say, Bertrand Russell, than with the values of the middle class liberal making common cause with the working class: 'The more we read history the less we shall doubt men's idealism and the more we shall doubt their perspicacity.'[48] Taken in isolation, the statement recalls in tone the heroic age of liberalism — it might, one feels, have been uttered by Stendhal. Taken in the context of the class struggle in the 1930s, its ironic detachment and its lucid refusal of both harmonious optimism and schematic pessimism echo Romain Rolland's aphorism made famous by Gramsci, 'pessimism of the intellect, optimism of the will'.

The voluntaristic impulsion is closely allied with a deep sense of the crisis and failure of bourgeois civilization. In spite of some conventional rhetorical flourishes to the effect that 'capitalism can continue to exist only . . . by attacking . . . not only the workers, but everyone who dares to support the eternal cause of human culture, of science and civilization itself . . .',[49] Strachey's central preoccupations during the 1930s are less with the defence of constituted liberal civilization (based on the claims of the individual) against the depradations of fascism and war, than with the need for collective action to effect a radical socio-cultural transformation:

> We inevitably long to be allowed to lead our own personal lives against the background of a society which, however imperfect, is at any rate stable. But the society in which we live is not stable. We can no more escape its perturbations by refusing to take part in the social struggles of our times, than a frightened passenger can escape from a shipwreck by locking himself up in his cabin . . . .
>
> The best men and women of every class in Britain and America will come to the conclusion that they cannot find a worthy purpose for their lives except by participation in the organized movement to change the world.[50]

The hyperbolic appeal, here, to 'every class' in society need not obscure the central points being made here about the immediate necessity of transcending the inherited fragmentation of bourgeois thinking about 'culture' and 'society', and about the class struggle as the agency for their progressive inter-relation and transformation. It is this sense of total activity which, for Strachey, distinguishes the commitment of the 1930s from that of the preceding period of the development of English socialist thinking, that of the Fabians in the 1880s and 1890s:

The Fabian's arguments for Socialism were, paradoxically enough for men who believed that they were pre-eminently social scientists, humanitarian, moral and aesthetic, rather than scientific or economic. Shaw, for instance, wanted socialism because capitalism outraged his strongly developed moral sensibilities. But none of the Fabians wanted socialism because they had realised that the alternative to it was not the calm continuance of capitalism but the collapse of human civilization.[51]

For the Fabians of the late nineteenth century, then, socialism was an *optional* commitment which could be — apparently — accommodated within the pluralistic structure of bourgeois culture. (And as such, it might be argued, though Strachey does not, its conformity to bourgeois norms in many respects tended to consolidate and perpetuate them.) For Strachey as a Socialist of the 1930s, on the other hand, it presents itself as an *imperative* — a total engagement in response to the total cultural breakdown in which 'the British capitalists let their characteristic cultural, moral and religious system collapse in the post-war years, putting up but a lackadaisical defence'.[52]

The instrument for the enactment of such a commitment — for the revolutionary interaction of intellectual and worker, individual and collective movement — put forward as the central proposal of Strachey's last major statement of the Popular Front period, *What are We to Do?* (1938), is a Leninist mass party adapted to British conditions of the 1930s. (Strachey's terms for this — 'The New Model', 'New Model Party', 'New Political Force' — recall as well, of course, the revolutionary armies of the 1640s.) In this organization the role and responsibilities of the revolutionary intellectuals are of cardinal importance not — as in liberal cultural theory — as the privileged bearers and defenders of an inherited tradition, but as, rather, a functional élite to guide the collective project of political and cultural transformation.

'... what the movement needs is not less leadership but, in one sense, more leadership. *Only this leadership must be a qualified leadership.* Socialism is now a science and only those who have mastered this science are qualified to have a decisive voice in the leadership of a Labour movement.'[53]

The legitimation of the élite lies in the paramount need to counter the tremendous force of hegemonic bourgeois ideology and, as the following passage makes clear, in the élite's inherent tendency to make its own very existence superfluous:

It is a prime duty of those who take on the heavy responsibility of leadership in a working class movement to take off the bandage with which capitalism blinds the eyes of the workers. But, instead, the existence of that bandage is made the excuse for every inadequacy, for every inaction and for every surrender.[54]

The precisely delineated function assigned to the élite within the revolutionary movement as a whole provides another significant point of comparison with the Fabians: having developed their ideology, as they themselves freely admitted, through an exclusively middle-class fraction operating, moreover, totally within the intellectual horizons of a class society (that of late nineteenth-century Britain) in which functions, duties and privileges seemed irreversibly distributed among the various constituted classes, the Fabians had no reason to question that the best achievable form of social organization should eternalize for them a tutelary role over the working class — a role in fact derived largely from inherited class-advantage but one for which they were increasingly to find warrant in the closed nature of the Stalinist bureaucracy and the restriction of effective working-class democracy in the Soviet Union.[55]

Nevertheless the dividing-line, in practice, between a provisional activist élite of the 'transmission-belt' type envisaged by Lenin and restated by Strachey, and a caste exerting power and influence deriving from accumulated privilege, can become extremely blurred — as the emergence of the Stalinist bureaucracy in the USSR, and the effectively conservative appropriation of its ideology by 'moderates' in the West such as the Fabian leaders, arguably demonstrate.

In Strachey's case, the tactical exigencies of the Popular Front movement could, on occasion, lead to an acceptance of middle-class opportunism into revolutionary politics even more brazen than that of Pollitt: 'The middle classes of any country are swayed by the same motives as other classes; and one of the most important, and most human, of the motives upon the strength of which men choose their political alignment, is the desire to be on the winning side.'[56] The clear perception of the need for a dialectical unity of intelligentsia and proletariat within the revolutionary movement as a whole, can, then, atrophy into an opportunism which tends to obscure class differences rather than genuinely resolve them, through a denial of their real history (how can one class be said to have 'the same motives' as another, except in the context of rhetorical abstraction?). Through a related and comparable process, the provisional function of the élite can harden into a new form of romantic individualism, its voluntarism turned inwards to support a renewed cult of the hero.

The phenomenon is observable throughout both Soviet and Western artistic production of the period: notably in films such as the Vassiliev brothers' *Chapayev* and in Eisenstein's later productions, in the central figures of 1930s novels by writers close to the cultural politics of the Communists (Hemingway's *For Whom the Bell Tolls* and Malraux's *L'Espoir* for instance); and at its crudest in the presentation by writers such as John Lehmann of Stalin himself as a 'romantic hero' ('yes, romantic, if the words mean anything positive at all today . . .').[57]

In Strachey's case, the tendency is observable in his review of Brontman's account of the Soviet expedition to the North Pole, *On Top of the World*:

> Schmidt himself, the leader of the expedition . . . as everybody knows, is a professor. But what a professor. In our world the word professor carries the connotation of the man of books, the recluse, the sheltered, purely intellectual worker. But here is a professor, and a real professor mind you, with the very highest academic and scientific qualifications, who goes flying over the Pole, who leads a squadron of aeroplanes to the top of the world, signalling to each plane as it flies, to take its place in the formation, like an admiral leading his fleet into battle. . . . Here, in a word, is the very incarnation of that destruction of the barriers between intellectual and physical labour of which the great masters of scientific socialism have written.[58]

The political content of this is in one sense minimal (much of it could be applied, *mutatis mutandis*, to Scott of the Antarctic). The revolutionary sense of personal development through collective subjectivity has been radically reduced: politics here figures merely as the backdrop to a drama of individual self-realisation (one which reminds us of the ambiguous political status of the airman as represented in the work of T.E. Lawrence, Auden, Malraux, Rex Warner, Saint Exupéry — and which, moreover, ironically foreshadows Strachey's conventionally successful wartime career in the RAF).[59]

The political uncertainty latent in this text is manifest in a letter written by Strachey to his psychoanalyst in the same month, April 1938 — a letter whose expression of intense personal insecurity significantly complements the preceding image of the intellectual as hero: '. . . is the prospect of a world of war, fascism, or both . . . a result of neurotically motivated, hate-compelled, impulses from the left, producing their inevitable reaction from the right?' The only way out of this depressing psychologistic pendulum-motion is now, for Strachey, a surprisingly naive faith in the intervention of the psychiatrist god-figure in the political arena, to confer absolute meaning from without upon the confusing relativities of history:

> You have got, in your knowledge of psycho-analytic theory, and in your wide clinical experience, a unique safeguard against forming compulsive opinions on economics

and politics . . . insofar as a trained analyst has freed himself from these inhibitions, could he not come to economic and political science with unique objectivity and see relatively easily into the nature of its problems?[60]

To infer from this that Strachey's politics of the 1930s were in essence a product of neurosis would be to capitulate to the very psychologism which Strachey is at this point embracing. Rather it is the *political* significance of the form of the neurosis — manifest both here and in the remarks on the Soviet explorer — which must retain our interest. Both texts mark the reversion to a pre- or sub-political cult of personal authority, the abdication of any notion of collective political responsibility, the submission to mystification rather than its interrogation — a gravitation towards the psychology (if not altogether the formal politics) of the Right.

A glimpse of Strachey's loss of confidence in the integrated dynamic of a revolutionary movement of both intellectuals and workers — the factor underlying the shift — is perhaps apparent, in *What Are We to Do?*, in the language almost of fatalism in which setbacks are recorded; and which contrasts strongly with the active voluntarism of 1936: '. . . the immediate and universal expropriation of the capitalists . . . is not the subject which history has today written upon our agendas.'[61] The sense of collective dynamism disintegrates henceforth into, on the one hand, the individualist cult of the will already noted, and, on the other, a debilitated collectivism in the form of a vague populist sentiment, centring (after the Nazi–Soviet pact) on the USA: 'New, vigorous, rising working-class and popular forces exist in the United States. Our imperative duty is . . . to co-ordinate these American popular forces with our own, so that . . . it will be, not the capital, but the peoples, of Britain and America, who clasp hands.[62] The apologetics of the cold war are already (in 1940) perceivable in embryo, among the ruins of Strachey's once remarkably articulated Popular Frontism.

The central position occupied by Strachey in the intellectual history of British popular frontism is a result of both of his consistency of focus and magnitude of influence during the period, and of the centrality of the Popular Front to this intellectual development and reputation. Strachey at his best was the least conciliatory of radical social theorists of his time; his theory the most demanding in many respects, both of intellectuals and of the working class; expressed with great clarity — the fruit, itself, of great conceptual sophistication — it is moreover, notable among left-wing writing of the 1930s for its almost complete lack of talking down to an imagined audience, of condescension.[63]

By contrast with the best of Strachey's work, Hyman Levy's *A Philosophy for a Modern Man*[64] appears often mechanistic rather than clear, dogmatic rather than uncondescending. Aiming at a degree of textbook authority in its own sphere — an account of the principles of science and scientific method, and their applicability to society and political practice through the conceptual framework of dialectical materialism — comparable to a work such as *The Theory and Practice of Socialism*, its very title, perhaps indicative of an uncertainty of the audience to be reached (a hint of patronage even) is characteristic of the unease surrounding the political interventions of radical intellectuals at the time.[65]

The impression is borne out by the ingratiating jocularity with which the first chapter commences: 'Philosophers are not commonly regarded as men of affairs . . . . The man in the street is the only person who will treat them with due respect, with the respect he will give to any rare incomprehensible specimen.'[66] The uncertainty is significantly balanced by the affirmation elsewhere that 'mathematics, we are told . . . is *par excellence* the most telling illustration of how the mind in its free activity can form ideas that reach the highest pinnacle of human creativeness.'[67] (Levy was himself an eminent mathematician).

Quite apart from questions of special pleading — or even of the subjective sense of status of the scientific worker, significant though that may be — the uncertainty derives from Levy's hesitation in ascribing philosophy to the category of social *force* or of social *product*; commenting on contemporary society he states:

> In the effort to appreciate and control the forces that are moulding this changing situation there is a call that philosophy must help to provide understanding, and that understanding must offer guidance. It is to the readjustment in the economic sphere of Britain's relation to other nations, to the new wave of uncertainty and to the increasing awareness of the British people that the outlook and philosophy of security, isolation and unchallenged supremacy no longer reflects the modern *tempo* of wars and revolutions, that one must trace the new philosophical awakening.[68]

The shift from dominance to subordination — and back — of the role of 'philosophy', as registered in this brief extract, may legitimately be seen, in its instability, as correlative to that of the Popular Front alliance between intelligentsia and proletariat within the overall context of liberal capitalism. Not surprisingly, the instability is also present in a later discussion of art, where the notion of art — like philosophy above — as *reflection*, is rapidly supplanted by a familiar expression of humanist individualism:

> At the interregnum between two successive epochs a special responsibility rests on the shoulders of artists and writers. On them falls the duty of sensing the future, clinging

to the valuations that man is seeking to rescue from decay, expressing them in their work, applying the best of the past to the creation of the future.[69]

The mechanical see-saw effect between ideology and social formation, base and superstructure, would appear to result from the refusal of a thoroughgoing class-analysis which would be capable of seeing social change as entailing not merely changes in the dissemination and appropriation of superstructual phenomena (the arts, science, etc.) seen as pre-constituted and static in themselves, but as inter-relating with continuing developments internal to those phenomena.

It is true that in his account of change, causality, and the transformation of qualities Levy does at times outrun mechanist schematization: as in Strachey's *The Coming Struggle for Power*, socio-economic development is seen as a succession of over-lapping layers rather than a linear progression from one mode of production to another;[70] the actively interventionist role of the scientist in observing relationships rather than discrete phenomena is stressed;[71] the nature of causality is seen to be multiple rather than linear, to the extent that 'base' and 'superstructure' emerge as fluid and related determinant terms rather than, as in the mechanical Marxism of previous generations, as fixed poles in a relationship: circumstances are noted in which 'causal responsibility for the change shifts from what was the primary cause of the mere sharpening in quality, to a secondary internal cause which is in itself brought into being by that primary cause.'[72] Such dialectical complexity is, however, continually at odds, in Levy's work, with a tendency to a mechanistic reductionism (especially observable in his relation of scientific categories to contemporary social formations) to which the very language which he deploys seems pre-disposed — thus, ironically, throwing into question Levy's own mechanistic assertions about 'the inertia of speech and the way in which our thoughts and ideas are entangled within its framework'.[73] (The conflict, and the over-determination of its eventual outcome, may again be seen as conceptual enactment of the conflicting Popular Front motivations of revolutionary social transformation and, more powerfully, of accommodation to liberal-democratic cultural norms within the overall context of capitalist society.) Thus planets and atoms are both categorized as 'a group of *things*'; the validity of philosophy is seen as its relevance to 'the ordinary man in his *handling* of the world'[74] (a significant conjuncture of populism and self/world dualism, this); similarly, reference to 'pieces of matter' — a phrase which, as we shall see, was to arouse Bertrand Russell's antagonism — is defended thus: 'The word matter is here used for what we pick up as pieces and objects everywhere. Commonsense refuses to be violated by false interpretations of simple scientific discoveries.'[75]

The hesitation in Levy's discourse — between a dialectic inter-relating self and world (and by implication individual and collective, base and superstructure) and a monolithic and eventually determinant mechanism, is apparent from the fluctuations of the following passage:

We see the universe existing 'out there' apart from us . . . independently of the meaning it has for us. There is danger in this apparent independence . . . . In some sense (the universe) is different for our presence; the world is changed by our being here from what we may *imagine* it would have been without us. The thought is, of course, a mere fictitious idea; we are part of the universe in the sense that we are one of the cogs in its vast complicated machinery.[76]

The effect of such mechanistic thinking, when transposed into an account of the logic of social process, is debilitating to say the least: it manifests itself — after a long and conventional account of the Marxist theory of social development in the terminology of natural science — as characteristically liberal 'scientific detachment' leading to a bathetic, amost tautologous, conclusion:

Not only have we tacitly assumed that the democratic machine will function efficiently for this purpose, (that of social transformation) but we have assumed that the very people themselves will in their growing distress and in the confusion of schemes and policies that are insistently presented to them by contending groups be clear-sighted enough to elect a strong democratic and socialistic Government. We will not venture on the probabilities of such an occurrence; but failing it then the other route (that of fascism) is clearly that which will be trodden.[77]

Alternatively, the logic of natural science leads necessarily to the classless society: 'For us the problems of philosophy are resolved into those of guiding ourselves and others towards [the] classless society.'[78] Eventually scientific mechanism becomes transposed into a kind of social functionalism whose imperatives coincide with the class alliance of the Popular Front, its approach to the middle classes being justified as follows: 'The theory of class society, as we have tried to make clear, is a statistical theory. What is sharp under modern conditions is not the division into employers and employees, but the functions of exchanging labour power, and controlling the access of that power to machinery.'[79]

Bertrand Russell's review of Levy's work in the *New Statesman*, and the ensuing polemic with the author, constitute an intellectual document of some interest and importance.[80] The points initially made by Russell against the book — from a standpoint, as becomes evident later in the polemic, of individualist radicalism — represent in effect an inventory of many of the intellectual incoherencies and accommodations into which apologists of the Popular Front had, given the ambiguous nature of the project such as we have seen it, either been forced; or had willingly adopted. These may be characterized as follows:

1 The emasculation of the class-conflictual element in Marxist dialectics in the interests of harmony among 'progressives' of varying social backgrounds, seen as one more instance of the incorporative strategy of the ruling-class:

> Hegelianism becomes bland and sensible in the writings of Caird and Bosanquet, and so does Marxism in the writings of Professor Levy . . . . The English, when they have been aware of the existence of the Germans, have . . . either . . . treated them with contempt, or they have edited them and bowdlerised them until their systems seemed compatible with common sense.[81]

2 The element of both mechanism and political opportunism evident in the playing down of the class-struggle: Russell, as a liberal moralist, deplores as 'rather sycophantic' Levy's assent to Marxism on grounds of belief in its likely victory (opportunism of this kind was considered in different ways, as we have seen, by both Pollitt and Strachey). It might be argued that, whilst in conflict with ruling-class strategy (1 above) in the short term, it coincides with it in the long term.

3 Its ahistorical humanist individualism: Russell seizes on Levy's definition of 'Truth' as 'the summation of man's experience'; and comments tartly, in fact echoing Marx and Engels on the bourgeoisie: 'When people speak of "man", they are to be suspected of giving a fictitious universality to themselves.'[82]

4 Levy's dated and mechanist view of matter, as a substance rather than a process (his reference to 'pieces of matter' being evidently seen as cardinal, since Levy's project is to demonstrate the applicability of natural science to politics). Russell refers to quantum theory as increasing the amount of stress on *chance* now necessary in historical explanation; moreover stating that modern physicists need only to believe in 'the series of events', dismissing the 'material substratum' as 'metaphysical lumber'.

Significantly, Levy in his reply makes no attempt to refute Russell's points 1 to 3 — indeed it is difficult to conceive of a convincing reply by a committed defender of the Popular Front in practice. Rather, he concentrates on the, technically, admittedly central question raised by 4; ignoring Russell's stress on the significance for modern physics of the 'series of events' (possibly a means, one would have thought, of reconciling quantum theory with a notion of history and society as process rather than as a random grouping of phenomena — a reconciliation which, as we have seen, certain of the more dynamic aspects of his own work allow for); reaffirming rather, with an amalgam of mechanistic thinking and of philistine populist bluster, that his audiences were uninterested in 'the old philosophical issues', and crudely ascribing to Russell the view that all politics was 'metaphysical lumber'; proclaiming in a parody of Popular Front eclecticism: 'I refuse at a time like this to be party to increasing the confusion that already exists. Matter is simply what we pick up and handle . . . '; finally affirming Russell's belief in the immateriality of the world and hence necessary political impotence.[83]

Russell replies to these exaggerated denunciations reasonably enough — incidentally in a manner more reconcilable than that of Levy with the most rigorous materialism when he writes that he holds 'in common with Einstein that position in space is relative, that Spain, Italy, China, Abyssinia are relative terms; but I do not see how this view bears on my interest in the fate of Spaniards, Italians, Chinese and Abyssinians' — and repeats the assertion that 'the atom is more conveniently treated as a series of events, not as a persistent entity'.[84] He then, however, goes on to affirm the inconceivability of the notion's having any connection with politics — and then to attack Marxism from an apparent standpoint of random eclecticism: 'We can organise the food supply . . . without any particular theory of social dynamics'[85]; rejecting with aristocratic disdain Levy's remarks about his audiences: 'Professor Levy apparently holds that one should advocate a metaphysical doctrine . . . because it is supposed by some, owing to their incapacity for logical thought, to be useful to one's political party'.[86]

In the final contribution to the polemic, Levy — as might be expected — easily refutes Russell's crude dismissal of the significance of social theory: 'Every piece of social organisation towards a particular end involves some kind of theory of dynamics'.[87] Yet he makes no attempt to relate quantum theory to the class struggle, as might conceivably have been done by considering the significance, for an account of history, of the atom viewed as series rather than object. Yet, of course, this would have involved, ultimately, a consideration of base and superstructure in the same terms, and thus a genuine engagement with dialectics — and so Levy merely descends to vulgar abuse, accusing Russell of 'muttering commonplace scientific ideas at me about Relativity and Quantum Theory'.[88]

Clearly, Russell got the better of the immediate debate — and his revelation (and his inducement to complementary revelations by Levy) of the philosophical inadequacies of Popular Frontism — its quasi-bourgeois attempts to reconcile irreconcilables, its tendency to hypostatize an already insecure conjuncture of workers and intelligentsia, its populism and necessary tendency to seek the political (and theoretical) lowest common denominator — is all of it salutary enough. Yet a detailed account of the debate reveals, in Levy, a consciousness of the necessary relation of thought to social practice, however vitiated by mechanistic modes of thinking and by bad faith; and in Russell, a decided refusal to attempt to relate the structure of the physical universe to that of man's social experience, hardly less vitiated by individualism.

Yet it would not be entirely true to conclude that the era of the Popular Front could achieve no more, intellectually, than the confrontation — across an unbridgeable gulf — of reductive, mechanistic science and sociology, with the more plausible but, in fact, no less sclerotic philosophy of humanist individualism.

Attempts were continually being made to bridge the gulf through the social and political practice of Popular Frontism. For a final characterization of its manifold ambiguities we could do worse than compare the nature of their assent to it of two writers and political activists: Leonard Woolf and G.D.H. Cole — both members of the Labour Party throughout their adult lives (and in the 1930s of the Executive of the Fabian Society), whose attitudes had been formed in the 1910s and 1920s and who had, by the period of the Popular Front, achieved in each case a consistent range of preoccupations which was to be largely maintained throughout the ensuing war and post-war period. In contrast to Spender and Strachey (whose ideological divergencies in some ways paralleled their own, but for whom the problems of the 1930s represented a crucial series of occasions for self-definition as radical intellectuals), and still more to men such as Julian Bell and John Cornford or Ralph Fox (between whom, again, a similar set of political and cultural disparities may be seen) whose commitment, however dissimilar, to the politics of Popular Frontism as such led to death in Spain — for Woolf and Cole the Popular Front represented not so much a crucially new alignment of forces as a specific episode in which the claims of already established principles had to be reasserted and adjusted. In this sense, if perhaps in no other, they may be seen as more representative than the other writers discussed here.

Their continuing principles and motives of course, were radically divergent: Woolf's the maintenance and dissemination of the 'civilized' values of patrician Bloomsbury liberalism (the feasibility of which he came to consider, in the inter-war years, with an increasing elegiac scepticism, as both his contemporary writings and his retrospective autobiographical judgements in *Downhill All The Way*, published in 1967, make plain); Cole's the access to effective political and cultural power of the working class as a whole — a concern which had led him from opposition to the Webbs' autocratic Fabianism in the 1910s to the theorization, in reaction, of Guild Socialism, and to a perennial interest in issues of workers' control: an interest, incidentally, almost unique among British Socialist thinkers.

The language of the two writers provides a vivid contrast. Woolf's validation of the supposedly particular virtues of English politics — 'a system of government in which freedom, tolerance, and compromise — the foundations of a civilized life — have been slowly and painfully substituted for irresponsible power, violence, privilege and superstition'[89] — enacts, in its sonorous monotony of accumulated abstractions, the virtual hypnosis of liberal ideology, with its consistent and overt tendency (as here) to dissolve the acknowledged conflicts of the past into the pervasively suggested harmonies of the present.

On the other hand Cole's writing can have an aphoristic sharpness which recalls the best of Shaw: here the tense and conflictual reality of the politics of liberalism — as opposed to Woolf's soothingly formulated ideology — is actualized (rather than disguised) by the language: 'If Socialism, of a sort, is tolerated, even where Communism is not, that is because the defenders of capitalism identify Communism in their minds with the sort of Socialism that really means business'.[90] The contrasting languages are, of course, the articulations of fundamentally opposed definitions of the nature of culture in society, and consequently of the role of the intellectual. For Woolf, 'civilization is the social order secreted by men who are civilized'[91] — a commodity rather than a process or relationship, evoked here in terms of restriction and mystification ('secreted'), and of self-validating circularity. The intelligentsia are, accordingly, defined in essentialist terms, forever guarding the accumulated treasure which is human culture from inter-active contact with human society: 'They are not concerned with getting things done, with politics and power, but with *things* of the mind, truth, speculation, morality, art'.[92]

Cole characteristically refutes any such fetishization of the intelligentsia with an analytic precision which, like much of Strachey, derives from an advanced and sophisticated Popular Frontism which avoids both Fabian élitism and crude workerism:

It is neither possible nor desirable in a democratic community for the specialists to have the last word about what is to be done. The last word should rest with the people themselves and with their representatives . . . . Where democracy half-exists, as in Great Britain today, the people and the vested interests contend for the last word; and the chances of popular success depend mainly on the spread of clear knowledge among the people and of sympathetic co-operation between them and the scientific specialists.[93]

Woolf's monolithic liberal humanism reveals itself, politically, in unquestioning acceptance of the similarly monolithic notion that human history is not that of conflict, but of an eternalized ruling class: 'The objectives of a society are revealed in its organisation or in the aims, declared or concealed, of its government or governing classes'.[94] The lack of any genuine historical sense, the bourgeois compulsion to negate substantive conflict, now display their effective politics — a debased Popular Frontism which achieves the incorporation of Marxism within the hegemonic discourse of the liberal boureoisie: 'It sounds almost indecent to say it, but it is almost certainly true that the ultimate social end of Stalin is the same as that of Mr. Winston Churchill; they are both on the side of Western civilization'.[95]

The occasion for such a vertiginous convergence had, of course, been provided in the 1930s by the reversion of the USSR to something resembling bourgeois cultural norms — a reversion moreover based on the effective repression of collective proletarian democracy and the re-establishment of individual authority in so many ways. Thus Marxism could be accommodated, through Stalin, to liberalism — and Woolf could insert an affirmation of bourgeois humanist individualism into a paraphrase of the *Communist Manifesto*:

The ultimate end of Stalin's policy . . . is not . . . the establishment of a classless society . . . the ultimate end is the widening and enrichment of the individual's existence, the creation of an association in which the free development of each is the condition for the free development of all.[96]

Yet against this process — of the incorporation of revolutionary potential, the perpetuation of patrician liberalism and of middle-class cultural authority, towards which, as we have seen, so much Popular Front activity tended — must be set the recognition of much real intellectual dynamism: of Strachey's central awareness (its over-audacity, it may now seem, leading to frustration and reaction) of the possibility, in the 1930s, of a new basis for a newly articulated socialism; of Cole's perception of the achievability, through a genuinely mass-controlled Popular Front, of a socialism avoiding the *impasses* of both élitism and workerism — an awareness which could fall forth again something very like the voice of Winstanley:

> We therefore, with no other help than our will to express honestly what is in us of help towards meeting the troubles of a world that is sorely beset, must do what we can to find the words that will enable us to get on terms one with another, and, having discovered wherein we think and feel together, to act together as well.[97]

The incapacity of such men as these to translate theory into practice calls less for Orwell's splenetic denunciation of the Popular Front as 'the nauseous spectacle of bishops, Communists, cocoa-magnates, publishers, duchesses and Labour MPs marching arm in arm to the tune of *Rule Britannia*'[98], than for something like the lucid critical sympathy of C. Day Lewis for those caught in a later, and perhaps even more intractable dilemma:

> It is the logic of our time,
> No subject for immortal verse,
> That we who lived by honest dreams
> Defend the bad against the worse.[99]

Notes

1 For an account of the problems of the *Front Populaire* in France, notably those of reformism and of the relationship between mass-movement and political leadership, see D. Guérin (1970), *Front Populaire, Révolution Manquée. Témoignage Militant*, Maspéro, Paris, esp. chap.III.

2 Compare for instance the accounts of the economic context given by H. Noguères (1977) *La Vie Quotidienne en France au Temps du Front Populaire 1935–1938*, Hachette, Paris, chap.IV; and N. Branson and M. Heinemann (1973), *Britain in the Nineteen Thirties*, Panther, London, chap.I.

3 J. Lewis (1970), *The Left Book Club. An Historical Record*, Gollancz, London.

4 V. Gollancz (1936) 'Editorial: The Left Book Club', *The Left Book Club News*, May 1936, 2. See the reverential account of the political influence of French intellectuals in H. Fluchère (1936), French Intellectuals and the Political Crisis', *Scrutiny* Vol.V no.3, December 1936.

5 H. Laski (1938), 'A Communist Leader', *New Statesman*, 27 August 1938, 319–20.

6 'The Popular Front', *New Statesman*, 8 August 1936, 179.

7 cf.'Guérin, *op. cit.*, 110.

8 H.G. Wells (1939), 'A Forecast of 1939' in *Travels of a Republican Radical in Search of Hot Water*, Penguin, Harmondsworth, 24.

9 See especially G. Orwell (1941), 'The Lion and the Unicorn: Socialism

and the English Genius', in *Collected Essays, Journalism and Letters II* (1968), Secker & Warburg, London, 56–109.

10 H.G. Wells, *op. cit.*, 71.

11 H.G. Wells, *ibid*, 77.

12 G.B. Shaw (1935), 'Freedom', in Dan H. Laurence (ed.) (1962) *Platform and Pulpit*, Rupert Hart-Davis, London, 266.

13 S. Webb and B. Webb (1935), *Soviet Communism: A New Civilisation?* NALGO Edition, London, 1114.

14 For views inclining to the consensus, see (for France) standard histories such as: L. Bodin and J. Touchard (1961), *Le Front Populaire*, A. Colin, Paris; G. Lefranc (1965), *Histoire du Front Populaire*, Payot, Paris and H. Noguères, *op cit.* Critical views are to be found in L. Trotsky (1974), *Whither France?*, New Park Publications, London, see too his remarks in Part VII of *The Struggle against Fascism in Germany*, Penguin, Harmondsworth, (1975). See also Daniel Guérin, *op. cit.* French sources have been quoted on problems of Popular Frontism since, obviously, its relative underdevelopment in Britain in the 1930s has led to little retrospect consideration of the problems in general. See however E. Hobsbawm (1976), 'Forty Years of Popular Front Government' in *Marxism Today* July 1976 — and for a contemporary critical view, the virtually unobtainable A. Fenner Brockway (1937), *Workers' Front*, Secker & Warburg, London.

15 R. Fox (1932), 'Comrade Stalin's Letter and the C.P.G.B.', *Communist Review*, April 1932, 204–5.

16 R. Fox (1935), 'Communism's Fight on the Cultural Front', Daily Worker, 11 September 1935; reprinted in Lehmann, Jackson, Day Lewis (eds) *Ralph Fox: A Writer in Arms*, Lawrence & Wishart, London, 181 (emphasis added).

17 R. Palme Dutt (1932), 'Intellectuals and Communism', *Communist Review*, September 1932, 422.

18 R. Palme Dutt, *ibid*, 428.

19 R. Palme Dutt, *ibid*, p.424.

20 H. Pollitt (1936), 'Building the People's Front', *Left Review*, December 1936, 798, 802.

21 H. Pollitt, *ibid*. 803.

22 Richard Acland in a speech to the Left Book Club Albert Hall Rally, 7 February 1937, reported in *The Left News*, March 1937.

23 The Alpha Group (1936), 'Artists and the People's Front', *Left Review*, October 1936, 677.

24 A. Williams-Ellis (1936), 'Soviet Literature', in *Britain and the Soviets: The Congress of Peace and Friendship with the U.S.S.R.* Martin Lawrence, London, 144.

25 A. Williams-Ellis, *ibid*. p.150. For a theorization of the fulfilment of this prophecy, see H. Marcuse (1971), *Soviet Marxism. A Critical Analysis*, Penguin, Harmondsworth, chap.VI: 'Base and Superstructure — Reality and Ideology'.

26 Anon (1937), 'Marxism and the Arts', *Arena*, October/December 1937, 196.

27 Anon, *ibid*., 195. A comparison between the (explicit) organicism of Leavis and that implicit in the Popular Front literary criticism of Georg Lukács would yield much of interest.
28 S. Spender (1951), *World Within World*, Hamish Hamilton, London, 210–11.
29 J.P. Tuck (1934), 'English Criticism and the Soviet Writers' Congress', *Cambridge Left*, Autumn 1934, 12.
30 S. Spender (1935), *The Destructive Element. A Study of Modern Writers and Beliefs,* Jonathan Cape, London 224 (emphasis added).
31 S. Spender *ibid.* cf. C. Bell (1938) *Civilization*, Penguin, Harmondsworth, *passim.*
32 S. Spender, *ibid*. 223.
33 S. Spender (1937), *Forward from Liberalism*, Gollancz/Left Book Club, London, 50.
34 S. Spender, *ibid*. 70.
35 S. Spender, *ibid*.20–21.
36 S. Spender, *ibid*. 21–22.
37 S. Spender, *ibid*. 27.
38 S. Spender, *ibid*. 71. A description of the May Day crowds in Tiflis, Georgia, by Spender's close friend John Lehmann, actualizes the complex of attitudes with unintentional but graphic precision: 'Not that the crowd was disorderly; on the contrary, with one or two exuberant exceptions, it did the expected and the reasonable thing the whole time, with a lively instinct for just the right amount of discipline': J. Lehmann (1937), *Prometheus and the Bolsheviks*, The Cresset Press, London, 47.
39 S. Spender, *op cit. World Within World*, 290.
40 'When they [i.e. the Communists] lectured unctuously about our "cultural heritage" they meant wealth which they proposed to debase and squander, inherited from ancestors whom they would have regarded as their worst enemies in their own lifetimes', S. Spender, *ibid*, 251.
41 Notably in *The Coming Struggle for Power* (1932), *The Nature of Capitalist Crisis* (1935), *The Theory and Practice of Socialism* (1936) and — perhaps most influential of all — the pamphlet *Why You Should Be a Socialist* (1938, new edition 1944).
42 Quoted in H. Thomas (1973), *John Strachey*, Eyre Methuen, London, 158. The vituperative tone — as with Spender's paradoxical implication that it was the *Communists* alone who were 'unctuous' about culture, may be seen to derive from a will to avoid self-recognition. When Strachey says that 'even I was staggered' by the Webbs' defects but nonetheless praised their work, all we can reasonably conclude is that he would rather be thought a liar than a dupe, retrospectively.
43 In H. Thomas, *op. cit.*, 58.
44 J. Strachey (1932), *The Coming Struggle for Power*, Gollancz, London, fourth edition, 29–30.
45 J. Strachey (1936), *The Theory and Practice of Socialism*, Gollancz/Left

Book Club, London, 359–61.

46 J. Strachey (1938), *What are We to Do?*, Gollancz/Left Book Club, London, 67–8.

47 J. Strachey, *ibid.* 385.

48 J. Strachey, *op. cit. The Theory and Practice of Socialism*, 131.

49 J. Strachey (1932), 'The Education of a Communist', *Left Review*, December 1934, reprinted in E. Allen Osborne (ed) (1938), *In Letters of Red*, Michael Joseph, London, 221.

50 J. Strachey, *op cit. The Theory and Practice of Socialism*, 10, 16.

51 J. Strachey, *op cit. What Are We to Do?*, 83.

52 J. Strachey, *op. cit.* 'The Education of a Communist', 217.

53 J. Strachey, *op. cit. What Are We to Do?*, 280.

54 J. Strachey, *ibid.* 285.

55 Shaw's statements in his Fabian Society lecture of November 1932 'In Praise of Guy Fawkes' are both characteristic of Shaw and representative of many of his generation. Here, as so often, Shaw has the merit of revealing, with almost childlike simplicity and glee, frequent but unspoken social and ideological assumptions: 'The [New] State will be a hierarchy, like the Corporate State of Italy and the Communist State of Russia . . . self-election, provided you eliminate all corrupt inducements, is the best sort of election, for the willing worker is the best worker . . . . In such a system as I have sketched for you, the ruling hierarchy culminates in a Cabinet of Thinkers' (in G.B. Shaw, *op. cit: Platform and Pulpit*, 245–6).

56 J. Strachey (1936), 'Topic of the Month: France', *The Left Book News*, May 1936, 7.

57 J. Lehmann, *op. cit. Prometheus and the Bolsheviks*, 119.

58 J. Strachey (1938), in *The Left News*, April 1938, 767.

59 H. Thomas, *op. cit. John Strachey*, 215 ff.

60 Quoted H. Thomas, *ibid.*, 170–1.

61 J. Strachey, *op. cit. What are We to Do?*, 314.

62 J. Strachey (1941), 'The American Question', in V. Gollancz (ed) *The Betrayal of the Left*, Gollancz, London, 105.

63 A certain degree of condescension becomes evident, significantly, simultaneously with the drift towards populism, in Strachey's contributions to *The Betrayal of the Left*, especially the essay on 'Totalitarianism' (chap. VII).

64 H. Levy (1938), *A Philosophy for a Modern Man*, Gollancz/Left Book Club, London. Local groups of the Club were encouraged to discuss it at their meetings; it was obviously considered a 'key' publication by the Club.

65 cf. Shaw's *Intelligent Woman's Guide;* Wells' *Experiment in Autobiography: Discoveries and Conclusions of a Very Ordinary Brain since 1866*; Cole's *Intelligent Man's Guide through World Chaos* and *What Marx Really Meant;* etc. etc.

66 H. Levy, *op. cit. A Philosophy for a Modern Man*, 11.

67 H. Levy, *ibid.* 228.

68 H. Levy, *ibid.* 18.

69 H. Levy, *ibid.* 239.
70 H. Levy, *ibid.* 94–5.
71 H. Levy, *ibid.* 105.
72 H. Levy, *ibid.* 110.
73 H. Levy, *ibid.* 23.
74 H. Levy, *ibid.* 10, 12–13 (emphasis added).
75 H. Levy, *ibid.* 31.
76 H. Levy, *ibid.* 24.
77 H. Levy, *ibid.* 226.
78 H. Levy, *ibid.* 269.
79 H. Levy, *ibid.* 279.
80 B. Russell, 'Philosophy and Common Sense', *New Statesman*, 12 February 1938; 26 February 1938; 5 March 1938; 12 March 1938.
81 B. Russell, *New Statesman*, 12 February 1938, 252.
82 B. Russell, *ibid.* cf. Marx and Engels: 'For each new class which puts itself in the place of one ruling before it, is compelled, merely in order to carry through its aim, to represent its interest as the common interest of all the members of society . . . to give its ideas the form of universality, and represent them as the only rational, universally valid ones'. C.J. Arthur (ed) (1970), *The German Ideology*, Lawrence & Wishart, 65–6.
83 H. Levy, *New Statesman*, 26 February 1938, 325.
84 B. Russell, *ibid.* 365.
85 B. Russell, *ibid.*
86 B. Russell, *ibid.*
87 H. Levy, *New Statesman* 12 March 1938, 405.
88 H. Levy, *ibid.*
89 L. Woolf (1935), *Quack, Quack!*, The Hogarth Press, London, 106–7.
90 G.D.H. Cole (1937), *The People's Front*, Gollancz/Left Book Club, London, 326.
91 L. Woolf (1939), *Barbarians at the Gate*, Gollancz/Left Book Club, London, 42.
92 L. Woolf, *Quack, Quack!* 109–10 (emphasis added).
93 G.D.H. and M.I. Cole (1937), *The Condition of Britain*, Gollanz/Left Book Club, London, 18.
94 L. Woolf, *Barbarians at the Gates*, 43.
95 L. Woolf, *ibid*, 95.
96 L. Woolf, *ibid.* 69–70.
97 G.D.H. Cole, *The People's Front*, 306.
98 G. Orwell (1938), Review of Fenner Brockway, *Workers' Front* (February 1938), reprinted in *Collected Essays, Journalism and Letters I*, 305.
99 C. Day Lewis (1943), 'Where are the War Poets?', *Word Over All.*

4 CHANGING THINGS: ORWELL AND AUDEN

Frank Gloversmith

Part I: Orwell

The critical estimate and the popular esteem for Orwell — the man and the works taken together — have long since converged to sustain a major emphasis on integrity, on 'character' in a traditional sense. The career and the writing are taken to exemplify and to articulate a difficult ethic of decency and virtue in bewildering times. So the 1950s saw an intellectual hero, a generation's conscience reluctantly depicting its savage disenchantments — *Animal Farm*[1] and *Nineteen Eighty-Four*[2] — a hero who was a good man, 'a social saint'. As a man of commitments, though grittily independent, surviving the scarifying experiences of 'a low dishonest decade', Orwell was remarkable in authenticating his words by his deeds. Since he forbade biography and detested attention such as T.E. Lawrence received, George Orwell could all the more readily be taken into the select band of those writers who *are* what they write.

So a form of response was set, its limits able to accommodate a sense of Orwell's difficultness — his contradictions, prejudices, and tensions — so that the composite 'Orwell', works and personality, could be presented as a mirror for Anglo-Saxons. The bluntness, and contrariness, the not-to-be-fooled straightforwardness of the ordinary man had been raised to qualities of genius, composing a model to emulate, in living and in writing. The ambiguities, the opinionatedness, and changes in stance only enhanced this appeal, displacing unreal adulation by deep respect for an all-too-human example, valued exactly for this truculence and this mental awkwardness. The turbulence of the individual life, and the contradictions intrinsic to writing to the moment by a man immersed in the destructive element of a disturbed historical moment: these could be totalized, and the confusions all explained, coherently represented. So, for example, we have Orwell as the artist who creates in suffering, living a life of allegory with the works as comments on it. (This is a rough-and-ready version of how Shakespeare seemed to Keats; and Thomas Mann's artist-hero in *Dr Faustus* has this role in an age of Fascism.) His development as a representative artist of his age is seen as that of a politically aware Stephen Dedalus, recording responses to the disintegration of personal and public values. Alternatively, in terms subdued to a practical, neo-Freudian tone, an Orwell whose total activities, aesthetic and practical, are comprised in a struggle between a fundamental pessimism, and an equally 'given' wish to promote Socialism.[3]

So, in various ways, the received image of the embattled iconoclast is confirmed by critics estimating positively the collisions and tensions of a kind which Orwell himself would so sharply single out, especially in his contemporaries. Even when the contradictuions are deplored as irritating, damaging, or colossal, they are subsumed in the closing stress on the good and passionate man, whose stripped speech and verbal compression are moral achievements. These commonly made claims can be tested by a foregrounding of Orwell's contradictions, inside the works, and without any invidiously personal implications about Orwell the man. Ultimately, as his critics, his admirers, and Orwell himself all suggest, there are the closest affiliations and consonances between the work and the life. But, in the first instance, it is the contradictions and the confusions demonstrable in the writing that must be explored and tested by Orwell's own principles and procedures; and their relevance to the quality and status of the work itself must be assessed. So much of his writing is immediate and personal, autobiographical either by design or implicitly, the experiences feeding the imaginative effort. Yet the life and the work must be detached, and the contradictions in question be located inside the autonomous structure and movements of the books.

Orwell himself fostered a sense of a profound dilemma in his career as a writer, insisting repeatedly on his reluctance to write about contemporary issues — seen as topical, social, contentious. He is keen to present the notion of the thwarted aesthete, the stylist struggling to discard his propagandist's pen. He is the first to sketch his own development as that of the spoiled artist, a Stephen Dedalus in reverse, moving from the pre-political and apolitical concerns to the reluctantly social and political issues thrust upon him. This 'contradiction' is repeatedly stressed, and many (including Orwell himself) assume that it gives the work its stamp of necessity, resilience, authenticity. There is an assumption behind this that the openly, freely committed approach will be entrammelled by the partisan, the tendentious; impartiality is to be more readily attributed to the enforced, begrudging participant in the turbulent issues. Orwell's claims along such lines are echoed in both scholarly and popular assessments of his objectivity and detachment. Yet behind Orwell's discussions of aestheticism versus commitment is a critically naive sense of what may be constitutive of aesthetic effect and form; and there are continuities and connections between his 'practical' and his 'aesthetic' compositions which make his distinctions irrelevant.

The theme of change can be used as a wide-angled focus for Orwell's work, to redefine and to relocate his dilemmas and contradictions. In some ways, Orwell wrote about nothing else except the nature and necessity of *change*, and the insistent blocks and checks attending it. Without giving a political specification or partisan context to the term, such a focus can suggest a great deal about Orwell's understanding of commitment as a concept, and help to indicate whether he could have really chosen to work otherwise as an artist than he did. To keep the term 'change' as general as possible avoids the tracing of Orwell's concerns and projects to a psychological compulsion or fixation. Considering his insistent treatment of change in all forms — personal, social, political, spiritual — implies no searching out of the concealed or fugitive, no cracking of unconscious coding in the works. What matters is what is visible in the images, in the fictive structures, in the enacted and represented situations of the works' surfaces.

The movement that structures the first book, *Down and Out in Paris and London*[4] now seems peculiarly Orwellian, though it embodies one mode of perception of their times repeatedly adopted by writers in the early 1930s. Change is here the motion of exploring subtended social areas: the observer/protagonist is a visitant to an underworld, where experiences that transform him are recorded for the overworld, for the inconscient. They are to be shocked into awareness, and so into action. The journey is deliberate, the report is a considered one: change, of all kinds, is insistently looked for. Yet the tone of presentation, and Orwell's development of the material — a sophisticated, ambitious mixing of literary models and edited personal experience — these have distinctive, ambiguous features. Notably, the varieties of prose in the language itself: it moves from Balzacian evocations, through jaunty, bohemian picaresque, to journalistic survey of work conditions. The wish to entertain, to excuse the anecdotal passages as the trivial interest of a 'travel diary' (p. 189), clashes with the moral indignation of sensational revelations about poverty. A limp moralism is the precarious linking of these contradictory movements — as in the *plongeur* section (pp. 103–8), and the ending. The diversity exemplifies a recoiling from the starker implications. This endemic vacillating between humorous acceptance and horrified rejection is yet inevitably true to the bifocalism of Orwell's apperceptions. For he totalizes his vision of poverty — as in the book's epigraph — but reifies that term. He sees an absolute condition — that of tramps, *plongeurs*, drop-outs, street-people, the abject poor — yet one which good-hearted reform can possibly ameliorate. Beyond that, he offers, and increasingly so in later books, only the spectacle of a struggle *against* society, seen from an excluded position as a monolithic institution, with individuals or exiled groups resisting assimilation. Orwell exposes in society the flaws and incoherence, the impositions and subjugation which he simultaneously accepts as innate, as somehow extra- or suprasocial.

Two works from 1936 to 1937, the period taken as crucial in Orwell's development, further exemplify this bifurcated vision: *Keep the Aspidistra Flying*[5], and *The Road to Wigan Pier*[6]. They were produced in the period which supposedly sees Orwell's politicization, culminating in his commissioned journey to the North; stating his radical commitments, however thornily, in the concluding discussions to the second book. Yet fundamental affiliations and convergences between two such apparently disparate books, and their shared development from the earlier works of 1933 to 1935, sharpen further the sense of irresolutions and contradictions central to the imaginative creation. Central; the paradox being that the bifurcated vision — persisted in, developed, given its own order and shape — is the enabling force of Orwell's project. It is the origin of his distinctive imaginative appeal, even as it must ultimately prompt fundamental questions about 'integrity', about the unity and meaning of Orwell's position.

Keep the Aspidistra Flying

The novel could have used the epigraph from *Down and Out in Paris and London*: its obsessive referral of everything whatsoever to money makes it a more earnest and consistent redaction of the earlier subjects. The willed-for change, the turn-around of a life by seeking out the excluded and the subjugated: this journey immerses Gordon Comstock in society's depths. It is precisely the orderliness, the much improved plotting and fictive patterning of the action, that clarify the reader's sense of Orwell's own double vision. In the earlier fiction, the uncertainty finally crystallizes into a disrupting, evasive strategy: the choosing protagonist commits suicide — Flory, in *Burmese Days*[7] — so cancelling the drama's problem, annulling the imaginative issues. Or the breakaway and turn-around of life are evacuated of import by a mere story-device — as in attributing amnesia to the central character, Doris Hare, in *A Clergyman's Daughter*[8]. With Comstock's story, the uncertainty is itself, paradoxically, sustained, structured, ingrained in the situations, in the action, and (above all) in the presentation of the protagonist, Comstock. The most acute and continuous indicator of the distended and structural debilitation is Orwell's tone: it seems to detach the author from situation and character while simultaneously involving and directly implicating him. So Orwell's description of a working-class pub (pp. 93ff.), or of a cinema (p.78), modulates into ambivalent responses about them; as, in turn, the character's distasteful reflections, about women, for example, (pp. 110ff.) become absorbed into authorial viewpoint. Comstock's high opinion of his verses is not ironically attributed to his rabid self-conceit — and its being elsewhere (earlier) printed as Orwell's own work makes the reader's embarrassment more acute. And so with all of Comstock's attitudes, opinions and values: just as Orwell seems to distance them, the narrative absorbs and so endorses them.

For this fiction, extensively and intensively concerned with protest, change, and rebellion, is profoundly ambivalent in its representations. This is not the result of artistic purpose being overwhelmed by social and political views.[9] It is rather that Orwell's aesthetic aims, taking in social and political representations (as with this novel's progenitors, Dostoievsky's *Notes from Underground* and Joyce's *A Portrait of the Artist*) give imaginative form and potency to conflicting perceptions. One is an actively critical, satirical perception: contemporary society as drab, commercialized, greedy, degenerate. The other is an anguished, recoiling, impassioned perception: the individual without communal sustenance commits metaphorical suicide. Insofar as Comstock is the satiric hero, his journey to the lower depths endows him with the knowledge and the authority to rebuke his society's moral impotence. Insofar as such a rebellious course isolates him, Comstock loses power, is prone to self-pity, and increasingly self-destructive. Where Dostoievsky shows all these impulses as inextricable, composing a unified, strangely compassionate yet ironical portrait, Orwell fashions an underground man whose indigation becomes hollow, self-pitying, distasteful. Comstock, instead of growing in awareness, becomes even more stunted, and his despairing rebelliousness becomes a smug capitulation.

This moment of Comstock's return (to marriage, familial and social responsibility, to a resumed career) is indeed a crux: it conjoins complex narrative movements. The nature and dramatic logic of the character's choice, however, and Orwell's mode of situating, assessing that resolution, only deepen the text's confusions (pp. 252–6). Since all the indeterminacy, ambiguities and tensions are promoted together, a textual fracture 'ends' the development. That is, the protagonist's journey circles back, and the amnesia is not that of an ironized or valorized individual figure: it is textual, signalling occlusions of Orwell's own. At one moment, Comstock seems to be making a sneering mock-surrender, retaining some shred of his bitter refusal to live in a degraded society: 'He would sell his soul . . . he would be a law-abiding little cit . . . a soldier in the strap-hanging army'[10] (p. 254). Almost simultaneously, religiose phrases (narrator's and protagonist's together) condemn the two years' protest as intrinsically futile: 'To abjure money is to abjure life' (p.253). The Biblical terms are seriously (if uneasily) proferred, and rebellion is labelled 'blasphemy' (p.253), as an organ-voiced text climaxes these reflections and resolutions: 'Out civilization is founded on greed and fear, but in the lives of common men the greed and fear are mysteriously transmitted into something nobler'.

Inside the question of how to view Comstock, how to respond to the closing movement, is the more intriguing issue of how Orwell's treatment of his themes produces inadvertently contradictory characterization of this sort. Given the dichotomies of the book — society/underworld, conformity/rebellion, marriage/sexual abstinence, careerism/idleness, money/destitution — the confusions of plotting, characterization, and thematic development follow ineluctably. For each term in the many sets is both positively and negatively dramatized by Orwell. He creates an action in which choice is limited to leaping to one side or the other of his social polarities, a moral melodrama in which — as in the earlier work — each term is good and is evil. It seems that the central figure is agent and actor in a situation which (ultimately) appears unmoving, fixed. These are the conditions of the fable directly indicating Orwell's own occlusions and blockage: his abstractions — Money, Poverty, Belief, Decency, Society itself — are reifications, static, detemporalized. The positive rhythms in Orwell's fictions are those of the central figure's seeking change, and looking not for a raising of consciousness, nor for isolated, individual salvation, but for external, general alteration. The counter-rhythms, confusing and disrupting, are those which establish the external, socially general as natural, innate, timeless: Greed, Poverty, Money and (later) Power.

Nowhere, then, does Orwell represent his selected themes to suggest how they comprise relation, interchange, principles of action, modes of behaviour. Poverty in *Down and Out in Paris and London* is alternately the ambience of a bizarre, jaunty bohemian subtopia; or the appalling context of dishwashers, waiters, and tramps in London 'spikes'. Money, the god-term in *Keep the Aspidistra Flying*, is presented alternately as omnipotent but sterile, the absolute of a degraded commercialized society; and, paradoxically, as the sustainer of decency, honour, respectability, of the 'aliveness' of ordinary people. What money mediates is absent: the relations and ownership of the means of production, and the systems by which private and public wealth create social connections, opportunities or dependencies. What the book simply labels 'money', its own action represents as issues about kinds of work, about class differentiation — and as the impingement of wealth, power and class upon all values and all behaviour, however intimate to the self.

How to deal with issues so reductively reified as to seem as single, natural, and fixed as the emblematic homologue, the aspidistra? What agency or mode of change is feasible? If the book's action cannot alert the reader to alternatives or degrees of choice, then the story's figures will be artificially contained, restrained.

Details of image, situation, action or character lead insistently, through whatever sophisticated mediations the particular artwork demands, to the enabling imaginative experience. Here, briefly, the incoherence and the blockages evident in this novel can be instanced by two features, implicit and explicit. First, the discussions between Comstock and the middle-class intellectual Ravelston, a would- be revolutionary. Though graceless, irritated, and self-pitying, Comstock is shown to put his friend to shame, in the debate about Socialism, the middle classes, belief, and the significance of money (Chapter 5, *passim*). Comstock's thoughts, and the experience they are rooted in, are given from inside, and endorsed by the narrative manner. Ravelston, given neither thoughts, debating points nor a demonstrated position rooted in experience, is represented as passive and deferential. This is Orwell's depiction of the theorist and theorizing, and crystallizes his implicit evaluation throughout the action of the inefficacy of any systematic critique based on analysis of social systems. This friendship with Ravelston, shot through with condescension and intellectual contempt, leads to the second illustrative feature. For Ravelston, like Comstock's girlfriend Rosemary, is a source of material as well as emotional support. Each is resented precisely because of the money and help provided, and the relationships they offer are imaged as burdens, as irksome debts. Money permeates everything, and here seems to metamorphose friendship and sexuality itself. The disturbing ambiguity is that a fictive action based on a critique of society's degenerate obsessions with wealth is itself implicitly representing the alternative values as profoundly corrupted in the same way. Human individuality, friendship, affection, and sexual passion itself are bleakly represented. The anger against money is displaced bitterness about the human condition, a bitterness so often to sour Orwell's representations of society.

To reject and to rebel bring, necessarily, 'not only misery, but also a frightful emptiness, an inescapable sense of futility' (p. 253). A good or great fiction might plot such a movement, but Orwell's outcome suppresses the braver insights and enriching experience of his rebel. In addition to ambiguously representing his venture,

Orwell abrupts the alternative choices and values. In Ravelston, he parodies intellectual criticism and political theory, naively and rather crudely; in the relations with Rosemary, apparently unwittingly, he parodies the power of sexual love to sustain and to enrich relationships. Most of all, and perhaps least guardedly, Orwell underwrites Comstock's individuality, his apartness, his separate vision: the reader sees everyone else only, and exactly, as the protagonist sees them. The mental world, and distinctive consciousness of Comstock, and those of Orwell's book, are co-incident, co-defining. Ravelston, Rosemary, Gordon's family, as individuals, exist only as Gordon sees them: which means that Socialism, sexual love, friendship, the everyday lives around him have to be valued as he values them. For Orwell's barely maintained distance from his ambiguous character is enmeshed in the assumptions of his own bifurcated vision. The struggle for a free existence, the desire to break away, this engages dramatic sympathy — while the total action builds up an overwhelming sense that human individuality, love, and society are what they are, unalterably so. The resigned wisdom of a relieved surrender (p. 252) has been called 'a vote for health, a democratic gesture'.[10] It marks, rather, the exhaustion of a conflict within the book, a massive collision of values which swamps the individual project of a Comstock. However drained of meaning, degraded, or sickening, the culture of contemporary society cannot be abjured. Its wasteland existence is 'mysteriously transmuted' into a nobler one; and a single word, '*mysteriously*', is meant to bridge the incredible abyss that Orwell's thoughts and feelings have created, objectified, and projected into his writing.

For a considerable shift and an emotional blurring is evident when Orwell struggles to locate the authentic living values of ordinary people. There is a marked difference of pitch between common existence in the Paris sections compared with that of the English sections, in *Down and Out in Paris and London*. The realities of social class, work and wealth, touched on in the *plongeur* sections, become the whole context, the oppressive climate, of the English experiences. Such authenticity is the characteristically Orwellian aim of Comstock's journey; yet the refreshment of spirit converts to distaste and despair. Conversely, the abandoned ordinary people, unloveable, impotent, and degraded, peremptorily acquire decency, honour, spiritual force. It is as if a massive miscognisance has been rectified: the authentically alive are not outside, but inside society: 'They would be, for example, small clerks, shop-assistants, commerical travellers, insurance touts, tram-conductors' (p. 255). 'For example' — a strikingly condescending phrase here — the tenants of Mrs Wisbeach's apartment house (Chapter 2), Flaxman and Lorenheim, both commercial travellers; Mr Erskine and Mr Clew, at the New Albion Company (Chapter 3); Uncle Walter and Aunt Angela (pp. 64–77); customers at McKechnie's bookshop, like Mrs Penn and Mrs Weaver (Chapter 1). What is striking about these guardians of the aspidistra is that Orwell first edgily, sometimes savagely, caricatures them, before redeeming them at the close; and secondly, with blurred feeling, sets them out as the decent ordinary people to whom Gordon Comstock longs to return. Though living in 'typical lower-middle-class' streets, they have inviolable standards, are 'bound up in the bundle of life'; to be away from their living is to be an anchorite, to be 'thrust out of the stream of life'. That this resolution is not a clarification, a newly attained insight, is clear from these moral exemplars' being still called 'the ruck of men', living by a degenerate code, neither knowing nor caring that 'they were only puppets dancing when money pulled the strings' (p. 255). Totally irreconcileable attributions and responses are co-mingled, jammed into bogus harmony. The intended beneficiaries of Comstock's experience of alternative social values seem beyond the reach of even the need for change.

The Road to Wigan Pier

The Road to Wigan Pier, apparently so very dissimilar as a work, further develops some of the disconcerting elements in the earlier fiction, and so particularly evident in *Keep the Aspidistra Flying*. Mrs Wisbeach's rooms are replaced by the Brookers' lodging-house with tripe-shop, though the closer parallel is with Madame F's Parisian lodging-house (*Down and Out in Paris and London*, Chapter 1). All three sections are carefully structured, composed scenes which have acute significations in tone and imaginative feeling. Poverty, noise, odd personalities, smell, filth, disease, bugs: all are common to Madame F's hotel and the Brookers', but only at the English house are they unfunny, repulsive and nauseating. The low farce of Parisian shabbiness becomes the savage exposure of a near-excremental filthiness: the reader is to comment with Orwell and the Cockney traveller — 'fellow-Southerners' — 'The filthy bloody bastards'. Yet who and what is being recognised and excoriated here? The opening of a specifically commissioned report on the situation of the northern working-classes in the mid-1930s must be a keynote, a distinctive marker. Orwell's *Diary*, in *Collected Essays, Journalism and Letters of George Orwell, Volume I*, pp. 194–243), reveals that the Brookers' house is a synthesis of various unpleasant places and experiences: it here becomes a working-class underworld, subhuman, below any level to which a Comstock could wish (sentimentally) to sink. These lowest depths are peopled by the old and the unemployed, wasted or dying; and they, along with the commercial travellers, are seen to by the Brookers. The husband, an unemployed miner, runs the shop and the lodging-house because Mrs Brooker is always unwell. Does the reader take this as representative of working-class conditions, or of the degradation that everywhere surrounds and threatens the Northerner? Perhaps Orwell suggests one extreme, balancing it with the positive and ideal home at the close (pp. 104–5)? If so, the acute, insistent images of revulsion and disgust are given all the imaginative force; and the later, literary and generalized images of approval, being mere clichés, show the disengaged sensibility.

Given the specific occasion, and given Orwell's quickening response to socio-economic and political issues, expectation (after shock) might have been that it was exactly *this* condition that called for radical remedies. The sour and bitter tones of the Brooker chapter linger on, behind the business-like reports, figures and descriptions. Some of its implications, however, are beyond statistics or reform: for existence at the Brookers is insect-or animal-like. The husband is a dirty, small-boned creature; the wife is dehumanized: 'Upon a shapeless sofa, our landlady lay permanently ill, festooned in grimy blankers — a big, pale, yellow, anxious face' (p. 6). One son remains, 'a large, pig-like young man', since many children 'had long since fled from home' (p. 11). The references to grime, urine, excrement, beetles, waste food, and tripe are obsessively repeated, so that the Brookers and this 'setting' are inextricable. Whatever is there because of Orwell's neurotic hypersensitivity, more significant is what is absent. Brooker, after all, is a miner — out of work for two years — who copes with a shabby, small-scale business; his wife's illness from heart-trouble (C.E.J.L., I, p. 203) is re-attributed to gluttony by Orwell (pp. 6, 7 and 11). There is no sign of any attempt to understand the Brookers' situation, no sympathy for its origins or even its real nature. The disgust lets the hostility show through; where the lodgers bore him, the working-class family fills him with uncontrollable disgust and loathing. (Compare the attitude to Madame F. and her husband.) The pathology of this concern with smell and sensuous disturbance, or the analysis of this deployment of insect and animal imagery, are here decidedly secondary matters. Primarily, these elements contribute to expression of an extreme feeling about a group of figures — possibly typical rather than actual — whose context defines them precisely as they create, indeed, *are* that context.

Orwell's journey (to a dozen industrial towns) made a physical, social, reality of the metaphorical journeys given form in his fictions. There, exposure to any experience outside the known and contained social decencies produced, along with distress, sympathetic insights and social compassion. Looking back from the mid-1930s, however, we can see that the more Orwell feels that the 'fringe' groups are close to, or even within, the accepted social area, the more the sympathies are hesitatingly expressed. Street-folk in Parisian suburbs are coarse, vigorous, amusing; but tramps like Paddy are worrying, self-pitying, envious, contemptibly dependent (*D.O.P.L.* pp. 133–4). Comstock's expedition to the social underworld does not take him among the street-folk, or into nightmare experiences like Doris Hare's in London (*C.D.*, Chapter 3). Yet his sudden, agitated return to familiar (lower-middle-class) settings annuls the compassionate anger and the insights that had provoked his departure.

It is as if the identifying of groups and classes outside the lower middle class (as depicted in *Keep the Aspidistra Flying*) is fraught with difficulties due to their amorphousness. Fringe-groups, drop-outs, and street-folk move in and out of these 'lower' classes. Brookers' house compares unfavourably with some of the tramps' spikes: it seems to be both hostel and working-class house. In this opening to a report, then, the plethora of physical detail carries a load of apprehension, resentment, and it signals an imbalance. It repeatedly evinces Orwell's defensive self-distancing.

The notion of an oppressively contiguous existence, bewildering, coarse, physically impingeing, drawing in the intrigued observer: this also permeated Comstock's adventures, in apartments, back streets, pubs, cafés and cinemas. The absence from the novel of named, specific representatives of that life is indicator and consequence of the unrestrained concern with Comstock's own responses, *per se*. Orwell now names the figures, though it is startingly clear that no one individual engages his full interest. The perfunctoriness about Reilly, the old age pensioners, Joe and the Scotch miner, is never replaced by any fuller, warmer sketching-in of a particular person. The almost brute and coarse physicality of presentation (converted to an admiring response to working, but still unindividualized, miners) foregrounds his baffled response. The reader is clearly meant to respond with considerable shock to the revelations of this report on the condition of Northern England. Orwell's self-presentation is that of the mediator, the disturbed observer in a harsh climate whose exposure gives the reader chance to recover to absorb and reflect. 'You realize . . . what different universes different people inhabit' (p. 29). The amount of new data on housing, income, work conditions, food, health and unemployment, flat enough to read now, indicates a significant, positive function of the report. It witnesses to a vital need for connections between the 'different universes', and its tone of address suggests how, in part, such ignorance and such separateness were constituted and maintained.

At its mildest, the tone suggests the uneasy reassurances of a social anthropologist, keen to show that the customs and manners, the behaviour and the speech habits should not really be so disconcerting: 'Hence the Southerner goes north, at any rate for the first time, with the vague inferiority-complex of a civilized man venturing among savages, while the Yorkshire man, like the Scotchman, comes to London in the spirit of a barbarian out for loot' (p. 98). This now passes, perhaps, for facetiousness; but Orwell trundles out the feeblest music-hall and picture-postcard clichés as if they deserve serious reflection. He markedly offers little other way into understanding Northerners — factual information apart — than contravening or modifying these crude prejudices. So when Orwell himself feels that Sheffield has 'a population of troglodytes' (p. 86), he spends pages relating this to the modern physical degeneration of the English as a race. He explains that the working class actually do like to work (pp. 33–4), do not prefer the slums (pp. 57 and 62), and are not parasites with a dislike of work (pp. 78–9). There is clearly a different family structure, different ways of relating, a life with its own forms of loyalty (pp.103ff.). Working-people's directness may disconcert (apart from their dialect and uneducated speech forms); however, Orwell explains, it represents their tendency to treat others as equals (pp. 102–3). They also usually refuse things they do not want, rather than politely accepting. They do grossly and habitually misspend, and Orwell attempts a rationale. Chocolate, fish and chips, beer, smart clothes, cinema-going, gambling: all are excused as compensations, 'cheap luxuries, which mitigate the surface of life'. Even marrying on the dole is part of the indirect protest (pp. 77–81).

For underlying the apparent concern with superficialities and irrelevancies is an attempt to give fundamental reassurance. The condition of Norther England being insistently as Orwell reports it to be, then reform and massive changes must anticipate and forestall any rebellious moves. What Comstock felt as weirdly intriguing, degraded, fearful, Orwell — showing apprehensiveness with his evidence — attempts to rationalize as features of an alternative culture. What is so naively singled out, so fatuously commented on, is taken to witness the reality of displaced hostile energies:

> But it may be that the psychological adjustment which the working-class are visibly making is the best they could make in the circumstances. They have neither turned revolutionary nor lost their self-respect; merely they have kept their tempers and settled down to make the best of things on a fish-and-chip standard. The alternative

would be God knows what continued agonies of despair; or it might be attempted insurrection which, in a strongly governed country like England, could only lead to futile massacres and a regime of savage repression. (R.W.P., p. 80).

In an essay coming, say, after World War II, these strictures would strike the usual Orwellian note. Coming where they do, they articulate that apprehension, so widely shared, that the situation of the industrial workers might well provoke an extreme response. The edgy bewilderment before this alternative culture of the North projects a sense that the workers are difficult to reach, to understand; and the anxiety feeds into impressions of a physically menacing and repellent breed. Their houses smell, and, as Orwell offensively reiterates, so do they: it perhaps elides matters of health, housing, food into a personal fault?

As *The Road to Wigan Pier* and the *Diary* both make clear, a journey to the industrial North is a tour of 'Special Areas', thrust out of the stream of life, into misery and destitution. In *Keep the Aspidistra Flying*, poverty could be contained, and a fixed condition, 'Money', could be hypostatized, seen as a sterile, blighting deity. Health might mean to abjure it. In this documentary, Orwell transmits the shock of seeing ways of living without money that do not mysteriously dignify existence — as Comstock admitted finally, and with great relief. For Orwell, first-hand witness, cannot deny the multiplicity of ways in which absence of money blights the social landscape: health, housing, employment, individual development, community-life. Though intermittently, the report manifests an acute awareness of the social, economic and political realities that money determines. Money now, that is, can be demystified, seen as distribution of wealth, as a question of ownership, as power, as agent of change. Working at problems, issues, and seeing them in quantifiable terms, Orwell guardedly confronts public systems, responsible institutions, and the effects of general attitudes. Circumspectly indeed, for such a blunt, not-to-be-fooled commentator, valuing his independence; since the sense of two nations is being reinforced rather than dissolved. These arguments, descriptions and statistics are not meant for inhabitants of 'Special Areas', but for those whose interest and action can be engaged on behalf of such people. The repeated note of condescension about the working classes is part of a plea for large-scale, good-hearted social condescension, for awareness and practical response by others. The morally distasteful patronage is intrinsic to seeing the workers as apart, as separable, as others.

Everything in the long run comes back to Money; so runs the insistent thesis of the Comstock novel. Everything in the short run comes back to Money, is the disturbing discovery of the documentary report. But the move forward from a static notion to a radical, dynamic understanding of the nature and function of wealth is suddenly suspended, and the development of the findings interrupted. For *The Road to Wigan Pier* has a major fracture of the kind that so often collapses Orwell's works. The fissure is clearly marked, since it is the division between Parts I and II. The project had always been to follow facts with generalizations, the investigation of problems with proposals and resolutions. Orwell clearly intends, however idiosyncratically, to deduce from the empirical observations composing Part I, some principles of socio-political commitment to form the conclusion. Then, as so frequently since, such principles were assumed to be markedly Socialist, regardless of any prickly reservations. That Orwell himself assumed his intentions were not only clearly of this kind, but also satisfactorily carried out, is again a mark of his amazingly bifurcated vision.

Briefly, the major fracture is created because Part II is a shying-away from generalities, an ultimate refusal of theorizing. If there is commitment, it is not one to fundamental change in a spirit of radical Socialism. (Whether others made such commitment is not here the point.) Part II is an apologia for not making inferences apparently consequent upon the experiences detailed in Part I. There is a turn-about as pointed and vertiginous as the climax of *Keep the Aspidistra Flying*, and, equally, the achieved and defended position is offered in terms of insight and difficult acceptance, prompted by experience. The assumed debater's role with Orwell's offering to be devil's advocate in sketching a case against Socialism, converts into a total position, and there is an attack in earnest, sustained, unopposed. Orwell's right to question so searchingly is unassailable: it is here a matter of establishing what survived his scrutiny, and what form of scrutiny really composes his Part II summary. The question of Russian Communism apart, perhaps the notorious Foreword (11 January 1937) by Victor Gollancz was much more to the point than it seemed at the time.

What is Orwell's working definition of Socialism? Gollancz is puzzled by its absence, by the startling inadequacy; truer to say, perhaps, that the definition is there, but discards the expected intellectual rigour, logical exposition, or discussion of concepts. Orwell, plain-man-as-thinker, propounds two forms of Socialism: one of the working classes, one of the middle-class intellectuals. What he offers as the first form matches the implications about Socialism in Part I: 'For it must be remembered that a working man, so long as he remains a genuine working man, is seldom or never a Socialist in the completely consistent sense' (p. 154). Here, the 'politics' is agitation for better wages, shorter hours, freedom at work; moving on, for some, to hunger marches, to resistance against oppression and, at its sharpest, 'a vague threat of future violence'. But the run-of-the-mill, Labour-voting Socialist looks to a reformed society, the worst abuses of the present being dealt with, thus clearing space for his interests: 'family life, the pub, football, and local politics'. Though he alludes to 'the more revolutionary type', Orwell categorically claims that 'no genuine working man grasps the deeper implications of Socialism'. More than that, none has ever had any interest whatsoever in Marxist theories, Marxist ideology, in the intricacies of dialectical materialism. Revolutionary changes, then, are certainly not envisaged by such Socialists as Orwell describes, in these sweeping and disingenuous allegations. With relief, not impatience, he concludes that the first type cannot grasp the 'immense changes in our civilization and his own way of life' that the orthodox Marxist discusses.

The other form of Socialism, as Orwell quaintly puts it, 'is that of the book-trained Socialist higher up'. The theory of Socialism is 'confined entirely to the middle class': this theory consists of 'the usual jargon of "ideology" and "class-consciousness" and "proletarian solidarity" and all the rest of it'. This off-handed, contemptuous, and jejune approach to Marxism justifies Gollancz's dismay: nothing more substantial follows. Instead, with a troubled pitch of intense personal feeling, Orwell reiterates his rather shrill caricature of representative Socialists — moving rapidly through a sliding argument identical to Comstock's mode of reflection. A tentative position is sketched, then attributed to a friendly figure whose stance conjoins contradictory attitudes. 'I am making out a case for the sort of person who is in sympathy with the fundamental aims of Socialism, who has the brains to see that Socialism would "work", but who in practice always takes to flight when Socialism is mentioned'. Such a type begins, apparently, with a 'semi-frivolous' attitude, objecting to Socialists, but not to Socialism. Though admitting this is logically poor as an argument, Orwell asserts that it nevertheless 'carries weight with many people' (p. 152). The remainder of the section (Chapter 2) shows the very considerable weight that this 'argument' has for Orwell himself. The 'tentative position' (with its unexplained contradictions) becomes his aim. The inventory of middle-class Socialists it comprises is as extraordinary and startling as Gollancz indicated; whatever the personal elements and motives, it remains a rather unintelligent assault on intellectuals and on political theory.

So there are hits at the authoritarians inside Fabianism (Shaw, the Webbs), out to impose mechanical social and cultural order: they are typified by 'the intellectual, tract-writing type of Socialist, with his pullover, his fuzzy hair, and his Marxian quotation'. Still more typical, Orwell asserts, is the prim white-collar Non-conformist intent on professional status; along with the young 'Snob-Bolshevik' who is out to marry very well and become a Roman Catholic. The zany randomness of these thumbnail sketches suggests deep uneasy resentments, and leads to the notorious directory of Socialist and Communist adherents: 'Fruit-juice drinker, nudist, sandal-wearer, sex-maniac, Quaker, "Nature-Cure" quack, pacifist, feminist'. Time and fashion may have converted many of Orwell's unlovely villains into heroes, or even into ordinary people; but the irrelevance of his stifled feelings to political discussion is eventually saddening. As even more clearly with his repeated jibes about homosexuals, 'the pink Nancy-boys of the left', there are gross equations between physical features or behaviour, repulsive to Orwell, and what he alleges to be innate characteristics of 'typical' Socialists. The disgust is itself distasteful, as in the animus against two elderly men (pp. 152–3) — (what if they were Tories?); and against the I.L.P. champions of the working class, 'mingy little beasts', insufferably marked by middle-class superiority and snobbishness.

Wit and humour have always a place in debate, functionally and historically; political arguments are serious, but preferably not solemn. Orwell's humour is marked, however, by sour resentments, unfounded prejudice, near-hysterical allegation, and incredible snobbishness. These tones increase in pitch and volume when the topics are political; and however complex and overdetermined its origins, it evinces Orwell's response to intellectual theorizing. The negative treatment of Ravelston, throughout the previous book, fits in with the milder sketches of middle-class literary leftwingers: he might well have published or edited Orwell's postulated 'Marxism for Infants' (p. 31). That Ravelston has so many physical traits of Orwell himself is suggestive for psychological approach; as if Orwell attempts to annull such interests in himself. But *The Road to Wigan Pier* has developed several other related attitudes to intellectuals and political theory that place the discussion firmly back in a context of public debate.

The book is far more than a straightforward expansion of the jottings in the *Diary* (C.E.J.L. I), or a compilation of reports, discussions, descriptions and essays. It is carefully structured, one of its cohesive rhythms being strongly autobiographical. Interweaving events and encounters on the journeys with recollections of the radically different setting of his own upbringing, Orwell's questioning the ingrained attitudes of his class can strike readers as genuine frankness, even humility: 'In a way it is even humiliating to watch coal-miners working. It raises in you a momentary doubt about your own status as an "intellectual" and a superior person generally'. The very phrasing still tingles with the tone and assumptions that show Orwell trapped, as Gollancz remarked, by the mental habits he claims to discard (Foreword, xvii). Still, the fuller patterning and range of styles in the work as a whole suggest comprehensiveness, openness, and authenticity. Here, comparison with the fragmentary jottings of the *Diary* can test this implicit structural claim, and very revealingly so with the treatment of working-class activists, organizers, and intellectuals.

Orwell's travels through northern England depended on a great deal of assistance from friends; especially from Richard Rees (a model for Ravelston in the novel), who had many contacts with Socialists. But particularly helpful were organizers and members of the National Unemployed Workers' Movement, who provided him with a great deal of information, arranged many visits (to the mines, factories, and members' houses) and gave him contacts in each town. A letter to Rees (C.E.J.I. I, p. 188) is the first of many references to this generous help: all pared down in the book to one paragraph, without names, but with the comment that N.U.W.M.'s organizers show great talents, but not much capacity for leadership (pp. 74–5). Orwell registers surprise when a working-men's club conference turns out to represent 10, 000 members in South Yorkshire alone (C.E.J.I. I, p. 228). Surprise becomes admiration when he learns more about the way Tom Degnan and Ellis Firth, both miners, organized opposition to a Mosley ralley — getting hurt and being fined; and when he hears Degnan speak so well at a Communist Party rally in Barnsley (C.E.J.L. I, pp. 232–3 and 241). This incident is re-shaped (R.W.P., p. 154) with the 'broad lingo' of the (unnamed) Degnan, allegedly an unorthodox Communist, being set off against the bookish middle-class speech of the visiting speaker. There is no allusion at all to activities like the N.U.W.M.'s social evening to raise money for the imprisoned Ernst Thoemann, leader of the German Communist Party. The *Diary* notes (C.E.J.L. I, pp. 206–7) sneer at Wigan's 'cross-section of the more revolutionary element'; and at Wal Hannington, founder of N.U.W.M., for being both 'bourgeois' and speaking with 'the wrong kind of cockney accent'. (C.E.J.L I, p. 201). Even general discussion groups, on writers and thinkers, or attendance at *Adelphi* Summer Schools, prompt only irritated jottings, and are omitted altogether from the book (see *C.E.J.L., I*, pp. 219, 225 and 244).

Orwell's mixed feelings about working-class interests and activities, political and cultural, are revealed by his *Diary* jottings, and the subsequent omissions from the full text. This hesitancy is peculiarly marked with the outstanding individual organizers, leaders, writers and activists that he met. A group of these were connected with the Workers' Northern Publishing Society in Manchester, both printing and contributing to the *Adelphi* magazine, since its editor Middleton Murray was leading a splinter-group from the I.L.P. known as the Independent Socialist Party. The Manchester circle included Sam Higenbottom, historian of the Society of Woodworkers, who wrote for the *Adelphi*; another, with whom Orwell stayed, was Frank Meade, a union official with the Society of Woodworkers. He ran both *Labour's Northern Voice* and the northern office of the *Adelphi*. The Liverpool group included the J.S. Deiners and George Garrett, ex-seaman and docker, a story writer and Marxist critic. (*C.E.J.L. I*, pp. 198, 213–124). Orwell's friendlier responses to the personalities, talents and activities of these intellectuals and writers takes in their associates and friends: Joe (Jerry) Kennan, electrician; Paddy Grady, a miner, the Searles, husband and wife; and the unnamed 'B' in Sheffield. All are thoroughly working class, all are committed politically to fundamental social change, all are activists, all impress Orwell; but all are omitted, ungenerously and gracelessly, from his discussions of working-class socialism and working-class consciousness and intelligence.

The *Diary* shows a genuine curiosity and concern about situations like that of the man he called 'B'. A convinced, embittered Socialist, B is full of hatred for the middle classes. Given no dole, merely some pittance from the parish, B is a social discard, having a withered hand. His Marxism is too insistent for Orwell; but B reads, thinks, discusses, attends the Summer Schools. His own room surprised Orwell by its tastefulness, since B makes furniture and is also a painter. Orwell, having been accompanied and considerably helped in Sheffield by this man, confesses in his notes that B is of a much more forcible character than himself. He says it also of Searle, B's friend; and in Searle's wife, he is amazed at 'a grasp of the economic situation and also of abstract ideas' going with what he thinks is near-illiteracy. Mrs Searle, working as a charwoman, takes for granted ideas about social change, particularly in attitudes to women, which are those of the modern feminist (*C.E.J.L. I*, pp. 217–23).

Yet Orwell's general discussion eventually excizes these experiences, and implicitly discounts the attitudes the values and achievements of these individuals. They do not illustrate his argument; or, rather, they are made (anonymously) to illustrate it by a rhetorical shift, a re-categorizing. First of all, Orwell claims that 'the working-class intelligentsia is sharply divisble into two different types'. One kind, though an adherent of I.L.P. or even C.P. policies, retains his accent, habits, and working-class behaviour; but, 'in his spare time', such a man 'improves his mind' (*R.W.P.*, p. 143). The other kind alters his accent and behaviour, and, via State scholarships, 'succeeds in climbing into the middle class'. This is usually the literary highway to social success; and the irascible pages on the 'poisonous jungle' of literary London and middle-class Socialism display unrestrained dislike of the socially superior intelligentsia and the assimilated intellectuals from below. Since Orwell imperiously disallows any other choices, and stresses the exceptionalness of D.H. Lawrence's career, the point is solidly rammed home. Only the intellectual who stays fixed is a genuine one: 'The first is one of the finest types of man we have'. But the definition does not comprise the careers and attitudes of a Joe Kennan, a Paddy Grady, a Tom Degnan, or a man like 'B'. None chooses spare-time study merely to 'improve the mind'. Orwell's definitions would be shockingly patronizing if they were at all relevant to his experiences. 'Improving the mind' might, in any case, lead to radical convictions and political awareness like that which Mrs Searle acquired in other ways; or to the interests, abilities, tastes, and embittered social criticism of men like 'B' and Mr Searle. Orwell certainly knew neither category included writers like Jack Common, Sam Higenbottom, Frank Meade and George Garrett.

All of these people had, as the *Diary* shows, the mental energy, the awareness and the capacities that mark the intellectual; and they were all radical, committed left-wing thinkers, Socialist or Communists. The frequently repeated claim that nobody in the working class could read or understand Marxist works, or could claim to be 'ideologically sound' is (to put it mildly) disingenuous. Clearly, the accomplished *Adelphi* group, like Jack Common, were considered as somehow distinct, apart, not really working class, though not emulating London's 'verminous little lions'. With the non-writers, the rhetorical shift operates: mere possession of good furniture, books, or a piano — these indicate adhesion to the middle class. In Barnsley, the working-men's club organizer, Wilde, an ex-miner, is immediately declared detribalized since he has little marked accent, and carries gloves and an umbrella: 'As usual, has been bourgeoisified' (*C.E.J.L. I*, p. 226). Possession of a wage of four pounds pwer week means, asserts Orwell, an immediate shift into an ideology appropriate to such a level of income. What could a Mrs Searle or a Frank Meade say to such an unintelligently mechanical materialism?

The working-class Marxist and writer who should have given Orwell's ideas and conclusions a real jolt was the ex-sailor and docker, George Garrett, whose (punning) pseydonym was 'Matt Low'. He wrote reviews, articles and stories for many magazines, especially the *Adelphi*. His earlier experiences of a Jack London style of life intrigued Orwell, but Garrett preferred to discuss social issues and political ideas. This was the working-class intellectual who had to stay put: he lived with his wife and several children, in two rooms. His Communism meant he was blacklisted for work in the docks, and had only dole pay. When Orwell suggested that he write his autobiography, Garrett told him that his home-conditions prevented his writing anything except short stories (*C.E.J.L. I*, pp. 213–15). His choices and conditions were not those Orwell categorized.

Orwell's exclusion of these acquaintances and exchanges is more noticeable because of the autobiographical cast that he gives to the book. Its lack of close contacts and any warm individual interests is the more surprising since the *Diary* has intimations of both. The embarrassments and the ungenerosity of his responses are indexes of some deep-seated hostility to what they represent. That Orwell spoke and wrote 'with particular loathing' about working-class intellectuals has been often remarked (see Toynbee, 1959). His hostility is masked by condescending praise of 'the warm-hearted unthinking Socialist', but blatantly betrayed in sneers about 'historical necessity', 'dictatorship of the proletariat', and 'the pea-and-thimble trick with these three mysterious entities, thesis, antithesis, and synthesis' (*R.W.P.*, p. 155). For the thinking working-class socialist deeply troubles Orwell. The organizer or union-official, the activist, the intellectual and the writer: each may be the agent of revolutionary change. Any change that is backed by articulated theory (and therefore by 'intellectuals') is anathema to Orwell. He attempts to dismiss intellectuals (of any class), to dismantle theories of change as intrinsically authoritarian, and to redefine Socialism by locating it inside his experience of the northern working-class — or this experience interpreted to exemplify his account of a major movement in English morality.

One answer to theorizing is empiric observation, the socio-political enterprise of Orwell's seeing-for-himself. But his account of the subworld of the Brookers, the devastating poverty of caravan, hut, and slum wilderness, is not balanced by a sense of how the Garretts, Meades and the Searles would envisage its transformation. There is the compensatory, idealized image of the contented home — given full employment, of course — with its 'sane and comely shape'. Not only the phrase is quaintly nostalgic: Orwell admitted he was thinking here of his own childhood home. This superimposed image, however, is to draw together the sense of the working-classes as one huge family. The peroration of Part I (pp. 103–5) — going against the grain of all its own facts, figures and observations — is presenting a class which knows how to combine, has coherence, has its own forms of loyalty. This is, ultimately, what *The Road to Wigan Pier* wishes to represent as 'Socialism': the ways and the values of the working-class. This is a belief as lived, humanized, 'when the nonsense [sc. theory] is stripped off' (p. 193). The working class are guardians of common decency, respectability; what *Keep the Aspidistra Flying* attributed to the middle classes is here relocated as definitive of those below them. In depressed and degraded conditions, the population of the Special Areas has been commendably restrained, and has clung on to its customary values. Greenwood's *Love on the Dole*[12] is quoted to demonstrate that all the workers demand only to be given work; there is no political rallying-cry. Yet Greenwood above all had demonstrated that the working-class family had completely disintegrated.

Again, as in the novel, all the ambivalent tensions and the ambiguities of Orwell's purposes break into the open. The reader is to be jolted by the extremity of this report on the condition of the northern working classes: there must be immediate action and large-scale reform. Simultaneously, the reader is shown a population ignorant — or at most naive — about political action and revolutionary theories; and a people hostile to education, to time wasted away from 'real work'. Orwell emphasizes the rectitude of this supposed working-class rejection of education as an occupation merely contemptible and unmanly. In the context of this book, Orwell's agreement with such an attitude is not only reactionary, but hypocritical. Its rhetorical function however is to suggest the quietism of the workers, whose genuine intelligentsia use any spare time to improve their minds, and eschew social criticism or political activism. This set of reassurances and guarantees explains the nervous paradoxes on how conscious efforts at removing class barriers, which have definite results, only intensify class prejudice (pp. 140–2). This is a deadlock, insofar as Orwell writes at a time when the map of class divisions and the charting of educational opportunity would have the closest possible correlation. Change in one is inextricably connected with change in the other. The aim seems to be to stress how little fundamental change is involved in improving matters. Life styles, behaviour, and values will not be surrendered: 'The only sensible procedure is to go slow and not force the pace' (p. 147).

The sustained ambivalence of *The Road to Wigan Pier* is precisely comparable to that of the novel: each is nominally making an exploration of lower classes, and deploying that experience to sustain a bitter attack on the middle classes. The authenticity of the exploited, bleaker life throws the inauthenticity of the abandoned alternatives into sharp relief. The ambiguity that leads to a confused reversal of intention comes from apprehension and distaste released and intensified by the immersion in the lower, raw experience. As the novel's central figure bolted back to the securities of the lower middle classes, so Orwell himself, the social commentator, increasingly appeals for the restitution of such ethical supports. Orwell throughout this report takes himself as a typical, representative figure, and occasionally discusses his entrapment inside class values. This is demonstrated most, of course, in the hypersensitivity to surface details of working-class habits, speech, behaviour and appearance. It goes with the pervasive, if muted, tone of the sensationalism of the observer's investigations and findings. The concern is insistently (as in the novel) with response, with the observer's feelings, with the disturbance caused to the sensibility. The objects, situations and the actual people are in a more remote focus. Orwell foregrounds his immediate personal response (often of recoil) in a way that transmutes the problems into a disturbingly private form.

The strange convolutions in treating Socialism fit in with this tilting of the report away from the subject figures themselves, and towards the rebuked reader. Orwell accommodates Socialism to the ethic of decency and respectability, setting it free of working-class militancy and of middle-class theorizing. In one astoundingly casual phrase, he sums up: 'Socialism is such elementary common sense that I am sometimes amazed that it has not established itself already'. The Socialism of the working-class intelligentsia is suppressed; its manifestations in the (mainly left-wing) literary intelligentsia are ridiculed and caricatured. Its contemporary widespread form as a belief is, throughout one lengthy section (Chapter 12), equated with industrialism, machine worship, and the theory of Progress. (Here, Stalin's Russia and Wellsian Utopia are conflated as the Socialist dystopia.) So this is dismissed as proto-Fascism. All this pares away the possibly alarming trappings of Socialism, and redefines it in forms acceptable to the morally earnest middle-classes. The appeal is throughout to the liberal-minded who want reforms, to 'the ordinary decent person who is in sympathy with the *essential* aims of Socialism' (p. 160). Even the cranky docrtinaires can be incorporated — their failings now said to be merely in externalities (pp. 195–6). Everyone is to abandon their *Punch* magazine comic image of the workers (p. 109), and abandon snobbish attitudes (pp. 145–8), though Orwell anxiously stresses the gradualness of any such alteration. He wants to avoid Lawrence's mistake of directly condemning the failings of those who can end the antagonism between proletarian and bourgeois (pp. 146–8).

This is the end-result of Orwell's vigorous, incisive study of the condition of the northern working-classes in the mid-1930s. The profound and extensive changes called for necessarily involve Socialist programmes. The strategy of this ambiguous and puzzling report is to justify this call for radical change by de-politicizing the concept of Socialism and deconstructing the concept of change itself. The 'unthinking Socialism' of the majority of workers calls for no structural changes: all will be as before, once the rank abuses are dealt with. The other forms of Socialism are displayed as fashions, eccentricities, or concealed authoritarian ideals. The 'essential aims of Socialism' are identical with the ethical norms of the average (i.e. middle-class) Englishman, and theories (especially Marxist) are dispensed with. Orwell's own theories are sweepingly moralistic: all is gathered under the slogan of Justice and Liberty: 'The only thing *for* which we can combine is the underlying ideal of Socialism; justice and liberty . . . . Justice and liberty! *Those* are the words that have got to ring like a bugle across the world' (pp. 189–90). Never mind that historic crimes and contemporary injustice were/are perpetrated under that banner: it raises the issues above social practicalities and political insistence. Universalized as the struggle of the Oppressed against the Oppressors (p. 195), the hard-won specific insights of Part I dissolve into a call to overthrow tyranny, and Socialism converts into anti-Fascism.

These rapid and colliding shifts in perspective reveal Orwell's hostility to any sustained analysis of social ills and evils, and to any developed critique sustained by political theory. Having sometimes sneered at thinkers of the 'change-of-heart' school, he can yet claim that the method chosen has no particular significance, for 'economic injustice will stop the moment we want it to stop and no sooner' (p. 130). All the inconsistencies, hesitations, and withdrawals in his discussion come back to this incapacity to think and feel that many powerful groups have every wish for things to stay just as they are. This report would neither disturb nor change their attitudes; and it peters out in an embarrassingly jocular appeal, to representative middle-class figures, to drop their anxieties about other (i.e. lower) classes. Change is not seen as objective, public, calling for analysis, study, careful planning; but an (ultimate) consequence of more friendly attitudes and individual behaviour. The refurbished ideals of respectability, consideration and decency are prior to anything that a theory of change could possibly effect.

Part II: W.H. Auden

The early poetry of W. H. Auden is marked by brilliant evocation of restlessness, questioning, tension, the struggle for change:

> Will you turn a deaf ear
> To what they said on the shore,
> Interrogate their poises
> In their rich houses? (*Poems*[13] I)

The following poem, a version of the Anglo-Saxon *The Wanderer*, gives a universality to the urgent quest, the confronting of menace, the conflict, and the apocalyptic change:

> Bring joy, bring day of his returning,
> Lucky with day approaching, with leaning dawn. (*P.*, II)

In the first half of the decade, Auden gives precision and intensity to the very distinctive elements of his earliest verse. The clipped, imperative syntax carries a mode of address susggestive of insistent danger, immediate action, obscure threat:

> Means that I wish to leave and to pass on
> Select another form, perhaps your son;
> Though he rejects you, join opposing team
> Be late or early at another time,
> My treatment will not differ — he will be tipped,
> Found weeping, signed for, made to answer, topped. (*P.*, III)

This elliptical idiom, making even archaic echoes into the brusque and instantaneous, creates a note of exhilarating and almost brutal decisiveness for which the obscurity becomes a strategic mask. The basic simplicity of the vocabulary and the sentence structure — verbs and nouns packing main clauses, a minimum use of qualifying words or subordinate clauses — these all fashion a stripped rhetoric whose mode declares a meaning. Everything is urgent: the address is immediate, the listener must respond, now.

The imperious, knowing utterances concern conflict, feud, suffering and pain; everything occurs at borders and boundaries, with furtive groups,spies, defectors, and heroic individuals. All the detritus of a disintegrating industrial civilization composes the wasteland where the conflict nears its climax:

> Who stands, the crux left of the watershed,
> On the wet road between the chafing grass
> Below him sees dismantled washing-floors,
> Snatches of tramline running to the wood,
> An industry already comatose. (*P.*, XI)

The depiction of these trappings of a threatened or doomed society is itself, in part, a lingering review of what has been valued. The ambivalence is enriching the verse with images and rhythms that suggest how difficult a surrender is involved in the changes that now have to be made. The speaker's being entangled in what he must deplore gives his dismissive tones the tinge of regret which makes the air of bewilderment appropriate and moving:

> Go home, now, stranger, proud of your young stock,
> Stranger, turn back again, frustrate and vexed:
> This land, cut off, will not communicate . . . .
> . . . . Near you, taller than grass,
> Ears poise before decision, scenting danger. (*P.*, XI)

Poems of sensitive balance, such as "*Who Stands* . . . . (*P.*, XI) or *From Scars Where Kestrels Hover* (*P.*, XXIV), give way to bolder, brasher writing, such as *Get There if You Can* . . . . (*P.*, XXIII). The wasteland of an industrialized society in decay is vigorously represented, a colloquial, broadly satiric answer to all the prophets of progress through technology:

> Smokeless chimneys, damaged bridges, rotting wharves
>   and choked canals,
> Tramlines buckled, smashed trucks lying on their side
>   across the rails;
> Power-station locked, deserted, since they drew the
>   boiler fires;
> Pylons fallen or subsiding, trailing dead high-tension
>   wires;
> Head-gears gaunt on gross-grown pit-banks, seams
>   abandoned years ago;
> Drop a stone and listen for its splash in flooded
>   dark below. (*P.*, XXIII)

But the exhortation to change now combines threat, caricature, pleading and prognostication in a style that Gavin Ewart so well parodied in *Poetry of the 1930s*[14] (p. 67) and many, like C. Day Lewis, admiringly and frequently imitated:[15]

> Have things gone too far already? Are we done for?
>   Must we wait
> Hearing doom's approaching footsteps regular down the
>   miles of straight;
>
> Or, in friendly fireside circles, sit and listen for the
>   crash
> Meaning that the mob has realised something's up and
>   start to smash;

> Engine-drivers with their oil-cans, factory girls in
> overalls
> Blowing sky-high monster stores, destroying intellectuals? (*P.*, XXII)

This is revealing self-parody: along with bumptious moral commentary, the crude jocularity suggests uncertainty of aim. Poise and tension give way to ambiguity; partly because the imminent change is both welcomed and feared. The 'you' addressed becomes 'we': as with the typical *dramatis personae* of the early verse — travellers, fighters, spies, the enemy — there is vacillation about how the opposing parties are to be defined. One of the later (temporary) retitlings nervously points to the dilemma: 'Which Side Am I Supposed to Be On?'

This very ambivalence is contributory to the best and the worst elements in Auden's early work. Whatever gaffes it leads to, having allegiances in both camps is constitutive of strengths in detail and in structure. What in the Orwell books is evidence of fractures and contradictions, of his bifurcated vision, is here turned often into poetic virtue. This is partly an outcome of the nature of verse itself, rhythmic, highly figurative, compressed. Partly it is due to Auden's foregrounding the issue: responses and choices, in the face of impending change, are themselves the direct material, the surface subjects. Much is further due to Auden's not sharing Orwell's implicit assumption that his positions and values are largely coincident with those of radical Socialism. Auden may show, in the relevant poems, concern to understand or adopt some of these values; but he does not have Orwell's irksome task of explaining disparities in his commitments. Where Orwell gives a trajectory to his protagonist's quest that has ultimately to be defensively redefined, Auden allows the uncertainties and contradictions to emerge in, and for, the poem's persona.

This can be clearly seen in the best poems of the period, many in *Look, Stranger!* (1936),[16] in which the clash of possible allegiances is given precise imaginative force. The poem dedicated to Geoffrey Hoyland, *Out on the Lawn* is exemplary; it has all the ease, control and wit that marks Auden's better work, and these qualities are directly connected with its self-imposed limits; it speaks to, and about, a close circle of privileged people. Its intimate allusions produce some whimsy (stanza 6), even coyness (stanza 5), but equally sustain the lyrical delicacy of the controlled regret for the perfection of the passing moment:

> That later we, though parted then
> May still recall these evenings when
> Fear gave his watch no look;

The lion griefs loped from the shade
And on our knees their muzzles laid,
  And Death put down his book.

(*L.S.*, II, st.4)

The self-regard and the preciosity of this insulated existence is focused in turn, as Auden's images allude to European tyranny and political violence, to poverty, Hunger Marches, and the fatal indifference of the cultured, governing classes. Revolution seems unavoidable:

Soon through the dykes of our content
The crumbling flood will force a rent
  And, taller than a tree,
Hold sudden death before our eyes
Whose river-dreams long hid the size
  And vigours of the sea

(*L.S.*, II, st.13)

The closing stanzas, with a sigh of resignation, express the hope that the privileges and privacy of the élite will not be wiped out, but included in the new order that the poet and his friends accept, understandingly forgive, and would support. The images of flood, drowning, and the destructive speed of the tigress outweigh the apologetic hopefulness of the speaker, and pre-figure the inevitability of total change.

The shapely and persuasive movement of such poems is the result of Auden's skill in giving reflective unity to the tensions, and rhetorical impetus to competing elements. When he artificially suppresses any of the doubts and anxieties, then he produces the crude and strident simplifications of verse such as *A Communist to Others*,[17] with its callousness and its hollow pretension to strong feeling. It is also the welding of private and public, the personal and social, which gives the authentic ring to Auden's verse at the time. His strength is in placing the specific details of his immediate experience in the setting of some wider perspective, creating an idiosyncratic form of generalization. Something of this marks Christopher Isherwood's Berlin stories; Auden displays his form of it in the birthday poem he wrote for his friend:

Pardon the studied taste that could refuse
The golf-house quick one and the rector's tea;
Pardon the nerves the thrushes could not soothe,
Yet answered promptly the no-subtler lure
To private joking in a panelled room,
The solitary vitality of tramps and madmen;
Believed the whisper in the double bed:
Pardon for these and every flabby fancy.

(*L.S.*, XXX, st.7)

This stanza subtly interweaves the autobiographical and the topical observations of the poem into an unpretentious but pointed commentary on how the times are set. It seems all the more betrayed when capitalized abstractions — Courage, Calculation, Slim Truth — displace such an intriguing balance: moral stridency annuls the tensions, the ambivalence, the self-questioning. Returning to this earlier balance allows the poem to end on personal reflections that flow easily into those about crisis, the nature and urgency of action, the balanced, acutely felt moment of historical decision.

Much of Auden's early work has pointedness and strength when its contemporaneity is given full play. The teasing obscurity of some poems is at least lessened when they are given the immediate context of their original setting: *Poems* (1928): *Poems* (1930, revised edition 1933): *Look, Stranger!* (1936): and the earlier verse plays. Poems such as *Who Will Endure* and *To Ask The Hard Question* gain impetus from the full sequence of related verse in the 1930/1933 collections. This is part of the legitimate demand upon the readers: and the support is that of a common mood and a complex of related concerns. The mood is that of restlessness, apprehension, questioning, an insistence on the need for change.. That it comprises psychological and social, personal and public, inner and outer conflict, does not mean that one end of the spectrum annuls the other. The vacillations and the tensions are an enrichment of the poetic action and its structure; the better the verse, the less is one set of terms allowed to work as metaphor for its counterpart. That the frontiers to be riskily crossed are internal as well as national, or those of social class; that the love always invoked may be erotic and personal, as often as it is comradely and social; these are, more often than not, poetic gains that compensate for the blur or incidental vagueness.

The context that sustains and nourishes the early verse, however, could not be simply the printed one. Auden's poetry has always a tang of the immediate, the instantaneous, and the contemporary about it. The subjects and the tone are given the inflection of urgency, the pressure of the occasion. In its original placing even, the modernized Anglo-Saxon verse takes on the same insistence: it distills a sense of how men now feel, in the early 1930s. This responsiveness to the mood of the moment, the social turbulence, may meet and match the poet's pre-occupations, his fantasies, or his nightmares. But in projecting one, he etches in the other, as with his deployment of images of industrial breakdown, poverty and hunger, or his sketches of nervous aristocrat, harassed financier, or furtive revolutionary. So, in the mode of W.B. Yeats (mainly his *Meditations*), the verses later titled '1929' (*P.*, XVI) run through the spectrum of topical interests: personal and historical development; psychosomatic symptoms, social malaise, political unrest, catastrophe and apocalyptic change, of all things and everyone. Such a mélange seems a prescription for amorphous versifying: yet the controlled development from section to section, and the cunning interweaving of autobiographical with social and political commentary is both peculiarly Audenesque and distinctively of its time and place. Its tone, rhythms and images anticipate the finest of his early 1930s poems, and they do so by catching up the topical, the feelings of that moment:

> We know it, we know that love
> Needs more than the admiring excitement of union, ...
> Needs death, death of the grain, our death,
> Death of the old gang; . . . .
> The hard bitch and the riding-master,
> Stiff underground; deep in clear lake
> The lolling bridegroom, beautiful, there.
>
> (*P.*, XVI)

In his Hopkins pastiche, *Sirl No Man's Enemy*, success of a sort comes from the bravado with which the fashionable jargon of psychological analysis is converted to an extended set of poetic conceits to celebrate total change — in personality, in behaviour, in the forms of society. Its total immersion in the topical gives it some coherence and effectiveness. (*P.*, XXX)

Certainly this poet's skill and instinct in catching the tones and the topics of his time do not of themselves prove any deep engagement in the current socio-political concerns. The propaganda verses alone would indicate a very loose connection, even an indifference. However, the overt socio-political references, the allusions to specific personalities, incidents, and phenomena, are not exclusively the stuff, the constitutive material of political writing, for the imaginative playwright, novelist, or poet. That many of Auden's poems between 1928 and 1934 are political, without being dotted with topical allusions, would only be surprising if 'political' is narrowly construed as, say, concerned with the doctrines of parties and the practice of governments, rather than with the condition of the whole social organism. Reflections on the English situation are formative of manner and matter of these years; but argument, concepts and theory are assimilated to poetic form and rhythmic enactment:

> Our hunting fathers told the story
>   Of the sadness of the creatures,
> Pitied the limits and the lack

Set in their finished features;
Saw in the lion's intolerant look,
Behind the quarry's dying glare,
Love raging for the personal glory
That reason's gift would add,
The liberal appetite and power,
The rightness of a god.

(*L.S.*., III)

In one stanza, Auden creates a fable which condenses man's account of evolution, and his pride in the rationality that assures his control of Nature and history. Love, individuality, and power are his god-like attributes:

Who nurtured in that fine tradition
Predicted the result,
Guessed love by nature suited to
The intricate ways of guilt?
That human ligaments could so
His southern gestures modify,
And make it his mature ambition
To think no thought but ours,
To hunger, work illegally,
And be anonymous?

(*L.S.*, III)

The query is amused bewilderment at a complete turnabout: romantic, sensual love gives way to love that is impersonal, dedicated to others, at the cost of guilt, devious struggle, and deprivation. The stanzas contrast two great estimates of human purpose, and the poem's logic endorses the modern, difficult interpretation. Its wit and rhetoric compose a sophisticated representation of two views of history: the Renaissance estimate of man's status and qualities, as formulated in nineteenth-century Romantic liberalism; and the reaction against that, the politicization of history by the Socialist revolutionary. The superb compression of the language, the rich, playful use of idiom and metaphor, the disciplined stanza form, all make paraphrase very flat: but they give incisive shape to a political meaning. This is itself being implicitly shown to be a matter of the whole sensibility, of values comprehended in attitude and action. A poem such as this, coherent and independent, still gains from relation both to other poems alongside it in the original volume, and to the issues and concerns of its time, the early 1930s. Images of social transformation, of radical changes in living, of the need to abandon failing practices and institutions, these crowd the verse of Auden and his contemporaries. *Our Hunting Fathers* effectively metaphorizes the theory of such change. Though everything it implies is consonant with the views of genuinely radical Socialists, this is obviously (despite its closing paraphrase of Lenin's words) not a matter of exposition of doctrine in any form at all. Its structure of feeling is what matters, and what qualifies it, in the broader sense, for description as political writing.

There is no better confirmation of the significance of Auden's varied treatments of change and revolution than his own pointed return to them during the 1940s. He undertook a large-scale re-ordering of his work, the results clearly determining the shape of the 1945 *Collected Poetry*[18] and the 1950 *Collected Shorter Poems*.[19] The alterations range from those to single letters and short phrases, through every other step, including deletions and total excisions. Besides rewriting or eliminating, Auden repositioned short and long pieces in such a way that he effectively creates a new setting and fresh contexts. Though so apparently various in kind, the revisions do show a common tendency, and reveal specific purpose and direction.

Certainly poets have revised their work quite extensively; but none has perhaps carried out such a single-minded overhauling, with such distinctive results. It is not a matter of revision to work-in-process, or of recently composed verse. Auden is implicitly making fundamental claims about the nature and development of his poetic work. The outcome also involves basic critical issues about the reader's response to a much-revised poem. Has such revision its own inner perspectives and limits? Does the radically altered piece still have determinate relations with the poem as first printed, the Ur-text?

The Prologue to the volume *Look, Stranger!*, in its original form (May 1932), was akin to *Our Hunting Fathers* in its witty imagistic encapsulation of views of history. Nineteenth-century man offered his worldwide conquests and industrial empire as fulfilling Nature's plan; the exhaustion of that dream is

> Leaving the furnaces gasping in the impossible air,
> The flotsam at which Dumbarton gapes and hungers.

All the 1930s stagnation, waste and breakdown, outcome of a 'crude . . . sense of glory', is temporary, occasion now for the alternative fulfilment of Nature's purpose in History:

> Some possible dream, long coiled in the ammonite's slumber
> Is uncurling, prepared to lay on our talk and kindness
> Its military silence, its surgeon's idea of pain;
>
> And out of the Future into actual History,
> As when Merlin, tamer of horses, and his lords to whom
> Stonehenge was still a thought, the Pillars passed

> And into the undared ocean swung north their prow,
> Drives through the night and star-concealing dawn
> For the virgin roadsteads of our hearts an unwavering keel.
>
> (*L.S.*, Prol.)

The confident sweep of the rhythms has its climax in an image from legend forefiguring the splendour of total revolution. Auden's first revisions, from a text in *New Country*, had sharpened the Marxist certainties of the verse. The later revisions are all the opposite way: 'Future' and 'History' lose their capitals, 'love' gains one. The sense Auden so often gave it — comradely, social love — is replaced by vaguer, grander conceptions, while the Marxist implications about history are annulled. For the changes are part of the excising of confident heralding of revolution. 'Our hopeless sigh' becomes 'a hopeless sigh', as the poet disengages: and a fullstop to close Stanza 12, at the cost of ungrammaticalness and incoherence, aborts the sweep of exhilaration building up through the last four stanzas. The somewhat mangled poem is entitled 'Perhaps', instead of 'Prologue' (see v. *C.P.* and *C.S.P.*).

Out On The Lawn . . . . was retitled *A Summer Night 1933*, being written that June. It underwent a similar editorial treatment: three stanzas (10, 11 and 12) were excized. One of these, alluding to the Hunger Marches, sharply exposed the poet's circle for its 'metaphysical distress', its 'kindness to ten persons'; the next evokes the impending, exciting changes, which the same group can imagine and accept, but give no help to; the third confesses how feeble their own cherished cultural values have become. Their omission, unlike the removal of the coyly evasive stanza about a lover (Stanza 5), cannot be justified on stylistic grounds, since they are graphic, witty, effectively composed. The closing stanzas are made grammatically vague, by alteration of the pronouns, and the disengagement signalled by converting 'our privacy' to 'this privacy'. By making the other pronouns plural (it/they, its/their), the poet befuddles the sense of what is to survive the great change. Far from any stylistic clarification, an obfuscation of the movement and a blurring of the sense has resulted. Where Auden's revisions do not wreck the grammar or fudge the sense, then there is a general tendency which can be illustrated by what happens, for instance, in the conclusion to the sequence, *In Time of War* in *Journey to a War* (1939).[20] Among sounds of guerilla fighting, the poet bears the invocation of the voice of mankind, rallying the forces of the will:

> Till they construct at last a human justice,
> The contribution of our star, within the shadow

Of which uplifting, loving, and constraining power
All other reasons may rejoice and operate.
(*J.W.*, p.301)

This is metamorphosed into:

Till, as the contribution of our star, we follow
The clear instructions of that Justice, in the shadow
Of Whose uplifting, loving, and constraining power
All human reasons do rejoice and operate.
(*C.P.*, p. 349; *C.S.P.*, p. 296)

Apparently small changes — justice/Justice; which/Whose — with capitals; or displacing an adjective — 'other reasons' becomes 'human reasons' — have, along with other rewriting in the work, and some omissions — effected a major change. The Socialist humanism of a work that endorses the struggle to bring about justice in society, fair-dealing, and brotherly love, is baptized, Christianized.[21]

The critical plea that the changes are, dictated by stylistic, aesthetic considerations can often conceal assumptions of a dichotomy between aesthetic and ideational, between form and content. Certainly, Auden is sometimes working for more appropriate sound, more precise language; so 'Forests of green have done complete' gives way to 'As congregated leaves complete'. (*C.P.*, p. 96). This is not the kind of textual crux that creates critical disagreement. Yet even the adding or subtracting of capital letters, a non-audible change of the printed text, can make a tremendous difference, and contribute to giving the verse a completely altered cast. Even the miniscule alterations have altered purport, since they are incorporated in this very large-scale post-war rerepresentation of his work. For the two volumes *Collected Poetry* (1945) and *Collected Shorter Poems* (1950) — resituate all the selected pieces. Printed as they are in an adventitious order — alphabetically — all traces of the original context are sloughed off. The valuable interconnection of pieces in the same volume is lost; and the relation of each poem to its time of composition is denied. In a poet supremely responsive to the occasion, like Auden, the loss is considerable. For the work between 1928 and 1936, this relation is so often central, decisive, constitutive of meaning.

This neutralizing of his career and development, abolishing chronolgy,stabilizes everything on the poetic plateau of a 'Collected Poetry'. It is not only that Auden suppresses, excizes, or rewrites verses that celebrate, invoke, or fatalistically welcome change and social transformation. It is that the nature and importance of change *itself* is brought, contradictorily, into question. Auden is acting as though what he meant in a 1930 or a 1933 poem, and what readers at that time understood him to mean, is now (in the mid-1940s) utterly clear to him. In the light of this understanding, he amends and rewrites. This is contradictory, since such a process, with new insights, could occur at five-year intervals, say; and it goes against the shared understanding of readers, not only of the first versions then, but of critics and scholars comparing the rescensions of the text. The history of writers' revisions suggests that an initiating idea attains a self-validating form, a degree of dramatic autonomy which any further alterations have to respect. Persistent revision, like Wordsworth's of *The Prelude*, even though it pre-dates publication, can begin to misrepresent the original conception, and even damage its integrity — as Wordsworth violates the truth about his youthful ardour for revolutionary political change. When W.B. Yeats altered *Three Marching Songs*, he consciously intended to slight the group they had been meant for. He knew how and why he altered, and aimed to subvert his own verses.

Auden's revisions can damage the integrity of his work in various ways. They can obscure the phases of his artistic development, concealing innovatory power, exploratory skills, relatedness to other work. They can mislead, as do some of Yeats' revisions made long after composition, but printed over the original date. (e.g. *The Sorrow of Love*.) They can, with a disconcerting righteousness, free the early work from its uncertainties, its contradictions, and its ambiguities. These may all have, directly and indirectly, contributed to the specific forms of the earlier achievements. Above all, and most paradoxically, the revision and resetting of the work implies that the poet's vision, his interpretation of experience, and his imaginative ideas have been constant. A naive and paradoxical claim, since the alterations have to be of so many kinds, and on such a large scale. However, this is incidental to a larger claim that ideas are not related to particular times and places, to a specific, initiating situation. This temporal rootedness — obviously a simple determinism is not in question — is to be inked out, treated as a flaw, a regrettable distraction from the poetic instance. The outcome is to remove the oeuvre from the realm of the social, the political, and the historical. The paradox is the obvious one: this is itself an ideological operation, and carried out to promote those new ideological adhesions and fidelities that interest the older writer.

Part III

The elegy composed upon the death of W.B. Yeats, as 1939 began, exactly charts Auden's current feelings about the name and nature of the poetic art:

For poetry makes nothing happen: it survives
In the valley of its saying where executives
Would never want to tamper; ....
.... it survives,
A way of happening, a mouth.

(*C.P.*, p.50)

The artwork fashions its own realm, one apart: the verbal change from 'the valley of its saying' to 'its *making*' seems to move back the emphasis even one more stage, to the self-vindicating creative moment. The world of executives — administrators, business-men — is curtly dismissed. Art is precious just because of its inefficacy and non-relevance to the world of telegrams and anger, the civilization of luggage:

In the deserts of the heart
Let the healing fountain start,
In the prison of his days
Teach the free men how to praise.

(*C.P.*, p. 51)

The 'praise' is the transposing into art of the distress and failure of the life outside and beyond art.

The formal beauty of the ordered language is one of the achievements by which the human spirit survives. It fashions a counter-world to that of 'the brokers roaring like beasts on the floor of the Bourse', one in which revolution becomes a metaphor for the great man's dying (p. 49, st. 3), not a political event.

Yeats' own career had the contrary pattern, an accelerating movement away from inherited, refined modes and verbal beauty, towards a spare, passionate rhetoric, imprinted with the immanent presence of the poet. Whatever his resistances are, Yeats presents them, and propels them dramatically to a declarative form. The verse of his middle and later years is that of the artist giving complex aesthetic shape to his vision and insights. He authenticates the images; he shows his proud responsibility for them. The achieved art is the declaration; the complex, passionate verse is the insight and vision, Yeats' contribution. That it did not cure Ireland's madness does not remove it to 'the valley of its saying'. It has an ascertainable place as an action inside that troubled history, as it explores and creates responses and values vital to the conflict, in the way only available to poetic art.

This Yeats is, of course, implicitly celebrated in the ambivalent elegy of his admirer and follower:

In the nightmare of the dark
All the dogs of Europe bark,
And the living nations wait,
Each sequestered in its hate;

Intellectual digrace
Stares from every human face,
And the seas of pity lie
Locked and frozen in each eye.

(*C.P.*, p. 51, ss. 11 & 12)

Here, Auden is on the edge of moving into his poem, pressing through the images he makes, to a passionate, responsible vision of his times. That is itself the artist's action, without leaving the 'valley of saying' for some public rostrum, or the amorphous realm of opinion or doctrine. The autonomy of the artwork is not some ontological discreteness. Rather its distinctiveness is to use rhythm, image, and formal intricate patterning to fuse the poet's impassioned insight with things as they are, as the poem now presents them with objective validity. There, Auden's own images dramatize a truthful perception, and that they did not prevent the European madness does not diminish their composing an action. They are not, any more than Yeats' images, merely removed, if spiritual, consolation.

The elegy reveals Auden's wrestling with his convictions; he converts the discussion into more systematic terms in the article called 'The Public vs. the late Mr. William Butler Yeats'.[22] The Auden of the mid-1930s now speaks the weaker lines of the Prosecutor, pleading the case for art's commitment; the Auden of the present dismisses 'the fallacious belief that art ever makes anything happen'. History, claims this Defence, has never been changed one iota by an artwork. Within a few months, Auden is sharpening this attack on his old positions:

Art is not life and cannot be
A midwife to society.
For art is a *fait accompli* . . .
An abstract model of events
Derived from dead experiments

(*C.P.*, p. 267)

That the meaning is fossilized in verse is to be balanced by the positive force of the language, its virtues separated out from the content, that 'algebraic formula' it seems fated to transmit. Undemocratic in ideas, a poet such as Yeats paradoxically achieves 'a true democratic style' through the continuous development of his diction: 'The social virtues of a real democracy are brotherhood and intelligence, and the parallel linguistic virtues are strength and clarity'. By a sleight of hand, Auden moralizes matters of diction and style (seen as separable), and gives socio-political weighting to aesthetic form and qualities (seen as autonomous). Auden's critical logic, in the vindication of his new beliefs, and new practice as a poet, involves a new theory of language, language hypostatized, set apart, reified:

> (Time ......)
> Worships language and forgives
> Everyone by whom it lives;
> Pardons cowardice, conceit,
> Lays it honour at their feet.
>
> Time that with this strange excuse
> Pardoned Kipling and his views,
> And will pardon Paul Claudel,
> Pardons him for writing well.
>
> (*C.P.*, p. 50, 'him' is W.B. Yeats)

It can seem sometimes as though the holder of reactionary views — a Kipling, a Claudel — is specially qualified in this hypothesized aesthetic realm, 'the valley of saying'. Auden's own best use of language, both locally in the Yeats elegy, and generally in his early work, is, however, the best disconfirmation of both points. Whatever the unevenness of the tribute to Yeats, it is not reducible to an algebraic formula, to the fossil of some once vivid experience; its language has no virtues of force or elegance separable from its poetic efficacy in erecting Auden's perceptions. At other times, when he is not entertaining versions of art-as-game, Auden abandons this notion of poetry as verbal organization inside a semantically-free space:

> It is both glory and the shame of poetry that its medium is not private property, that a poet cannot invent his words, and that words are products, not of nature, but of a human society which uses them for a thousand different purposes .... However esoteric a poem may be, [language] makes it testify to the existence of other people.[23] [24]

Language is neither a totally objectified, independent system; nor only subjective, expressive, individually creative. Seeing the poem as a particular form of language-practice, itself constitutive of social behaviour, is a restoration to poetry of its power to mean, to constitute a form of action.

Auden and Orwell share common confusions about how to treat the presence of beliefs in literature. Each considers that personal freedom and political liberty is somehow bound up with good writing and the force of art:

So in this hour of crisis and dismay,
What better than your strict and adult pen
Can warm us from the colours and the consolations
The showy arid works, reveal
The squalid shadow of academy and garden,
Make action urgent and its nature clear?
Who give us nearer insight to resist
The expanding fear, the savaging disaster?

(*L.S.*, p. 65)

What Auden wrote of Isherwood might have been written by or about George Orwell. It certainly is an epigraph suitable for Orwell's project in his later works, *Animal Farm* and *Nineteen Eighty-Four*; despite his persisting general sense that socio-political issues, beliefs, ideological conflict has all been foisted on to modern man — the eruption of a contemporary malaise. In a milder form, Orwell hankered for the 'poetic life' that would transcend all these concerns; echoing in this, the project of Edward Upward's protagonist in his trilogy about this period, *The Ascending Spiral* (1977). Auden's emphasis on the saving graces of 'writing well' which offset unsympathetic ideas, was largely a temporary one, and preceded a total conversion about ethics and aesthetics.

The critical practice of Auden and Orwell, in assessing the ideas and beliefs of other writers, is much more unified, forceful and precise than their loose generalizations about it. Orwell implicitly answers Auden's debating points in the Yeats' elegy and the accompanying prose dialogue. He concludes that good art could be produced from almost any coherent position — Catholic, Communist, Fascist, Anarchist, Conservative. (His exceptions are the fanatical, grossly limited positions of the Ku Klux Klan, of Buchmanites.) Throughout this study of Swift,[25] Orwell precisely pin-points the co-ordination in effective artworks of intensity of representation, formal aesthetic qualities, and unified, committed vision. Clarity, strength, wit and elegance are not separable components: they are critical descriptions of how Swift fashions his work, or how the Catholic or the Communist creates his meanings in the novel or the poem. Auden's early criticism (e.g. in *Scrutiny* articles) makes such assumptions; in his later articles (*The Dyer's Hand*) he displaces radical and humanist interests by ethical, moral and spiritual concerns. The works, however, of Dickens or Ronald Firbank, of Ibsen or Cervantes are treated in holistic fashion. Their structure of feeling, their representative, mythopoeic figures, the author's sensibility, the fineness of language; all are brought together, and placed in a context of general ideas. Orwell, on the other hand, looks to the particularity of Swift or Dickens, or to the structure of feeling created in gangster fiction or in boys' magazines.

Each in his way, and with a variety of methods, is assuming and asserting the significance of beliefs in shaping the literary work. Each is concerned with the personal, even idiosyncratic vision, as realised and visible in the action of the work. Orwell asserts that a book is primarily an individual thing: 'It is either truthful expression of what one man thinks and feels, or it is nothing'.[26] The bluntness is not Orwell's taking literature as self-expression, opinion or revelation; but asserting the full responsibility of the artist for what the work is. With more indirections, Auden shares the same sense, with an insistent stress on the interrelations between artistic skill and moral achievement (see *D.H.*, 'Genius and Apostle').

If we accept the notion of Auden's art as a series of games, in which the poet wears a different hat for each 'Poetic performance', interrupted by his alter-persona, the Anti-poet; or if each work is an imaginary 'As if', a provisional situation imaged for our pondering; then there is still the clinching element of how each posture is assessed, its instrumentality and its significance. The poet's distance or nearness, his detachment or participation, are inevitably signalled in every contributory detail. He is as accountable for the flip epigram, the academic graffitti, as he is for an extended sonnet-sequence or verse play. Auden's revisions and re-contextualizing of his 1930s work displays his sense of accountability, and shows his awareness of the ideological cast of that work. But his new accountability, apart from making this work quite puzzling for new readers, has drawn other charges. One commentator remarks: 'There will always be something mildly shocking in the idea of altering records'.[27] For Auden 'is virtually misrepresenting the thought which actually informed the earlier writing'.[28] All traces of development from poem to poem were suppressed, notes Spender, who then concludes: 'His development seemed largely a disowning of his own past'.[29] In the first instance, it is not a matter of the disaffection from radical thought and from Socialism, whatever one's personal regrets; it is the question of the actual blurring of a distinctive achievement, of uprooting work from its context. The local, temporal, and the topical were far from negligible components in that achievement. They channelled an excitement, the passion, perhaps, of a Byronic radical:[30] but the poetic force was in that commitment, however wavering and ambivalent.

The approach to Auden's work through the specifically narrowed focus of his textual revisions leads to consideration of the widest possible implications. The poet is clearly and strongly reacting against the earlier balance of his responses, and revealing his sharp sense of accountability in ensuring that his verse shall be taken as free of certain significations, or even free of certain *kinds* of meaning. The major erasure is of all images of social revolution, of all notions of possible change.

With Orwell, it is the ambiguities, the massive reservations, the confusions, that are more and more to be pondered. His accountability in his fiction — which constitutes a surprisingly large part of his output — is of the kind he scrutinized in others. The hero — a Comstock or a George Bowling — may be small, with none of Orwell's toughness or force. But the book itself is a total action, with movements of sympathy or of recoil, the index of the engaged sensibility of the man making the work. The structure of feeling in *Keep the Aspidistra Flying* has been shown to be similar to that of *The Road to Wigan Pier*, where Orwell's responsibility is continuously clear. The reservations about change have been singled out, because they themselves signal much more than the declared specific disenchantments with Soviet Communism. These fundamental reservations are an index of a sensibility shared by minds as different as Auden's and Orwell's, and by a host of their contemporaries during that key-decade, the 1930s.

Notes

1 G. Orwell (1945), *Animal Farm* (hereafter cited as *A.F.*), Secker & Warburg, London.
2 G. Orwell (1949), *Nineteen Eighty-Four* (hereinafter cited as *1984*), Secker & Warburg, London.
3 Zwerdling (1974) *Orwell and the Left*, Yale University Press, Yale.
4 G. Orwell (1933), *Down and Out in London and Paris* cited as *D.O.P.L.*), Gollancz, London.
5 G. Orwell (1936), *Keep the Aspidistra Flying* (hereafter cited as *K.A.F.*), Gollancz, London.
6 G. Orwell (1937), *The Road to Wigan Pier* (hereafter cited as *R.W.P.*), Gollancz/Left Book Club, London.
7 G. Orwell (1935), *Burmese Days* (hereafter cited as *B.D.*), Gollancz, London.
8 G. Orwell (1935), *A Clergyman's Daughter*(hereafter cited as *C.D.*), Gollancz, London.
9 Steinhoff (1975), *The Road to 1984*, Weidenfeld & Nicolson, 139.
10 Steinhoff, *ibid.*
11 G. Orwell, in S. Orwell and I. Angus (eds) (1968) *Collected Essays, Journalism and Letters of George Orwell, Volume I: An Age Like This 1920–1940* (hereafter cited as *C.E.J.L.I*), Secker & Warburg, London, 194–243.
12 W. Greenwood (19), *Love on the Dole.*

13 W.H. Auden (1930), *Poems* (hereafter cited as *P.*) Faber & Faber, London.
14 W.H. Auden in R. Skelton (ed.) (1964) *Poetry of the 1930s*, Penguin, Harmondsworth.
15 W.H. Auden, in R. Skelton (ed), *ibid.* 63, for example.
16 W.H. Auden (1936), *Look Stranger!* (hereafter cited as *L.S.*) Faber & Faber, London.
17 R. Skelton (ed.), *op. cit.* 54.
18 W.H. Auden (1945), *Collected Poetry* (hereafter cited as *C.P.*), Random House, New York.
19 W.H. Auden (1950), *Collected Shorter Poems 1930–1944* (hereafter cited as *C.S.P.*), Faber & Faber, London.
20 W.H. Auden (1939), *Journey to a War* (hereafter cited as *J.W.*), Faber & Faber, London.
21 J. Warren Beach (1957), *The Making of the Auden Cannon*, Minnesota.
22 W.H. Auden (1939), 'The Public vs. the Late Mr. William Butler Yeats', in *Partisan Review*, Spring 1939.
23 W.H. Auden, in E. Mendelson (ed) (1977), *The English Auden: Poems and Dramatic Writings 1927–1939*, Faber & Faber, London.
24 W.H. Auden (1963), *The Dyer's Hand* (hereafter cited as *D.H.*), Faber & Faber, London, 23.
25 G. Orwell, in S. Orwell and I. Angus (eds) (1968), *Collected Essays, Journalism and Letters of George Orwell, Volume IV: In Front of Your Nose 1945–1950* (hereafter cited as *C.E. J.L IV*), Secker & Warburg, London, 241–61.
26 G. Orwell, in S. Orwell and I. Angus (eds) (1968), *Collected Essays, Journalism and Letters of George Orwell, Volume II: My Country Right or Left 1940–1943* (hereafter cited as *C.E.J.L.II*), Secker & Warburg, London.
27 B. Everett (1964), *Auden*, Oliver & Boyd, London.
28 J. Warren Beach, *op. cit.*
29 S. Spender (1951), *World Within World: An Autobiography*, Hamish Hamilton, London, 300.
30 F. Duchêne (1972), *The Case of the Helmeted Airman: Auden's Poetry*, Chatto & Windus, London.

5 PRESENTING 'THINGS AS THEY ARE': JOHN SOMMERFIELD'S *MAY DAY* AND MASS OBSERVATION

Stuart Laing

In an article in *Left Review* in May 1935 Montagu Slater spoke of 'one of the conditions of literary advance' as a:

> knowledge of the ordinary world of people and of things, the world of work, the world of everyday economic struggle. A function which *Left Review* must learn to perform has been exemplified and then only partially in one number — the issue in which nine workers described a shift at work. Descriptive reporting is something which the tabloid press has almost replaced by wisecracks, which the revolutionary press often has no room for, and which for one reason and another has a particularly revolutionary import (we have even invented a jargon name for it, *reportage*). Certainly to describe things as they are is a revolutionary act in itself.[1]

The assumption here was that the transcription of the real ('descriptive reporting') was a relatively unproblematic task; the problem was rather that it should be made acceptable. Montagu Slater's definition of the term 'reportage' gave it two related meanings — truth to the facts ('things as they are') and a degree of implicit social or political comment.

In the following year the term was to be found again in *Left Review* — now in a more 'literary' context. Stephen Spender in a review of Auden and Isherwood's *The Ascent of F6* praised:

> the rhythmic contrast which the writers maintain between two entirely different methods of presentation: firstly realistic scenes of political reportage; secondly fables. There are two approaches to the contemporary political scene: the one is direct, or partially satiric, external presentation, the other is fantasy or allegory.[2]

'Reportage' was here defined in terms of a naturalistic style of *presentation* rather than of 'things as they are' in the sense of historical accuracy. It is a question of *realism* as a style, not, pre-eminently, of giving the verifiable facts, although clearly these might go together. As regards the novels of the period the 'reportage' style would have encompassed such writers as James Hanley, Walter Greenwood and even Orwell's fiction, as opposed to such Marxist 'fables' as Rex Warner's *The Wild-Goose Chase* and Edward Upward's *Journey to the Border*.

The term 'reportage' could then be applied both to a particularly observant and accurate form of descriptive journalism and to a style of literary presentation; this double reference in itself testifies to the convergence of and confusion between 'realistic' novel and 'documentary' as prose forms during the 1930s. Storm Jameson, in an article on 'Documentary' in *Fact* in 1937 was very much concerned to clarify the confusion and advance the convergence; the article addressed much of itself to novelists, instructing them on how to compose a documentary:

> A well-placed novelist might bring out a double-sided record; one day or one week in the life of a family of five living in one of the wealthier residential districts of the West End . . . set down opposite the life during the same length of time of a similar (in ages, size etc.) Paddington, Hoxton, Lambeth family.[3]

The novelist in doing this would, however, be working on a documentary, not a novel, even if he brought to it his technical skill as a writer:

> The number of documents to be got is infinite. How are they to be presented? This is the crux. A journalist can observe and report. No writer is satisfied to write journalism, nor is this what is wanted — visits to the distressed areas in a motor-car. Nor must the experience, the knowledge waited for and lived through, be fictionalized, in the sense of making up a story or a novel on the basis of facts collected (e.g. *The Stars Look Down* by Cronin). Perhaps the nearest equivalent of what is wanted exists already in another form in the documentary film. As the photographer does, so must the writer keep himself out of the picture while working ceaselessly to present the *fact* from a striking (poignant, ironic, penetrating, significant) angle.[4]

The determining features of documentary films, however, included not only the angles of the individual shots, but also the sequence of shots which, by juxtaposition of scenes and images, could imply or assert many kinds of relations and connections. Storm Jameson implicitly recognised this in her conclusion when referring to the problems awaiting the prospective documentary writer:

> One technical difficulty remains to be solved. The solution may turn up any day, in the course of the experiments going on all the time. This is the frightful difficulty of expressing, in such a way that they are at once seen to be intimately connected, the relations between things (men, acts) widely separated in space or in the social complex. It has been done in poetry. At certain levels of the mind we see and feel connections which we know rationally in another way. In dreams things apparently distinct are seen to be related (but Surrealism is not the solution). We may stumble on the solution in the effort of trying to create the literary equivalent of the documentary film.[5]

This requirement called into question the value of 'reportage' in Montagu Slater's sense — the description of 'things as they are' in the sense of how they immediately appear. What was called for was a going beyond, or rather beneath, immediate appearances (such as the description of a shift at work) to achieve the recognition and presentation of normally unseen connections.[6] The problem here, as Storm Jameson realised, was that to state the need was much easier than to develop a mode of writing which could fulfil it.

The desire for a literary equivalent of the documentary film represented one of the many and varied impulses behind the formation and growth of Mass Observation. At the same time as Storm Jameson's article in *Fact* was appearing, the first Mass Observation statements of intent were being formulated; and in the introductory pamphlet called *Mass Observation*, published in summer 1937, a passage appeared which — in reviewing the first batches of observers' reports — paralleled Storm Jameson's elevation of fact over fiction:

> The readability of the material is also borne out in the reports sent in on February 12th. Their fascination is akin to that of the realistic novel, with the added interest of being fact and not fiction. The most ordinary environment is rich in surprises, and in transcribing their environments, the Observers reveal the ultimately surprising character of life itself. Whereas fiction provides an escape into the worlds of wish-fulfilment, where the mill-girl always ends by marrying the mill-owner, these reports start from an acceptance of the real conditions of existence, an acceptance of the reality principle, the principle of adult life and of a modern scientific society.[7]

As in the phrase 'making up a story' used by Storm Jameson the assumption was that a novel would tend to impose an artificially neat and misleading pattern on the 'facts' and 'ultimately surprising character' of 'life itself'.

Overall, the 1930s novelist who sought to develop a reportage or documentary mode of writing faced a range of potentially antagonistic arguments, of which this neo-Platonic position was only one. For if on the one hand he could be accused of falsification and escapism in 'making up stories', on the other he would be open to the kind of criticisms made by Orwell in a radio broadcast in 1940. Referring to one particular novel he stated:

> It is about a young proletarian who wishes he wasn't a proletarian. It simply goes on and on about the intolerable conditions of working-class life, the fact that the roof leaks and the sink smells and all the rest of it. Now, you can't found a literature on the fact that the sink smells. As a convention it isn't likely to last so long as the siege of Troy.[8]

The debate about how to judge received literary values and 'great art' centred around the issue of whether they were inherently capitalist (or feudal) or rather represented a common human heritage.[9] Orwell was speaking partly about this problem and partly about his own uncertainties about the relative values of a 'naturalistic' and a consciously 'literary' style; these uncertainties are

'The struggle between combined Sheffield and Manchester ramblers and gamekeepers yesterday in which one keeper was injured' (Sheffield Telegraph, 25 April 1932)

'A gamekeeper receiving assistance from ramblers after being injured during the mass-trespass on Kinder Scout yesterday' (Sheffield Daily Independent, 25 April 1932)

'New Suburb' in The Heart of England (Batsford, 1935)

'Happy Hikers: "The England that is" ' (The Field, 24 September 1932)

Humphrey Spender: 'Pylons', 1932

(Mass Observation Archive, The University of Sussex)

The painter Graham Bell and photographer Humphrey Spender on the roof of Bolton Art Gallery, Spring 1938

(Mass Observation Archive, The University of Sussex)

Humphrey Spender: Bar Pumps Bolton, 1938

'A "Council of War" of ramblers before yesterday's skirmish with gamekeepers on Kinder Scout' (Manchester Evening News, 25 April 1932)

Cover of pamphlet Trespassers will be Prosecuted, by Phil Barnes (Sheffield, 1934)

manifested in *A Clergyman's Daughter* (1934) where 'reportage' accounts of tramping and hop-picking sit uneasily alongside the ostentatiously modernist scene in Trafalgar Square where the mode of presentation is based directly on the 'Nighttown' section of Joyce's *Ulysses*.

For novelists working within the milieu of the Left in the 1930s, (whether Communist Party, ILP, *Left Review* or other), these problems seem to have resolved themselves into the effort to reconcile three competing influences — influences which at times pulled in different directions. These were the need for reportage (describing 'things as they are'), the desire for a certain aesthetic or fictional structure, (at its crudest 'making up a story'), and the pull towards a literature of political commitment and political persuasion. When the status of reportage was also put in question then the difficulties of finding a solution became even more complex. One kind of solution, which found a number of adherents, was to organize the novel around a plot structure which would juxtapose a presentation of the typical 'ordinary world of people and of things' the everyday world with significant moments of political drama (the strike, and particularly the march or the demonstration) during which some sort of crisis within the structure of the novel could be presented.

This juxtaposition is to be found, for example, in two of the most celebrated 'proletarian' novels of the 1930s — Greenwood's *Love on the Dole* (1933) and Grassic Gibbon's *Grey Granite* (1935). In Greenwood's novel, the death of the hero, partly as a result of his injuries from the police during a Means Test march, signals the hopelessness of the situation, and opens the way for the cynical side of the novel's ending. On the face of it, the ending of *Love on the Dole* actually appears to conform to the Mass Observation strictures on novelistic plots — certainly the mill-girl Sally runs off with the wealthy bookmaker, Sam Grundy, even if the moral implications of this are the opposite of the conventional happy ending. It is a cold-blooded act of prostitution, justified by the way in which it then enables Sally to secure jobs for her father and brother. It is by this inversion of the normative happy ending that Greenwood solves his problems of structural integration, although arguably at the expense of a clear political commitment.

The novel is full of 'reportage' in the sense of 'the ordinary world of people and of things, the world of work, the world of everyday economic struggle'. Greenwood had to adapt his style very little (removing perhaps some of the Dickensian caricature) in writing a documentary — *How the Other Man Lives* — for the Labour Book Service in 1937; the novel contains much of poverty in the home, the world of the engineering factory, the experience of the dole queue, and working-class leisure activities. The plot, with the struggle into marriage of the average Harry and Helen and the tragedy of the exceptional Larry and Sally, is not incidental to the implicit social criticism of the 'reportage', since precisely what denotes the situation as so bad is the denial of an adequate home or marriage. The novel's reversal of the conventional happy ending serves to confirm the social documentation of intolerable domestic conditions. Both lend weight to the novel's explicitly political message as presented in Larry, a constitutional Marxist whose inability to control the violence between police and demonstrators signals his own death and the apparent destruction of any hope for change — a pessimism mirrored by the repetition of the novel's opening scene of domestic hardship at its close.[10]

The juxtaposition of the everyday world and the dramatic moment of political struggle forms then an important, but subordinate, structural element in *Love on the Dole* — subordinate to the conventional, marriage-centred, narrative form. It is subordinate also in *Grey Granite*, although here subordinate to the structure of the whole trilogy, which on the surface traces the life of Chris Guthrie from her origins in an agricultural peasant economy to the industrial city of *Grey Granite*; at a deeper level the structure is that of the process of transition, in stages, from the pre-industrial to the industrial capitalist social formation. Within *Grey Granite* the political demonstration occupies a similar place to that in *Love on the Dole*, with the crucial difference that in Grassic Gibbon's novel it marks not the defeat of the hero, but rather the moment of his conversion into political activity. Finally in *Grey Granite* Chris and her son Ewan are seen moving in different directions — Chris back towards the land as a source of value and individual fulfilment, and Ewan towards the industrial working class and political commitment. The novel closes with this dual perspective, Ewan about to lead a hunger march to London, while Chris returns to the farm of her origins.

As regards the 'reportage' element of the novel, however, Grassic Gibbon was, in the eyes of *Left Review* at least, not very successful; his lack of first-hand knowledge was particularly criticized: 'He had never been in intimate contact with the industrialized worker: he was unfamiliar with engineering shops; he did not know how the workers felt or how they reacted to their industrial, workshop environment. The lack of this vital and absolutely essential knowledge invalidated his chances of making *Grey Granite* the success it ought to have been.'[11]

The deficiency of *Grey Granite* from this perspective was that despite its aesthetic sophistication (seen as part of the whole trilogy) and its political commitment, it failed to portray the 'ordinary world' with enough authenticity. The nature of this criticism serves to confirm the implications of the remarks (already cited) of Montagu Slater and Storm Jameson with regard to the pressures on Left writers to build their writings on 'knowledge' and 'facts'.

This juxtaposition of the ordinary and the extraordinary formed then a valuable structural element for Greenwood and Grassic Gibbon in the attempt to integrate 'reportage', the aesthetic and the political; but for John Sommerfield in *May Day* (1936)[12] it constitutes the basic and continuous organizing principle of the whole novel. It is a novel with no single hero or small group of consistent central characters, but the fates of two of the characters — brothers James and John Seton — do parallel those of the heroes of Greenwood's and Grassic Gibbon's novels. In the May Day march which forms the climax of the novel one brother (like Larry in *Love on the Dole*) dies after being struck by a policeman, while the other (like Ewan in *Grey Granite*) simultaneously takes a leading part and finds his uncertain political commitment becoming firm.

Contemporary reviews of the novel disagreed quite widely in their attempts to describe its structure and its success. The *Times Literary Supplement* was able to categorize it with ease:

> The book contains Communist propaganda in the form of fiction. It is in a great many short scenes, in which the same characters appear and reappear, showing the lives of the factory workers of London, showing also the capitalists in their board-rooms and at their pleasures, in their 'plush' motor-cars and their 'plush' halls. Mr. Sommerfield writes with a coarse though at times effective vigour, but his book very soon becomes monotonous. His scenes are different but, like advertisements, they all lead to the same end: 'the workers will come out on strike on Mayday'. His style too is monotonous with the monotony of the one note of the steam siren. The Communist cells 'spray out leaflets like machine-guns scattering bullets' and even the alarm clock cannot simply ring — it 'sprays a jet of noise into the ear-drums'.[13]

The novel was politically and aesthetically unacceptable. In *Left Review* the valuation of the novel was, predictably, somewhat different, as was the description; whereas *The Times Literary Supplement* saw it as propaganda, for Jack Lindsay the novel was successful, particularly as 'reportage': 'the best collective novel that we have yet produced in England; the real protagonist is the London working-class, particularly as represented by one factory . . . . Sommerfield gives us the true London, smelt, seen, understood.'[14] Jack Lindsay's emphasis on the world 'collective' was deliberate in its recognition of the novel's rigorous attempt to break with the assumption that a novel must have an individual hero.

The review that was most sympathetic to the novel's method (in my view) was in *New Statesman*, where it was reviewed, with other novels, under the general heading of 'Proletarian Novels'.

> He has gallantly attempted to paint an impressionist picture of every stratum of, and interconnecting link in, the lives of all who go to make up the man power of a factory, and to relate the feelings and will of the workers with those of the rest of mankind who are struggling for better conditions. In quick and undeniably vivid snapshots he presents a number of characters, from the directors to the workers, and traces the movement of their private and public lives in the two days preceding May 1st, whose strike is described in the last section of the book.[15]

Also worth noting here is the text of an advertisement for the novel in *Left Review* of May 1936: 'A cross-section of the social pyramid, from the factory to the managing director's luxury flat. It's three days of life to-day, and it *moves* — it's got technique.'[16] Both the *New Statesman* review (explicitly) and the text of the advertisement (by implication as I shall suggest later in this article) drew attention to certain analogies which could be drawn between the novel and forms of visual representation (note particularly the phrases 'paint an impressionist picture' and 'undeniably vivid snapshots'). Storm Jameson was to call, a year after the publication of *May Day*, for the literary equivalent of a documentary film, and there was certainly a sense in which John Sommerfield's novel had already addressed itself to two of the particular issues raised in that article. These were the need for the selection of a 'striking (poignant, ironic, penetrating, significant) angle' of presentation and the need for the demonstration of 'the relations between things (men, acts) widely separated in space or in the social complex'.

With regard to the former the novel's 'snapshot' technique (as *New Statesman* termed it) consists both of varying the characters presented and the angle of presentation (for example, 'close-ups' on one individual or 'long-shots' of crowds). The novel is, as the *Times Literary Supplement* review implied, composed predominantly of sections of four or five pages in which the activities of separate groups of characters, or of the whole city of London grasped as a single complex, are presented. This was, of course, not innovatory in itself — both Joyce's Dublin and Virginia Woolf's London (as well as the America of Dos Passos in *USA*) are at times constructed in this way. However in *May Day* the technique is retained throughout and without any Leopold Bloom, Stephen Dedalus or Mrs Dalloway as a central reference point.

The novel also attempts to overcome what Storm Jameson termed: 'the frightful difficulty of expressing, in such a way that they are at once seen to be intimately connected, the relations between things (men, acts) widely separated in space or in the social complex.'

In *May Day* there is always a clear form of perceptible connection between one section and the next, but never a direct narrative link and very rarely, if at all, a connection that the novel's characters are themselves in a position to perceive. However, unlike many modern chroniclers of the city, John Sommerfield is not interested in making the readers share any sense of isolation or disconnection that the characters may feel; this novel's task is to *reveal* the connections and relations. Some characteristic examples of how connections occur between one section and another will illustrate this — characters passing in the street or a car passing a certain building (the text will move from one character to another as they pass or from the occupants of a car to a patient in the hospital being passed), common memory (two people in different parts of the city recalling a shared experience), newspaper headlines seen simultaneously by otherwise apparently unconnected people, a cinematic technique of 'moving over the roof-tops' from one end of a district to another, characters looking at the same star simultaneously from different parts of the city — very often, in fact, the connecting idea is that of unrecognized, shared experiences (although the interpretations of the experience may be very different). Beneath these immediate connections and making sense of them is the structure of social and economic relations which is focused by the involvement of many of the characters, at a variety of levels and in a variety of roles, in one particular factory.

All this constitutes one kind of answer to Storm Jameson's problem of demonstrating connections, and it is this technique which was highlighted by the use of the term 'cross-section' in the *Left Review* advertisement. David Mellor has noted[17] that the phrase 'cross-section' was important in the vocabulary of Mass Observation and links this usage with the influence of Ruttmann's 'documentary' film *Berlin: Symphony of a Great City* made in the late 1920s — a film whose structure provides some significant parallels with *May Day*. The film opens with a journey into the city by train, the novel with a traveller returning by sea; the film follows the pattern of just one day (in a now familiar documentary style), just as the novel follows the development of three individual days; and both use totalizing images of the city as a network of communication systems — a central image in *Berlin* is of patterns of wires, rails or tramlines, while in *May Day* the text returns throughout to descriptions of the underground railway system and the network of power cables. The novel literally, as well as figuratively, directs itself to the presentation of normally invisible connections.

However, along with this complex organization, there is no doubt that one function of the novel is seen as to reveal conditions 'as they are' in the Montagu Slater sense:

John went in. It was a tremendous room, shivering with the loud, undeviating music of machines, the air loaded with their oily breath.

The floor is slippery with oil and graphite, as with some horrible blood. After a while the noise comes to seem a fearful shattering silence.

Here, two hundred and forty girls in ugly grey overalls and caps live, breathe and think, their fragile flesh confused with the greasy embraces of steel tentacles. Each has a simple set of movements to perform for eight hours. The machines, Langfier and A.E.I. do the rest. Everything moves meaninglessly, repetitively — wheels, axles, shaftings, belts and drills, spinning and hurrying: rods, pistons and punches shuttling savagely exact rhythm.[18]

The presentation of the everyday is not always in a mode as dramatic as this ('tremendous', 'horrible', 'fearful', 'savagely'); it also at times resembles the approach of Orwell:

. . . He took shelter in a cafe.

It was a dingy little place, with marbletopped tables like slabs of old streaky bacon. The outstanding features were a tarnished tea-urn surmounted by a great ecclesiastical-looking tin eagle, and a flyblown bill of fare decorated with faded pink and blue watercolour scrolls. Behind the counter a billowing shapeless woman wrapped in a dirty white overall sat thinking about a film she had seen last night.

Two lorrydrivers were talking about motor engines. A small cabinetmaker with a gingery waxed moustache and a bowler hat was reading the leading article in the *Daily Herald*. At the next table a young mechanic in a clean faded blue boiler suit was talking to two unemployed youths (in rakish peak caps, knotted white scarves etc.) about dog-racing.[19]

The last paragraph in particular could almost be taken straight from the notebook of a mass observer, but the novel goes even further than this in purporting to render an accurate account of 'things as they are' by including one section headed — 'Some Statistics Relating to the May Day Demonstration'. Here figures concerning unemployment, industrial accidents, malnutrition, strikes, Communist Party membership and other aspects of social concern are given; the intention is to show that social conditions are deteriorating (and Communist activity and strength increasing) in this '*average* year between 1930–40' in which the novel, according to the author's prefatory note, is set.

Despite this appeal to the facts, John Sommerfield does not, like Storm Jameson, have a complete faith in journalism as an appropriate technique for the presentation of social knowledge — one character, a sub-editor, reflects: 'This was a human being, accurately observed, utterly remote and unknown, never before seen and never to be seen again. Pat was a journalist, a very good one: he saw, noted, wondered, but could not make the imaginative synthesis that goes beyond the facts and discovers the truth.'[20] As already noted in *May Day* this going beyond is in part achieved by the juxtaposition of many different scenes to present the 'cross-section' effect; it is also achieved by a certain variety of styles. The *Times Literary Supplement* charge of monotony of style is by no means justified, for if at times the language of the novel is that of a more up-tempo *Road to Wigan Pier*, at other times it is that of Virginia Woolf.

The London of Mrs Dalloway makes its appearance, appropriately enough, particularly in the accounts of upper middle-class social occasions:

> There's Peter Langfier, thinks Clara. Look how he stands against the wall, melancholy and alone. He wears a sad, a disillusioned air. Now I catch his eye, now I smile at him, a sympathetic smile that tells him I understand, that I too have leaned against a wall, forlorn and melancholy, waiting for someone who does not come.
>
> I have given up hoping that she will come, thinks Peter. But the door keeps opening with a premonitory rustle of women's clothes and every time my heart beats faster for the little space of time it takes to prove that it is not she. A girl does not come to a dance and life is meaningless . . . .[21]

A personal world in which consciousness and particularly self-consciousness can be seen as primary and virtually autonomous is presented in the novel very much as part of a field of particular class-activity. There are, however, some moments in the novel when this mode of writing is put to a more general use in the handling of time:

> But time passes, the earth turns, the sun declines, and the clock on the mantelpiece struck, a gentle ringing note repeated, and hearing it the players were brought to mind of time's flight and the turning earth, and in their minds began to expend perspectives of appointments to be kept, of dinners and theatres, the hands of other clocks in other rooms inexorably moving towards appointed moments.[22]

Here the Woolfian style is put to a very un-Bloomsbury-like purpose — to the demonstration of the novel's epigraph, 'Men make history; but not as they please'. The sentence construction makes subjects of inanimate objects (sun, earth, time, clocks), in a style resembling the 'Time Passes' section of *To the Lighthouse*, in order to emphasize the 'inexorable' movement towards May Day itself.

If Virginia Woolf's writings seem to constitute one available literary model, then so equally does Graham Greene's novel, *It's a Battlefield*, although here it is not so much a question of stylistic resemblance as of *May Day*'s seeming to offer itself as a kind of answer to the questions and doubts of Greene's novel. *It's a Battlefield* was published in 1934 and used elements of a cross-sectional perspective to present a range of representatives of different social groups, all involved in the fate of a bus-driver convicted of killing a policeman during a political demonstration in which the Communists have played a leading part. Greene's central metaphor of a battlefield is explained in his prefatory quotation: 'Insofar as the battlefield presented itself to the bare eyesight of men, it had no entirety, no length, no breadth, no depth, no size, no shape, and was made up of nothing except small numberless circlets commensurate with such ranges of vision as the mist might allow at each spot.'[23]

Greene's view of social organization is one familiar to students of early twentieth-century European fiction — recalling particularly Joseph Conrad in its lack of assured moral perspectives and in the ironic failures and self-deceptions of his characters. *May Day*, again with the London busmen's movement as a background element and a political demonstration foregrounded, uses the battlefield metaphor very differently, implying clarification rather than confusion. The opening section writes of London's people: 'These fragile shreds of flesh are protagonists of a battle, a battle where lives are wasted, territories destroyed, and populations enslaved. Every true story of today is a story of this struggle.'[24] This view of battle as a clarifying metaphor is confirmed early in the novel as James Seton (a character as close to a hero as the novel permits) reflects: 'Now these streets breathed to him the air of a battlefield. Here, in the shadows of the factory chimney, amidst the pulsating rhythms of millions of lives, once more he felt clearheaded, potent and full of purpose.'[25]

The final demonstration and the struggle outside the factory gates bring together all the elements of John Sommerfield's London, focusing the meaning of his battlefield, while in Greene's novel the confusion of the demonstration which precedes the opening of the novel is maintained throughout.

Despite this fundamental difference the novels do, however, share one particularly striking structural element — the use of newspaper headlines as a way of linking disparate groups of characters into a common experience,[26] and the implicit view of the newspaper as a new unifying and organizing social principle. This appears to have been an idea that informed much thinking, of various political persuasions, about the nature of urban society in the 1930s. In *May Day* the headlines are seen as providing an opportunity for collective experience: 'A million looks glanced upon these words understandingly, with varying thoughts, no two quite the same yet no two altogether different.'[27]

To turn from this passage to the opening lines of the introductory pamphlet, *Mass Observation*, is to recognize a similar mode of social analysis. The pamphlet opens with a newspaper headline about the abdication and then continues:

> Confronted with these headlines, a nation of fifty millions gasped in astonishment . . . . At last England had to face a situation to which there was no stock response. Millions of people who had passed their lives as the obedient automata of a system now had to make a personal choice, almost for the first time since birth.[28]

The role of newspapers here is two-fold. They are illustrating the fact that a situation of importance common to all exists; but also they are the agency that effectively generates the existence of that situation by making knowledge of it commonly available. For Mass Observation, it was the collective nature of the response that was of prime interest; Jack Lindsay noted that *May Day* had a collective hero and so, too, with Mass Observation: 'Collective habits and social behaviour are our field of inquiry, and individuals are only of interest insofar as they are typical of groups.'[29]

It was because both John Sommerfield (in *May Day*) and Mass Observation were focusing on the collective as the central point of interest that for both the term 'mass' became of particular importance.

In recent years the word 'mass' has had something of a bad press on the Left (apart from certain defences of it in relation to the work of some members of the Frankfurt school); it has been associated mainly with 'mass culture' and 'mass communications' theory which seeks to simplify the analysis of modern society, often at the expense of the concept of class. Twenty years ago Raymond Williams gave the word a very hard time in the conclusion to *Culture and Society*; he saw it partly as a way of seeing people as objects: 'I do not think of my relatives, friends, neighbours, colleagues, acquaintances as masses; we none of us can do. The masses are always the others, whom we don't know, and can't know.'[30] — and partly as a means of controlling the social system. 'The idea of the masses, and the technique of observing certain aspects of mass-behaviour — selected aspects of a 'public' rather than the balance of an actual community — formed the natural ideology of those who sought to control the new system, and to profit by it.'[31] This criticism, in particular, was one which had already been levelled at Mass Observation in the late 1930s; however John Sommerfield's use of the term in *May Day* was rather different from any of the uses noted by Raymond Williams.

In *May Day* the term 'mass' is important in its validation of the novel's technique of presenting reality as a collective experience; 'mass' implies the fact of a collective reality and the possibility of a collective organization. 'Mass' is both the analysis of a problem and its (revolutionary) solution. The factory-owner perceives the collective power of his workers as a threat:

A scene that fascinates him and yet one that he half fears — the workers in a mass, held together by a silent, unspoken force . . . . They are people who call him 'sir', who are sometimes timid before him, sometimes defiant, but who always face him with an unspoken, half acknowledged anger and resentment of the power that he has over their lives. But when they are together, in a mass, they exhale a sense of their own power, that deeply disturbs him.[32]

The experience of being a part of the mass is seen, for the workers, as potentially liberating: it offers a fuller life that can be had as a single individual. Elsewhere the novel tries explicitly to reconcile the two terms — 'mass' and 'individual' — in an account of the factory-girls:

Taken individually they were just a lot of ordinary, silly, laughing girls, some noticeably prettier or uglier than most, a few more full of vitality, a few more lustful, a few harder or kinder than the rest. But also the whole lot of them together shared in a group consciousness: beyond their own individuality was their individuality as a mass . . . .[33]

The mass is, crucially, not amorphous, but has a specific and positive identity; often this is associated with the collective experience and organization of the work place, particularly the factory. In one of the summarizing sections a conventional (by the mid-1930s) image of urban life is invoked:

In the morning the factories are magnetic points attracting vast converging streams that, taken over a large area at any given instant, will seem to be moving quite motivelessly. In the evening they are centres of dispersal from which pour hundreds of thousands of men and women in great tides that are quickly scattered and whose identities as masses are lost.[34]

This image (of crowds in London seen as water — 'flowing' or 'streaming') has often been given a negative connotation in twentieth-century writing,[35] but rarely for the reasons given here. The individual's losing his individuality in such a crowd is the usual lament; for John Sommerfield, positive identity is collective and not individual, and it is precisely the crowd's dispersal that constitutes a loss. The crowd, or mass, is positive — particularly in the final section of the novel during the march, James Seton reflects: 'Now I am quiet, I am serene. I sink my identity into the calm quietness of this waiting crowd, I am part of it, sharer in its strength . . . and the solution of my conflicts is bound up with the fate of this mass.'[36] Also in the final section the fears of the factory-owner are reiterated in a conversation with his son: ' "I like the working-class . . . but when they are together in a mass something gets into them, they become quite different, frightening somehow. Don't you ever feel that?" he asked abruptly in a different tone. "I'm just repelled by *any* large mass of people," said Peter. "It's a kind of agrophobia with me." '[37] Peter's sensitivity is an index both of his existence in a world consisting of his own individual fantasies, and of a failure to face the reality on which his life is built — collective labour. The May Day march acts, within the novel, as a means of making explicit that which was previously only latent — (this is the function of the juxtaposition of the ordinary and everyday with the extraordinary); it forces Peter to face the reality of factory existence and political struggle and it gives the marchers an opportunity to experience theit collective strength: 'They feel something strong within them, something huge and strong, an emotion that transcends their separate individualities and joins them into a single conscious mass.'[38]

In *May Day* John Sommerfield uses 'mass' then to suggest how collective consciousness and political strength should grow directly out of the living and working conditions of urban industrial society; it is, of course, not a matter of a purely spontaneous growth, but one aided and directed by the Communist Party — a party whose strength is presented as being its close relation to the working-class experience.[39] This use of 'mass' as a signifier of a positive social force is one to which Raymond Williams does not give enough weight, and one towards which Mass Observation was itself rather ambivalent.

As I have indicated, Mass Observation's concern was with collective experience and behaviour as observed by and within individuals. For Mass Observation, 'mass' seems to have had a number of connotations which are listed briefly below:

1 *New Social Conditions*. The railway has 'rendered possible mass activities — the Cup Final, the monster rally, the seaside holiday, the hiking excursion.': 'Since 1900 the daily newspaper, the radio and the film have all been busily celebrating the enormous field, until now a peak of mass-publicising has been reached.'[40] The implications here are clearly that a new kind of society had arisen in the twentieth-century for which the term 'mass' was particularly appropriate. The emphasis is on the increased amount of collective behaviour and common experience.

2 *Mass as the 'Common Man'*. 'There is a widespread fatalism among the mass about present and possible future effects of science, and a tendency to leave them alone as beyond the scope of the common man.'[41] The mass as the 'common man' whose behaviour was to be observed, as the object of study, constituted perhaps the

most central meaning of 'mass' for Mass Observation. There is a parallel to be drawn here with the use of the term in a *London Mercury* editorial of May 1936 which argues for the importance of 'proletarian literature': there it anticipates 'the enrichment of literature by the introduction into it of a new sort of awareness that has never yet permeated it, derived from the subterranean depths of the insufficiently explored mind of the inarticulate masses.'[42] It would be somewhat unfair to identify Mass Observation fully with this kind of formulation, but the anthropological language does find a parallel in Mass Observation statements of intent, and in the key influence of Tom Harrisson.

3 *Mass as Observers*. The mass were not only the observed but, ideally, also the observers; great emphasis was placed on the work of the 'untrained observer, the man in the street'.

4 *Collection and Organization of Material*. The aim of the Mass Observation project was to 'patiently amass material, without unduly prejudging or preselecting'.[43] For the 1937 Coronation Day study the Observers provided a 'mass of data, which had to be sorted, indexed and filed'.[44] This raised a very difficult problem of analysis and of presentation.

5 *Mass as Public*. This was in some ways a peripheral category and in some ways the most important in its completion of the circle. The initial pamphlet speaks of 'the masses to whom its studies are addressed.'[45]

The term 'mass' in Mass Observation did not, for public consumption at least, have any of the political, revolutionary, overtones found in *May Day*.[46] However what John Sommerfield and Mass Observation did share was the technical problem of how to organize and present the reality of this collective social world. The words of Storm Jameson seem particularly appropriate to Mass Observation (with their problems of 'a mass of data, which had to be sorted, indexed and filed'), 'the number of documents is infinite — how are they to be presented?'. One answer given by Mass Observation lay in concentrating on the significant and unusual public event:

> Everyday the social consciousness is modified by the news reported in the newspapers or on the wireless. The more exciting the news, the more unified does the social consciousness become in its absorption with a single theme. The abdication of King Edward VIII was a focusing point of this kind. The coronation of King George VI is providing another'.[47]

The pamphlet went on to announce the publication of two surveys — one on 'a normal day on which nothing of importance took place' and the other on Coronation Day itself; the outcome of this was the book *May 12, Mass Observation Day Survey*. Like the novelists Greenwood and Grassic Gibbon, but more particularly John Sommerfield, Mass Observation grasped at the idea of juxtaposing the normal everyday pattern with the experience of the exceptional collective occasion as one solution to their problems of presentation.

May 12 does exhibit a number of detailed parallels with *May Day*.[48] In both there is the focus on one important day with accompanying sections on the preparations for it and on a contrasting 'normal' day. In *May 12* the internal organization of the presentation of the day surveys, with the sequence of short reports from different observers scattered throughout London (and the whole country), contains a similar aim to that of *May Day* — to avoid focus on the individual and present the mass. The novelist allows himself a more elliptical form of organization than the social survey — particularly in trying to give a sense of simultaneous happenings at different parts of the city:

Here are some more things happening now: Peter Langfier was waking up with a headache . . . .

James Seton was talking politics with two firemen off the *Corinthia* in the reading-room of the Sailors' Home.

The Earl of Dunbourne was being shampooed.

Bill Riley's mother was having her temperature taken.

Jean, the Langfier's maid was repelling the advances of Henry McGinnis, the chauffeur.[49]

The list is organized to make a particular political point, but it still has something of the surrealist feel to it of Humphrey Jennings's famous list of subjects for study by Mass Observation:

Behaviour of people at war memorials.

Shouts and gestures of motorists.

The aspidistra cult.

Anthropology of football pools.

Bathroom behaviour.[50]

As with this list *May Day* at times seems to parody itself in the attempt to be inclusive in the presentation of all aspects of social behaviour. After describing the simultaneous activities of a burglar in the West End and a hungry child in Finsbury Park, the novel announces: 'In these three seconds 7,283 more souls are asleep.'[51]

In *May 12* simultaneous events are presented less spectacularly, but often with attempts at an equal precision. Reports are timed to the minute to allow the comparison of different accounts of life in London at 7 o'clock in the morning or 11 o'clock at night.

One final similarity between *May Day* and *May 12* refers back to a point already noted — the confusion between and convergence of novel and documentary techniques in the 1930s. *May Day* closes with two extracts — purporting to be from a London evening paper and a Communist Party document respectively — condemning and celebrating the May Day demonstration which has formed the novel's climax. Similarly the first section of *May 12*, dealing with Coronation preparations, closes with two extracts from *The Times* and the *Daily Worker* respectively, celebrating and criticizing the Coronation spectacle which is about to take place. As with all these points of comparison, it is worth recalling that *May Day* was published over a year before *May 12*.

May Day and *May 12* developed similar forms of presentation because they faced similar problems. The most fundamental problem was that of how to combine the detailed particularity required by Montagu Slater ('the things as they are'), by Mass Observation ('the lesson is to stick to the facts') and by the naturalistic novelist — (Grassic Gibbon's failure was in lacking 'this vital and absolutely essential knowledge' of the feelings and reactions of the industrial worker) — with a synthetic and generalizing perspective, which 'goes beyond the facts and discovers the truth' (Sommerfield), reveals the 'relations between things' (Jameson) or would achieve what Mass Observation more guardedly called 'co-ordination'. *May Day* is a novel which, in the context of its political perspective, deserves credit and attention for its answers to this problem.

Notes

1 M. Slater (1935), *Left Review*, May 1935, 364–5.
2 S. Spender (1936), *Left Review*, November 1936, 779.
3 S. Jameson (1937) *Fact*, No.4, 1937, 11.
4 S. Jameson, *ibid*, 15.
5 S. Jameson, *ibid*, 18.
6 The debate about the values of 'showing things as they are' was central to much Left artistic practice in the 1930s. In 1932 Workers' Theatre Movement had argued that:

> The naturalistic form, namely that form which endeavours to show a picture on the stage as near to life as possible, is suitable for showing things as they appear

on the surface, but does not lend itself to disclosing the reality which lies beneath. And it is just this reality existing beneath the polite surface of capitalist society that the Workers' Theatre must reveal.

This passage is taken from a 1932 conference statement reprinted in *History Workshop*, No.4, Autumn 1977, 131.

7 *Mass Observation*, London, 1937, 42–3.

8 G. Orwell (1968), in S. Orwell and I. Angus (eds) *Collected Essays, Journalism and Letters of George Orwell, Volume II: My Country Right or Left.* Secker & Warburg, London. This passage is taken from p.59 of the Penguin edition, 1970.

9 Again see Workers' Theatre Movement's slighting reference to other Left groups who had 'the belief that it is their mission to bring the working class into contact with 'great' art (i.e. capitalist art)', *History Workshop*, No.4, Autumn 1977, 129.

10 For the development of these arguments see S. Laing's (1973) article on Walter Greenwood in *Working Papers in Cultural Studies*, No.4, University of Birmingham.

11 *Left Review*, February 1936.

12 J. Sommerfield (1936) *May Day*, Lawrence and Wishart, London.

13 *Times Literary Supplement*, 13 June 1936, 499.

14 *Left Review*, January 1937, 915.

15 *New Statesman*, 16 May 1936, 772.

16 *Left Review*, May 1936, 403.

17 D. Mellor (1977), 'Humphrey Spender and the Visual Imagination of Mass Observation'. The article is contained in the catalogue to the *Work Town* exhibition of Spender photographs, Gardner Centre Gallery, University of Sussex, 1977. An earlier version of this article was delivered as a paper at a symposium held to mark the opening of the exhibition.

18 J. Sommerfield, *op. cit.* 28–9.

19 J. Sommerfield, *ibid*, 157.

20 J. Sommerfield, *ibid*, 52.

21 J. Sommerfield, *ibid*, 93.

22 J. Sommerfield, *ibid*, 70.

23 G. Greene (1934), *It's a Battlefield* London.

24 J. Sommerfield, *op. cit.* 4.

25 J. Sommerfield, *ibid*, 35.

26 Both Greene and Sommerfield use the idea of making the headlines tell particular stories which develop throughout the respective novels. The nature of these stories signify in relation to the authors' social analyses — Greene's tell of a murder and of Ramsay Macdonald's travels; Sommerfield's of an international air-race: 'The world is being girdled, the world is being changed: it grows smaller, it grows larger: men change the world and the world makes men to change it.' (J. Sommerfield, *ibid*, 73). Airmen were frequently symbols of social progress in the 1930s, and not just on the Left — see the 'rule of the airmen' in Korda's 1935 film *The Shape of Things to Come*.

27 J. Sommerfield, *ibid*, 36.

28 *Mass Observation*, 9.
29 *Mass Observation*, 30.
30 R. Williams (1958), *Culture and Society 1780-1950*, London. The passage is from p.289 of the 1961 Penguin edition.
31 R. Williams (1958), *ibid*, 301.
32 J. Sommerfield, *op. cit*, 19.
33 J. Sommerfield, *ibid*, 149.
34 J. Sommerfield, *ibid*, 170.
35 See T.S. Eliot (1922) *The Waste Land*, Faber & Faber, London; or C.F.G. Masterman (1909), *The Condition of England* (1909).
36 J. Sommerfield, *op. cit*, 212.
37 J. Sommerfield, *ibid*, 224.
38 J. Sommerfield, *ibid*, 241.
39 This discussion of *May Day* has not placed it as fully as is necessary in the context of the Communist Party in the 1930s. The meaning of 'mass' in *May Day* should clearly be understood in relation to the ideas of the Party on organization, and indeed the novel does give a valuable (idealized?) account of Party organization in the period. John Saville 'May Day 1937', in A. Briggs and J. Saville (eds) (1977) *Essays in Labour History 1918-1939, London* has recently reminded us of the difference between Labour Party and Left celebrations of May Day in the 1930s, and noted that the Chairman and Secretary of the May First committee for 1937 were Communists. His article suggests that the May Day march was of particular significance to the Party in allowing them to assume the leadership of a mass working-class demonstration. John Sommerfield's novel can be placed usefully in the context of these points (the issue of whether to join the Labour Party march, on the first Sunday in May, or whether to leave work to join the Communist-organized march on 1 May itself is debated by workers within the novel). *May Day* should certainly be read by any researcher into the Communist Party in the inter-war period.
40 *Mass Observation*, 19.
41 *Mass Observation*, 16.
42 *London Mercury*, May 1936, 1.
43 *Mass Observation*, 29.
44 *May 12, Mass Observation Day Survey*, London, 1937, 4.
45 *Mass Observation*, 41.
46 Although it should be noted that John Sommerfield himself became a Mass Observer for a time, when he joined Mass Observation in Bolton in 1937 after his return from Spain.
47 *Mass Observation*, 30.
48 John Saville notes that the London busmen's strike, which began on May Day 1937 'was felt by many on the May Day processions [to be] a fitting counter to the environment of bunting and tinsel that was celebrating the abdication of Edward VIII and the accession of George VI and his intelligent wife.' ('*May Day 1937*', 233.)
49 J. Sommerfield, *op. cit*. 137.
50 *New Statesman*, 30 January 1937.
51 J. Sommerfield, *op. cit*, 109.

6 POPULAR FICTION AND THE NEXT WAR, 1918–39

Martin Ceadel

Oxford Street, Piccadilly, the Mall, Trafalgar Square, the Strand, Fleet Street, Ludgate Hill, were carpeted with the dead. The entrance to every tube station was piled high with the bodies of those who had made one last mad effort to escape from the poison gas. In the City itself the Bank of England had been blown to pieces and in the narrow streets in the neighbourhood the stench was appalling . . . .

A wave of panic-stricken humanity, fleeing from the first bombs dropped by the raiding aeroplanes had stampeded inland; and this human wave had met another wave which had come running from London. At those points where the collision had taken place, fighting between the two panic-stricken mobs must have occurred . . . And then had come the rush of poison gas and the fighting and confusion had become suddenly stilled.[1]

Despite recent interest in the literature of the inter-war years and its relationship to the politics and society of the period, the prolific genre of prophetic and alarmist 'next war' fiction, of which the above passages are typical, has not merely been neglected, but ignored. Even I.F. Clarke's seminal study of *Voices Prophesying War 1763–1984* focused primarily on the didactic literature of the pre-1914 period and, secondarily, on the post-1939 era.[2] This was understandable in view of the fact that none of the inter-war novels in the genre was a best-seller; none, moreover had the immediate political impact achieved by the pre-war invasion scares, or haunted the imagination as lastingly as the Orwellian satires or the science fiction of the atomic era. Nor, with the possible and partial exception of the two most famous and reputable examples, Harold Nicolson's *Public Faces* (1932) and H.G. Wells's *The Shape of Things to Come* (1933), were they redeemed by literary merit. Indeed most of the novels were appalling and dreadful in both the original and modern senses of the word: readers coming upon them today are likely to be appalled more by the wooden and stereotyped characterization of the hero, the villain, and — normally superfluous except for the mandatory love-interest — the heroine, than by the dreadful air raids, gases, death rays, and unbridled destruction which were the staple ingredients of the plots.

Yet there are two related reasons why these examples of second-rate fiction merit a brief examination. Firstly, as contemporary historical evidence they shed light on attitudes to war, and especially on public fears and expectations about the nature of an impending World War, particularly about the role to be played by air bombardment. As historians of British defence policy have recently emphasized, the Air Ministry's astonishingly exaggerated faith in the war-winning power of a strategic air offensive was accepted by successive governments almost to the extent of neglecting the fighter defences that were to save her in the Battle of Britain. In part this was because of the public mind's obsession with the bomber.

But could evidence for this obsession be more profitably and pleasurably found in writing of higher literary quality? After all, most literature-and-society studies, and especially the increasingly common inter-disciplinary courses on this theme at universities, start from the assumption that the most historically significant aspects of a period will be conveniently and clearly reflected in its best literature. But in the case of inter-war Britain the answer — and, therefore, the second justification for this essay — is that to a surprising extent the unprecedented and all-pervasive fear of war is *not* clearly and straight-forwardly reflected in the major literature. In contrast the domestic issues, in particular the radicalization of politics and the social effect of the depression, can be easily related to the work of major writers such as Auden, Spender, Orwell, Warner and many others. Where these writers did deal with international affairs — most notably, of course, the Spanish Civil War — they seem to have treated them as an advance warning of the intensifying struggle between extreme Right and Left which Britain might itself undergo; in other words Fascism was treated as an internal disease rather than as an external military danger. This perspective still, moreover, conditions recent academic work on the literature of the period: the best recent study, for example, focuses on the domestic politics and is surprisingly unsure on the subject of fear of war.[3]

Why is this? The answer seems in part to be that some proponents of the literature-and-society approach have had an insufficient historical grasp of the periods they are studying and are simply ignorant about attitudes to war. What is more, they seem to have adopted too unsubtle a view of the way that good literature 'reflects' society: they have expected it to be self-evidently 'about' the major social and political issues. In the absence of any literature obviously of this sort about warfare, they have ignored the issue despite its historical importance. What they should have done is look for the many indicators of concern about air power, for example, to be found in the literature of the twenties and thirties which is not directly about fear of war. A major book of this type remains to be written; but this essay will not practise what it preaches. It will merely offer a *reductio ad absurdum* of the 'direct reflection' approach by examining the only 'literature' which can be said to be about the coming war in the same way that, for example, *The Road To Wigan Pier* is about unemployment.

Precisely to define and delimit this next-war genre is not easy since, as will shortly be noted, it encompasses three separate types of writing, one of which is the limitless field of science fiction. But an adequate working definition is provided by a reviewer in *The Times Literary Supplement* who wrote wearily in 1936 of the 'many novels forecasting the destruction of the next war. Most of them try to make our blood run cold by describing the effects of aerial bombardment and poison gas of awful potency'. Of the more than eighty futuristic novels I have examined, more than half can be regarded as falling into that reviewer's category of 'just another prophecy about the next war'[4] and, therefore, form the basis of this essay. Not included, however, either in these figures or in the essay, are foreign novels on this theme; also excluded are two other neglected types of popular fiction: stage plays dealing (sometimes allegorically) with the international situation,[5] some of which became popular on the London stage, particularly in 1938;[6] and political novels[7] (often dramatizing the struggle between liberalism and more extreme ideologies), which frequently included incidental speculation about the coming war.

The roots of the genre of the next-war novel can be traced back to the beginnings of a market for popular fiction in the last third of the nineteenth-century, in which three clear strands of prophetic or speculative fiction can be detected. The first, of which the best examples were the invasion scare stories of the 1870–1914 period — prompted by anxiety at the Bismarckian upheaval in Europe, at the Channel Tunnel proposals and, later, at the more concrete threat of German rearmament — can be called defence alarmism, since their purpose was to call attention to threats to national security. The second, in which future scientific developments were extrapolated as the basis for a good yarn, can be classified as a form of science fiction. Its most influential nineteenth-century exponent was Jules Verne, but the writer who is often regarded as his English equivalent, H.G. Wells, soon lost interest in futuristic speculation for its own sake, despite the brilliance of his predictions of mechanized warfare and the atomic bomb. His real interest lay in the question of whether man's social and moral evolution could keep pace with scientific advance, and his work falls, therefore, into a third category, anti-war moralism, which was more concerned about the threat of modern scientific warfare to the very survival of mankind than about Britain's defences or man's technological ingenuity.

Each of these strands was clearly detectable in the inter-war period, although there was an increasing tendency for novelists ot depict war in such extravagantly destructive terms that their books simultaneously preached the deficiencies of existing defences and the evils of war itself, whilst also overbalancing into science fiction. In part this was because of the technological advances of World War I, which seem to have left the public imagination in the early 1920s convinced that some sort of death ray would soon be invented. Even Winston Churchill, who had been commissioned to write on the future possibilities of war for *Nash's Pall Mall* magazine in 1924, approached his friend Professor F.A. Lindeman with a serious inquiry about 'the deadly ray'.[8] Lindeman, an Oxford physicist, impressed him with his vision of electricity playing a leading role in a future war, and in his article Churchill wrote that 'a vista opens up of electrical rays which could paralyse the engines of a motor car, could claw down aeroplanes from the sky and conceivably be made destructive of human life or vision'.[9] If an experienced warrior and statesman like Churchill could speculate in this way, it was not surprising that throughout the inter-war period novelists produced tales of atomic energy, flying submarines, tunnels dug from Japan to South America down which an invading force of super-tanks was sent, and flesh-factories for fabricating artificial soldiers to serve as the canon-fodder of future wars.[10]

This study will, as already suggested, ignore pure science fiction, except where it becomes impossible to disentangle from defence alarmism or anti-war moralism, in order to focus on the novels which were responses to what was believed to have been nothing less than a revolution in warfare set in train by World War I. For the English civilian, to whom wars had already previously been away-fixtures, even the limited Zeppelin and Gotha bomber raids of World War I seemed to mark a qualitative and irreversible change in the purpose of war, whereby the breaking of the enemy's civilian morale had replaced the defeat of his armed forces as the first military priority. As historians of air power are agreed,[11] two raids on London on 13 June and 7 July 1917 panicked the Cabinet into a premature commitment to the view that a long-range strategic bombing force would be the major weapon in any future war. This view was soon elevated into a doctrine by Sir Hugh Trenchard, head of the Royal Air Force — which was itself, of course, set up precisely to fulfil this strategic role and whose very survival as an independent institution thus depended on continued belief in the decisiveness of air bombardment.

The impact of this revolution in warfare on the novels can be introduced by establishing some continuity with the pre-war genre through two of its leading exponents whose work straddled World War I, H.G. Wells and William le Queux.

H.G. Wells' work shows remarkable consistency between his pre- and post-war novels — a consequence of his having as early as 1908 published the first and definitive air-power novel *The War in the Air*. Written before Blériot had flown the Channel, it had prophesied that an abrupt end to, and reversal of, what had previously been regarded as the inexorable progress of modern civilization would be administered by a bombing war launched by the airships and experimental aeroplanes of the Great Powers. Understandably, the book was re-issued in 1921, with a new preface in which Wells ignored the book's moral message in order to point out how far he had anticipated the change in warfare from an affair of 'fronts' to one of 'areas'.[12]

The abruptness with which this new strategic orthodoxy forced writers less far-sighted than Wells to switch from tales of invasion to tales of air power can be illustrated by the publication, also in 1921, of *The Terror of the Air* by that most skilful exploiter of invasion fears, William le Queux, author of *The Great War in England in 1897* (1894), *The Invasion of 1910* (1906), and other tales. The title referred to a mysterious and prodigious pirate seaplane which had solved the technological problems that made aeroplanes inferior in certain respects to airships: it was entirely silent and could stay airborne for weeks, thanks to its ability to liquefy air by processing radium. But only the technology had changed since pre-war days, for le Queux's plots still depended on the well-tried formula of German-led conspiracy. The pirate 'plane, which bombed the cities of the world, including London and New York, with aerial torpedoes, food-contaminating gas, and leaflets declaring its ostensible purpose to be the overthrow of capitalism and the social order, was in fact controlled by 'the uncivilized and uncivilizable Junkers of Prussia' who were bent on avenging the Treaty of Versailles. Significantly, the hero, who — using another new invention, radio — tracked down and destroyed the pirate 'plane, was the head of the British air force. When taken in conjunction with the novel's explicit reference to Germany's Gotha raids on London in 1917 and to the RAF's offensive on the Rhine towns in 1918, this indicates how Le Queux's novel was, in effect, propaganda for the Trenchard view that air power would dominate any future war.

More precisely, Le Queux's depiction of Londoners panicking under air bombardment, especially in the East End and Soho where 'Jews and foreigners' were concentrated, illustrated a particular corollary of the Trenchard doctrine that was taken up by novelists in the immediate post-war period: a realization that success in a bombing war pre-supposed that one's own nationals would not crack first. In the aftermath of the Russian Revolution, and with the novel-reading middle class making the acquaintance of the Bolshevik menace at the same time as the air danger, it was not surprising that in the early 1920s air war and revolution were widely linked by novelists.

A notable example was Hugh Addison's *The Battle of London*, which was written in 1920 although not published till 1923. Addison professed both 'the frank intention of shocking what the friends of Red Russia call the *bourgeoisie* into a realisation of the only means of meeting revolution if and when it should arise', and the subsidiary intention 'to give some idea of what a modern air raid on London would be like'. His story depicted a weak British government faced with a revolutionary armed uprising led by two Russian Jewish Commissars. The revolutionaries were acting in cahoots with the Germans — an interesting anticipation of the real-life secret Treaty of Rapallo — who launched a bombing attack with 'squadrons of heavy triplane bombers, many-engined and carrying huge torpedoes, and bombs of devastating power . . . led by a group of swifter and smaller aeroplanes' — a rare fictional acknowledgement of the vital role the escort fighter was to play twenty years later. However, since the revolution had been swiftly crushed as soon as the no-nonsense Liberty League had been allowed to put the boot in, Britain was not caught unawares. Though Westminster was destroyed by the German raid, the British, who had made wise preparations since World War I, were able to launch a decisive counter-assault. Berlin went 'through torment beyond imagining. For half an hour the pitiless rain of huge projectiles had fallen on Berlin, blotting out whole areas and causing incalculable damage and heavy loss of life'. Thousands died when a single air torpedo obliterated an entire railway station packed with Berliners trying to flee into the countryside. Their 'lurid hell' was exacerbated by bewilderment: 'They could not see — because London had been bombarded — why Berlin should be bombarded in return. It had for long been accepted that in times of international stress one of the chief functions of England's capital was to be a passive target for her bombs. There had been nothing in their experience to teach them that London might fight back.'

By describing 'the one-day war' in such loving detail Addison was propagating the Trenchard view that the known vulnerability of London made a strong British strategic bombing force the number one defence priority. Even without the sharp post-war cutback in defence spending to exacerbate inter-service competition for resources, it is inevitable that this analysis would have been challenged by the Army and, in particular, by the Navy. The resulting public debate over the relative effectiveness of new weaponry over old — which often degenerated into an emotional disagreement over the continued utility, or otherwise, of the battleship — was fought out also in novel form in the mid-1920s.

In 1926, in particular, there appeared a crop of crude fictional contributions to the air power versus sea power debate. Several of these were from the pen of a retired naval constructor, E.F. Spanner, who combined a strong belief in air power with the conviction that the Navy should control it. His first novel, *The Broken Trident*, was set in 1931. In that year the complacent British Prime Minister, Stacey Balgrove (who was clearly not a million miles away from the real Prime Minister of 1926, Stanley Baldwin), paid the price for concentration on the obsolete capital ship at the expense of the air force. Germany, ruled by the New Nationalist Party which was bent on overturning the Versailles Treaty, brushed aside the puny British air force, launched a paralysing but humane air attack on industrial and military targets, and sank the Royal Navy, before imposing a generous and lasting peace. 'They had broken Britannia's trident, but did not wish to bow her head', Spanner concluded, clearly hinting that Anglo-German partnership against Bolshevism was to be preferred. His military thesis, that air power was so important that it should be entrusted to the Navy, was made even more explicit in the second book he published that year: *The Naviators*, in which Australia was saved from invasion by the Japanese through an air force developed by the Navy in preference to its obsolete capital ship. It ended with the explicit moral: 'What utter and hopeless folly to persist in arguing Sea Power versus Air Power, when all the time the so obvious course is to unite these two great arms. And if united, how better than as "the Navy"?'

Also in 1926, another advocate of air power, this time a former soldier, Captain Frederick Britten Austin, published a collection of short stories dramatizing modern theories of warfare under the title *The War God Walks Again*. Carrying a solemn preface by General Sir Ernest Swinton (the well-known tank-pioneer who had just become Professor of Military History at Oxford and was himself author of a propagandist military novel),[13] the book's various scenarios depicted the total mechanization of armies through the development of 'land ironclads'; the use of gas shells to quell revolutionary uprisings; and — in a story that is unusual for its specific emphasis on the need for fighters — the ability of a strong air force, equipped with gas bombs, to win a future war without calling on the two senior services. Yet these stories cannot be dismissed as products of a novelist's febrile imagination; they were dramatizations of ideas that were being currently put forward by Britain's leading military theorists. For example, the most striking chapter in Britten Austin's book, describing the capture, intact and with insulting ease, of a force of battleships by the use of gas dropped from carrier-based aircraft, was an almost exact illustration of a passage in *The Reformation of War*, a serious and influential study which the pioneer tank commander, J.F.C. Fuller, had published in 1923.[14]

This belief that gas bombing might enable war to be fought in future with fewer casualties — like E.F. Spanner's assumption that precision bombing of military and industrial targets could decide wars without the need to bomb civilians — represented what might be called the optimistic school of next-war prophecy, which — it is now easy to forget — had influential adherents in the mid-1920s. As a professional soldier, J.F.C. Fuller seems to have hoped that modern science would give renewed scope to imaginative generalship after the frustrations of World War I; and, as a crude social Darwinist who was to become a pillar of the British Union of Fascists, he had particular reason to hope that what he conceived to be the inexorable and constructive human struggle for survival between 'supermen' and 'supermonkeys' could be prevented from escalating into the race suicide of another war. But his rejection of the prevailing sentiment that gas was an atrocity whereas bullets and shells were relatively humanitarian also found support on the other extreme of the political spectrum from J.B.S. Haldane, the distinguished scientist and Communist.[15]

Yet despite so varied an endorsement, and despite the irrefutable statistical evidence that gas had caused fewer deaths than conventional weapons during World War I, the public mind firmly resisted all optimistic views about modern war and refused to regard gas as anything other than the ultimate obscenity in the god of war's armoury. A majority of novelists agreed too; as one put it: 'sling, arrow, arquebuse, burning oil, flint-lock, cannon rifle-gun, T.N.T., flame-thrower, and last, his final triumph — gas'.[16] But perhaps it is not surprising that the public refused to stop worrying and learn to love gas, when it is remembered how terrifying even an optimist like J.F.C. Fuller could make a 'humane' gas war sound:

> I believe that, in future warfare, great cities such as London will be attacked from the air, and that a fleet of 500 aeroplanes each carrying 500 ten pound bombs of, let us suppose, mustard gas, might cause 200,000 minor casualties and throw the city into panic within half an hour of their arrival. Picture, if you can, what the result will be: London for several days will be one vast raving Bedlam, the hospitals will be stormed, the city will be in pandemonium. What of the government at Westminster? It will be swept away by an avalanche of terror. Then will the enemy dictate his terms, which will be grasped at like a straw by a drowning man. Thus may the war be won in 48 hours and the losses on the winning side may actually be nil.[17]

Taking their cue from expert 'optimism' of this sort, novelists took up gas warfare almost to the neglect of other types of weapon. This reflected a public obsession with gas which historians have tended to overlook but which was neatly summed up in E.M. Forster's contemporary comment that 'war has moved from chivalry to chemicals'.[18] A classic example of the gas novel, which appeared in 1926, was *Nineteen Forty-Four* by the second Earl of Halsbury. Though a barrister by training, Halsbury had done detailed work during World War I on the technicalities of air bombardment, at first as a member of the Air Department of the Admiralty, and by the end of the war as a Major in the newly-formed Royal Air Force.[19] In the 1920s he became the Cassandra of the gas menace, and his novel prophesied that in 1944 the Russian dictator, Kernin, would launch a perfidious series of air raids on the rest of Europe, using a colourless, odourless, but deadly gas. Britain, which, having ignored the warnings of the wealthy landowning hero, Sir John Blundell, MP, was defenceless and unprepared, soon collapsed into a state of total anarchy in which the population reverted to cannibalism. However, the Chinese attacked Russia, precipitating a world conflict which ended with hopes of a new world order emerging out of the resultant chaos.

Halsbury's novel was written out of serious concern for Britain's vulnerability and with the benefit of some, albeit out of date, inside expertise. And it was taken seriously by some at least: David Davies, the coal millionaire and ex-M.P. who regarded himself as an international affairs specialist, thought that, as a 'description of what is coming to us', it was 'restrained rather than exaggerated'.[20] Yet the novel can scarcely be distinguished from either science fiction or Wellsian anti-war moralism. In the international calm of the 1920s, when Germany was still disarmed and — bombing ranges being what they were — when France was the only possible air threat to London, it was hard to specify a realistic political and strategic dimension for a war story. But what made it particularly hard to stop seriously intended propaganda shading off into exuberant fantasy was the temptation, which seems to a greater or lesser extent to have affected even the most authoritative military analysts in the inter-war period, to neglect the existing limitations of the new offensive weaponry on the grounds that the pace of scientific advance would soon enable it to fulfil its destructive potential. Thus in his preface, which has already been mentioned, to Britten Austin's *The War-god Walks Again*, Sir Ernest Swinton had noted with approval that the book's intention was to 'awaken the national conscience' to the fact that 'the methods of waging war, far from having reached finality or having become stereotyped, are in reality more than every in a state of flux and liable to change'. And, similarly, when a 1935 novel postulated that in nine years time

Russia would be able to launch a pre-emptive strike against Britain with colossal, bullet-proof bombers with which the R.A.F. could cope only by ramming them with special fighters equipped with ejector seats, before sending off its own bombing force to attack Moscow, a retired Air Vice-Marshal, Sir Vyell Vyvyan, could endorse it in a foreword which cautiously pointed out: 'In view of the rapid advances that are taking place in the speed, range and carrying capacity of aircraft, it would be a bold person indeed who would say that the main outline of the story is at all fantastic'.[21]

With scientific licence thus compounding artistic licence it was inevitable that, in certain hands, the genre became so extreme in its predictions as to acquire an apocalyptic tone. A few authors who were making painful personal attempts to come to terms with post-war conditions were attracted to write about the next war because it could serve as a modern morality play's secular hellfire, deservedly visited upon a sinful world. One such writer called himself Martin Hussingtree, being in fact Oliver Baldwin, the unhappy and eccentric son of the Conservative leader. Having embarked on a period of travel and adventure after the doubly-unsettling experience of schooling at Eton and service on the Western Front, the restless Oliver found himself agreeing to serve as military adviser to the Armenian Army. Captured and imprisoned by the Turks, who thereupon handed him over to their allies, the Bolshevik Eleventh Army, he spent five months in captivity facing imminent death — an experience which gave him a mystical faith 'not in churches or priests or candles, but a Protective Power of Infinite Beauty'.[22] On his sudden release he found his nerves had been affected, and while recuperating he became converted to left-wing socialism and embarked on his novel, *Konyetz* — 'The End' in Russian. Published in 1924, this told the tale of Bolshevik aggression which, starting in Trans-Caucasia and aided by the machinations of the Jews of Europe and by the destructive power of gas, high-explosive bombs, shells filled with arsenic powder, and death rays, swept across Europe until finally England, whose socialist government was too trusting towards Bolshevism, was bombed and invaded. At this point politics gave way to mysticism, and after earthquakes and volcanic eruptions all the awful prophecies of the Book of Revelations were explicitly fulfilled.

A similar version of war as a judgement on mankind was expressed two years later in another oddly-entitled novel *Ragnarok* — which means Armageddon of the Gods in Scandinavian mythology, according to the author, Shaw Desmond, whose philosophy of life was less conventional even than Oliver Baldwin's. Brought up a strict Irish Methodist with an obsessive fear of hell, he had rebelled firstly against his religion, secondly against his comfortable job in the City, which he left in order to work for the ILP journal, the *Clarion*, and thirdly against the Labour movement itself for the loss of idealism which accompanied its increased political success.[23] He ended up as a spiritualist and a believer in reincarnation. *Ragnarok: A Novel of the Future* (1926) can be read as an illustration of modern theories of war: it contained references to J.F.C. Fuller's opinions, and put forward the view that a 'single airman in a single poison plane was worth a hundred army corps'. But the author's real purpose was to spell out the doom of a bankrupt civilization, and it was for this that he invoked wireless-operated planes, vomiting gas, atomic rays, and long-distance aeroplanes capable of being refuelled by submarines, which between them destroyed most of the world, and reduced Londoners, in particular, to an underground race living in the sewers and tube tunnels, eating mushrooms and battling for survival with the rats. The moral was explicit: 'White Civilization had died because man had made God in the image of a machine, had bowed down and worshipped him'.

Most writers were attracted to the genre, however, not because they had a message to impart, but because it seemed a commercially rewarding formula. This was undoubtedly the reason for the appearance in 1931 of what may be regarded as the definitive gas novel, *The Gas War of 1940* by 'Miles' — one of the pseudonyms of the prolific novelist, Stephen Southwold, who wrote most of his books under the name Neil Bell. Southwold, a struggling author living from hand to mouth, wrote the book at the suggestion of Henry Williamson, who had been intrigued by his passing reference in a science fiction story[24] to the Gas War of 3–10 September 1940, in which 150 million people died. His venture into science fiction had been a commercial flop, but his detailed account of *The Gas War of 1940*, which he published in May 1931 — by which time the death toll had increased tenfold to 1,500 million victims — sold 100,000 copies in all, despite indifferent reviews.[25]

Later, Southwold was to claim predictive significance for the fact that his story featured a Nazi–Soviet pact and that his world war started on the same day — albeit a year later — that Britain declared war on Germany. But that was as far as prophetic plausibility went, for the novel assumed that Britain — by 1940 a dictatorship — was merely one victim of a ghastly world gas war triggered off almost by spontaneous combustion out of the post-Versailles tensions, in which — with a fine disregard for real national strengths — a triumphant role was played by the Greek, Chinese, and Mexican airforces. This latter force attacked both New York, killing two million people in twenty-two minutes, and Rome — although, as one reviewer unkindly pointed out, the author's neglect of time-zones meant that his Mexican planes would have had to fly far faster than the futuristic 500 mph with which he endowed them in order to arrive an hour before they started out.[26] Having arrived, moreover, these prodigious aicraft dispensed gases of a nastiness that can be gleaned from this brief description of one of the book's many air-raids: 'A youngster had the face wiped off him down to the skull, nothing left in front but his teeth. And he was alive and screaming for several minutes'.

Appearing as it did in May 1931, *The Gas War of 1940* owed its relative success partly to its timing. Although in the absence of reliable and comprehensive sales figures[27] such judgements are tentative, it seems that in the 1928–30 period, when the novels and memoirs about World War I were in full spate, there was a temporary decline of public interest in next-war literature even from the modest level of the early and mid-1920s. But by 1931 revelations of trench life were drying up and attention had firmly shifted to future wars, particularly as a result of the progressive deterioration of the international situation that became evident after the outbreak of the Manchuria crisis in September 1931. More important for the revival of next-war literature, however, was the announcement in January 1931 that the long-awaited World Disarmament Conference was finally to meet at Geneva in February 1932. This was the signal for the peace movement to bring to a climax its disarmament campaign, in the course of which reputable scientists and politicians made predictions about future wars that seemed to corroborate much of what the novelists had already claimed, and therefore to stimulate more writers to take up their pens.

The next-war novels of 1931–3, the years in which disarmament was being seriously discussed by governments, fell for the most part into the category of anti-war moralism. Scientific marvels were described not, as in the 1920s, primarily to warn against the Prusso–Bolshevik conspiracy, fight inter-service battles, adumbrate the apocalypse, or boost sagging plots, but to draw attention to the problem of unrestrained scientific competition in the means of destruction.

In marked contrast to the optimistic view of science which prevailed before 1914, many novelists now saw it as essentially dangerous. In 1932 — the year in which Aldous Huxley published his pessimistic satire on the scientific planning of society, *Brave New World* — John Gloag, the distinguished writer on architecture and design, published his first novel in order, as he remembered it forty-five years later, 'to wake people up and end the stupid belief that science must always be beneficient'.[28] His book, *To-morrow's*

Yesterday, described an attempt to alert people to the danger of war through an avant-garde film depicting the regression of human civilization to primitive tribalism and eventual extinction as a result of the World War of 1997 in which remotely controlled French aeroplanes drop gas bombs on Britain. The author's explicit thesis was that the 'mechanical accomplishments' of the twentieth century were too much for a civilization whose international relations had not progressed out of the eighteenth century, and the book ended with the film's warning having been ignored and an air raid by an unspecified enemy beginning.

Fear that the scientists of one nation might develop a supreme weapon enabling it to terrorize its rivals was the theme of two other novels published in 1932. In *Empty Victory* by George Godwin, a barrister, novelist and pacifist, a Cambridge scientist discovered the secret of 'a gas so powerful that one part to ten million of air produces instantaneous death' and, before dying, passed the secret to the Prime Minister. But in the enlightened Britain of the 1950s the incumbent of that office who was thus entrusted with this lethal secret was a Quaker pacifist, who decided to suppress it. But rumours of the discovery spread to the other nations of Europe and the French (arbitrarily chosen by Godwin to be the aggressors 'rather than fall back upon the Ruritanian device') launched a pre-emptive air strike on London because they were convinced that, behind the ingenious façade of a pacifist government, Perfidious Albion was secretly manufacturing the gas. The French killed 950,000 Londoners in one hour with their own 'arsenic fog' (eighteen times the real figure of 58,000 Britons killed by air attack during the whole of World War II) and then invaded Britain. Godwin's pacifist message became explicit as he described how 'defeated' Britain became a more compassionate, classless and productive society, while the 'victorious' French became ever more demoralized until they finally abandoned their occupation.

More satirical in tone was Harold Nicolson's rare but successful venture into fiction, *Public Faces*, which he wrote in the spring of 1932 to earn some money, drawing for his setting on his diplomatic experience, for his characterization on his acquaintances, and for his central idea — the explosion of an atomic bomb — on his own imagination and the technical assistance of the scientific journalist Gerald Heard.[29] Apart from rewarding his centrist political friends by postulating a political realignment in which the Churchill–Mosley coalition was beaten at the polls by a Centre Block consisting of Noel Baker, Hore-Belisha, and others, the novel focused on the diplomatic consequences in June 1939 of the British discovery, on an island in the Persian Gulf, of a mineral which made possible the rocket plane and the atomic bomb. The League of Nations demanded the internationalization of the island, and a political crisis in the British cabinet ensued, in the course of which the Air Minister exploded the atom bomb on his own initiative. A futuristic epilogue suggested that the bomb had set up climatic changes, moved the Gulf Stream, and helped to end capitalism.

Nicolson's anticipation of the atomic bomb occurred in the year (1932) that has been described as 'the *annus mirabilis* of nuclear physics'[30] because of the splitting of the atom and the discovery of the neutron in that year. By the outbreak of World War II enough theoretical nuclear physics had been published for the possibility of a bomb to be recognised by novelists, some of whom were even investigated for possible security leaks when the Manhattan project began to close the thirty-year gap between scientific practicality and fictional fantasy.[31] With novelists — even in Germany — able to spot the implications of freely-available technical research, leading scientists became alarmed at the danger of nuclear technology falling into totalitarian hands, and from 1939 onwards they made attempts to see that Germany did not win the atomic race.[32]

The possibility that the international scientific profession might attempt, on its own initiative, to prevent its inventions being used against the interests of justice and peace was a solution to the problems of the arms race which had strongly appealed to novelists during the disarmament period. It was one form of the Fabian (or Wellsian) conception of the expert elite imposing correct solutions on an indadequate world, but by the early 1930s it was accepted that things were going to have to get far worse before the experts could start to make them better. Thus the catalyst for the eventual imposition of peace-by-scientist in Bernard Newman's 1931 novel, *Armoured Doves*, was the horrific Russo–Polish War of 1942 in which bacteriological warfare was used — a surprisingly unusual occurrence in a genre dominated by gas. Newman, who was one of the writers to predict an atom bomb and fall, therefore, under security suspicion (which was perhaps not surprising since he was a civil servant who wrote prolifically in his spare time),[33] gave his novel an overt peace message, partly because he was anxious, as was his publisher, Victor Gollancz, to correct the impression gathered from his one previous novel by some critics, that he was insufficiently anti-war.[34] He used the events leading up to the 1942 war to make amusing political predictions about real politicians — notably Oswald Mosley, whose Labour Government was brought down in a war scare by a mass demand for Winston Churchill as war leader — but his main purpose was to trace the career of the hero, Paul de Montigny, who though English-educated had been born (with obvious symbolism) as the result of the rape during World War I of a French lady by a German officer. Furnished in this way with impartial blood, Paul became a brilliant scientist and invented a 'peace ray' capable of immobilizing all electronic and metallic equipment, which enabled the League of Scientists of his creation to defeat attempts by Italy to attack France in 1954, and by Germany and France to go to war in May 1961.

A variant on this Wellsian theme was put forward in 1933 in *Man's Mortality*, whose plot seemed to be prompted by the widely discussed disarmament proposal for the abolition of all military — and the internationalization of all civil — aviation, since it dealt with the development of an international civil aviation authority into a full world government. The novel is interesting mainly as an attempt to keep up with changing public preoccupations on the part of its author, Michael Arlen, whose best-known novel, *The Green Hat* (1924), had so neatly caught the fashionable mood of the 1920s that it had been a best-seller.

Man's Mortality suffered also from being overshadowed by a novel on a similar theme by the maestro himself, H.G. Wells. Having (in 1930) toyed with the device of a peace gas in his unsuccessful political satire, *The Autocracy of Mr Parham*, Wells three years later produced his best known novel in the inter-war period, *The Shape of Things to Come*. Written after the Nazis had come to power, it predicted a horrifying world war, arising out of a trivial incident in Danzig between Germany and Poland in 1939: a Pole with recalcitrant false teeth was shot dead by a Nazi who thought he was making faces at his uniform. But for Wells (in what was in some respects a more didactic updating, after a quarter of a century, of *The War in the Air*) the debilitating war was significant not for itself, but as a solvent of the irrational old order which, he argued, would give way, after a period of post-war chaos and the gradual accumulation of authority by the technicians in control of vital services such as the transport combines, to a planned scientific Utopia. The novel thus reflected Wells' characteristic but complex blend of short-term pessimism — he declared explicitly that progress had come to a halt in 1933 — with long-term optimism about science. This blend proved too subtle to adapt well to the screen and, despite three attempts at writing a screenplay, Wells was never satisfied with Alexander Korda's film version, *Things to Come*, which was released in 1936.[35] His views were so crudely dramatized as to lose all appeal, and the public's interest in the film seems to have focused on its visual warning of the short-term physical and social dislocation to be expected in an air war.[36] The film was, moreover expensive to make and lost money, which perhaps explains the surprising reluctance of film-makers to venture into the visually exciting field of next-war prophecy.

A shift from moralizing about the longer-term consequences for mankind of failure to disarm to worrying about the imminent threat of war can be easily detected in the novels as they took cognizance of the nature of Nazism and (particularly after the German walk-out from Geneva in October 1933) of the collapse of the Disarmament Conference. The flood of novels that appeared in 1933–4 differed from previous novels in two respects. Firstly, although Germany was rarely actually named as the aggressor, there was no longer any suggestion that France would be the enemy and only the very occasional suggestion that it would be Russia. Secondly, there was a growing questioning of the deterrent value of the bomber, reflecting the re-opening within government circles of the immediate post-war debate over the use of air power — a debate which, however, ended with the same decision: to implement the programme of air force expansion recommended by Trenchard a decade previously but which had been postponed for economic reasons. For their plots these novels of 1933–4 depended on two ingredients: jitteriness about the possibility that current international tension might lead to a 'bolt from the blue' — a pre-emptive air strike to knock out London; and the material and social disintegration that Britain would suffer as a result.

Ladbroke Black's *The Poison War* (1933) — the source of the horrific description of the bombardment of London with which this essay began — opened with England totally unaware of the danger of a war that would overwhelm it within hours. Indeed the only advance hint was news of a world coconut shortage — coconuts having been used in World War I for box-respirators against gas. That very night, however, and without any warning, the 'Central Powers' launched a raid on London, provoking a terrified mass trek into the countryside which precipitated a struggle for survival in which Englishmen killed each other for food and only the army maintained any discipline. Although the novel focused on this social chaos, it put forward a clear military thesis: the mechanized British Expeditionary Force — making a rare appearance in such novels — was annihilated on the Continent by a superior bullet; and a British airman who had returned from a costly but effective counter-attack on the enemy confirmed that the RAF had been forced into this policy of reprisals by the impossibility of defending London in any other way.

In 1934 the same ingredients — an international crisis erupting into war by fear alone and resulting in Britain and her enemy both being reduced to anarchy — were given a more political treatment by

Frank McIlraith and Roy Connolly in *Invasion from the Air: a Prophetic Novel*. Professing a serious anti-war purpose, the book incorporated documentary material about the likely nature of a future war, and cast Germany as the villain 'because, with the coming of the Nazi regime, there has been a deepening of the European crisis which may express itself in another world war with France and Germany as the leading combatants'.

The novel thus dramatized the very real public unease, following the collapse of the Disarmament Conference, about whether Britain's Locarno commitments would entangle her in a Franco-German quarrel; and it began with what in 1934 was a real worry, a crisis in the Saar, where French occupation under the terms of Versailles was due to expire early in 1935. The debate within Britain over whether to intervene — which enabled the authors to indulge in the satirical conventions of the *roman à clef* — was, however, cut short by a German bolt from the blue. The effects of the various German gases and the indirect effect of what the authors called 'gas fear neurosis', reduced the population to violence and revolution. The British dropped their own 'Breath of Death' gas on Germany, with similar results, but although the governments called a halt to the war on the eleventh day of the crisis, the irony was that by then they had lost control of their countries.

Whether offence was the only defence, or whether Britain would have made better use of the money spent on her air force by converting her sewers and underground railways into a comprehensive shelter system, was debated at length by cabinet ministers, press lords, journalists, and other characters in the first half of *Exodus A.D.: A Warning to Civilians,* published in 1934 by the novelist Princess Paul Troubetzkoy in collaboration with the well-known war artist, C.R.W. Nevinson. In the second half of the book an international crisis, caused by the death of an international financier, led for no very clear reason to the bombardment of Britain by gas and high-explosive bombs, which — largely owing to unnecessary panic — reduced the population to savagery: within two days starving men were ripping live chickens to pieces and consuming them raw. The book thus came down in favour of deep shelters as the only policy for suvival — a moral that was graphically endorsed in another novel of 1934, Moray Dalton's *The Black Death*, in which a group of ordinary British holidaymakers emerged from a visit down into the Cheddar caves to find themselves the only survivors of an impressively efficient German gas attack.

As civilians began thus to feature as the front-line heroes of next war novels, it became clear that for the first time that another war would be, to quote the title of another 1934 novel, a *War Upon*

Women. Written by Maboth Moseley, a self-styled specialist on women's subjects, this allegory about a war-crisis provoked by a Mussolini-style Ruritanian dictator toyed, among other ideas, with the argument that women could prevent war by refusing to have children. The ability of women to prevent war was taken up by other novelists, perhaps because the updating of Aristophanes' *Lysistrata* offered one of the few humorous perspectives onto an increasingly grim subject. George Cornwallis-West's 1935 melodrama, *The Woman Who Stopped War*, took its cue from the liberated role of the post-war woman. The beautiful war-widowed heroine swallowed her pride and became the mistress of an armaments millionaire in order to finance her women's peace movement, which — at the appropriate time — declared a general strike of the economically indispensable women workers, thus halting a war crisis and saving Britain from a gas that 'rots you into black filth if ever you breathe a drop of it'. In Eric Linklater's *The Impregnable Women*, published three years later, women withdrew labour of a different sort and a world war was halted by an international sex-strike led by Lady Lysistrata Scrymgeour, wife of a British cabinet Minister.

In general, however, the tone of the genre became understandably less whimsical as World War II approached. Although some technological romances of the sort common in the 1920s still appeared — such as Joseph O'Neill's *Day of Wrath* (1936), which depicted an extravagantly futuristic world gas war in 1952 — the category of defence alarmism made a notable come-back. Hitler's claim in March 1935 that the Luftwaffe had already attained parity with the RAF seems to have caused novelists finally to lose interest in the Trenchard doctrine, and two other pre-occupations came to the fore in the second half of the 1930s: predicting the likely *casus belli*; and, more especially, warning of the need for better air raid precautions.

One of the most successful adventure stories incorporating prophecy was the trilogy of novels published by Sidney Fowler Wright, an accomplished thriller writer and editor of *Poetry* (later *Poetry and the Play*). The first part, *Prelude in Prague: A Story of the War of 1938*, was published in 1935 and predicted a crisis in 1938 between Germany and Czechoslovakia after the former had already taken over Austria. Wright failed, however, to anticipate Chamberlain's peace initiative and his crisis led to war between these two countries, with an inadequately prepared Britain agonizing over whether or not to intervene. The second part, *The Four Days War* (1936), revealed that Britain did intervene but, handicapped by inadequate defence measures and by a secret Russo–German Pact, suffered heavy German bombing.

Having exhausted the predictive possibilities of the European situation, the final novel, which appeared late in 1937, reverted to being a conventional story of the activities of an English secret agent during the war, which — in contrast to the assumptions of earlier 'bolt from the blue' novels — still continued, despite Britain's ordeal by fire, high explosive, and gas in the opening German air raids. Indeed London was rebuilding improved air defences and the whole civilized world was uniting against Russia and Germany. The title of this third part — *Megiddo's Ridge*, which means Armageddon — was justified by its cliff-hanging climax, with the forces of good and evil poised for a final decisive air battle.

Despite this apocalytic ending, despite the speculations about freezing gases and nerve-powders, which — seemingly — no thriller writer could resist, the trilogy clearly reflected a serious and increasingly realistic awareness of the deficiencies in Britain's air raid defences. Wright's claim on the dust-jacket of *Four Days War*, that his work was 'not intended in any way as a prophecy but rather as a warning of the danger in which England lies and must continue to lie until she has been adequately equipped for her own protection . . .', was borne out by his incorporation into his story of references to the use of decoy-lights to deceive enemy bombers, the evacuation of cities, the need to give the production of anti-aircraft guns priority over gas masks, and — most graphic of all — the lynching of Glasgow's socialist city councillors for having failed to implement the government's air raid precautions scheme.

This new concern among novelists for air raid precautions was an almost immediate reaction to the government's first A.R.P. proposals in the summer of 1935. For Frank Fawcett, the epitome of the hack novelist whose output was at times as high as a novel a fortnight,[37] these official proposals, and the derision they provoked, provided a ready made plot that he laced with gruesome speculations about gas raids, which would leave the pavements spattered with 'pieces of lung-tissue . . . like over-cooked meat in a devil's stew'. His 1935 novel, *Air-gods' Parade*, which he wrote under the name of Simpson Stokes, concerned an MP's campaign for 'air-locks' — huge air-tight shelters which he considered the only true protection, particularly for children, against gas.

The novel's cover and frontispiece featured a gas-masked mother and child alongside a monkey and its baby, drawn so as to make the masked humans ape-like, and captioned 'Twentieth-century culture'. In the late 1930s the ugly and dehumanizing gas-mask became for the novelist and the artist a vivid symbol of the horror of war. In 1937, for example, Sarah Campion, daughter of the historian G.G. Coulton, wrote a book debating in fictional form the validity of pacifist views; she entitled it *Thirty Million Gas Masks*, and in it the debate was resolved symbolically and pessimistically by the facifist heroine committing suicide by removing her gas-mask during an air raid.

By 1938, however, faced with the evidence of the Spanish Civil War that high-explosive (and incendiary) bombing was more likely than gas, novelists began to advocate precautions against these more easily imaginable menaces. One was the much-decorated World War I hero, Captain A.O. Pollard, who had won the VC, MC and DSM, but then found peace too much for his nerves until he found a niche as a writer of thrillers.[38] In his 1938 crime novel, *Black Out*, an anti-air-raid-precautions league turned out to be a cover for gangsters; and in his war thriller published in the same year, *Air Reprisal*, 15,000 Londoners were killed in three raids by the Vandalian air force and the book's hero was made to lament his apathy in not having trained as an ARP warden. An interesting feature of the book, before it relapsed into a straightforward adventure, was the realistic moderation, by the standards of the genre, of its casualty figures, and its belief that anti-aircraft guns and fighters would play a significant role.

By 1938 also, Shaw Desmond had significantly revised his former opinions about the nature of the war that would be visited as a judgement upon a sick civilization. Instead of the reduction of London to a colony of starving sewer-dwellers as the result of a gas attack, which — as has already been noted — he had prophesied twelve years previously in *Ragnarok*, his 1938 novel, *Chaos*, explicitly rejected the widespread view 'that whole cities would be wiped out in a twinkling of an eye'. The war he now described 'was all so different from what had been anticipated' being a more conventional war of attrition involving trench warfare, naval battles, and prolonged air raids with which the population of East London learned to cope — although Desmond could not resist his customary apocalyptic ending, complete with atomic rays and cosmic changes.

A similar reaction against the idea of the knock-out blow can be found, also in 1938, in Eric Linklater's otherwise whimsical novel, *The Impregnable Women*, which criticized 'the prophets and the experts' for believing 'that the next war, though unbelievably horrible, would be almost incredibly short'. His novel suggested rather that, partly because of better air raid precautions, the war would outlast the opening air raids and end in 'a return to the conventional use of trenches and the orthodox principle of attrition'. Although going too far to the other extreme, Linklater was right to dissent from the exaggerations of next-war prophecy, though he still accepted that war would begin with a bolt from the blue: 'They were wrong when they pretended that there was no defence against aerial attack, and wrong when they said the majority of people everywhere would be defeated by panic. They were right only in foretelling a sudden beginning to the war. In this, on which they had all agreed, they were pitilessly accurate.'

It was not just novelists, but virtually all Englishmen, who suffered from the masochistic egotism of assuming that the Luftwaffe had been designed especially for them and would, therefore, be directed against them as the opening move of the war. This assumption was made in what was otherwise the most accurate of the fictional 'forecasts of what may be coming to us'.[39] This was *What Happened to the Corbetts*, published in the Spring of 1939 but written late in 1938 by Nevil Shute, a professional engineer who had just ended an eight-year stint as managing director of an aircraft factory and wanted to use this inside knowledge to warn a gas-obsessed public 'of the devastation that would be caused by high explosive or by fire'.[40] Shute's emphasis was on the mundane but often neglected hazards caused by the collapse of essential services — in particular, the danger of disease. In his novel the high-flying enemy bombing force, navigating by the stars, made repeated raids on Southampton, where the Corbett family lived. The sewers were hit, cholera broke out, and food distribution broke down, creating chaos from which the Corbetts escaped on their private boat. Politically, however, the novel was more complacent: while the Navy safeguarded Britain against invasion, world public opinion united in revulsion against the 'unnamed' nation which launched this aerial atrocity.

One thousand free copies of Shute's novel were given away by his publisher to A.R.P. workers, and those who read it would indeed have been given advance warning of the breakdown in local services in Southampton in November–December 1940, which proved one of the most serious episodes in the Blitz.[41] Shute's detailed analysis of the Corbett family's problems was both more chilling than the exuberant exaggerations of earlier novels, and proved to be a better prediction of what was to come. Nevertheless it still combined political optimism with the genre's characteristic failure to notice the difficulties in delivering a sustained bombing offensive.

Indeed, taken as a whole, the genre neglected, except for the occasional reference in the later 1930s, the mundane problems of navigation, bomb-aiming, repairs and crew-training that were to afflict all bomber forces — but then so too, it could be pointed out, did the Air Ministry to a surprising extent. The key factors of the air war — radar and the need to establish air superiority by engaging the defence fighters with escort fighters — were also missed. Nor despite their enthusiasm for cataclysmic horrors, did the novelists predict the most murderous horror of the war — the fire-storm raids — although they could claim credit for anticipating the atom bomb. Perhaps their major failure, however, was their inability to foresee how limited was the contribution air power would make to the overall war. With few exceptions (such as Nevil Shute's belief in the continued importance of the Royal Navy) the Army and Navy were normally mentioned only in order to demonstrate their obsolescence: and the obsession with air power seems to have made the novelists somewhat blasé about the dangers of invasion, in marked contrast to the pre-1914 period.

The genre's main mistake had been to extrapolate warfare too far into the future on the basis of the rapid pace of air power's early development, whereas in the event World War II was to break out before it potential had been consolidated into an effective and fully practical weapon. Nor was this mistake compensated for by literary success; its failings in this respect being too obvious to need comment. More surprisingly, however, its imaginative vision was often blinkered: it could fantasize about future scentific marvels, while still assuming that society and its institutions would remain unchanged so that, for example, the people would still follow the progress of these future wars by such technologically primitive means as the afternoon editions of the newspapers.

But this limited imagination improves their value as documents of inter-war history, by showing that the books were concerned not with the future as such but with the threat of air war to society as it then stood. It might be objected that trying to derive evidence of popular attitudes from such a stereotyped genre is like assuming that an interest in crime novels is a sign of a society alarmed about law and order, when it is probably more true that it is the escapist response of a society that feels tolerably secure about its police system. But the conventions of next-war fiction were not stylized and timeless. It was only in the inter-war period that the genre developed its particular obsession with the bomber and gas attack, and this can be shown from numerous other sources to be a major public concern — indeed one such piece of evidence is the marked reluctance of reviewers to criticize these novels for exaggeration and alarmism. What is needed now, therefore, is a study of how this public concern was more subtly reflected in literature which, unlike the neglected novels dealt with in this essay, was not written especially for the purpose.

Notes

1 L. Black (1933), *The Poison War*, 252,269.
2 I.F. Clarke (1966), *Voices Prophesying War 1763-1984*. It contains,

however, a useful bibliography, based on his earlier work, *The Tale of the Future* (Library Association Bibliographies No.2, 1961).

3 For example, in his otherwise excellent book, *The Auden Generation: Literature and Politics in England in the 1930s* (1976), Samuel Hynes seems to believe that there was no writing about future war before 1929–30, and also fails to understand important distinctions between different strands of thinking about war, such as that between the Peace Ballot and the Peace Pledge Union. See 61,100,194.

4 *Times Literary Supplement*, 12 December 1936, 1033.

5 Such as Beverley Nichols, *Avalanche*; Robert Sherwood, *Idiot's Delight*; Bernard Shaw, *Geneva*; Leonard Woolf, *The Hotel*(never performed); and Karel Capek, *Power and Glory*.

6 See *Peace News*, 25 June 1938; 17 September 1938.

7 Such as Storm Jameson, *In the Second Year*; Joseph Gordon Macleod, *Overture to Cambridge;* Barbara Wootton, *London's Burning*; Geoffrey Gorer, *Nobody Talks Politics* — all published in 1936.

8 M. Gilbert (1976), *Winston S. Churchill, Volume V: 1922–1939*, 50–1.

9 M. Gilbert, **ibid**, 61–2.

10 See respectively: 'J.J. Connington' (pseudonym of A.W. Stewart, Professor of Chemistry at Belfast), *Nordenholt's Millions* (1923); E. Van Pedroe Savidge, *The Flying Submarine* (1922); Gawain Edwards, *The Earth Tube* (1929); and Philip George Chadwick, *The Death Guard* (1939).

11 See, for example, N. Frankland, *The Bombing Offensive Against Germany* (1965), 32–3; Barry D. Powers, *Strategy Without Slide-Rule: British Air Strategy 1914–1939* (1976), 52–8, 94–5.

12 Writers on Wells have not always made clear that this preface represents his *post* World War I interpretation of the book's significance; *e.g.* I.F. Clarke, *Voices* (1970 edn), 100–1; T.H.E. Travers, 'Future Warfare: H.G. Wells and British Military Theory, 1895–1916', in Brian Bond and Ian Roy (eds), *A Yearbook of Military History*, I (1975), 75.

13 E. Swinton (under the name 'Backsight Forethought') (1903) *The Defence of Duffer's Drift*.

14 Compare *The Reformation of War* (1923), 146–7, with *The War-God Walks Again* (1926), 167–204.

15 See J.B.S. Haldane (1925), *Callinicus*, 5,32–3.

16 G. Godwin (1932), *Empty Victory*, 260. For an explicit repudiation of the Haldane view about gas, see Princess Paul Troubetzkoy and C.R.W. Nevinson (1934), *Exodus A.D.: A Warning to Civilians*, 29–31.

17 J.F.C. Fuller, *op. cit*, 150.

18 *Spectator*, 17 March 1933, 368–9.

19 N. Jones (1973), *The Origins of Strategic Bombing* is dedicated to his memory. I am grateful to the 3rd Earl of Halsbury for informing me of the small collection of papers in the R.A.F. Museum relating to his father's work during the Great War (at which time he was known by the title Viscount Tiverton) which give a fascinating insight into the origins of the exaggerated picture of the effects of air bombardment.

20 Davies to Halsbury, 6 Jan. 1931, Davies of Llandinam Papers, National Library of Wales.
21 L. Pollard (1935), *Menace: A Novel of the Near Future.*
22 O. Baldwin (1932), *The Questing Beast: An Autobiography*, 128.
23 He is probably best known now for his 1921 book *Labour: The Giant with the Feet of Clay*. This account is based on his 1951 autobiography, *Pilgrim into Paradise*.
24 'Miles' (1930), *The Seventh Bowl.*
25 See N. Bell (1955), *My Writing Life*, 129–33, 145–8.
26 *The Times Literary Supplement*, 25 June 1931, 512.
27 My systematic efforts to find out sales figures have been largely unsuccessful, but I am grateful to the following publishers for their help: George Allen & Unwin, Barrie & Jenkins, Constable, Peter Davies, Duckworth, Eyre Methuen, Victor Gollancz, Robert Hale, George G. Harrap, Hodder and Stoughton, Hutchinson, and John Long.
28 Letter from John Gloag to the author, 20 April 1977.
29 Nigel Nicolson (ed) (1966), *Harold Nicolson: Diaries and Letters 1930–1939*, 115–9.
30 M. Gowing (1964), *Britain and Atomic Energy 1939–1945*, 17.
31 A. R. Michaelis (1962), 'How nuclear energy was foretold', *New Scientist* No.276, 1 March 1962, 507–9.
32 M. Gowing, *op. cit*, 33–4.
33 B. Newman (1960), *Speaking from Memory*, 116–7.
34 B. Newman, *ibid*, 60–4.
35 For the making of this film see N. Mackenzie and J. Mackenzie (1973), *The Time Traveller: The Life of H.G. Wells*, 389–92.
36 See, for example, C.E.M. Joad's comments in *Times and Tide*, 2 May 1936, 630.
37 According to his entry in J.M. Etheridge (ed) (1964), *Contemporary Authors, Volume IX–X*, 147–8. This, and the 1934 edition of the *Authors and Writers Who's Who*, have been useful sources of biographical information for this essay.
38 Capt. A.O. Pollard (1932), *Fire Eater: The Memoirs of a V.C.*, 272–3.
39 N. Shute (1939), *What Happened to the Corbetts*. Epilogue; see also N. Shute (1954), *Slide Rule: the Autobiography of an Engineer*, 246–7.
40 N. Shute, *ibid*, Preface, 2nd ed.
41 See T. Harrisson (1976), *Living Through the Blitz*, 143–80.

7 BRITISH ART IN THE 1930s: SOME ECONOMIC, POLITICAL AND CULTURAL STRUCTURES

David Mellor

I: Modernism in Recession

The economic crisis in the late summer of 1931 — the crisis which led to the formation of the National Government — was to have a direct and immediate impact on many British artists. 'Since the war [World War I] the English school of painters has increasingly tended to live in exile',[1] complained a writer in *The Studio*. This was an exaggeration, but many British upper-middle-class artists had, in the 1920s, settled into a bohemian and cosmopolitan existence in Paris and the South of France.[2] Their idyll was punctured when the National Government, in one of its first acts, suspended the Gold Standard. The painter, Tristram Hillier, encountered this economic reality in Marseilles harbour in September 1931:

> There fell a mortal blow which put an end to all our hopes and dreams. None of us read the newspapers in those days — we were far too busy with our own lives to be concerned with matters that did not directly affect us — and thus we had no inkling of the financial crisis that was shaking the western world. Suddenly we were told that the pound sterling had been devalued in relation to the franc and that its purchasing power would thenceforth be approximately halved . . . the problem now was to find enough money for the bare support of my family.[3]

Under these economic pressures, Hillier was forced to return home and his paintings began to bear the definite, but coded, imprint of his changed circumstances. In 1932 and 1933 their dominant theme was a pronounced melancholy and deprivation. His earlier, more lyrical, pictures celebrated his French idyll through a traditional iconography of harvesters, bedroom nudes, boule players and cubist still lives.[4] This now became dislodged by disconsolate images of beached machinery,[5] ruins[6] and, in Hillier's own words, 'broken chairs, abandoned newspapers and other things evoking (desolation)'.[7]

Hillier's change in iconography was typical of many British artists in the 1930s. Images of loss, abandonment and catastrophe were to recur more and more frequently as the decade continued, gaining reinforcement as an iconography from such imperative cultural commonplaces as industrial dereliction and fears of aerial bombing. There were also, as we shall see, strong counter currents to seek consolation in the homely, familiar British pastoral and a new humanitarianism.

The immediate effects of the economic depression were quickly registered: in January 1932 Paul Nash warned, 'The economic situation of the artist today is distinctly precarious'.[8] The United States slump had already destroyed the flourishing market in contemporary British etchings; so much so, that Graham Sutherland, who was to develop as a major painter in the late 1930s and 1940s, abandoned etching as a livelihood. Another example was the drop in gallery receipts from sales. There were some responses to this. One of the leading London galleries, Tooths, introduced hire purchase terms for paintings by Sickert, Matthew Smith and John Nash, in November 1935, 'to help British artists to sell more pictures and to assist a larger public to purchase them'.[9] The pursuit of a wider public for art, ultimately linking with ascendent Populist ideologies, would be another direction for British art in the 1930s.

This essay is chiefly concerned with the values, attitudes and formal strategies generated by some British artists in the context of the economic, cultural and political environment of the period. We have seen that the devaluation of the pound forced some expatriate artists to return fromthe Continent. One of the key themes of British cultural history in the 1930s, in its relation to British painting, is the tension between internationalism and nationalism. It was a tension felt acutely in the first six months after the National Government was formed. In November 1931 a 'Buy British' campaign, directed from Whitehall, began on a massive scale. In this, and in other things, as A.J.P. Taylor observed, 'the National Government told English people that their own country came first. English people unconsciously drew the moral'.[10] Paul Nash in December 1931 diagnosed a cultural crisis which 'accentuates our insularity . . . . May we not be required next to "Paint British"?'[11]

Paul Nash, Edward Wadsworth and Edward Burra were a few amongst many British artists who had learned from Continental vanguard sources and were in the process of renovating their art through these contacts. Now the onset of the economic and political crisis seemed to open onto a larger cultural crisis in which the anglicization of Continental styles and values was being openly contested by a militant cultural nationalism — as it had at an earlier critical moment in British modernism in the period during World War I. The leading established art magazine, *The Studio*, led the attack with a series of articles in the early months of 1932 around the general title, 'What is Wrong with Modern Painting'. 'Internationalism' was singled out as the first evil when *The Studio* inveighed against the 'denationalised'[12] painter open to estranging alien influences. *The Studio* prescribed: 'Painters would be better advised to stay at home . . . and to study life for a change . . . .

Britain is looking for British pictures of British people, of British landscapes . . . a thorough-going nationalism'.[13]

This conservative statement was, in fact, prophetic and ironically prophetic of much Populist, Social Realist and Documentarist art that was to emerge in the second half of the decade. Yet, in the context of 1932, it certainly reeked to Paul Nash of 'the blustering denunciation and carping of our own reactionaries . . . referring to "British" art as if it only came into being with Protection or to speak of "going" modern as if it were synonymous with going to the dogs'.[14] Nash pondered the question of whether it was even possible in the contemporary intellectual climate to 'go modern and still be British'.[15]

John Betjeman had announced the death of modernism at the end of 1931[16]; and neo-Victorianism seemed an attractive historical Utopia to some,[17] redolent of Britain's golden age. This nostalgic fall into the past was symptomatic of another element in the attack on modernism — the assumption that the onward progress of history was halting. The view was well expressed in the huge tableaux comprised in Noel Coward's *Cavalcade* (premiered in Drury Lane in late Autumn 1931). This reviewed British history with the pious hope for a return to pre-twentieth-century verities. And within the vanguardist camp this kind of regression and disbelief in positive historical progress took root as well. During the economic crisis of 1931, Humphrey Jennings was painting in Paris, making scarf designs for a London firm.[18] He noticed a personal shift away from his own former feelings about progress extending indefinitely into the future. Trying to convey his new thoughts to his wife, he wrote: 'I see no future and that leaves it open. I feel I have always assumed that things would inevitably get better and people more understanding, but [I] don't now — people and things will continue to be stupid and wrong for ever . . .'.[19]

This new wave of cultural pessimism reached a high-water mark with those artists who had been converted in the late 1920s to the optimistic myths of a more hygenic, constructed, essentially 'modern' world, in the area of design and architecture; artists who now recanted in the early 1930s. Francis Bacon had been one; deeply impressed with German achievements — for Germany was being perceived by many in Britain in the period 1927–31 as a 'modern utopia'[20] and Berlin also rivalled Paris as the primary continental art capital. Bacon's designs for geometric, glass, steel and mirrored furniture had been hailed as the epitome of the '1930 Look'.[21] But, by 1933 he had become a painter of grim, miserabilist oil paintings, dragging with him a train of archaic iconographic figures — Crucifixions and romantic ghosts.[22] Bacon's recoiling movement from design to despair, in four years, depended on the eclipse of the promise of Constructivist perfection of the environment. Following the crisis of 1931, no such perfection seemed likely on a cultural, political or economic plane.

Thus functionalism and technology might appear deathly — as it did in Hillier's painting *The Pylons*.[23] The frailty of recent Utopian hopes enshrined in the promise of a modernism now in disruption cast a chill over the visual imagination. In Anthony Powell's 1932 novel, *Venusberg*, the capital of a gloomy Baltic state with fossilized ceremonials, is shown to boast an extensive modernist town planning scheme — a project which, however, has been discontinued, leaving rusty girders and decaying masonry. Powell's protagonists 'seemed to be making their way among ruins of another civilization now passed away and of which there would soon be no trace'.[24] This description of age and ruin paradoxically overtaking the paradigms of modernism could apply to the oils of one of Paul Nash's colleagues, John Selby Bigge. Nash chose Bigge's painting *Leviathan*, of a giant ocean liner, to illustrate one of his articles in *The Listener* in February 1932.[25] On the part of Continental and British architects, painters and writers, there had been a high ideological investment in the image of the liner as a floating Utopia — the prototype dwelling of the future, a model for the community, white, pure and orderly.[26] Moreover, the great liner, in actuality, had become early in the Depression an emblem for the fortunes of national prosperity, as Cunard's first abandoned then resumed work building the *Queen Mary*. Bigge's *Leviathan* is dreamily cross sectioned — gigantic but gutted and unseaworthy, its name carrying connotations of the state and the *Titanic*, resonating political enormity and disaster. Again a utopian icon seemed blocked and negated.

II: The Cultural Politics of Unit 1

But Bigge, with Paul Nash, Tristram Hillier and eight other artists and architects[27] regrouped around Unit 1, formed in 1933, in an attempt to renew and consolidate the mythology of modernism; to renew a myth of progress and the future through, among other things, constructivist 'Design . . . considered as a structural pursuit'.[28] The internationalist creed was also reasserted; . . . 'the spearhead of contemporary European painting and sculpture'.[29] Nash argued that Unit 1's formation was 'a hard defence, a compact wall against the tide' [of Nationalism][30] and Herbert Read echoed the vanguardist vocabulary.[31] The decorum of Unit 1 was to be 'the shape of things to come' from the point of view of art, design and architecture. It was no coincidence that when an exhibition of their work, which had started at the Mayor Gallery in London in April 1934, began its provincial tour in Liverpool in June, it was opened by the science fiction author Olaf Stapledon, writer of *First and Last Men* (1930).

When he had visited Germany in 1929, the art critic William Gaunt believed that architects and designers like Erich Mendlesohn were forming a Wellsian caste of 'intellectual samurai' to build a new future order.[32] The theme of the totally redesigned environment was given a political inflection by a *Punch* cartoon of 1932 which showed John Bull dithering while a futuristic, black-shirted Mussolini pored over models of a reconstructed Rome. When Cabal, the aviator survivor of the old order comes back to reconstruct the ruined world in the Korda film of Wells' *The Shape of Things to Come* (1935) — for which John Armstrong of Unit 1 had done designs — he appears dressed in a uniform close to that of the Blackshirts of the British Union of Fascists.[33] Thus Unit 1's attempt to seize an image of the future from a strongpoint, to break with a conserving and decaying order, was symptomatic of certain other areas in British culture in that moment of 1932–5. The imagination of Unit 1 began to intersect with Mosleyian universe of a 'new' Britain, planified, regulated and unitary. For the most convincing iconography of the future seemed at that moment, to some, to be Fascist in origin (although it would be very soon ousted, in appeal by more 'human' and sentimental, Soviet and Popular Front images). Tristram Hillier's friend, Roy Campbell, who had written the catalogue Foreword for Hillier's 1933 Lefevre Gallery exhibition, praising his severe hard-edged forms, began to adhere to the political extreme Right. And, commenting on Ben Nicholson's proclamation of Unit 1 membership, a reviewer in the *New Statesman* in November 1933 confessed he was depressed by 'this passion for commufascist nomenclature'.[34]

However, in terms of actual voting preferences the majority of Unit 1 members — particularly Moore, Hepworth and Armstrong — were sympathetic to the Labour Party. Yet it was indicative of the contemporary political and cultural conjuncture, that, when Herbert Read produced a questionnaire for Unit 1 in 1933–4, Question 16, on policy, asked: 'Have you any political convictions of a party kind (conservative, fascist, communist)'.[35] Read's range of political choice, on first sight baffling in its omission of the Labour Party, only reflected the actual political conditions of that moment, when, following the National Government landslide in November 1931, the parliamentary Labour Party had been decimated — reduced to 52 seats. In the aftermath of the emergency of 1931, the cultural and political options appeared to be presented, by Read at least, in terms of conservatism or extremism.

'There is nothing naive about Unit 1', Nash wrote, comparing them with the Pre-Raphaelite Brotherhood; 'these [i.e. Unit 1] are a Unit; a solid combination standing by each other'.[36] The connotations of a 'tough' identity was in contrast to the Seven & Five Group, formed in the 1920s, whose 1932 exhibition was denounced for 'effeminacy'.[37] An indication of Unit 1's reputation can be found in Tristram Hillier's memory of a friend of Paul Nash telling him, half jokingly: '.. I saw you the other evening marching your stormtroopers into the Cafe Royal'.[38] An underlying totalitarian ethos was also detected by Brian Howard when he reviewed the book-cum-manifesto in April 1934. ' "Purist", "Purity", "Pure" — they have a familiar, a faintly folk song ring . . . . I am sure there is nothing more dooming in the world than a partiality for Absolutes'.[39] As desired ends, purism and absolutism were, for Nash, part of the vanguardists wish to 'construct, in however apparently small a space, an ordered, independent life'.[40]

Unhappily, Nash and Read's image of Unit 1 as a strategic bastion against conservative 'national' art was being eroded. In his letter to *The Times*, Nash had warned that the tide running against the Unit 1 bastion favoured an indigenous 'British' Culture which would probably take the form of a revival of 'the Nature Cult'[41] — a regression to traditional landscape genres and representationalism. Only two months afterwards he visited the Avebury megalithic remains in Wiltshire, and, fascinated, succumbed to the mystique of the romantic pre-historic landscape. Even as Unit 1 was being organized Nash was, in fact, in recoil, like Francis Bacon, from the ordered, constructed, purist Utopia. Nash's switch to pre-historic models was occasioned by something of the same drive which led Humphrey Jennings to admire pre-historic rock paintings from South Africa, which he had seen exhibited in Paris at the end of 1930. Both Jennings and Nash suspected that the central modernist style, post-Cubist, orderly and architectural, was in disrepair, and might be superseded by a more fluid pictorial space — like that found in the Surrealist organization of a picture — one that, moreover, could allow the representation of myths. Jennings found precisely these qualities in rock painting and in 1931 he forecast a Lawrentian future for modernist art, in terms of regaining the 'heroic sense . . . producing a world of heroic mutations parallel to the heroic proportions of African painting'. This goal of an 'heroic', irrational space, rhythmic, elemental and chthonic, Nash discovered in 1933 at Avebury, albeit framed in a British cultural context of antiquarianism.

Nash retreated into conservative genres — the genres which had previously supported his work before the trauma of the Western Front — the Antiquarian and the Picturesque, supplemented by Surrealist pictorial space. But in 1933 there was a strong cultural drift towards the 'national landscape', foregrounding it as part of the contemporary art repertoire, which was the very 'tide' Nash referred to. In June 1933 Maxwell Armfield exhibited large murals of National Trust properties at the Leicester Galleries in London. Since 1931 the British landscape had been extensively promoted as the location for patriotic holidays into the past, in articles like *Bournes of Pilgrimage in the Homeland*[42] and *Exploration at Home*.[43] Nash's friend and associate Edward McKnight Kauffer had designed a poster, using Braque's style, showing Stonehenge, with the caption *Stonehenge: See Britain First on Shell*, introducing a tie with the new art patrons, the giant petrol industries and public corporations.[44] And in 1934 Graham Sutherland followed Nash's initiative in search of the 'heroic' national pastoral, by painting in the Pembrokeshire countryside and, like Nash, resolving the cultural tension between 'going modern' and 'being British'. *The Studio*'s remedy for 'a healthier and a saner development'[45] in art — the medicine of British pictures of a British landscape — was apparently being followed.

III: Humanitarian Realism and Populism

Despite the significant shifts in Paul Nash's choice of iconography in the first years of the 1930s — from constructivist grids and 'ordered interiors' to nature myths of pre-history and the moon — his formal methods remained more or less the same. He seemed fundamentally concerned with objectified, de-natured aspects — a dry and distant portrayal of things. His paintings were depopulated; as early as August 1926 he set out his position with the statement . . . 'My anathema is the human close-up'.[46]

In the recoil from modernism that had set in, an alternative form took the place of 'alien' geometrics and purism. It was the same 'human close-up' which Nash abhorred. A 'neo-Humanism'[47] (which was favourably opposed by critics to 'mechanism') was expressed by a return to a representational Realistic art which offered moral values of altruism, sympathy, sincerity and consensual truthfulness. This return to Realism consolidated a powerful middle ground in the terrain of British visual culture and repudiated stylistic 'extremism'. Poster designs and photographs which showed the influence of German 'new objectivity' teaching, began to fall out of favour, being resented as 'ugly' and 'kolossal',[48] crude and eccentric.[49] The 1920s heritage of steep-angled, purist, mechanical images that had been resisted by conservative opinion was now checked. 'The late fad for leaning towers, skew-gee compositions . . .

arrangements . . . are making way for representations of persons, things and places as objects of beauty'.[50]

The check came from a complex of sources. It was to be found in the compassionate photo-journalism of Humphrey Spender from 1934; in the portraiture of Howard Coster and Shaw Wildman from 1932; amongst the Euston Road School of Painters especially; in the humantiarian paintings of urban low life by Robert Medley from 1934; and in the Christian Socialist morality play drawings of Arthur Wragg from 1933. Pathos and soulfulness were re-asserted as pictorial values after modernist objectivity. Not only did the 'human close-up' repopulate contemporary visual imagery in a decisive way, but formal means changed from the objective, dead, finish of modernism to more relaxed styles. In the course of 1935 Howard Wadman noticed this tendency in advertizing — 'instead of sans serif, dashing brush script letters . . . and loose and lively drawings nearer to the spirit of charcoal and water colour than the dry precision of the camera and scraper board'.[51] Wadman was a leading apologist for this neo-humanism, which made its first entry in Howard Coster's, publicity photography for the *Daily Herald* in 1931–2. This took the form of posters featuring enormous photographic close-ups of ten-foot-high heads of the *Herald*'s political commentators and colunists, Hannen Swaffer and Sidney Moseley.[52] It was primarily based on Continental — German and Soviet — techniques; but its international derivations Wadman chose to ignore when he introduced Coster: 'He is the modernist who stayed at home. He calls himself, "photographer of men" '.[53] Prominent writers and personalities like Aldous Huxley and T.E. Lawrence had photo-portraits made by him from a realist point of view depicting them as humane and relatively 'ordinary' people.

From 1933 some photographers became convinced that there was a connection between the prevailing socio-economic situation and the Realist style that was being favoured. In another call for cultural 'sanity' — in this case *Back to Sanity in Portraiture*, Paul Tanquerey admitted: '. . . It may be that the depression has had the psychological effect of bringing us hard up against fact and reality'.[54] This was certainly true in the case of Stephen Spender's brother, Humphrey Spender, who trained as an architect until 1933, and then, finding no work, began as a photographer for the *Daily Mirror* as 'Lensman', roaming Britain for photographs of the social scene. There were, of course, limits to the *Mirror*'s desire for realism: it was limited by a picture editor's preference for sentimental social types. 'I had been up to Tyneside and had been rather horrified by what I'd seen there',[55] Spender has said. Some of his pictures of unemployed men in the Special Area were rejected by the *Mirror* as too coarse for publication in the Autumn of 1933.[56] Sentimental constraints also operated on Arthur Wragg's art, beginning in 1933 with a collection of his newspaper drawings[57] that were introduced by the Pacifist leader, H.R.L. Shepherd (who recorded that, when he was first shown them by Wragg, he had to turn away; 'Lest Wragg should observe the lump in my throat'.[58])

But around the end of 1934 this evangelizing, humanitarian, visual code began to assume a political and Social Realist inflection, when the first Artists' International Association (AIA) exhibition was held in Charlotte Street in London. Overtly Marxist in direction, the fortnight long exhibition was called 'Social Conditions and Struggles of Today'. A Soviet influence in aesthetics was now in the ascendent. In the debate on 'Art and the State' in the *Listener* in the Autumn of 1936, the Russian, N. Malyutin claimed: 'Soviet art was naturally humane because its object was man and the masses'.[59] Robert Medley was one of the leftist artists who exhibited with the AIA from the time of its first exhibition. His 1938 oil *The Butcher's Shop* — a street scene with a butcher's shop in front of which a young working-class couple are walking with their children, is a resumé of the new current of social realism — with a flavour of miserabilism in its alternative title, *The Poor are Also with Us*.[60] The well-established painter, Walter Sickert, showed a number of definitely Populist oil paintings at the Leicester Galleries summer exhibition in 1936. Their Populist orientation lay in the source and appeal of the images; one showed a coal miner re-united with his wife; the other, an informal Edward VIII getting out of a car. But both were oils based on newspaper photographs. Graham Bell, the Social Realist painter and critic, had written acutely of Sickert: '[His] art has little connection with contemporary painting: it is far more related to contemporary photography'.[61] The factualist and democratic character of photography in art began to be stressed[62] and younger painters like Graham Bell began to incorporate news-photo images in their paintings. His *Red White and Blue*[63] of a demonstration in Whitehall, was displayed in the same exhibition as Medley's *Butcher's Shop*, at the Storran Gallery in November 1938, where both were subjected to the strictures of the critic Clive Bell:

> Obviously working from a photograph, the painter has not succeeded in recreating the scene. . . . There is no reason why a painter should be a communist painter or a fascist painter . . . but it is essential that his message should be implicit in the paint. Once he allows it to flap out like a bit of untucked-in shirt the picture is lost. Unadjusted sociology is, I fancy, what is the matter with a picture by Robert Medley. Propaganda must be properly assimilated'.[64]

Graham Bell's Populism extended into questions of working-class access to his paintings. He confided to Tom Harrisson, a co-founder of Mass Observation, that he believed that 'the test of his sort of art is if the workers like it'[65] — for Bell wished to be regarded primarily as a representationalist, a moral painter of recognisable scenes, rather than a Social Realist. Harrisson collaborated with Bell on the issue of wider social accessibility to his paintings, for this was an area of particular interest to Harrisson who had, for example, designed leaflets for the Bolton Council elections of October 1937 based on Football pool coupons. All this was part of the essentially Populist, Mass Observation project which had been organized to find ways of making civic information more legible and widening access to democratic processes. For the Storran Gallery exhibition, Harrisson, with Bell's aid, invited hundreds of anonymous Londoners, choosing them at random to attend the show in order to see painters' versions of their metropolis. At this same moment, in November 1938, Harrisson helped sponsor an exhibition of Unprofessional painting by amateurs at the Peckham Health Centre, with the painter Julian Trevelyan and Robert Lyon, the educationalist. He drew up a manifesto, which took the Populist thrust in the visual arts in Britain to a new level with the bold print assumption, 'Anyone can Paint', at the head of the catalogue.

'Art for the People' had already become the guiding slogan of the British Institute for Adult Education (BIAE), when in 1935 it announced the organization of travelling art exhibitions. Robert Lyon subscribed to the Populist ideal of public access to art — both traditional and experimental. In his view:

> The public are anxious to learn its [i.e. modern art's] alphabet; they are ready to consider experimental work; they are curious about the methods and intentions of painters, designers and sculptors . . . . No doubt those who reveal an interest in art are a minority of the population, but it is also certain that they are a substantial minority and one which is rapidly growing in numbers.[66]

As a conclusion to this populist movement, it is important to recall its fulfilment in the 1940s. The BIAE's policy of travelling exhibitions accompanied by lecturers became an important constituent of the Arts Council's programme, once it was established from its roots in BIAE and the Council for Encouragement for Music and the Arts (CEMA) at the close of World War II.

IV: Corporate Patronage and New Roles for the Artist

One channel for such 'popular visual communication in the 1930s was through the multi-national petrol company, Shell Mex. In February 1933 its huge new offices, Shell Mex House, were opened in London with decorations by the Unit 1 artist, John Armstrong. A commentator noted that the building was 'typical of an age whose motto is "centralization", . . . [with] something eternal almost in this huge palace of commerce'.[67] Like the new *Daily Express* Building (opened in 1932) and the Olympia site, Shell Mex House appeared part of Unit 1's imaginary environments of the future — flush surfaces, clean lines, Absolute, purist and orderly. Arthur Wragg presented Shell Mex House as a hard-faced and brutal palace of industry in his illustration for the words in Psalm 30; 'And in my prosperity I said, I shall never be moved'.[68] This was some unjustice to Shell Mex's enlightened policy of subsidising artists: to be sure, John Armstrong, in August 1933, was to contrast the collapse of private patronage by rich individuals who cared only for portraiture, with the development of a new public patronage. The Shell Mex company, he felt, represented a new type of patron, immensely large and wealthy, a patron of the future — 'commanding resources that make the present ducal incomes seem just pin money'.[69] One of Herbert Read's great anxieties when he introduced Unit 1 in 1934, was that the artists had to combine into group units because they lacked 'a corporate existence of any kind in the state'[70] in the post-Liberal economic, and cultural climate, concentration was an important tendency of the period. There had been massive state intervention in art from 1916 to 1919 to record, dramatize and project the war-time struggle through the Official War Artists scheme. Now it seemed that Shell Mex, as well as the large railway companies, the Empire Marketing Board (EMB), the BBC, the public corporations, the great daily newspapers and the London Passenger Transport Board might offer new identities and substantial roles for artists in the cause of corporate publicity.

Already the most inventive designer working in Britain in this period, Edward McKnight Kauffer, an American expatriate living in London, moved almost exclusively in the area of publicity for government agencies and the great corporations and companies. Kauffer's composite of romantic national propaganda and petrol company publicity — *Stonehenge: See Britain First on Shell* — was the most reproduced poster from the first Shell Mex advertising exhibition, held not on their commercial premises but in an art gallery — the Burlington Galleries — in June 1931. The show became an annual event, showing the publicity executed by established artists such as Edna Clarke Hall and Vanessa Bell with young vanguard Surrealists like John Banting. 'How easily the modernist adapts himself', observed a critic in *Commercial Art*.[71] The person behind Shell Mex's intervention in art patronage was their publicity manager, Jack Beddington, who favoured the national pastoral as an icon for advertising purposes. Sir Kenneth

Clark, at the opening of the fifth Shell Mex exhibition said; 'Mr. Beddington . . . is content that Shell should simply be associated with a beautiful landscape'.[72] By the time of the fifth exhibition, Clive Bell was prepared to believe that Shell Mex was now a more important institution in fostering art than the Royal Academy.[73] Sir Kenneth Clark bonded the new Populist thrust in the arts to Shell's publicity designs when he rejected murals in favour of posters. Large-scale public works programmes involving murals were to be part of the American New Deal treatment for the ailing condition of art in the United States; and in the Spring of 1934 Sir William Rothenstein also advocated the painting of civic murals in major British cities.[74] Clark's criterion for preferring posters to murals was that posters were 'necessary and popular'[75] a utilitarian as well as populist rhetoric that he applied as a test to the art of the past hundred years and since it was 'a luxury designed to attract a few rich people', found it wanting.[76]

But such Populist and corporate beliefs concerning patronage and the types of art that might be encouraged in Britain in the 1930s, had been anticipated by the leading spirit of the National Government, Stanley Baldwin. In 1926, the same year the BBC and EMB were formed, Baldwin outlined a case for the management of art through 'the great corporations and municipal authorities of this country'.[77] The kind and style of art employed ought to be 'our own native art'.[778] He followed with a plea for moderate art after the 'extremist' reaction to Victorianism. Once more the ideology that had been enthroned by the National Government was being reproduced through the structures of contemporary art.

While artists like John Armstrong and Graham Sutherland were kept financially afloat by Shell Mex, many sought other careers in the period 1931–6. In the first years after Sir William Coldstream left the Slade School at the beginning of the 1930s, two of his painter friends abandoned art. One of them, Clive Branson, joined the ILP and then became a Communist activist — only returning to painting after volunteering for the Republican side in the Spanish Civil War. The other took up work as a door-to-door salesman. Eventually Coldstream stopped painting too, when his money ran out in 1934 and he joined the GPO[79] film unit.

Coldstream's art was part of a general pattern — Humphrey Jennings, another painter, joined the GPO in 1934; Paul Rotha, a fellow Slade graduate had joined earlier. By 1936 the ex-painters inside the GPO film unit begun to be 'plagued by . . . painters who would like to hump our tripods'.[80] W.H. Auden left teaching to work with the unit for a year in 1935, as did Benjamin Britten. For a moment around 1935 it seemed quite possible that traditional, manual pictorial art might contract and cease, for many of its makers were now absorbed in forms of production that were photo-mechanical and mass-reproduced — at the new photomagazine *Weekly Illustrated*, in the *Daily Mirror*, and in the GPO and Shell Mex film units. A generation of artists were propelled into the mass media to gain employment. 'The year 1934', wrote Gilbert Cousland, 'saw a change, of draughtsman, of painters turning to photography'.[81] It was against the emerging pattern of corporate patronage and the dissolution of painting in favour of photo-mechanical media that Sir Kenneth Clark began a renewal of private patronage to such artists as Graham Bell, Victor Pasmore, and Sir William Coldstream, giving them an allowance of a monthly cheque of £10. Coldstream was thus enabled, in 1936, to leave the GPO and resume oil painting.

Despite this, reassertion of liberal and individualistic roles, a new image of the British artist as culture hero was in formation, under pressure from the social and economic structural changes of the early 1930s. The cultural and economic framework of Liberalism had broken down and with it the *laissez-faire*, bohemian model of the artist — the one that had been serviceable until 1931 — was in decline in the face of collective seriousness and social responsibility. Myfanwy Piper remarked on this crucial shift in attitude which seemed complete by 1937: 'We are more serious now, not really playboys but agents'.[82] This fantasy artist-agent who had recaptured under institutional guise, the efficient unitary 'commufascist' aura that Unit 1 had hoped to assume, could now be found in Humphrey Spender's disguise as the *Mirror's* Lensman; or in Graham Bell's or Sir William Coldstream's assumed identities as volunteer Mass Observers; or in the appearance of the architects Wells Coates and Morton Shand as the agents of MARS.[83]

V: Exploring the Industrial Interior

This new figure, the artist-as-agent, conscious of his part in making a public art on (possibly) a mass scale, became drawn into the role of reporter and social detective — a diagnostic role sketched out in the point of view of Auden's *XXX Poems* of 1930: the artist-agent who must visit, witness, record and diagnose the vast cultural crime of the slump and its disfigurement of Britain. It was this experience that so affected Coldstream's attitudes, 'travelling about . . . and meeting people I would not normally have met . . .'.[84] Coldstream was, though his work in films, put into contact with the world of industrial labour. The artist-agent's pilgraimage into the industrial interior became a feature of the ascendent Documentary style in British art from 1935 to 1939.

Slums were re-erected at the Olympia Building Exhibition in 1934, striking the *Studio's* critic as '. . . the most horrifying indictment of the existing social system I have seen'.[85] However the derelict urban interior had to be experienced at first hand by Spender, Brandt, Coldstream, Bell and Medley as much as it was by J.B. Priestley and George Orwell. The earlier, conservative demand for 'British pictures of British people, of British landscapes'[86] was taken as an ironic cue in social reportage. The British urban landscapes that were produced by Bill Brandt and Humphrey Spender were not affirmative pastoral images of the kind preferred by Shell Mex. When the *News Chronicle* ran a competition in 1935 for photographs of Britain there were two categories . . . 'the picturesque old Britain . . . its traditional pastimes and toil; its ancient houses and shady lanes' and 'the new Britain embodying all that is best and worst in twentieth century work, life and social customs'.[87] There was an admission that an 'other' Britain existed besides the 'old' timeless landscape which now fixated Nash and Sutherland.

A strong link existed with the literary pilgrimages initiated by J.B. Priestley in his 1933–4 *English Journey*. This became a handbook for the Documentarists, and in particular for the cameraman Bill Brandt. Brandt had spent much of his early life on the Continent in Germany and Paris. In 1931, like Hillier he returned home, and in 1934 he began photographic work for the *Weekly Illustrated*. It was reading Priestley's *English Journey* that decided him to make a photo-tour in the industrial North of England, during the summer of 1935.[88] His photographs were then published in the spring of 1936 in *The English at Home*. This book set out the social contrasts Brandt had uncovered by juxtaposing photographs of working-class life with more priviliged life-styles on facing pages: 'Does anyone seriously maintain that the squalor exposed in these photographs is necessary?', Raymond Mortimer asked in his introduction to *The English at Home*.[89] Brandt is described by Mortimer as an anthropologist viewing British society objectively; and it was this anthropological side of social reportage that coloured the work that Humphrey Spender and others did for Mass Observation. The model of the expatriate's returning home on a redemptive pilgrimage into the British interior was established, and, significantly, established within the marketable and expanding genre of Documentary. Many artists and photographers felt distanced by class barriers and, therefore, viewed Britain from an imaginary exterior, 'foreign' in their own country. Julian Trevelyan, who volunteered as a Mass Observer to aid a project surveying social patterns and public opinion in, Bolton in 1937, became 'aware of the gulf of education, language, accent and social behaviour'.[90] which separated him from Bolton's inhabitants. For Trevelyan, Bell, Coldstream and Spender to overcome this gulf entailed a similar move to that made by Robert Medley in 1936 — to go and live in a 'mass environment'[91] to paint and photograph in order to escape the 'narrow and remote environment'[92] that composed the traditional setting for the artist. Medley lived with miners in South Wales and he was followed by the painter Sochachewsky the following year.[93] Edith Tudor Hart, who like Medley was a member of the AIA, had photographed most of the badly depressed 'Special Areas' in Britain: she had been in the Rhondda in 1935[94] and on Tyneside. Her belief in the candid camera's ability to penetrate hitherto unpictured social situations[95] was shared by Humphrey Spender, who was familiar with the origins of radical photo-reportage from his stays in Germany in the late 1920s and early 1930s. The master of German candid photography, Erich Salomon, had been given a retrospective exhibition at the Royal Photographic Society in 1935. Spender admired him, but he inverted Salomon's concentration on political élites. With his Leica camera secreted under a shabby raincoat, Spender assumed a contrary guise to Salomon's urbanity; Spender became the ordinary man, the man of the masses, who 'built himself into the environment'[96] in working-class Bolton and Blackpool. As a member of Tom Harrisson's group, he set about mapping behaviour in pubs, cotton mills, abattoirs and amusement arcades.

Tom Harrisson also persuaded Graham Bell to volunteer for Mass Observation's survey in April 1938, and the painter by the end of his stay had produced an elaborate iconographic programme for a series of paintings of Bolton's social life, which included houses of the middle classes with rubbish in the foreground; the interior of a cotton mill; chapel; pub; market; a Bolton wedding and a Bolton funeral; dance hall; mill workers and a derelict iron foundry. Bell journeyed up to Bolton with Sir William Coldstream, and both painted the industrial landscape from the roof of the local art gallery. Coldstream's notions about the kind of landscape they found are symptomatic of the motives and desires of that Northern pilgrimage: 'The choice of a Bolton factoryscape with chimneys was for social reasons — that the industrial landscape was inherently a better subject than a still life — although this was not logically so.'[97]

In the visual imagination of the volunteer painters and photographers, Bolton fused with *The Waste Land*, with the vistas of dereliction in the poems of Auden too, and the dead cityscapes of de Chirico and the Surrealists. For suddenly, at the end of 1936, the iconography of industrial ruin and social catastrophe had gained momentum — it was signalled by the unprecedented photographic and newsreel coverage given to Edward VIII's visit to the Special Area in South Wales. In James Jarchés epic photograph for the *Weekly Illustrated*[98] and Steven Spurrier's double-page Piranesian drawing in the *Illustrated London News*,[99] the King was shown dwarfed in an overwhelming waste-land of disused and wrecked steel blast furnaces, with in the *Illustrated London News*, a caption saying, 'Loyalty in the Ruins'.[100] When Coldstream and Bell came to Bolton they, too experienced it in terms of a revelation — a catastrophic wasteland: 'About 5 we could be seen in a huge canyon surrounded by rubbish dumps of great height, by the sewage system of the town, standing between a cemetery and a squalid little river full of old tins and dead things'.[101] Spender, also, eventually responded to Bolton through painting sinister landscapes of disused factories.

VI: Apocalypse: Re-armament, Spain and the Bomber

In 1938 Graham Bell had described waking one morning from the minor unpleasantness of the dream world to a 'real nightmare' of life in Bolton.[102] As the 1930s progressed, the derelict iconography of the slump came into conjunction with images of political apocalypse and war. Amongst the more established artists perhaps it was C.R.W. Nevinson who gave the fullest account of fears of another world war, through the increasing prominence he gave to icons of armaments and war paraphenalia in his paintings. In 1930, in an oil, *With Nothing to Lose – Not even Chains*,[103] marching soldiers are present in a composite self portrait with his wife in his studio, but they are still only memory traces of his World War I paintings as an Official War Artist. The picture's title, with its anti-communist swipe, asserted Nevinson's political opinions, and he was to be an outspoken supporter of the National Government in the autumn of 1931. In 1933 his lithograph, *The Spirit of Progress*,[104] showed the same studio with palette, easel and window, but overwhelmed by insurgent soldiers and rioters with a screen of bayonets and howitzers in the foreground, while, in the sky beyond the studio windows, aeroplanes passed in formation. Between *With Nothing to Lose . .* and *The Spirit of Progress* had fallen the worst effects of the slump, the Japanese invasion of Manchuria and the Nazi revolution in Germany. Later that same year in *Ave Homo Sapiens*,[105] Nevinson dissolved the studio, and, from amongst the seething ranks of soldiers one has been enlarged, centre, with gas mask and respirator, surrounded by howitzer barrels and bayonets. Blood rains from the sky along with bombs from military aeroplanes. Douglas Goldring in *The Studio* considered it was, 'A slick piece of journalism in the *Cry Havoc* style'.[106] Goldring's strictures were similar to Clive Bell's criticisms of Graham Bell's and Robert Medley's paintings. But a diagnostic status for a hybrid form of art/journalism was being deliberately sought by some of the artists in this period. The association of *Ave Homo Sapiens* with a literary text, — Beverly Nichols' best selling tract against armaments *Cry Havoc!* — was apt, for the following year Nevinson was co-author, with Princess Paul Troubetzkoy, of *Exodus AD: A Warning to Civilians*, a novel which dealt with the horrendous consequences of a bombing attack on London. In his melodramatic paintings and in his book, he acknowledged the worsening international situation, the likelihood of conflict and the prospect of the bombers' getting through, as Baldwin had warned.[107]

World War I and its images — revived at the end of the 1920s in popular novels and films — generated still further images of a future war. In November 1934 the *Daily Express* assembled a version of World War I in a large photographic exhibition at Dorland Hall in London. Some photographs dominated by virtue of their sheer size — some of the earliest and biggest photo-murals in Britain, over thirty feet long and twenty feet high.[108] Visual propaganda for disarmament had the example of the French advertizing designer Carlu, whose 'scare' poster, *Pour le Désarmement des Nations* was widely reproduced in Britain[109] at the end of 1932. There was also a Pacifist exhibition in Cambridge at the end of 1933, and AIA shows had a section for the Peace Publicity Bureau, for which Edward Bawden, a Shell Mex artist, did a design in May 1937.

With Christian Socialism as Arthur Wragg's primary ideological drive, aided by his collaboration with H.R.L. Shepherd, it was no surprise that the issues of Disarmament and Pacifism formed major themes in his illustrated books — especially *Jesus Wept* (1934) and *Thy Kingdom Come* (1939). Wragg would often mount contemporary newspaper cuttings, detailing gas warfare or conscription, onto his inky black scenes, sometimes grotesquely amending religious images by overlaying them with profane newsprint. He wrote: 'Most of the drawings are backed by cold figures . . . statistics are always dull unless they can be flicked into life'.[110] This was a tactic he shared with the Marxist artists of *The Left Review*. In October 1935 James Fitton's cartoon from *Left Review* showed a dove of peace with R.A.F. roundels carrying a newsclipping of Handley Page bomber contracts. Wragg's illustrations for *Jesus Wept*, dating from 1934, belonged to the same sort of visual imagination found in the first half of the film, *The Shape of Things to Come* (1935), with its repertory of news placards, of air armadas, gas-masked children, and the ruined city slipping into barbarism. The Unit 1 artist, John Armstrong (another painter, like

C.R.W. Nevinson and Paul Nash, who had experienced World War I) found that his work on designs for *The Shape of Things to Come* overflowed into his paintings. A world of ruins, gutted houses and empty streets, in depopulated post-bombardment cities transferred from the film, were the subjects for paintings like *Sunrise, Pro-Patria* and *Forsaken Street*, that he exhibited at the Lefevre Gallery in 1938.[111] With these adaptations of the romantic ruin genre in the age of the bomber, went a deliberate rejection of military-industrial technical progress, a rejection which he symbolized in his series of *Icarus* paintings begun in 1939. The first *Icarus* presents a silver grey globe cut open to reveal a circular metal framework. The globe is impaled on a pole around which lie fragments of broken metal skin in a surrealist desert/waste-land. Like Hillier's and Bigge's paintings of c.1933, it seemed to confer negative values on technology. It is an emblematic wreck of a machine; but, globe-like, it echoes Arthur Wragg's illustration *Journey to the End of the Night*,[112] where the Earth's globe has become condensed with a runaway locomotive, driven by a skeleton, hurtling to a crash. Such images of destruction,[113] as pictorial signs for the instability of civilization, were decked out with traditional references to Icarus and a medieval, skeletal personification of Death, to anchor a contemporary pessimism.

It is important to notice that not all the paintings with anti-war sentiments were produced by artists sympathetic to the Left. In the Royal Academy of 1938, William Russell Flint, a pictorial and political conservative, exhibited *In their Own Homes*,[114] subtitled *Spain's Agony of Civil War 1936–8*. Russell Flint had made his reputation from high kitsch scenes of alluring gypsy women in folkloric mediterranean locales. *In their Own Homes* showed a group of such women being lined up against a wall and shot by Republican riflemen. 'Cheerfully rich in colour, its theme is a little horrific', wrote F.C. Tilney in his ultra-conservative art magazine *Art and Reason* under the motto, 'For a Sane and Competent Art':. . . 'The theme is tragic enough and must bring home to visitors Spain's agony . .'[115]

One of the first British volunteers to the Republican side to die in Spain was an AIA artist, Felicia Browne, in the autumn of 1936. Two years later Picasso's large mural panel *Guernica* was exhibited at the New Burlington Galleries in London, and then in Manchester. Picasso's style and visceral imagery fermented in the style of British artists and especially affected Julian Trevelyan, revealing itself later in his small oils of Hammersmith in 1939-40 based on personal anxieties about air raids. The Picasso-derived heads in Trevelyan's paintings[116] — fractured and expressionistically coloured red and green — are gazing into the sky. 'We all thought', Trevelyan recalled, 'something was going to come from there'.[117] Paul Nash, too, looked to the sky in apprehension '. . . suddenly the sky was upon us all, like a huge hawk, hovering, threatening . . . . I hunted the sky for what I dreaded in my imaginings'.[118] The intensified, apocalyptic cultural pessimism of 1938–9 and the onset of the war emergency can also be detected, mediated in Paul Nash's painting *Earth Home*. In this picture from 1939 the Earth's surface has been exposed, revealing plant roots and in the centre a huge, rounded deep bunker for air raids, labyrinthine, its scale impossible to gauge, and its model a mole's nest. It underlines the conjunction of Nash's nature romanticism of the middle and late 1930s with the omnipresent actuality of the hurried building of air raid shelters and the widely held fears of holocaust from aerial bombing.

Notes

1 'What is Wrong with Modern Painting?', *The Studio*, February 1932, 63.
2 See, for example, the careers of Christopher Wood and Edward Wadsworth in the late 1920s.
3 T. Hillier (1954), *Leda and the Goose*, Longmans, Harlow, 119.
4 See Tristram Hillier's drawings and paintings in the collection of Rochdale and Doncaster Art Galleries.
5 See his lost painting *Mouth of the Rhone*, reproduced in *Unit 1*, Portsmouth City Museum and Art Gallery, 1978, 36.
6 See *Demolitions*, No.26, Mayor Gallery Unit 1 Exhibition April 1934.
7 T. Hillier (1934), 'Statement', in *Unit 1*, Cassell, London.
8 P. Nash (1932), 'The Artist and the Community', *The Listener*, 20 January 1932, 100.
9 Catalogue, *Contemporary British Painting*, Tooths Gallery, 21 November 1935 to 14 December 1935.
10 A.J.P. Taylor (1977), *English History 1914–1945*, Penguin, Harmondsworth, 26.
11 P. Nash (1931), **'Nature Life and Art'**, *The Weekend Review*, 5 December 1931, 715.
12 *The Studio*, February, 1932, 63.
13 *The Studio, loc. cit.*
14 P. Nash (1932), 'Going "Modern" and "Being British" ', *The Weekend Review*, 12 February 1932, 333.
15 P. Nash, *ibid.* On the topic of early 1930s cultural nationalism, see John Selby Bigge's remarks in his statement, *Unit 1, op. cit.*
16 J. Betjeman (1931), 'The Death of Modernism', *Architectural Review*, December 1931, 172–4. There he claims: 'The word "modern" is becoming old-fashioned . . .'
17 For examples of neo-Victorian sentiment in 1931–2, see Brian Howard's letter quoted in M.-J. Lancaster (1968), *Portrait of a Failure*, Blond, London, 319, and *Punch Almanack for 1932*, which contrasted

ultra-moderns with neo-Victorians at current cocktail parties. Wyndham Lewis was particularly antagonistic towards the neo-Victorian tendency: 'It . . . has become thorough as a fashion . . . the world has slowly been encouraged to return to its nineteenth century weakness and philistinism'., Rose (1963), *The Letters of Wyndham Lewis*, Methuen, London, 189.

18 Jennings had yet to become a Documentarist film-maker.

19 Unpublished correspondence, 2 September 1931.

20 William Gaunt, 'A Modern Utopia', *The Studio*, December 1929 859 *et seq*.

21 *The Studio*, August 1930, 140.

22 See his oil *Crucifixion* (1933) reproduced in Herbert Read (1933), *Art Now*, Faber & Faber, London.

23 Reproduced Plate XXXIV, *Unit 1, op. cit.*

24 A. Powell (1932), *Venusberg,* London Duckworths, Chapter 19, 93. At this time Powell knew Tristram Hillier and John Armstrong. Powell also replied to attacks on modernist painting through the correspondence columns of *The Listener*.

25 P. Nash (1932), 'The Painter's Subject', *The Listener*, 17 February 1932, 227. *Leviathan* is illustrated 226.

26 See the writing of Erich Mendelsohn and Le Corbusier in particular. Paul Nash became photographically infatuated with the purist possibilities of an Atlantic ocean liner in 1930.

27 Unit 1 was composed of Barbara Hepworth, Henry Moore, John Armstrong, John Bigge, Edward Burra, Tristram Hillier, Paul Nash, Ben Nicholson, Edward Wadsworth, Wells Coates and Colin Lucas.

28 P. Nash letter to *The Times*, 2 June 1933.

29 T. Hillier quoted in Charles Harrisson (1978), Introduction, *Unit 1*, Portsmouth City Museum and Art Gallery, 2.

30 P. Nash, *The Times, op. cit.*

31 H. Read, *Unit 1, op. cit.* 12.

32 W. Gaunt, *op. cit.*

33 The transparent overlay of Raymond Massey/John Cabal/Oswald Mosley was something commented upon when the film was first shown in February 1936. I am indebted to Professor Quentin Bell for this information.

34 *The New Statesman*, 4 November 1933, 551.

35 H. Read, *Unit 1, op. cit.* 15.

36 P. Nash, *The Times, op. cit.*

37 *The New Statesman*, 27 February 1932, 263.

38 T. Hillier, *op. cit.* 129.

39 B. Howard (1934), 'Absolutism and Unit 1', *The New Statesman*, 21 April 1934, 716.

40 P. Nash, 'Nature Life and Art', *op. cit.*

41 P. Nash, *The Times, op. cit.* Humphrey Jennings' thoughts on pre-historic art are found in H. Jennings and G. Noxon (1931). 'Rock Painting and La Jeune Peinture', *Experiment*, Spring 1931, 27–30.

42 *The Illustrated London News*, 3 October 1931, 322–3. For discussion

of the concept of 'cultural drift', see G. Kubler (1960). *The Shape of Time*, New York.

43 G. Hadon (1933), *The Listener*, 7 June 1933, 887.
44 *Commercial Art*, Vol. XI, June 1931, 43.
45 *The Studio*, February 1932, 63.
46 Letter to Martin Armstrong quoted in A. Bertram (1955), *Paul Nash*, Faber & Faber, London, 149.
47 H. Wadman (1936), 'Mechanism of Humanism', *Penrose Annual 1936*, 40–3.
48 *British Journal of Photography*, 28 February, 1930, 128.
49 *British Journal of Photography*, 5 August 1932, 478.
50 'Back to Beauty', *Photography*, May 1933, 30.
51 H. Wadman, *ibid.*
52 H. Wadman (1932), 'Howard Coster — Photographer of Men', *Commercial Art*, June 1932, 242–5.
53 H. Wadman, *ibid.*
54 P. Tanquerey (1933), 'Back to Sanity in Portraiture', *Photography*, 15 March 1933, 16.
55 H. Spender, in an interview with Derek Smith, 27 July 1977, in *Worktown: Catalogue of Humphrey Spender's Photographs of Bolton and Blackpool 1937–8*, Gardner Art Centre, 1977.
56 One of the photographs was subsequently printed in *The Listener*, 5 December 1933.
57 A. Wragg (1933), *Psalms for Modern Life*, Selwyn & Blount, London.
58 H.R.L. Shepherd (1933), Introduction, *Psalms for Modern Life, ibid.*
59 N. Malyutin (1936), 'Art and the State', *The Listener*, 2 September 1936, 423–5.
60 Medley's style was heavily dependent on Picasso's pre-cubist humanitarian painting and Bébé Bérard's neo-Romantic Parisian style of the 1920s and 1930s.
61 G. Bell (1933), 'The Sickerts and the London Group', *The New Statesman*, 25 November 1933, 662–3.
62 By, for example, Humphrey Jennings: 'The system by which the people can be pictured by the people for the people', *London Bulletin*, October 1938, 22.
63 Alternatively called *Sunday Afternoon in Whitehall*, the painting was destroyed in the Blitz.
64 C. Bell (1938), 'The Euston Road School', *The New Statesman*, 5 November 1938, 722.
65 T. Harrisson (1938), Memorandum, 30 March 1938, The Tom Harrisson Mass Observation Archive.
66 See R. Lyon (1935), 'Art and the Ordinary Man', *The Listener*, 3 April 1935, 556.
67 P. Jordan (1933), 'Shell Mex in three Cities', *The Listener*, 15 February 1933, 236.
68 A. Wragg, *op. cit.*
69 J. Armstrong (1933), 'The Evolution of Transport Mural Paintings at Shell Mex Building London', *The Studio*, September 1933, 73 *et seq.*

70 H. Read, *Unit 1, op. cit.* 12.
71 *Commercial Art*, July 1931, 47.
72 K. Clark (1934), 'Painters turn to Posters', *Commercial Art*, August 1934, 65–72.
73 C. Bell (1934), *The New Statesman*, 23 June 1934, 946.
74 W. Rothenstein (1934), in his Romanes lecture, Oxford, 1934.
75 K. Clark, *Commercial Art, op. cit.* 69.
76 K. Clark, *Commercial Art, ibid.* 69.
77 S. Baldwin (1928), *Our Inheritance*, Hodder & Stoughton, London, 190–1.
78 S. Baldwin, *ibid.*
79 See W. Coldstream, in R.S. Lambert (ed) (1938), *Art in England*, Penguin, Harmondsworth, 99–104.
80 See P. Rotha (1936), *The Studio*, Vol 112, 144.
81 G. Cousland (1935), 'Expressionism in Photography', *Penrose Annual 1935*, 86–7.
82 M. Piper (1937), *The Painter's Object*, Gerald Howe, London, 3.
83 MARS, the Modern Architectural Research Group was formed in 1933.
84 W. Coldstream, *op. cit.*
85 *The Studio*, November 1934, 263.
86 *The Studio*, February 1932, 63.
87 As reported in *Photography*, July 1935, 36.
88 Unknown to Brandt, two leading Continental photographers, Carl Hubbacher and Gisèle Freund were making similar surveys in Britain during that year.
89 B. Brandt (1936), *The English at Home*, Batsford, London, 7.
90 J. Trevelyan (1937), *Indigo Days*, McGibbon & Kee, London.
91 T. Harrisson and C. Madge (1937), *Mass Observation*, Frederick Muller, London, 47.
92 S. Spender (1938), Letter to Tom Harrisson, 23 March 1938, Tom Harrisson Mass Observation Archive.
93 See report of Sochachewsky's exhibition at the Bloomsbury Gallery, in the *Daily Worker*, 11 May 1938.
94 For her photographs see *The Geographical Magazine*, March 1936.
95 E. Tudor Hart (1934), 'More Freedom for the Photo-Reporter', *Photography*, February 1934, 39.
96 Tom Harrisson in an interview with the author, July 1973.
97 Sir William Coldstream in an interview with the author, March 1974.
98 *The Weekly Illustrated*, 28 November 1938, 16–17.
99 *The Illustrated London News*, 28 November 1938, 50–1.
100 *The Illustrated London News, ibid.*
101 G. Bell (1938), Unpublished correspondence, 21 April 1938.
102 G. Bell *ibid.*
103 Illustrated in *The Studio*, October 1930, 276.
104 Illustrated in *The Studio*, October 1933, 258.
105 Illustrated in *The Studio*, August 1935, 78.
106 D. Goldring (1934), *The Studio*, February 1934, 100.

107 Baldwin had told the House of Commons (10 November 1932) that 'the bomber will always get through'.

108 See *The New Statesman*, 24 November 1934, 747, and *Photography Yearbook 1935*, 390, for illustration of the erection of one of the photo murals.

109 See *Photography*, December 1932, 27 and *Commercial Art*, December 1932, 228–9.

110 A. Wragg (1939), Introduction, *Thy Kingdom Come*, Selwyn & Blount, London.

111 *Forsaken Street* is illustrated in J. Armstrong (1975), *John Armstrong, 1893–1973*, Royal Academy, London.

112 A. Wragg (1935), *Jesus Wept*, Selwyn & Blount, London. The title clearly refers to Céline's contemporary novel, *Voyage au Bout de la Nuit*.

113 Other painters who were motivated by Pacifist ideology did not always present convulsive images of the world in this period. Algernon Newton's quietist views of London and country houses were painted by a deeply convinced pacifist working within the genre of urban topography, rather than exploiting those pictorial categories Nevinson and Wragg had chosen to work within — the academy 'problem picture' and political satire.

114 Reproduced *Royal Academy Illustrated, 1938*, Royal Academy, London, 37.

115 F.C. Tilney (1938), *Art and Reason*, Vol. IV, No.41, May 1938.

116 They were shown at the Lefevre Gallery in May 1940.

117 Julian Trevelyan in an interview with the author, July 1973.

118 P. Nash (1954), *Outline*, 262.

8 IN SEARCH OF A REAL EQUALITY: WOMEN BETWEEN THE WARS

Jane Lewis

In 1918, the feminist movement rejoiced at the granting of the vote. *Punch* captured the moment in a cartoon of a St Joan-like figure, eyes uplifted and holding a banner enscribed 'Woman's Franchise'. The caption read 'At Last'.[1] Natural justice had triumphed and natural rights in areas such as morality, employment and wages would surely follow. But in 1936, when five active feminists sat down to write an account of women's progress since 1918, the tone was subdued.

They stressed the legal measures of benefit to women which had followed the vote: the Sex Disqualification (Removal) Act of 1919, which had had the immediate effect of opening the legal profession to women; an equal divorce law in 1923; an act giving equality between the sexes with respect to the guardianship of infants in 1925; and in the same year the granting of widow's pensions. Yet, the editor admitted that: 'None of the writers say that we can yet judge what it all amounts to: none of them feel that the freedom of women in society is either really achieved or really stable . . .'.[2] This realization did not bring with it new solutions, perhaps because these women faced even greater obstacles during the 1930s than they had in the Edwardian period. The impetus given to the movement by the suffrage fight had disappeared, and young women regarded feminists as dowdy and faintly ridiculous.[3] In addition, by the mid-1930s, feminists felt dwarfed by the threat of political forces beyond their control in the form of war, fascism and communism.[4]

To what extent was this feeling about the insecurity of women's position justified? The most immediate concern of the feminists writing in 1936 was to assess the position of middle-class women, who were trying to expand their activities beyond the home. The war had delivered the vote, and Parliament and the professions had been opened to women, but the number of women entering either had been disappointingly small. The war had also brought great changes in the nature of working women's employment, but these also proved largely transitory. The social and economic mechanisms structuring and controlling the fabric of women's lives had gone virtually untouched by the women's movement, a fact which feminists were only beginning to understand. For most women in the 1930s, work was still low-paid and undertaken to assist the family exchequer rather than for its own sake. A formidable ideology of motherhood stressed the importance of home, childbearing and childrearing. Health levels were low and the figures for maternal mortality were rising. Any assessment of women's position during the 1930s must focus on the realities of these experiences.

In a study such as this, it is inevitable that women's life at home be considered separately from life at work. But it is important that the relationships between the two and the way in which they interacted to form the fabric of women's lives should not be forgotten. In the case of Mrs P, who lived in St Pancras during the inter-war years, marriage came at the age of eighteen in 1926. The eldest of twenty children, she was a proficient housekeeper, and in her own words: 'Only by sleeping with a man was it [marriage] different'.[5] One year later, she gave birth at home with a midwife in attendance, and breast fed for a year, even though cracked, sore nipples made it 'hell' for the first three months. In 1928, her lorry-driver husband got a job in Welwyn Garden City, which meant a move from their two rooms (rent 17/6d. from an income of 32/6d.) to a small house with a bathroom. But by 1932 Mr P was out of work and would remain so for ten years. Mrs P was again pregnant. They returned to their two rooms. The baby was born in a local authority hospital because: ' 'ee [her husband] was out of work and I 'ad to go on the assistance'. The hospital 'done their job for you but there was no food, no good food . . . but it didn't matter to me because I've always been used to no food at times, you know what I mean'. Mrs P went out charring as soon as she could, taking the younger child with her. After a couple of years she got a job as a guard on the Underground and could have got promotion, but her husband 'said "no" '. In 1938, the third and last child arrived, delivered in hospital. This one was taken to a clinic, although Mrs P never attended for herself. She returned to domestic work as soon as she was able.

No one case is 'typical'. But an example such as this is valuable for the questions it raises. Exactly *how* typical was Mrs P's work experience, a family of three children, the hospital as a place of birth, the apparent lack of maternal and child health services, and her living conditions? Answers to these questions must be located in the context of the social and economic pressures bearing upon women and their responses to them.

In 1931, the female participation rate[6] was lower than in 1911, although slightly higher than that of the post war depression year of 1921 (see Table 8.1). Both married and single women's participation rates rose slightly between 1911 and 1931, but the rate for widowed and divorced women dropped; an important factor here was the introduction of widows' pensions in 1925 by which widows received 10/- per week plus 5/- for the first and 3/- for all subsequent dependent children. The way in which single and married women

Table 8.1. Participation rates in Great Britain by sex and marital status, 1911–31 (percentages). *Source*: A.H. Halsey (1972), *Trends in British Society Since 1900*, MacMillan, London, 115 and 118.

	Male	Female			
		Single	Married	Widowed and Divorced	Total
1911	93.5	69.3	9.6	29.4	35.3
1921	91.8	68.14	8.69	25.62	33.7
1931	90.5	71.6	10.0	21.62	34.2

maintained their levels of participation in the workforce is surprising in view of the male participation rate, which declined steadily between 1911 and 1931. 1921 and 1931 were both depression years, and it might have been expected that the participation of women, whose labour has always been marginal, would have shown a decrease. Obviously, this did not happen. To explain this, we need to look more closely at the pattern and character of women's work: how women might have responded to the economic crisis, how the nature of their work affected their employability and what role the attitudes held by government, employers and the public towards women's work played.

Ashworth suggests that the number of women seeking paid employment during the 1930s probably declined.[7] Yet increasing numbers of married women were certainly able to seek work. The birth rate dropped sharply from 21.8 between 1911 and 1920 to 18.3 in the 1920s, reaching a record low of 14.8 between 1931 and 1940.[8] The crucial factor in this decline was the conscious decision to have smaller families. The average completed family size in late-Victorian England was just over five and of those in the 1930s, slightly over two. Thus married women had more free time than ever before. Wilmott and Young suggest that the decrease in family size would have prompted many women to look for work had it been available.[9] However, unemployment never fell below 10 per cent throughout the 1930s.

This theory of the effect of unemployment on participation rates, known as the 'discouraged worker' theory, has not been tested for the inter-war period. Neither has its converse, the 'added worker' theory, which posits a response such as Mrs P's, who went to work because her husband was unemployed.[10] That married women in particular will work to supplement the family wage as and when necessary has been well established for an earlier period.[11] Moreover, limited evidence indicates that both this motive for married women's going out to work and the traditionally part-time and temporary character of their work[12] persisted during the inter-war years. Of seventy-four working-class women interviewed in Camden, Hull, Birmingham, Liverpool and Frome, Somerset,[13] eighteen had worked (24 per cent), a figure well above the average. But eight of these did odd charring jobs, hawked goods or worked for friends; in other words, did jobs that would not necessarily be counted in the census returns.

The participation rates show that younger married women, especially those aged between twenty-one and twenty-four were going out to work more by 1931, unlike those over thirty-five. It would, of course, have made economic sense for women with small children to work, this stage of the family life cycle being difficult financially. But it is equally possible that married women were working more only *until* the birth of their first child. After all, women with young children would be inclined to seek the kind of part-time work outlined above, because of the problem of child care. Day nurseries opened during World War I were closed shortly thereafter, the justification being that the state could not be expected to look after children of women who merely preferred working to staying at home.[14] Nursery education was promoted during the 1930s, especially by Labour women, but more with an eye to equalizing educational opportunity than to providing assistance to working women.[15] In fact, in the north west, it seems that it was only acceptable for married women to work either if they were childless, or if they had a single child and the woman worker's mother could help with child care.[16]

The nature of the work women did was as important a determinant of the female participation rate during the 1930s as women's own responses. Behind the fairly constant participation rates lies a change in the distribution of employed women between occupations. During World War I employment opportunities for women increased, only to contract again afterwards, forcing a return to more traditional forms of women's work.

The character of women's work was transformed during World War I. The biggest employer of female labour had always been domestic service, and in 1911, 2,127,000 women had been involved in personal service. This dropped to 1,845,000 by 1921 (still 32.5 per cent of the female workforce).[17] Of the 400,000 domestic servants who entered the munitions factories, for example, only 125,000 returned to service.[18] The numbers of women working in textiles, another traditionally large area of female employment, decreased from 825,000 to 602,000. Here the female experience was similar to the male, and the decline of this and the other staple industries continued to be a major cause of male and female unemployment throughout the inter-war years. Major areas of increasing female employment during the war were metals, engineering and shipbuilding.[19] Most dramatic of all was the war-time expansion of clerical opportunities for women. The number of women in the Civil Service increased from 33,000 to 102,000. Another feature of women's war experience was an increase in wage rates, especially by those whose positions were controlled by dilution agreements, which laid down that women replacing men were to receive a man's wage.[20] However, many of these gains proved transitory. Women affected by dilution agreements were obliged to leave their jobs when war ended, and women's wage rates failed to show any sustained increase, especially where unionization was weak.[21] In 1931, women's weekly wages averaged half the male rate in most industries.[22] A more lasting change was the large numbers of women who remained in the lower grades of the Civil Service. Light engineering also became a large employer of female labour in the South and Midlands during the 1920s and 1930s. But many women were forced back into traditional areas of work: by 1931, the number of women engaged in domestic work had risen again to 2,129,000 (34 per cent of the female workforce).

During the 1930s, the vast majority of women were still doing either specifically women's work (for example, paid domestic work), or unskilled low paying jobs. Women workers exhibited all the signs of a marginal workforce. It was not only that they tended to leave the labour force on marriage or on becoming pregnant, but also that their economic dependency, before as well as after marriage, made their commitment to work secondary. Young women textile workers in Colne, for example, would often be found jobs by relatives and pay all their wages to their parents, while their brothers paid board.[23] Married women usually saw their wage as a supplement to the family wage, that is, the wage of the husband. Thus women remained a cheap and elastic source of labour.

Male attitudes towards women's work show clearly the pressures on all women to restrict themselves to appropriate women's work, and for married women not to work at all. After World War I, heavy pressure was exerted on women to leave their new jobs, particularly in the Civil Service. The outcry in *The Times* during 1921 may be seen as typical. The employment of 2,200 women at the War Office, for example, was called 'a monstrous injustice'.[24] In reply, the War Office pleaded that of a staff of 9,160, only 1, 182 were women, of whom 700 did women's work (charring) and of the rest, 200 did mechanical jobs not particularly suitable for men.[25]

The heaviest pressure of all was for women to return to domestic service. In 1921, the government decided that Labour Exchanges could refuse out-of-work donation to anyone who had been a domestic servant in the past. An editorial in *The Times* welcomed the move thus: 'If they refuse the employment that is open to them because it is not exactly to their taste, they ought not to be paid out of the public purse and so enabled to live a life of idleness'.[26] Later the same year, when the unemployment insurance scheme was extended, domestic servants were one of the few groups excluded, unemployment being thought to be impossible in their case.

In 1920, when the Central Committee for Women's Employment was given £500, 000 to maintain centres for training women, the main concentration was on domestic service.[27] Still, fears were expressed that the Committee would nonetheless train women for work in areas in which men were unemployed.[28] Thus, in May 1921, when another £150, 000 was given to the Committee, it was designated for domestic service training only. In 1927, one member of the Committee resigned as a protest against the policy of training women at all; and female MPs, such as Margaret Bondfield and Ellen Wilkinson, who had opposed the narrowing of training schemes for women, were put in the position of defending them rather than face the total shut down of the centres.[29] Opposition to this concentration on domestic service training weakened still further during the depression years of the 1930s.[30]

Domestic service was believed to be the most suitable employment for working-class women. It was the most 'natural' kind of work and it was claimed that the happiest, best-kept working-class homes were ones in which the wife had at one time been a servant.[31] Moreover, the work was believed to be crucial in providing the middle class with help in bringing up a family. *The Times* saw the main danger of the servant shortage as 'the degradation of the middle class woman into a mere household drudge when she wants to rear a large family'.[32] During the inter-war period, the average wage for servants rose faster than the income of the servant-keeping classes. On the other hand, the price of labour-saving devices fell sharply between 1920 and 1938.[33] Inevitably live-in servants would be replaced by machines and daily 'helps', but this was only just beginning in the early 1930s. The domestic technology displayed in household manuals tended to be primitive. Moreover, advertisements for appliances such as vacuum cleaners usually showed them being used by a maid.[34]

Middle-class women could not work outside the home during this period unless someone else performed their household tasks. The Committees appointed by the government to inquire into the servant shortage during the early 1920s were weighted heavily in favour of mistresses rather than maids and their conclusions reflected the interest of the former in defending and maintaining the status quo. The committee members heard plenty of evidence condemning the appalling conditions of service, yet both advocated 'more training' in order to raise the status of the work as the preferred solution.[35]

Attitudes to middle class women's work also reflected the prevalent opinion that only certain types of work should be opened to women. During the war hospitals had opened their doors to female medical students — only to exclude them again in the 1920s. Women had been 'financially useful' during the war years, but afterwards St Mary's Hospital led the way in resurrecting the old objection to women on grounds of modesty.[36] Similarly, the National Association of Schoolmasters came out with the slogan 'men teachers for boys', a protest grounded in their fear of the number of women teachers and their opposition to the women's campaign for equal pay.[37]

It was generally agreed by employers that middle-class women became instantly unemployable on marriage. It would appear that pressure was exerted on working-class women more by their husbands than by their employers,[38] although, during the 1930s, the threat of unemployment among Lancashire textile workers led to the introduction of a de facto marriage bar, so that women hid the fact of their marriage.[39] Pressure on middle-class women was more formal. The marriage bar in the Civil Service was made legal in 1921 and supported by women in the lower grades because they feared competition from married women.[40] In 1924, the London County Council made its policy quite explicit when it changed the phrase 'shall resign on marriage' to 'the contract shall end on marriage'.[41] This was prompted by the refusal of some women doctors and teachers in its employ to resign. During the course of a legal case in which the right of the Poole Corporation to dismiss a married woman teacher was upheld, the Corporation expressed the view that if the woman married and did her duty at home, she had no time for anything else.[42] When a Married Women's (Employment) Bill was introduced into the House of Commons by Sir Robert Newman, the House voted it out largely because of objections to: 'The travesty put before us of the reversal of the sexes, where the mother goes out to work and the father stays at home to look after the baby'.[43]

During the course of the debate, MPs were also warned that in giving assent to the Bill they would be voting for a further reduction in the birth rate.[44] Concern over the quality and, more critically, the quantity of population was a major political issue during the whole inter-war period and one which had profound effects on women. If women were to have more and healthier children, it was inevitable that policies would be hostile to married women's work and that stress would be laid on the domestic duties and childbearing function of women. To this end, child and maternal welfare services were improved and efforts were made to remove the threat of death in childbirth, but the scope of maternal and child welfare work was necessarily limited. The demand of some women for free access to birth control obviously could not be accommodated if population was to be increased, and attention tended to focus on maternal deaths rather than on the less dramatic but widespread ill-health among women.

Concern over the quality and quantity of population may be traced back to the Boer War, when army inspections revealed a large number of working men to be unfit for service. The subsequent outcry over 'physical deterioration', led to the setting up of an Inter-Departmental Committee on the question.[45] The Eugenics Education Society, founded in 1904, popularized the idea of physical degeneration. Eugenists believed that hereditary qualities were vastly more important than environmental ones and that evidence of degeneration was therefore proof that the quality of the race was doomed to decline. The Galton Laboratory (for eugenics) equated 'quality' with high socio-economic status,[46] and when the report of the Registrar General for 1911 showed conclusively that the birth rate was indeed declining more rapidly amongst the middle and upper classes than among the working class, it was considered a proof of racial deterioration. (The fertility of the Registrar General's Class I was 80 per cent of the overall rate; of class II, 88 per cent; of class III, 99 per cent; of class IV, 102 per cent and of class V, 114 per cent.) Working class women were shown to marry earlier than middle- and upper-class women (three quarters of all miners' wives married before they were twenty-five years old, but less than one third of middle-class women did so) and, because they did not use birth control as much, had larger families.[47]

In fact, the class differential in fertility began to disappear during the inter-war period, and had all but gone by the late 1930s. However, contemporaries did not know this and fears were constantly expressed that the middle class would not reproduce itself. Middle-class women were condemned for entering 'masculine occupations of every kind' rather than concentrating 'upon making their own homes more interesting and more racially valuable'.[48] In 1932, the Obstetric Registrar of the Westminster Hospital stated that: 'Though the modern emancipated woman plays many parts in our social system, her most important function — and it is well she should remember it — is the perpetuation of the race'.[49] Women's magazines, which became more middle class in their orientation during the inter-war period, also played their part in encouraging a domestic role for women. The 'feminine mystique' described by Betty Friedan as an invention of the 1950s was in fact a product of the 1920s and 1930s. Even *The Lady* cut its employment features and substituted home-making articles.[50]

The falling birth rate, together with the loss of population resulting from the Boer War and World War I, gave impetus to the maternal and child welfare movement. Infant mortality rates were very high in the early part of the century;[51] and the special reports of the Local Government Board on this question, published in 1910 and 1915, made it clear that because of the population issue, infant mortality had become a question of 'national importance'.[52] In the 1915 report, the Chief Medical Officer of Health to the Board, Arthur Newsholme, pointed out that the welfare of infants depended in large measure on that of their mothers. Thus the promotion of maternal welfare and in particular the reduction of maternal mortality was also important, because it was as much in the interest of the race as the mother.[53]

After a sharp rise during 1918 and 1919 due to an outbreak of influenza and sepsis, the maternal mortality rate fell to pre-war levels. But from 1923 onwards, it rose again, remaining at over five per 1, 000 until 1936 (see Figure 8.1). Death in childbirth was by no means the main cause of death of women aged from fifteen to forty-four. It accounted for 5.9 per cent of deaths in 1931, while T.B. killed 24.6 per cent and circulatory disease 9.8 per cent. However, it was the only major cause of death to show an increase during the inter-war period. The government issued five reports on the subject between 1924 and 1937,[54] the aim being to stimulate action on the part of local authorities, who bore the responsibility of providing services under the Maternity and Child Welfare Act of 1918. Politically, though, maternal deaths were difficult to handle. Motherhood was sacred and a woman's prime duty; the 1927 debate on married women's employment had made that clear. The whole emphasis of the maternal and child welfare movement until the end of World War I had been on 'mothercraft' and the importance of proper child care in bringing down the infant mortality rate. Moreover, if motherhood was so dangerous, how could women be persuaded to have more children?

This question became crucial during the 1930s, when it was projected that by 2033, England and Wales would have a population no larger than that of the County of London in 1936.[55] These projections had a great impact. In his budget speech of 1935, Chamberlain warned that an Imperial power must view the decrease in the birth rate with grave apprehension.[56] It was also feared that an ageing population (a by-product of a declining birth rate) would have an adverse effect on consumption and result in even greater unemployment.[57]

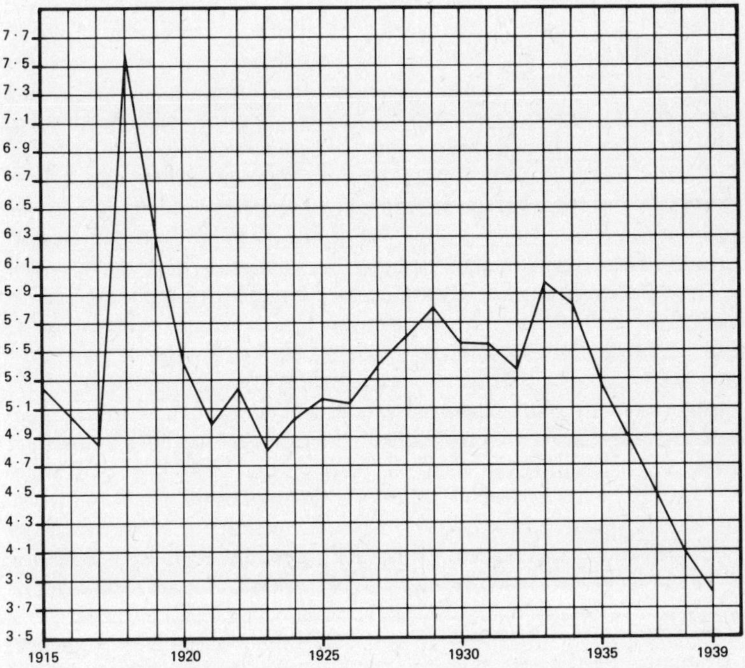

Figure 8.1. Maternal mortality rate, England and Wales 1915–1939. *Source*: Reports of the Registrar General, 1916–1939.

The media exploited these fears to the full. A radio series called 'One Generation and Another' explained that while the citizen naturally saw the question of birth control only in terms of family welfare, he must be educated to the wider, national and imperial aspect of the problem.[58] Beveridge also went on radio to persuade people to fill in a 'family form' to help demographers get a more accurate picture of the characteristics and numbers of people.[59] The government responded by passing the Population Statistics Act of 1938, which required such information as the mother's age at birth of each child to be recorded so that a more accurate check could be kept on population trends. During the course of the debate on the Bill, two points were made clear: that the dissemination of birth control information should not be encouraged, and that steps should be taken to remove the fear of maternal mortality and pain in childbirth.[60]

Political parties vied with one another in expressing their concern. During the economic crisis of 1930–31, Arthur Greenwood, the Minister of Health, reminded the Cabinet that the Labour Opposition were committed to a policy on motherhood, making cuts in this area difficult.[61] During the debate on population in 1937, a Conservative tersely reminded a Labour MP that the Labour Party had 'no monopoly of care or concern as to the health of mothers'.[62] The problem was that the more maternal mortality was talked about, the more prevalent the fear of childbirth was likely to become and the birth rate to fall. Thus, while the 1924 government report adopted a strongly critical tone, a 1937 circular on the subject sought to reassure women: 'The young woman can be told with confidence that if she is in normal health and will take ordinary and sensible precautions . . . the risk she will run in childbirth need be no matter of anxiety'.[63] The Ministry of Health had to tread a fine line; publicity on the issue was necessary if full co-operation in bringing down the death rate was to be exacted from local authorities and the medical profession. On the other hand, the lack of any marked improvement would only heighten public concern.[64]

The causes of death in childbirth were complex. Most commonly identified were sepsis (accounting for 32 per cent of puerperal deaths in 1931) followed by toxaemia (24 per cent) and haemorrhage (11 per cent). Young mothers were particularly susceptible to toxaemia and mechanical difficulties at birth and older women to a general loss of muscle tone leading to prolonged labour and haemorrhage. But these clinical causes of death were determined in large part by biological (relating mainly to age and parity), environmental and social factors. For example, the height of women has been found to be a good indicator of obstetrical performance, and height depends on environmental and social as well as hereditary factors.[65] In its studies, the Ministry of Health displayed singular reluctance to consider anything but clinical causes of mortality. The extent of general ill-health amongst women tended to be overlooked. Moreover, neglect of the effects of pregnancy on ill health and vice versa led to services being offered that did little to effect any immediate improvement in the maternal mortality rate or the health of women generally.

The response of the medical profession to maternal mortality was to advocate the hospitalization of childbirth. Specialists also insisted that to make childbirth safe every labour must be treated as 'a major surgical procedure'.[66] Nor was it coincidental that leading obstetricians, such as Victor Bonney, insisted on women's being delivered on their backs, a position convenient for the surgeon, rather than on their sides, a better position for slowly delivering the head and preventing tears.[67]

The justification for the hospitalization of childbirth rested in large part on the necessity for specialized aseptic and antiseptic routines common in surgery to prevent sepsis. Semmelweiss, a Veinnese physician, had shown the importance of such procedures as early as the 1860s, but the profession had been extremely slow in adopting them.[68] Sepsis could follow interference in labour or haemorrhage, or could follow a normal labour, in which case a throat or nose infection on the part of the attendant was often to blame. This latter source of infection was only confirmed in the mid-1930s, when strains of the same virus were identified in attendant and patient. That sepsis could follow interference in labour should logically have led to an emphasis on traditional midwifery methods, because the midwife delivering in the home was less likely to use instruments. However, the new emphasis on ante-natal care revealed toxaemic conditions and pelvic deformities earlier, and thus made intervention in the form of induction or caesarian section more likely. In fact, the proportion of births taking place in hospital rose from 15 to 35 per cent between 1927 and 1937.[69]

Most articulate women supported the move towards the hospitalization of childbirth. Government reports stressed the need for specialist care and women began to demand what they were told was the best. A voluntary committee formed by May Tennant (formerly Chief Lady Inspector of Factories) and Gertrude Tuckwell (a leading woman trade unionist) to lobby the government on the question of maternal mortality, believed hospital births to be safer and asked the Ministry of Health to make more maternity beds available.[70] Labour women stressed the value of hospital care in providing a much needed rest for working women.[71] Appropriately, the heroine of Vera Brittain's novel *Honourable Estate* (who is employed by the Labour Party) reflects:

> Suppose I'd been a working man's wife, with no salary to help me pay my doctor's bills, and no private income to meet the expense of staying in this nursing home till the

twins are safely over their first weeks and I've had all the rest I need? What if I'd been pushed out of hospital after ten days or a fortnight, hardly able to stand, with two delicate babies to care for and the housework to do and perhaps other young children to look after as well?[72]

Another reason for going to hospital was the availability of anaethesia. The National Birthday Trust campaigned for midwives to be allowed to use chloroform capsules in the home, but permission was refused by the Royal College of Obstetricians and Gynaecologists in 1936.[73] The only alternative permitted by the College was gas and air, but the apparatus required for its use was expensive and few independent midwives could afford to buy it.

It is hard to assess how common these positive feelings about hospital birth were. On the question of anaesthesia, for example, there is some evidence that working women in particular disliked the idea long before natural childbirth became fashionable. The Annual Report of the General Lying-In Hospital for 1932 commented that: 'In the locality [Westminster and Lambeth] a definite stigma is attached to any mother who has had an abnormal confinement — that is to say, an anaesthetic.'[74] A similar opinion was expressed by one working-class woman interviewed. Also, many working women preferred to be at home for births other than the first because of the difficulty of caring for other children. Women's organizations recognized this problem, but their strenuous campaigns to have home helps included in the maternity service offered by local authorities made little headway. In 1928, local authorities were spending only 0.1 per cent of their maternal and child welfare budget in this way.[75]

The hospitalization of childbirth had little impact on the maternal mortality rate. Mortality due to sepsis did not fall until the new chemotherapy became available in 1936; haemorrhage only ceased to be a major danger after blood transfusions were introduced during World War II; and potential toxaemia victims were only identified when ante-natal care became more widespread, again after World War II. Proposals for an improved maternity service, including the ones set out in government reports, were drafted by specialists and inevitably favoured large hospitals as the place of birth. The government report of 1932 recommended that all new maternity hospitals have seventy beds, the minimum needed for the appointment of a consultant.[76] There was nothing conspiratorial in this, for specialists genuinely believed hospital to be the safest place for childbirth and during the 1930s many women agreed with them. Home conditions could certainly be primitive. Women had to provide everything needed for the birth and the items listed in the

Motherhood Book of 1934 cost £4/1/11½, way beyond the reach of working-class women, to whom one bowl and jug (let alone the five recommended) was a prized possession.[77] But during the inter-war years, the key to safe childbirth was the presence of a careful attendant; and that this could just as easily be a midwife working in the home was proved by the excellent record of the Queen Victoria Jubilee Institute midwives, who never had a maternal mortality rate of over 2.[78]

All the evidence suggests that a generally low level of health prevailed among women and that pregnancy exacerbated this. The problem of maternal morbidity was much more widespread than that of maternal mortality and the hospitalization of childbirth did little to alleviate it. One doctor estimated that 60 per cent of hospital gynaecology derived from vitiated childbearing, and another that 600, 000 or 10 per cent of all mothers were 'more or less crippled' by childbearing each year.[79] This was in keeping with the kind of damage brought to light by the early birth control clinics. Marie Stopes, the leading proponent of birth control during the 1920s, reported that 31 per cent of her first 10, 000 patients had serious untreated gynaecology problems.[80] These, incidentally, often made the use of a diaphragm, and therefore the prevention of further pregnancies, impossible. Obviously, such problems resulted from lack of adequate post-natal care. Neither Mrs P nor the other women interviewed received any. As late as 1937, official statistics showed that only 10 per cent of women were attending post-natal clinics. More attention was given to provision of ante-natal care, which was received by 54 per cent of women.[81] This reflects the initial bias of the maternal and child welfare movement towards the health of the baby rather than the mother.[82]

The Medical Women's Federation stressed the importance of the general health of women. In evidence given to the Departmental Committee on Maternal Mortality in 1929, Rhoda H.B. Adamson, who had investigated the health of women munition workers during World War I, said: 'The Maternal Mortality Committee of the Medical Women's Federation is of the opinion that insufficient attention is often given to the investigation of the general health of the patient'.[83] This opinion was shared by the influential voluntary committee on maternal mortality led by Tuckwell and Tennant, which pushed strongly for an inquiry into the causes of morbidity rather than mortality. However, the response of Sir George Newman, the Chief Medical Officer at the Ministry of Health, was that such an enquiry could only prove 'embarrassing', because it could 'have but one ending, namely, the demonstration of a great mass of sickness and impairment attributable to childbirth, which would create a demand for organized treatment by the state'. He added that:

> Childbirth has always been womens' travail, and always will be . . . the broad fact remains, first, that childbirth is a heavy strain on the physique of any woman and the bodies of many must therefore be impaired; secondly that there is in modern civilized nations an insufficiency of organized facilities for effective treatment.[84]

The problem was admitted to be too large to tackle.

Unaware of Newman's feelings, the voluntary committee wrote again to say that what they really had in mind was 'an enquiry into the generally excessive sickness prevalent amonst married women'. This was curtly dismissed as 'impossible'.[85] Yet there was no doubt that this burden of sickness greatly affected women's reproductive experience. Gertrude Tuckwell's interest in maternal mortality only developed when she was sitting on the Royal Commission on National Health Insurance during the 1920s and noticed how prevalent sickness was among married women.[85] National Health Insurance records provide one of the few pieces of statistical evidence on women's sickness experience. During 1931–2, unmarried women covered by the scheme experienced 25 per cent more sickness and 65 per cent more disablement (long-term sickness) than had been expected by the government actuaries and married women a colossal 140 per cent more sickness and 60 per cent more disablement than had been allowed for. (Men's rates on the other hand, were lower than expected.)[87] The sickness rate of young married women was especially heavy,[88] and a similar pattern is revealed by the age specific death rates for single and married women of childbearing years: for the year 1921, the death rates of married women were consistently higher than those for single women up to the age of 37 and in 1931 up to the age of 25.[89]

It is true that only women working outside the home were covered by National Health Insurance and it might be argued that the sickness experience of these women would have been particularly bad, carrying as they did the burden of two jobs. However, this must be balanced against the fact that married women who did not work were not covered by health insurance and therefore had to pay for medical attention, a great disincentive to seek it. Also, it must be remembered that many women not covered by insurance still undertook casual, part-time work, often in inferior conditions to those experienced by full-time workers.

Undoubtedly, the additional burden of pregnancy was an important determinant of married women's high sickness rate. Yet, despite the current interest in the question of maternal mortality, the response of the government's actuary was to accuse women of malingering and to recommend that women's insurance be put on an actuarily sound basis.[90] In 1931 Parliament agreed to this and cut rates of benefit for women. Eleanor Rathbone, an active feminist, spoke out against the cuts in the House of Commons, but sympathy was limited.[91] After all the actuary's reports made it clear that according to records of maternity benefit claims, the birth rate of married women workers was only one half that of women who stayed at home.[92]

Clinical investigations and social surveys of the period lent support to the view that married women experienced particularly poor health. Some of these surveys also described the conditions of married women's work in the home, the context in which their sickness experience must be located. The most comprehensive account was published in 1939 by the Women's Health Enquiry Committee, who undertook the enquiry because they believed morbidity amongst working-class wives to be 'extremely widespread and enduring' and that women tended 'to become progressively less fit with the birth of each child'.[93] They received 1, 250 replies to their questionnaire. Many women did not consider themselves to be in poor health, and yet there was every indication that they were so, for example the thirty-eight-year-old woman in Cardiff who had severely decayed teeth, bronchitis every winter and a prolapsed uterus dating from her second pregnancy. Most common of all was anaemia, from which 44 per cent of all the respondents suffered.[94] The high incidence of anaemia was well documented during the period. In a sample of women examined in Durham and Tyneside, 50 per cent of wives of unemployed men and 44 per cent of wives of employed men showed a low haemoglobin count. The Pilgrim Trust Report on unemployed men found an increased incidence of bad teeth, anaemia and debility amongst their wives.[95] The saying 'for every child a tooth' was common during the period.

The prevalence of anaemia and debility was to some extent a result of poor nutrition in childhood. This was also true of pelvic deformities, resulting from rickets contracted in early childhood. As late as 1931, this caused 3 per cent of deaths in childbirth. However, as leading obstetricians recognized, a good diet during pregnancy could still have averted many difficulties.[96] But the diet approved by the BMA for pregnant women cost 5/- a week, which was quite beyond the means of the women who needed it most.[97] Women rarely got even their fair share of the food normally available in the home. As early as 1913, a group of Fabian women showed that in the case of certain Lambeth families the husband always got more and better food, chiefly because the wage-earner had to maintain his capacity to work.[98] A later study showed that this tradition continued even when poverty was no longer the major factor; of sixty-one women studied only fourteen ate adequately.[99] In her autobiography, Dorothy Scannel recalls her mother having what she called a 'kettle bender' for her evening meal. This consisted of hot water, crusts and a knob of margarine and was always eaten before her husband arrived home for his meal.[100] The elastic standard of living of wives served as a buffer for their husbands and for the larger economic system as well.[101]

Wives often did not know how much their husbands earned. Moreover, housekeeping money tended to stay constant regardless of changing family size and increases in pay received by the husband.[102] As housekeepers, women had to solve the food/rent equation. The Ministry of Labour felt that rent could fairly absorb 16 per cent of income,[103] but in the case of the Women's Health Enquiry Committee's survey the average figure was 25 per cent.[104] Yet often women would prefer to economize on food and pay for a good house (especially if it had a bathroom), despite the decline in health standards that this often entailed.[105] Three women interviewed mentioned the lack of a bathroom as a reason for moving during the 1930s. Leonora Eyles' picture of life in a terraced house during the early 1920s makes this preference understandable. Saturday baths in the zinc tub on the kitchen floor and no hot water for bathing or washing made housework very arduous.[106] Facilities seem to have varied widely between regions. Women interviewed in London and Birmingham had gas cookers by the 1930s, but in Hull and Liverpool ranges were still common and some women in Liverpool and Frome still cooked on open grates. In Birmingham, women in terraced houses often used communal wash houses for washing (called 'brew-houses') and one respondent told how she had had to get up a mere three days after the birth of her child to use the brew-house because her turn fell on a Monday and with a large family she could not afford to miss it.[107] Outings for these women were few. Of the seventy-four interviewed, ten went to the cinema fairly regularly, either by themselves, with a friend or very occasionally with their husbands. Only two went to the pub with their husbands on a regular weekly basis. The most frequent form of entertainment was family visiting.[108]

Had health officials investigated the amount of morbidity rather than mortality among women, they would have been forced to confront the problem of poverty. Most of the social surveys of the 1930s were prompted by the fear of the effect of long-term unemployment on physical and mental health. The health levels of women and children thus became major factors in the politics of nutrition. The government took the position that since infant mortality was falling there was no malnutrition. But, as Titmuss showed, the gap between the mortality rates of the highest and lowest social classes was widening during this period.[109] The effect of malnutrition on maternal mortality was an even more vexed question.

In the opinion of leading obstetricians, even a slight blood loss in an anaemic, debilitated or undernourished woman could be disastrous.[110] The Advisory Committee on Nutrition set up by the Ministry of Health in 1931, admitted that the 'feeding of the pregnant woman was at the base of the problem'.[111] But its later work never reflected this belief. Nor did that of the BMA, even though it too subscribed to the idea of a special diet in prenancy. No provision was made for buying these special foods in any of the minimum diets published during the period.

The Ministry of Health was eager to seize on the fact that in the East End of London maternal mortality was as high among the middle as the working class, and claimed that the diet of the well-off was as bad as that of the poor, because it was more likely to result in toxaemic conditions.[112] On the other hand, two unpublished studies carried out by government officials in Wales, and Sunderland and Durham showed that maternal mortality did increase in the Special Areas during the early 1930s.[113] It was hard to identify malnutrition clearly as the cause, though. The most common measure of malnutrition was subjective assessment by the Medical Officers of Health producing wide variations. Haemoglobin counts were rarely used by health officials. However, when mothers in the Special Areas were given extra nourishment during the course of two independent studies carried out by the National Birthday Trust and the People's League of Health, mortality rates dropped sharply. The People's League claimed that the incidence of toxaemia fell by 30 per cent in primigravidae.[114]

The government's own answer to the problem of nutrition was public education. A memo issued in 1934 by E.P. Cathcart, a member of the Advisory Committee on Nutrition, asserted that 'everything turns on the women', and in most cases they had received insufficient education to do a good job.[115] The Advisory Committee eagerly seized on Dr Elwin Nash's proposals to investigate methods of cheap cookery and to give demonstrations in working-class areas. Dr Nash promoted deep-fat frying and hay-box cookery (a slow method of cooking which conserved heat), and specialized in recipes for broken biscuits and windfall apples.[116] The BMA also gave a public cookery demonstration using their diet sheets, but apparently the quantities of food to be used were so remote from the realities of the weekly working-class budget that it was a fiasco.[117]

Groups who could agree on little else agreed on the need for education. Lady Baldwin (an active member of the National Birthday Trust) declared herself willing to go and demonstrate hay-box cookery.[118] The campaign to educate women extended beyond cookery to the proper care of children. Special emphasis was laid on the duty of mothers to breast feed. Mothers were told that if they followed the rigid instructions of Truby King (the most popular writer of infant care manuals of the day) on feeding schedules, they could not fail in this important regard.[119] In fact, this aspect of the campaign often proved particularly oppressive for middle-class women, who tended to be assiduous readers of advice literature. John and Elizabeth Newson quoted two letters they received from professional women on the subject: 'My daughter was born during the Truby King period, and it took a month of untold agony for myself and the child before I threw every book I had out of the house . . .' and:

> *I* was caught up in the Truby King Mothercraft doctrine of 1935 . . . . The health visitor prated and bullied; one's baby screamed and tears splashed down one's cheeks while milk gushed through one's jersey. But one must *never* pick the baby *up* — it was practically incestuous to enjoy one's baby . . . .[120]

Attention was also directed towards the education of school girls. In 1931 it became possible to offer domestic subjects for the School Certificate and in 1937 the Board of Education established a departmental committee on cookery. Teachers were urged to make their lessons practical, definite, systematic, progressive and simple.[121] But there was nothing very progressive about the kind of lesson Dorothy Scannell received for a year before leaving school (at fourteen years old) in the late 1920s. She recalls: 'As we entered, facing us was a large blackboard on which was permanently written, "A nourishing meal for a poor family of six: Three fresh herrings, 2 lb. of potatoes"; underneath were the words, "If a pudding is needed and able to be provided, then a suet pudding with black treacle".'[122] Girls often regarded these lessons as vocational training for domestic service, and hence heartily disliked them.

This educational solution has a long history. Before World War I, a similar approach had been advocated to deal with the problem of infant mortality. Girls were to be educated in infant care in school and their mothers in schools for mothers.[123] Yet in conditions where families could afford neither the utensils nor the fuel for cooking, such solutions were ridiculous. In 1938, it was even proposed to appoint a woman officer to instruct women how to spend Unemployment Assistance money efficiently.[124] Yet studies showed that the vast majority of women achieved as balanced a diet as was possible, given the circumstances.[125]

One way women could ease the double burden of work and ill health was to limit their families.[126] Women's attitude to frequent pregnancies was made quite clear by their recourse to abortion.[127] The BMA estimated that between 16 and 20 per cent of all pregnancies ended in abortion.[128] In industrial centres where large numbers of married women worked, the figure was probably much higher. The prevalent belief was that if the woman aborted herself, it was not an illegal operation. Abortion became an important issue in the 1930s because it was thought that the incidence of both criminal and spontaneous abortions was increasing. The mortality rate accompanying abortion was particularly high (due to septic infection), and it was feared that this was inflating the maternal mortality rate. An Inter-departmental Committee was set up to investigate the question in 1938: it revealed the widespread use of 'female pills', sold by manufacturing houses, and of savin, ergot, lead, pennyroyal and slippery elm, all of which were potentially poisonous. Some of these were more effective abortifacients than others. Women were often charged as much as 7/6 for one 'female pill' or 10/- for a bottle of what turned out to be washing soda and stout,[129] items commonly used anyway in abortion attempts. (It is worth noting that birth control devices purchased at the local voluntary birth control clinics were sometimes just as expensive.)[130]

Birth control societies used the issue of abortion to plead for freer access to birth control information through government clinics. But the report of the Inter-departmental Committee concluded that first: birth control failures would only encourage abortions; and second: that free access to birth control information would lead to a further decline in the birth rate.[131] The Committee recommended instead, better maternal and child welfare facilities with education for women on the evils of abortion, and family allowances to ease any economic incentive to abort. Mrs Dorothy Thurtle (the daughter of George Lansbury) was alone in feeling that it was indefensible that: 'The State has recognized the necessity for family limitation on grounds of health, but has not yet been prepared to recognize a high fertility rate as a reason for imparting birth control knowledge'.[132]

It was indeed well established that women giving birth to their fifth or any subsequent child were more likely to die in childbirth, and that their infants were more likely to be still born. Marie Stopes made use of this material in her argument for birth control.[133] However, it was argued that since working-class women in the East End of London had a low maternal mortality rate, frequent childbirth could not be a factor. Rather, the low birth rate of middle-class women meant that they had proportionately greater numbers of first births (always more dangerous than the second, third or fourth) and therefore a higher mortality rate. In fact, other factors intervened. The death rate of working-class women in the East End was lower only because the incidence of sepsis was so low, due to the excellent record of the East End maternity hospitals. The Government's own reports contained case histories which indicated that fatigue and undernourishment often preceded septic infection,[134] but nevertheless it held firm on its refusal to allow birth control information to be distributed in maternal and child welfare centres.

The main aim of birth control groups throughout the inter-war period was to change this policy. The 1920s saw a mushrooming of organizations concerned with birth control; Stopes founded her Society for Constructive Birth Control and Racial Progress (CBC) in 1921, the Workers' Birth Control Group formed in 1924 and the National Birth Control Association (NBCA) in 1930. Women's organizations also came out in public support of birth control, led by the Women's Co-operative Guild in 1923, and followed by the National Union of Societies for Equal Citizenship (NUSEC) in 1925, the Women's National Liberal Association in 1927, and the National Council of Women in 1929. The primary aim of such groups was to ease the lot of working-class women still subject to frequent and debilitating pregnancies. As early as 1911 the Women's Co-operative Guild had welcomed the decrease in the birth rate[135] and in 1915 had published a moving collection of letters from its members describing the cumulative effect of frequent childbirth, poor wages and home conditions.[136] Stopes and the NBCA also used an argument which became more common during the 1930s (and which was never opposed by women's groups), that birth control should be used to control the fertility of the poor. In 1929 the Wood Report on mental deficiency identified the existence of a 'social problem' group,[137] defined in greater detail by C.P. Blacker (a physician and leading eugenicist) as having the following characteristics: insanity, epilepsy, occupational instability, inebriety and social dependency.[138] A NUSEC deputation to the government in 1932 asked for an extension of birth control and sterlization on behalf of the social problem group. In this case it was clear that the unemployed were the group in question.[139] Lady Maureen Stanley of the NBCA asked the Government's Commissioner of Special Areas, Malcolm Stewart, to make a grant to the National Council of Social Services to allow the NBCA to set up birth control clinics in the Special Areas. Birth control information would be given on medical grounds, which would include evidence of malnutrition. Stewart was in full accord with this, but his desire to give the grant was thwarted.[140] Across the top of his correspondence on the subject with the Minister of Labour was scrawled: 'But the Chancellor of Exchequer appealing for more babies',[141] a reference to Chamberlain's budget speech of 1935.[142] By the mid-1930s quantity had become more important than quality.

The only government move towards making birth control information easier to obtain came in 1930. It was decided to allow information to be given to nursing and expectant mothers at maternal and child welfare clinics when further pregnancy was deemed to be detrimental to health, and to women attending special gynaecology clinics, again on medical grounds.[143] In other words, women had to be very sick to qualify. The measure was further limited by the refusal to allow gynaecology clinics to be held in the same building as maternal and child welfare clinics for fear of disrupting the educational work being done among mothers and infants. Birth control was not made an integral part of the maternal and child welfare system until the passing of the National Health Service (Family Planning) Act in 1967.

Full appreciation of the circumstances under which working women lived came only from working-women's organizations. In the introduction to their 1917 Memo on the National Care of Maternity, the Women's Co-operative Guild, an organization of some 70, 000 women during the 1930s, stated:

> ... During the months of pregnancy, the woman must learn by experience and ignorance, usually being told that all her troubles are 'natural'. In order to scrape together a few shillings she often goes out to char or sits at her sewing machine or takes in washing; she puts by pence in money boxes, she saves little stores of tea, soap, oatmeal and other dry goods; when times are bad she goes without, providing for her husband and children before herself. If not working long hours in a factory, her home work may be more injurious, when ill or well, she washes, mangles, lifts heavy weights, and may still be carrying an infant in arms. She may at the same time, have to nurse a sick husband or child. Up to the last minute before childbirth she has to wash and dress the children, cook the meals she's sometimes too tired to eat, and do all her own housework.
>
> At her confinement often only an untrained midwife is available, who sometimes has to make use of a child's help . . . . In the areas where bad housing causes the family in hundreds of thousands of cases to live in two or three rooms . . . privacy and quiet are impossible.[144]

Both the Guild and the Women's Labour League insisted that women needed a complete maternity service with home helps and free milk and dinners. Emphasis on the latter was particularly strong during the 1930s. At a meeting of the voluntary maternal mortality committee called in 1934, Mrs Barton, General Secretary of the

Guild, insisted that the health of mothers would inevitably be undermined by poor nutrition, and at the Labour Party Conference of 1934, a female delegate referred to the 'unchallengable evidence that one of the contributory causes [of maternal mortality] is the under-nourishment of mothers'.[145] The Guild and the Women's Labour League talked of 'safeguarding motherhood' and 'protecting the mothers of the race' in much the same way as the government did, but the concern was always the situation of the individual mother, as their stand on birth control proved. Labour women had brought this issue before the Labour Party Conference in 1928, but their demand had been ignored.[146]

During the inter-war period, the organized feminist movement, which was predominantly middle class, also gave more attention to the position of wives and mothers. In 1917, with the granting of the vote imminent, the National Union of Women's Suffrage Societies met to discuss its future work. Two distinct philosophies emerged. One section of the society wanted to continue to promote 'equalitarian' reforms which would make women politically, socially or economically equal to men. The other, led by Eleanor Rathbone — who became President in 1919 — argued that women must seek 'a real equality', demanding reform 'not because it is what men have got, but because it is what women need to fulfill the potentialities of their own natures and to adjust themselves to the circumstances of their own lives'. Rathbone called this approach the 'new feminism'.[147] In part it was a response to the lavish praises of women's war work, which showed how women's often heavy work in the home had been ignored.[148]

Middle-class feminists also felt that the gulf between the aims of working-class and middle-class women, so accurately sensed by Virginia Woolf when she attended a Women's Co-operative Guild meeting in 1913,[149] could only be bridged by a programme that addressed itself more to the problems faced by the majority of women. The new programme of the NUSEC, as it became in 1919, therefore included calls for birth control and family allowances.

'Equalitarian' feminists could not agree that such matters should take priority and in 1927 the split became public, the occasion being a vote on the issue of protective legislation. The traditional feminist view demanded that women ask for 'a fair field and no favour' and opposed all protective legislation, including maternity leave, on principle. Rathbone and new feminists felt that each case should be judged on its own merits, and condemned if it was a ploy of male workers to rid themselves of female competition; but welcomed if the work was genuinely dangerous, as in the case of the lead paint industry, from which women were excluded in 1926. Feminists and trade union women should then join in working for the extension of protection to men.[150] Many of the women who left NUSEC in 1927 joined the Open Door Council, which together with the Six Point Group and the Women's Freedom League were dedicated to removing 'all artificial barriers to women's progress', to which might have been added 'in the public sphere'.[151]

During the inter-war years, feminists such as Rathbone, Mary Stocks, a prominent member of the Labour Party, and Eva Hubback, Principal of Morley College, concentrated much of their attention on the campaign for family allowances. Originally, allowances were envisaged as a feminist reform. Rathbone had formed the Family Endowment Council in 1917, believing that the mother should be paid 12/6 a week during the eight weeks prior to the birth of her child and for as long as she had a child under five, plus 5/- a week for the first child and 3/6 for subsequent children.[152] To a family of five living on a subsistence wage of 53/- a week, this would have represented a substantial addition. The payment of the mother was crucial to feminists, because it involved recognition of her services to the state. Also, if men were no longer held responsible for the support of their families, the main impediment to equal pay would be removed. Women teachers demanding equal pay during this period faced opposition from the National Association of Schoolmasters over the issue of family responsibility; and the Royal Commission of the Civil Service, which reported in 1930, were divided on the question for the same reason.[153]

The feminist principle behind family allowances was eroded during the inter-war years. Many socialist women felt that child poverty alone was the central issue, a point of view that won many adherents during the 1930s. Rathbone's own argument for the payment of allowances rested heavily on the analysis of the cycle and extent of family poverty. The average family of five, which was the basis for most of the calculations in the poverty surveys of the period, accounted for only 8.8 per cent of families. On the other hand, 9.9 per cent of families had more than three children, and here was found no less than 40 per cent of the child population. Moreover, these large families were usually the poorest.[154] Rathbone moved further away from the feminist principle when she founded the Children's Minimum Council in 1934, at the height of the nutrition controversy. The CMC demanded family allowances, rent rebates for large families, sufficient Unemployment Assistance Board benefits to enable purchase of the minimum dietary laid down by the BMA in 1933 and free milk for mothers and infants.

When family allowances were implemented in 1945, it was as part of a Conservative programme. Conservatives hoped that allowances might increase the birth rate of the middle classes, who were believed to be limiting their families for economic reasons,[155] and they realized that allowances offered the possibility of giving money to those who needed it most without increasing wages. The latter point proved to be the crucial incentive during World War II.[156] Thus in two important areas of reform for women, family allowances and birth control, the feminist principle was submerged. In the campaign for family allowances other motives proved stronger and in the struggle for birth control feminists were never in the forefront, but rather followed the lead of the CBC and the NBCA.

In the case of an individual life, such as that of Mrs P, it is easy to see that family considerations played a role in her decision to go out to work, and that her reproductive experience meant more than the act of parturition; the care of the new baby and its siblings had repercussions on Mrs P's own health and dictated the nature of the work she sought. The decisions of MPs and policy-makers on issues of special interest to women were not informed by any such awareness of the realities of women's experiences, so that their motives usually bore little relation to women's needs. Thus policies on maternity care were affected by rivalries within the medical profession, and were eventually dictated largely by the interests of specialists, while problems of health and nutrition were ignored for political reasons. It is interesting that after World War II, when it was perceived that a change in the number of women in the workforce might become desirable, marriage bars were lifted.[157] Also, in 1949, the Royal Commission of Population supported the idea of women's doing two jobs and as a natural corollary, endorsed the use of birth control; an adequate population would be secured by inducements such as tax breaks and family allowances.[158]

Controversies over issues such as maternal mortality and nutrition and birth control in the 1930s were related to concern over population and the effects of unemployment, not the position of women. But the nature of evidence adduced during the course of the debate revealed much about the fabric of women's lives and showed how far women were from a real equality.

Notes

1 C. Rover (1969), *The Punch Book of Women's Rights*, (A.S.Barnes & Co., New York, 115.

2 R. Strachey (ed.) (1936), *Our Freedom and its Results*, Hogarth Press, London, 9.

3 R. Strachey, *ibid.* 10.

4 R. Strachey, *ibid.* 153. Winifred Holtby (1934) makes a similar point in *Women in a Changing Civilization*, John Lane, London, and it is this

feeling that makes the sentiments expressed in Virginia Woolf's (1938) *Three Guineas*, Hogarth Press, so exceptional.

5 Interview with Mrs P, 29 September 1977.

6 The participation rate is the percentage of the population of working age in the labour force.

7 W. Ashworth (1960), *An Economic History of England 1870–1939*, Methuen, London, 418.

8 D. H. Wrong (1967), *Population and Society*, Random House, New York, 50–51.

9 M. Wilmott and P. Young (1973), *The Symmetrical Family*, Pantheon, New York, 104.

10 D. Werneke (1978), 'The Economic Slowdown and Women's Employment Opportunities', *International Labour Review. Vol.117*, January/February 1978, 41–2, defines both these theories in greater detail.

11 See L. Tilly and J. Scott (1975), 'Women's Work and the Family in Nineteenth Century Europe', *Comparative Studies in Society and History Vol.17*, January 1975, 36–64.

12 See S. Alexander (1976), 'Women's Work in Nineteenth Century London: A Study of the Years 1920–50' in A. Oakley and J. Mitchell (1976), *The Rights and Wrongs of Women*, Penguin, Harmondsworth, 64.

13 Six interviews were conducted in Frome, fifteen in Liverpool, eleven in Birmingham, twenty-four in London and eighteen in Hull during September and October 1977.

14 PRO, MH 55/288, Memo 17 November 1921.

15 *Labour Woman* Vol.7 September 1929, 137, and Vol.20, December 1932, 185.

16 E. Roberts (1977), 'Working Class Women in the North West', *Oral History* Vol.5, Autumn 1977, 7–30.

17 The census category includes employees in restaurants as well as charwomen and laundry workers.

18 A.C. Pigou (1947), *Aspects of British Economic History, 1918–25*, MacMillan, London, 19.

19 On these changes in the structure of industry, see H.W. Richardson (1967), *Economic Recovery in Britain, 1932–39,* Weidenfeld & Nicolson, London, 70, 73, 82, 87.

20 S. Anthony (1932), *Women's Place in Industry and Home*, Routledge, London, 73–5.

21 S. Lewenhak (1977), *Women and Trade Unions*, Ernest Benn, London, 178.

22.N. Branson and M. Heinemann (1971), *Britain in the 1930s*, Weidenfeld & Nicolson, London, 145.

23 J. Bornatt (1977), 'Home and Work: A New Context for Trade Union History', *Oral History* Vol.5 Autumn 1977, 101–123.

24 *The Times*, 20 January 1921.

25 *The Times*, 22 January 1921.

26 *The Times*, 3 March 1921.

27 Ministry of Labour (1923), *Second Interim Report of the Central Committee on Women's Training and Employment for the Period Ending December 31, 1922*, HMSO, London, 26.
28 *The Times*, 3 March 1921.
29 *The Times*, 30 June 1923.
30 S. Lewenhak, *op. cit.* 203.
31 *The Times*, 4 August 1921, 20 December 1922, 28 December 1922, 14 April 1928, 18 April 1925.
32 *The Times*, 18 March 1919.
33 J. Myerscough (1978), 'Domestic Leisure: Labour Saving in the Home During the Inter-War Years', Paper given at the Institute of Historical Research, 17 February 1978.
34 See for example, R. Binnie and J. Boxall (1926), *Housecraft Principles and Practice*, Pitman, London.
35 Ministry of Reconstruction (1919), *Report of the Women's Advisory Committee on the Domestic Service Problem*, HMSO, London, 4, and Ministry of Labour (1923), *Report of the Committee Appointed to Enquire into the Present Conditions as to the Supply of Female Domestic Servants*, HMSO, London, 10.
36 *Woman's Leader*, 31 September 1924, 288.
37 National Association of Schoolmasters, *The Why and Wherefore of the NAS,* NAS pamphlet #1, n.d.
38 P.N. Stearns has suggested that this was the case for a slightly earlier period, 'Working Class Wives in Britain, 1890–1914', in M. Vicinus (ed) (1972), *Suffer and Be Still*, Indiana University Press, Bloomington, 113.
39 S. Lewenhak, *op. cit.* 215.
40 H. Martindale (1938), *Women Servants of the State, 1870–1938*, Allen & Unwin, London, 152.
41 *The Times*, 21 January 1924.
42 E. Reiss (1934), *The Rights and Duties of English Women,* Sherratt & Hughes, London, 235.
43 Debates, House of Commons, 205, 1927, col. 1185.
44 *Ibid.* col. 1204.
45 PP (1904), 'Report of the Inter-Departmental Committee on Physical Deterioration', Cd. 2175, 1.
46 E.M.E. Elderton, A. Barrington, E.M.M. de G. Lamotte, H.J. Laski, and K. Pearson (1913), *On the Correlation of Fertility with Social Value*, Dulau, London.
47 Census of Great Britain for 1915, *Summary Tables*, HMSO, xix and xiii.
48 M. Booth (1929), *Women and Society*, Allen & Unwin, London, 206.
49 *Mother and Child* Vol.3, 1932, 43–44.
50 C. White (1970), *Women's Magazines 1693–1968*, Michael Joseph, London, 93–119; R. Schwarz Cowan (1976), 'Two Washes in the Morning and a Bridge Party at Night', *Women's Studies* Vol.3 143–172; B. Friedan (1963), *The Feminine Mystique*, Norton, New York.

51 See G.F. McCleary (1935), *The Maternal and Child Welfare Movement*, P.S. King, London. Infant mortality rates for the period were: 1905: 128, 1910: 105, 1915: 110, 1920: 80, 1925: 75, 1930: 60, 1935: 57.
52 PP (1910), '39th Annual Report of the Local Government Board, 1909–10. Supplement' Cd. 5213, XXXIX, 973, 1, and (1914–6) '44th Annual Report of the Local Government Board, 1914–15. Supplement', Cd. 8085, XXV, 157, 4.
53 Cd. 8085, p.3.
54 H.M. Campbell (1924), *Maternal Mortality, Reports on Public Health and Medical Subjects #25*, HMSO, London; J.M. Campbell (1927), *The Protection of Motherhood, Reports on Public Health and Medical Subjects #48*, HMSO, London; Ministry of Health (1930), *Interim Report of the Departmental Committee on Maternal Mortality and Morbidity*, HMSO, London; Ministry of Health (1932), *Final Report of the Departmental Committee on Maternal Mortality and Morbidity*, HMSO, London; Ministry of Health (1937), *Report of an Investigation into Maternal Mortality*, HMSO, London.
55 PEP (1936), *The Coming Fall in Population,* PEP Broadsheet #75, London, summarizes these projections. The most-quoted were those made by E. Charles (1934), *The Twilight of Parenthood*, Watts & Co., London and Dr. Grace Leybourne's made for the Population Investigation Committee. Many other popular works were also published, for example, G.F. McCleary (1937), *The Menace of British Depopulation*, Allen & Unwin, London, and *Race Suicide*, (1945) Allen & Unwin, London; Eva M. Hubback (1947), *The Population of Britain*, Penguin, Harmondsworth.
56 Debates, House of Commons, 300, 1934–5, col. 1634.
57 J.M. Keynes (1937), 'Some Economic Consequences of a Declining Population', *Eugenics Review* Vol.XXIX, 1–5 and E.C. Snow (1935), 'The Limits of Industrial Employment. The Influence of the Growth of Population on the Development of Industry', *Journal of the Royal Statistical Society*, Vol.98, 239–73.
58 T.H. Marshall (ed) (1938), *The Population Problem*, Allen & Unwin, London.
59 Beveridge Papers, Box IX, f. 6, 'Changes in Family Life', TS 1932.
60 Debates, House of Commons, 320, 1936–7, cols. 508 and 530.
61 PRO, Cab. 24/213, 225 (30).
62 Debates, House of Commons, 320, 1936–7, col. 526.
63 PRO, MH 55/679, C. 1622, 7 May 1937.
64 For example women's magazines began to mention the subject openly: *Women's Own*, 11 July 1936, 517; and *Home Notes*, 7 July 1928, 4–5 and 4 July 1936, 8–9.
65 See for example, V.R. Butler and Denis G. Bonham (1963), *Perinatal Mortality. First Report of the 1958 British Perinatal Mortality Survey*, Livingstone, Edinburgh, 278–80.
66 J. Hay Ferguson, J. Young Thomas and J.M. Munro Kerr (1923), *A Combined Textbook of Obstetrics and Gynaecology*, E & S

Livingstone, Edinburgh, 320.

67 V. Bonney (1919), 'The High Mortality of Childbearing: The Reasons Why and the Remedy', *Proceedings of the Royal Society of Medicine* Vol.12, pt. III; 75–97.

68 A. Oakley, 'Wisewoman and Medicine Man: Changes in the Management of Childbirth', in *The Rights and Wrongs of Women*, 17–58, provides an account of this and a good analysis of the medicalization of childbirth.

69 Royal College of Obstetricians and Gynaecologists (1944), *Report on a National Maternity Service*, Royal College of Obstetricians and Gynaecologists, London, 25.

70 PRO, MH 55/262, deputation, 28 November 1935.

71 *Lansbury's Labour Weekly*, 29 January 1927, 15, article by Leonora Eyles and Mrs Hood's (1928), Women's Co-operative Guild Speech at the Annual National Conference of Maternal and Infant Welfare, 72–7.

72 V. Brittain (1936), *Honourable Estate*, MacMillan, London, 513.

73 PRO, MH 55/625, 'British College of Obstetricians and Gynaecologists Investigation into the Use of Analgesics Suitable for Administration by Midwives, 1936'.

74 General Lying-in Hospital (1932), *Annual Report for 1932*, 35.

75 PRO, MH 55/260, 'Notes on Home Helps', 17 January 1930.

76 *Final Report on Maternal Mortality*, 41.

77 Anon. (1934), *The Motherhood Book*, Amalgamated Press, London, 104.

78 *Nursing Notes, Vol.XLII* September 1929, 144.

79 J. Young (1928), 'An Address on Maternal Mortality from Puerperal Sepsis', *British Medical Journal*, 9 June 1928, 967–9 and W. Blair Bell (1931), 'Maternal Disablement, Pt. I', *Lancet*, 30 May 1931, 1171.

80 M. Stopes (1930), *Preliminary Notes on Various Technical Aspects of the Control of Conception based on the Analyzed Data from Ten Thousand Cases*, Mothers Clinic for Constructive Birth Control, London, 20–21.

81 Ministry of Health (1938), *19th Annual Report of the Ministry of Health, 1937–38*, HMSO, London, 241.

82 J.W. Ballantyne's classic manual (1904) on ante-natal care concentrated entirely on the welfare of the foetus, *Manual of Ante-Natal Pathology and Hygiene*, William Breen, Edinburgh.

83 Medical Women's Federation, Minutes Vol. II, 1 November 1929, and 2 November 1929, f. 271–8.

84 PRO, MH 55/262, Newman to Sir Arthur Robinson, 26 September 1932.

85 *Ibid.*, Tuckwell to Robinson, 14 December 1932 and Robinson to Tuckwell, 6 January 1933.

86 TUC Archives, Tuckwell Papers, Unpublished autobiography of Gertrude Tuckwell, TS, Chaper 28.

87 PP (1931–2), 'Report by the Government Actuary on the 3rd. Valuation of the Assets and Liabilities of Approved Societies, Cmd. 3978, XIV, 879, 32.

88 PP (1929–30), 'Report by the Government Actuaries on an Examination of the Sickness and Disability Experience of a Group of Approved Societies in the Period, 1921–27', Cmd. 3548, XXV, 825, 10, Table C.
89 Registrar General (1931), *Decennial Supplement for 1931*, Pt. 1.2, HMSO, London, 13, Table J.
90 Cmd. 3548, 15.
91 Debates, House of Commons, 267,1931–2, cols. 288–90.
92 PP (1926), 'Report by the Government Actuary on the 2nd. valuation of the Assets and Liabilities of Approved Societies', Cmd., 2785, XIV, 717, p. 37.
93 M. Spring Rice (1939), *Working Class Wives. Their Health and Conditions*, Penguin, Harmondsworth, 20.
94 M. Spring Rice, *ibid*. 35–7.
95 M. I. Balfour and J.C. Drury (1935), *Motherhood in the Special Areas of Durham and Tyneside*, Council of Action, London, 20, and Pilgrim Trust (1938), *Men Without Work*, Cambridge University Press, 127–34.
96 L. McIlroy (1934/5), *Proceedings of Royal Society of Medicine*, Vol.XXVII, Pt. II, 1385–406.
97 Balfour and Drury, *ibid*. 19–20.
98 M.S.Pember Reeves (1913), *Round about a Pound a Week*, G. Bell, London, 140.
99 S. Instone (1948), 'The Welfare of the Housewife', *Lancet*, 4 December 1948, 899–901.
100 D. Scannell (1974), *Mother Knew Best. An East End Childhood*, MacMillan, London, 37.
101 L.Oren (1974), 'The Welfare of Women in Labouring Families: England 1860–1950' in Lois Banner and Mary Hartman (eds), *Clio's Consciousness Raised*, Harper & Row, London, 240.
102 See for example, M.S. Soutar, E.H. Wilkins, and P. Sargent Florence (1939), *Nutrition and Size of Family. A Report on a New Housing Estate prepared for the Birmingham Social Survey Committee*, Allen & Unwin, London, 31–2.
103 *Bulletin* of the Committee Against Malnutrition, No.3, June 1934, 8.
104 M. Spring Rice, *op. cit*. 147.
105 G.C.M. McGonigle and J. Kirby (1936), *Poverty and Public Health*, Gollancz, London, 108–18.
106 L. Eyles (1922), *The Woman in the Little House*, Grant Richards, London.
107 Interview with Mrs S, 23 September 1977.
108 Similar findings were recorded by two social surveys of the period. See B.S. Rowntree (1941), *Poverty and Progress*, Longman, London, 428–45 and D. Caradog Jones (ed.) (1934), *The Social Survey of Merseyside* V.III, Hodder & Stoughton, London, 273 and 275.
109 R.M. Titmuss (1943), *Birth Poverty and Wealth*, Hamish Hamilton, London, 26.
110 L. Fairfield (1938), 'Maternity Work in LCC Hospitals, 1931–6',

Proceedings of the Royal Society of Medicine, Vol.XXI, January 1938, 237–50.

111 PRO, MH 56/45, Minutes of Meeting, 12 February 1932.

112 GLC Archives, Hosp. 2/27, Report of Deputation by the People's League of Health, 1936, speech by Kingsley Wood.

113 PRO, MH 55/629, N. Howell and A.T. Jones (1936) 'Maternal Mortality in the Special Areas', 9 October 1936 and PP (1934–5), 'Report of and Inquiry into the Effects of Existing Economic Circumstances on the Health of the Community in the Cty. Borough of Sunderland and of Certain Districts of Cty. Durham', Cmd. 4886, IX, 627, 26.

114 J. Jackson (1936), *Maternal Welfare*, National Birthday Trust, London, and GLC, PH/Gen./3/7, Papers of Letitia Fairfield (1939), 'Interim Report of the People's League of Health'.

115 PRO, MH 56/44, Minutes of Meeting of Advisory Committee on Nutrition, 28 January 1931.

116 PRO, MH 56/46, Minutes of meeting of Advisory Committee on Nutrition, 23 April 1934.

117 PRO, MH 56/54, H.E. Magee to T. Carnwath, 19 September 1935.

118 PRO, MH 55/642, Baldwin to Kingsley Wood, 11 June 1936.

119 Mrs S. Frankenburgh (1934), *Commonsense in the Nursery*, Jonathan Cape, London, 23.

120 J. Newson and E. Newson 'Cultural Aspects of Child-rearing in the English Speaking World' in M.P.M. Richards (ed) (1974), *The Integration of a Child into a Social World*, Cambridge University Press, 62.

121 PRO, ED 11/249, 'General Hints to Teachers of Cookery', 29 December 1937.

122 D. Scannell, *op. cit.* 136.

123 See C. Dyhouse (1977), 'Good Wives and Little Mothers: Social Anxieties and Schoolgirls' Curriculum 1890–1920', *Oxford Review of Education*, Vol.3, 1977, 21–35; and A. Davin (1978), 'Imperialism and Motherhood', *History Workshop Journal*, Vol.5, Spring 1978, 9–65.

124 PRO, AST. 7/3/15 Memo 22 July 1938.

125 See for example, G.C.M. McGonigle and J. Kirby, *op. cit.* 236.

126 D. Gittens (1977), 'Women's Work and Family Size', *Oral History* Vol.5, Autumn 1977, 84–100 has many insights on the reasons for the decline in the working-class birth rate between the wars.

127 A. McLaren (1978), *Birth Control in Nineteenth Century England*, Croom Helm, London, 231-53, has a good chapter on abortion in Victorian and Edwardian England.

128 Ministry of Health and Home Office (1939), *Report of the Inter-departmental Committee on Abortion*, HMSO, London, 8.

129 PRO, MH 71/18, Evidence of the Ministry of Health to the Inter-departmental Committee on Abortion, January, 1938, Appendix 8b.

130 PRO, MH 71/25, Evidence of the East Midlands Working Women's Association, 24 February 1938.

131 Ministry of Health and Home Office, *op. cit.* 66.
132 Ministry of Health and Home Office, 144.
133 M. Stopes (1925), *The First 5000*, John Bale & Danielsson, London, 24.
134 For example, *Interim Report on Maternal Mortality*, 36.
135 *Co-operative News*, 18 March 1911, 335–6.
136 M. Llewelyn Davies (1978), *Maternity Letters from Working Women*, Virago, London.
137 Board of Education and Board of Control (1927), 'Report of the Mental Deficiency Committee', HMSO, London, 78–89.
138 C.P. Blacker (1937), *A Social Problem Group?*, Oxford University Press, 4.
139 FPA Archives, A8/19, NUSEC Deputation, 27 January 1932.
140 PRO, MH 61/10, Stewart to Brown, 15 July 1935.
141 *Ibid*, Addendum to Mr F. Tribe's Memo of 16 April 1935.
142 See above, 217–18.
143 PRO, MH 55/289, Memo. 153 MCW, March 1931.
144 Women's Co-operative Guild (1917), Memo on the National Care of Maternity.
145 Women's Co-operative Guild (1935), *52nd Annual Report, 1934–35*, 8 and The Labour Party (1934), *Annual Report of the Labour Party*, The Labour Party, London, 182.
146 Women's Labour League (1928), *9th Annual Conference Report*, Women's Labour League, London, 26.
147 E.F. Rathbone (1929), *Milestones: Presidential Addresses at the Annual Council Meetings of the NUSEC*, NUSEC, London, 28.
148 V. Gollancz (ed) (1917), *The Making of Women. Oxford Essays in Feminism*, Allen & Unwin, London, 29.
149 V. Woolf, 'Introductory Letter to Margaret Llewelyn Davies' in M. Llewelyn Davies (ed) (1977), *Life as we Have Known It*, Virago, London, xxi.
150 Fawcett Library, Minutes of the NUSEC Exec. Committee, 22 November 1927.
151 *The Six Point Group*, Six Point Group Leaflet, London, n.d.
152 K.D. Courtney, H.N. Brailsford, E. Rathbone, M. Stocks, E. Burns and E. Burns (1918), *Equal Pay and the Family*, Headley, London, 40.
153 S. Lewenhak, *op. cit.* 224–7 and H. Martindale, *op. cit.* 170.
154 E. Rathbone (1924), *The Disinherited Family*, Allen & Unwin, London, 16.
155 See for example, R. Rhodes James (ed.) (1974), *Winston S. Churchill. His Complete Speeches, 1897–1963*, V. II, Bowker, London, 7186.
156 PRO, T 161/1116, Lord Stamp's Memo, 30 November 1939.
157 Treasury (1946), *Report of the Civil Service National Whitley Council Committee on the Marriage Bar*, HMSO, London, gives a full account of the lifting of the marriage bars in the professions and private industry.
158 PP (1948–49), 'Report of the Royal Commission on Population', Cmd. 7695, XIX, 635, 159–60.

9 CLASS AGAINST CLASS: THE POLITICAL CULTURE OF THE COMMUNIST PARTY OF GREAT BRITAIN, 1930–35

Alun Howkins

On 1 January 1930 a new daily newspaper appeared on the streets of Britain — *The Daily Worker*. Its title was proudly decorated with the hammer and sickle and it proclaimed itself 'The Newspaper of the Central Committee of the Communist Party of Great Britain — British Section of the Communist International'.[1] To say it appeared on the streets is more than a figure of speech — from the first it was placed under a political ban by most of the major newspaper wholesalers, and was sold mainly on the streets and at the factory gates by Party members.

The first issue was twelve pages long. The front page covered news — mainly industrial — and pages two and three continued this with good foreign coverage including a major article on Germany. On page four there was an article by Ranjani Palme Dutt, the Party's main theoretician, entitled 'War on the Labour Government'. This article, along with a statement of aims drawn up by the Politbureau of the Party, and printed on page six, gave the Party's line on the economic crisis and the political conclusions to be drawn from it. Dutt's article began, 'Capitalism is today in decline all over the world, and nowhere more than in Britain . . . .'.[2] He pointed to mass unemployment, the rise of fascism, and the inability of the Labour government to deal with these problems. Characteristically he drew a parallel with the Soviet Union where, it was claimed, there was no unemployment and working-class living standards were rising day by day. It was not simply that the Labour Party could not resolve the contradictions of the crisis — they had themselves become the agents of capitalism's continuing survival. As the Sixth Congress of the Communist International had said in September 1928: 'According to changing political circumstances, the bourgeoisie resort either to fascist methods or to coalitions with social-democracy, while social democracy itself, particularly at crucial moments for capitalism, not infrequently plays a fascist part'.[3] Dutt echoed the International's statement almost literally: '. . . new methods have been found in post war Europe. In Italy and other countries they have taken the form of fascism; in Britain and other countries they have taken the form of the 'Labour Government' and the employers–TUC conferences. The appearances may differ; the essence is the same. They are forms to maintain the rule of capitalism in its decline.'[4] However, because the Labour Party was the creation of the working class, and because its

Left still appeared to represent the working class, the class was unwilling to abandon it. The main task of the Communist Party was therefore the 'fight against the Labour government' and the 'lefts' in particular because: 'The more the Labour Government exposes itself as the weapon of the capitalists, the more it relies on the "left" phrasemongers to delude the workers and hold them back from action'.[5]

Dutt's article was a classic exposition of the line of the Party in the so called 'Third Period'. At the theses of the Sixth Congress of the International said:

> After the first imperialist world war, the international labour movement passed through a series of phases of development, reflecting the various phases of the general crisis of the capitalist system.
>
> The first was the period of extremely acute crisis of the capitalist system, and of direct revolutionary action on the part of the proletariat. This reached its high point in 1921 . . . . This period ended with the defeat of the German proletariat in 1923. This defeat marked the . . . second period, a period of gradual and partial stabilization of the capitalist system, of the 'restoration' of capitalist economy . . . . Finally came the third period . . . this period will, through the further development of the contradictions of capitalist stabilization, increasingly shake that stability and lead inevitably to the most severe intensification of the general capitalist crisis . . . .[6]

The ramifications of this new line, adopted at the Sixth Congress of the International, were to be absolutely fundamental for the Communist Party of Great Britain. Prior to 1928, the Party, following the decisions of the founding congresses of the International, had broadly adhered to a united front line. Its main work had been with the rank-and-file of the Labour movement via non-sectarian, but Party dominated organisations, like the National Minority Movement, working in the trade unions, the National Unemployed Workers Movement, and the National Left Wing Movement, in the Labour Party. It also created various kinds of quasi-political organizations, like the Friends of the Soviet Union; and worked within others, set up by the broad Labour movement, like the British Workers' Sports Federation. Finally, again following Lenin's instructions, it sought to affiliate to the Labour Party. In this it consistently failed.

With the characterization of the Labour Party as 'social-fascist' and the TUC as tools of the employers, this tactic could obviously not continue. The effect of the change in line is seen at its clearest in relation to the National Minority Movement, the Party group which was probably its most successful in the 1920s. The new Party line on the trades unions emerged, after considerable confusion following the defeat of the 'rightists' lead by Bukharin in the autumn of 1928. In October 1928, Losovsky, head of the Red International of Labour

Unions (the union equivalent of the Communist International) following Bukharin's eclipse, wrote an article in *The Red International of Labour Unions* which outlined the new position, and concluded:

> The masses must be organised and led, if necessary *without* the trade union apparatus and *against* it; no fetish must be made of the trade unions; the reformist organisations must not be transformed into objects of worship; while it must always be kept in mind that the reformist organisations are tools in the hands of the bourgeois state and the employers' organisations to crush the revolutionary wing of the Labour movement and to enslave the broad proletarian masses.[7]

The logic of this line in Britain was clear. Work within the reformist unions must cease. The Party, via the Minority Movement, must take the initiative in strike situations by setting up an independent leadership of the struggle in the form of factory committees, 'that will represent all the workers, skilled, unskilled, men, women and youths, organised and unorganized . . .'.[8] Once the strike was over, these committees were to form a permanent leadership of the workers. It was this last point that caused the problems, since it opened the Minority Movement to the charge of 'splitting' — of setting up alternative unions — a charge which the movement found it very difficult to deny; although the recalcitrance of the leadership, especially Jack Tanner and Harry Pollitt, on this issue shows they were acutely aware of it.[9]

The new line of independent leadership was finally accepted at the Sixth, and final, congress of the National Minority Movement in August 1929. On the surface, the effect on the Party's industrial work was little short of disastrous. Crucially it alienated a whole area of 'left' support which had been the basis of the Minority Movement's success. Arthur Cook, for instance, at the time secretary of the Mineworkers Federation of Great Britain, resigned from the Minority Movement, as did a large number of influential Left supporters.

The experience of the Minority Movement could be repeated over and over again in Party-run or affiliated organizations, and it was the apparent Moscow domination that led to the change of line which has in turn led to the new line's universal condemnation by bourgeois historians of the Party, such as Henry Pelling and Roderick Martin. As Martin writes: 'The Communist Party and the Minority Movement were led into the arid isolation of introverted sectarianism'.[10] Criticism of the new line of the Left has been even more severe if only because it is more clearly thought out. As a Trotskyist historian, Hugo Dewar, has written:

> To have really probed into the problem [of the new line] would have been to reveal that they [the Soviet leaders] had misread the entire political situation in the most blockhead manner possible; and that, even worse, they had subordinated all the communist parties to themselves, used them in the interests of their own power struggle in Russia, in the guise of Socialism in one country, masquerading under the guise of internationalism.[11]

Even the Party itself, embarrassed by the 'ultra sectarianism' of the 'Third Period' has condemned it at least by implication. For example Monty Johnstone, a leading Party theoretician, wrote in 1976: 'Trotsky's criticism of the line of the Comintern were essentially correct. Trotsky was right in his refutation of the sectarian ultra-left theory of social fascism that had been developed by Stalin and Zinoviev'.[12]

Nevertheless it is important to point out that the left turn was by no means as unreasonable as subsequent historians have tended to point out. Even Martin is forced to write that, 'There were sound political reasons for the Comintern to repudiate the united front and adopt a more left wing policy at the end of 1927'.[13] Martin points to the consistent refusal by European and Asian social democrats to have anything to do with the Party, the failure of Social Democratic controlled initiatives, especially the General Strike and the Labour/Social Democratic governments of Europe, and specifically in Britain to the witch hunting of Communists in the Union movement, and the Mond–Turner talks which seemed to show the TUC moving in a class-collaborationist direction. Other elements could be added to this. Before the Leeds Congress of the British party had met and finally accepted the new line, Wall Street had crashed, apparently shaking world capitalism at its very foundations, while unemployment was beginning its steep climb towards the high point of 1932. None of this can have been lost on the delegates at that congress.

It is also frequently cited as evidence of the Party's failure that membership fall as a result of the change in line, as well as that of its front organizations. This cannot be denied. Membership fell from 10, 800 at the end of 1926 to 2,555 by November 1930. Yet some qualifications need adding here. Firstly, in November 1930 the Party had only adhered formally to the new line for eleven months, and the major loss in membership occurred between 1926 and December 1929. During this period (still one of united front) the Party lost 7, 600 members. In the first two years of the 'third period', i.e. up to 1932, it regained 6, 150 of them. This means that despite the 'sectarian and ultra leftist line' the Party recruited more members in those two years then any other period of two years in its previous history. Secondly the Party's decline should be seen against a general background of Labour movement defeat. Not only the Party but the Labour Party, the Independent Labour Party and crucially the Trades Unions suffered severe loss of membership in the period after 1926. None of this is to argue that the new line was correct, simply to point out that the picture is by no means as black and white as historians have tried to make it.[14]

Once the faction fighting had finished and the Party had finally accepted the new line in December 1929, a transformation in Party life began. It should be understood from the first that party membership was not a part time thing. As the Report of the 1922 reorganization committee said: 'There is no rank and file in a Communist Party; . . . every member has some special qualification which can be used in some sphere of the party's work.'[15] This meant that to a peculiar extent all aspects of a party member's life were bound up with the party; 'Communism was my waking time' wrote John Cornford;[16] and Edward Upward's brilliant trilogy *The Spiral Ascent* shows quite how total the identification of a party member with the party could be. Upward himself, considered by Auden and Isherwood to be the most talented of their 'group', gave up creative writing, his friendships with his Oxbridge contemporaries and all that entailed, to become a party member. His party work was directed largely at the teachers' movement and he edited *The Ploughshare*, the journal of the Teachers' Anti-War Movement, a party front organization. But it is in the texture of the *novel* that Upward's real commitment, and the total dedication of a serious party member is made clear. Sebrill, the novel's main character, joins the party, marries a woman comrade, who is the antithesis of everything he believes 'beauty' to be, and gives himself wholehearted to the party's work. His social life becomes party dominated — party organized rambles and socials — and his friends are all party members. Social contact in his work has the sole end of winning members for the party — his breaks and lunchtimes are devoted to raising money for the party and its organizations and organizing and arguing on political issues. This all pervasiveness drove Bob Dark to leave the Party after nearly 20 years membership in 1951: 'During all my years as a member of the party I frequently had an uneasy feeling that my personal life was not all that was expected of a Communist. And if I was not happy about it neither was the Party. On and off my home and family came under severe criticism from other party members.'[17] Criticism could go further. Ernie Trory, a prominent Brighton Party member, was occasionally in trouble because in the opinion of the branch he was spending too much time in pubs and playing cards.[18] It is significant that the whole tone of Trory's account (*Between the Wars*) is very similar to the 'spiritual autobiographies' of nineteenth-century non-conformist working men.

This total society was of course neither new on the political Left nor accidental. In *What is to be Done?*, and in the famous *21 Theses on the Founding of the Third International*, Lenin had clearly laid down the role of the Communist militant, but there were many other historical precedents from both the British labour movement and abroad. Since the end of the eighteenth century radical movements had sought to create for their members a social as well as political environment, but perhaps the most striking example was the pre-World War I German Social Democratic Party. In his article in *Past and Present* Peter Nettl has written of the SPD: 'Right from the start it kept itself apart from society, first by emphasizing philosophical and moral differences, later completing the social containment of its members by organisational means. Thus the whole ideology of separation had strong moral overtones, which equated participation in society with corruption, and claimed to provide within itself a superior alternative to corrupt capitalism'. While the organization of the SPD was much larger, and, in some sense more all embracing, than that of the third period CPGB, Nettl's characterization of the party is useful.

The comparison is useful because with the change in line the Communist Party was forced to isolate itself from the rest of the Labour movement. The 'non-sectarian' contacts of the past came to an end, the social and especially cultural movements which the party had supported, but which were largely social democratic, now became the enemy, and areas of support which the party had come to rely on, the Left of the trade unions, sections of the Labour press and so on were now denied to it. In this situation they were faced with two alternatives. They could either simply abandon the whole periphery of 'non-political' organizing which had characterized much of the British (and indeed European) socialist tradition until then, or they could create new organizations which accorded with the changed line. They chose, not surprisingly, the second course.

In doing this, I would wish to argue, they created the foundations at least of a visible revolutionary and oppositional culture. For the rest of this paper I want to look, if only briefly, at some of the manifestations of that culture and then offer, at the end, some general thoughts arising from that discussion.

The most important of the new cultural forms was the *Daily Worker*. Since its foundation, the Party had produced various papers, usually weekly, but had relied heavily on other Left papers, especially the *Daily Herald*, to give sympathetic coverage to their policies and events. Following the left turn, this was no longer possible. Firstly, the *Herald* became a 'social fascist rag', and former allies like Maxton and Kirkwood 'police socialists'. Secondly, the party's own insistence that the period was one of revolutionary advance demanded that, at the very least, the party should be able to support its own paper. Like so much of the politics and so many of the organizations of the third period, the *Worker* was a result not of observation of the British political scene, but of a theoretical proposition.

Yet this did not make the paper or the organizations a failure. Had the theory been correct the opposite may well have been the case. The party's self-appointed role as the vanguard of the British working class necessitated they should be ahead of the class. But, above all, the paper they produced — despite its uncompromising, and ultimately tragic sectarianism — was in many ways, a remarkable piece of revolutionary journalism and represented a flourishing (if limited) revolutionary culture.

For those familiar with the *Morning Star* or the *Daily Worker* of the early 1960s, the *Worker* of the early 1930s is a surprise. Its layout, for instance, although showing signs of modern typographic developments and making good use of display, was very different from the popular press of the 1930s, even the *Daily Herald*, its major rival, which had been much more influenced by the Harmsworth revolution in illustrated papers. The reason for this is clear. The paper carried a much larger number of feature-length articles than was usual. Although few of these pieces were on theory *per se* they were of an unusually high standard. There was wide coverage of European affairs, including pieces translated from German and French (the former being a markedly higher level theoretically); and excellent material on the colonial question. This included articles by people like George Padmore and Jomo Kenyatta, as well as material from the well organized Indian Communist Party. This coverage of the colonial struggle is a marked contrast to the paper in the late 1930s, when the CPI rejoined the INC and the primary struggle was seen not as the fight for a workers' and peasants' revolution, but for the attainment of a constitutional national independence, at best. At worst, the national question was totally subordinated. As *World News and Views* pronounced in 1939: 'While upholding the rights of colonial peoples to self determination . . . Communists follow the teachings of Lenin and Stalin in subordinating the actual realisation of the right of secession . . . to the interests of defeating fascism'.[21]

A more striking contrast, both with the contemporary socialist press and the *Worker* of the popular front era, was the serious attention paid to the political struggle of women and to the social and intellectual 'periphery' of political life. For example, from the first the *Daily Worker* carried a regular women's page, but it was about as different from the normal version as it was possible to be. After World War I many, if not all, popular papers carried a women's page which centred on fashion, 'health and beauty', child care and cooking. By giving women a separate status in accordance with their new role as voters and consumers, it actually reduced them and re-inforced the sexual division of labour established in the 1880s and 1890s. The trade union and labour press by and large followed this example. Many trade union journals of the 1920s and 1930s had a 'wives' page usually of recipes, with perhaps occasional remarks on politics and union affairs.

The *Daily Herald* was similar, as was the *Daily Worker* after 1935. This, of course, accords with the party's attitude to the woman question, which was simply to relegate it to a subordinate position in relation to the class struggle. However, in the third period, although that attitude is still basically dominant, there was at least a serious attempt to deal with the political struggles of women. The first issue, for instance, had on its women's page a play by a textile worker, Clara Robbins, about the Lancashire strike (then in progress) which urged the need for women to organize and fight against wage cuts and redundancies. It also carried a long article by Rose Smith (herself an ex-textile worker) urging the creation of a National Conference of Women Workers based on local committees in the factories and streets. Interestingly this appeal was free from the sectarianism of the rest of the party programme and spoke of 'a Women's United Front organization on the basis of a broad programme of working class demands', though what the demands were was not made clear.[22] In the fourth issue there was a long report (the first of many) on the position of women in the USSR, which emphasized women's work, the provision of creche and nursery facilities, as well as the usual better living standards, the absence of unemployment, and similar material.[23] Other articles in 1930 include a long piece on the women's strike at Crosse & Blackwell in Bermondsey,[24] a piece by Kath Duncan on equal pay in teaching,[25] an article on organizing unemployed women,[26] and so on. Most interesting of all perhaps is a Central Committee statement of April 1930 that said, in relation to the party's women's work: 'All passivity must cease and the whole Party must realize the importance of recruiting working women to our party, and of leading the struggle of working women.'[27]

This concern spread to children. From the early 1920s the Party had a youth section the Young Communist League. In the early 1930s the Young Pioneers, for children under thirteen years old, was added. In April 1930 a campaign was begun to win children and youth to the party. In an article in the issue of 15 April, entitled 'To

Organize the Children', the Central Committee argued: 'At the present time in England actual economic conditions provide for a real mass children's organization.'[28] On May Day that year the YCL and the Young Pioneers had special contingents on the Communist Party May Day March. 'No school on Mayday' was the slogan raised in the *Daily Worker*, '. . . the workers' children must not go to school on Mayday . . . And if teacher says "No! you must come to school" the workers' children must say, "No, teacher, we will go in demonstrations because it is May Day".' Young supporters were further urged to tell their friends and bring them out as well as organize a school paper.[29]

The concern to organize children found its place in the *Daily Worker*. From the first there was a Children's Corner which, apart from YCL and YP notices and statements contained a daily cartoon. Until 1932 this was a character called 'Micky the Mongrel'. This cartoon strip, though not always successful, was an attempt at political education for young children. Not for Micky the puerile adventures of his much later successor Pif. In the first months he went slogan chalking, for the *Daily Worker*, got chased by the police ('Of course he could run much faster, because he doesn't get so much to eat and drink'):[36] gave out leaflets with his Irish doggy mates — the Tyke twins; and eventually visited the Soviet Union. In 1932 Micky was replaced by two Young Pioneers (boy and girl) who did much the same kind of things as Micky. However, in a really interesting series of scripts, they are made to confront and deal with their own latent anti-semitism. There is a boy at school whom they don't like, but don't really know why, who then turns out to be Jewish. They then see him, with his father, on an unemployed demonstration, collecting money (a much superior role to their own), and so become friends. The struggle of the working class unites even children over racial hostility. Micky the Mongrel and the Young Pioneers are perhaps crude, but they do represent a serious attempt to bring politics to children. More importantly they are indicative of the kind of closed world the Party sought to create in the third period. It was no longer sufficient simply to recruit working adults and leave wives and children to their own devices — they had to be included in the party structure. To go outside it was to risk contamination.

In this case it is important to see the dual nature of the *Daily Worker*. It was in itself a part of the culture of British Communism. Its articles, its cartoons, its often good theatre, film and book criticism gave the party line on a wide range of subjects. Film criticism is interesting here. Two regular (or semi-regular) features covered films. One, 'Films Which The Workers May Not See' covered Soviet films like 'New Babylon' and 'Mother'; the other 'Films They Show You' dealt with the commercial cinema. Although neither developed a theory of film, or seldom attempted to go beyond simple assertions of the Soviet–Good, Hollywood-Bad, kind, both series represent an attempt to analyse and argue about the politics of mass culture and again to integrate readers into a revolutionary world (i.e. Soviet films).

The other aspect of the *Daily Worker* is that it presents, and consciously mediates, the activities of the Party and its satellite organizations in the early 1930s. Micky the Mongrel's supporters had penny collecting boxes for Micky's fund, and one Young Pioneer wrote that older YCL'ers read him Micky the Mongrel.[31] Articles provided the militant with the matter of polemic while the organizations reported in the paper encouraged emulation. Also the sale of the *Worker* and fund-raising events, like the 'Grand Fancy Dress and Carnival Dance', held in Shoreditch Town Hall to celebrate the paper's birth, were important as part of the alternative world provided by the Party.

If we look at this world more closely, it is helpful to divide it into the organizationally formal and the organizationally informal. It is worth sketching in some of the borders of the latter. It was a land of cafes, pubs, bookshops through which the party members moved. Added to these were places, like Shoreditch Town Hall, which were regularly used by the Party for social and political activity. Of the cafes, the most famous was the Nanking Chinese Restaurant in Denmark Street, 'A place for the Internationalist' as the advertisement in the second issue of the *Daily Worker* said.[32] It was at the Nanking that John Cornford met Ray, a fellow Communist, the woman he was to live with for four years.[33] There was also the more proletarian Manningtree Cafe in Manningtree Street in the East End. Many of these cafes were owned by Party members and sympathizers; one is described in Upward's *The Rotten Elements*.[34] Another, and larger place, used frequently by the Party, was the Chanticleer Restaurant in Frith Street. This was usually reserved for dances and fund raising. It was also near the Scala in Charlotte Street, where the London Workers Film Society and the left-influenced Film Society showed Soviet films.[35]

Crucially, there was the world of bookshops. Here a provincial coming to London could be sure of a welcome and a sympathetic ear. David Archer's Parton Street Bookshop near Red Lion Square was where the young Esmond Romilly 'hid up' when he ran away from Wellington School in 1934 aged fifteen. He was followed there in June 1934 by Phillip Toynbee, also on the run from the Public School system.[36] Most famous of all was Henderson's 'Bomb Shop' on

Charing Cross Road, taken over in 1934 by Eva Reckitt, who gave her long life to the socialist movement, and reopened as Colletts. There was also the Party-run Workers' Bookshop in Theobalds Road and Charlie Lahr's anarchist-surrealist bookshop in Red Lion Square.[37]

In this honeycomb of cafes and bookshops in the old artisan areas of Soho and Holborn one led often to another and eventually to Party membership. Ivor Monague bought Liebnecht's *Militarism and Anti-Militarism* in Henderson's in 1917 and, inspired by this, wrote to the BSP (the Communist Party's forerunner). He was directed by them to the Minerva Cafe in High Holborn where the local BSP branch met. Forced to leave by his parents, he made contact again, in the early 1920s, through another route, the 1917 Club in Cambridge, and then back to London and the Film Society in Charlotte Street.[38] John Cornford arrived in London in January 1933, escaping from Stowe School and took rooms in Parton Street, near David Archer's Bookshop — 'drawn there' by its presence. A month later he joined the Party and became Editor of *The Student Vanguard*.[39]

The informal world, charted through the advertising columns of the *Daily Worker* shows how far the Party's notions went on what it should provide for its members. In the first week of January 1934 there was an exhibition on Soviet Education at the University of London Club; lectures on Marxism to the Socialist Summer School Students Association; League of Socialist Freethinkers meetings in Glasgow and Edinburgh, and a Whist Drive for the same organization in Glasgow: an International Labour Defence Dance at the Avesta Cafe near Oxford Circus; a Grand Variety Concert in Battersea with Ben Shannon's Band; The Rebel Players social at the Pindar of Wakefield in Kings Cross Road; a London Friends of the Soviet Union Dance, with Jack Carson and the Hadleigh Rhythm Boys; a Federation of Student Societies 'Workers and Students United' Dance at Clerkenwell Workingmen's Club; and an RTD Twelfth Night Party, also at the Avesta.[40]

The formal network consisted of those organizations that the Party created as an alternative to the social democratic cultural and sporting bodies that they had left at the beginning of the third period. I want now to look briefly at two of these organizations, the Workers' Theatre Movement and the British Workers' Sports Federation.

In the last couple of years the detailed history of the WTM has begun to be written, but it is worth linking it to the specific history of the third period. As Raphael Samuel has argued, there was a long tradition of association between the Labour movement and theatre, and in the late 1920s there existed a number of London and regional theatre groups more or less committed to the production of socialist theatre.[41] With the left turn those working in theatre moved decisively away from the social democratic groupings towards a new theory and practice of theatre. Samuel quotes Morris Dobb writing in 1929 about the: 'so called socialist plays whose "labour" hero is so much at home with a baronet's daughter in a Mayfair drawing room, and whose *Fanatics* discuss the "sex problem" as though . . . the class struggle did not exist'.[42] Similarly the plays of Shaw were to the *Daily Worker* in 1930 the products of 'An old fashioned reformist'.[43]

The new line turned this criticism into action via the remarkable figure of Tom Thomas. From early 1930 it is clear from the *Daily Worker* and Thomas's weekly column that a new type of agitational theatre was spreading through the party. In August 1930 Thomas published a lengthy piece in the *Daily Worker* arguing for the development of 'Revue, Cabaret, Concert Party — call it what you like' to be used at meetings and related to local issues, 'as opposed to the naturalistic play performed by dramatic societies, and the W.T.M. hitherto . . .'[44]

By the middle of 1932 there were at least a dozen local WTM troupes, with names like Red Radio and Red Front, performing agitational non-naturalistic theatre throughout the regions and in London. Their plays were nearly all produced locally, and covered topics like the means test, the Invergordon Mutiny, the struggle in the Co-op, as well as specific strikes; and there were more nationally co-ordinated efforts, like the play by Charlie Mann on the Meerut prisoners, and the plays produced for the Lenin, Liebknecht, Luxembourg campaign of 1934.

By 1934 the WTM had a dance band, a choir, and a lorry for country performances, as well as groups up and down the country — but its end was only a year away. The WTM's aggressive political drama was geared to the third period. It was not only politically separate from the reformist drama of the ILP and the LP 'which show[ed] no way out and which therefore spread a feeling of defeat and despair',[45] but formally separate. A change in the political line of the Party could only mean a change for its theatrical form. By August 1934 the party line was changing, moving gradually towards the United Front policy which lead in turn to the Popular Front vacuousness of 1936 onwards. By that year it was all but over. In January the New Theatre League was established under the Liberal Earl of Kinnoal for all 'interested in Progressive Theatre'.[46] The WTM had no place in this. As Tom Thomas wrote:

I was very surprised when it was put to me in 1935 or 1936 that as the organiser of the WTM and as the author of so many lampoons on the Labour Party, my continued leadership might be considered in some quarters a minor obstacle to the development of the popular front. . . . The Workers' Theatre Movement continued for some time, but it didn't really fit in with the popular front campaign and . . . by 1938 was, I believe, dead.[47]

Its epitaph appeared in *Discussion*, the Communist Party popular front journal in March 1938: 'In the past, several attempts have been made to organize theatre groups . . . the most successful being the WTM. The ultimate failure of the movement can be attributed to many reasons . . . . The most important for us today is in the intense sectarianism that enveloped it, whereby an immense swing away from trends of other amateur dramatic societies was made . . . .'[48] The very reasons that had commended the WTM in 1930 were now, in the new period, the reasons for damning it.

The history of the British Workers' Sports Federation (BWSF) is similar. Sport, especially rambling and cycling, had formed an important part of the social activities of the Labour movement since the 1900s. The ILP had its cycling club, the Leader Scouts; but the most famous of the workers sports organizations was the Clarion Club, which still supported a considerable cycling section in the 1930s. The BWSF was a body designed to bring together local clubs, and in the late 1920s its secretary was George Sinfield, a Communist Party member. Thus when the new lines were accepted in 1929 the BWSF became the Communist Party's sporting organization.

A sports organization was necessary partly because of the tradition which linked socialism with sport, especially cycling and rambling, and partly because of the growth of working-class spectator sports, especially football. The BWSF set out to organize 'real workers' sport'. In the first issue of the *Daily Worker* Sinfield wrote that a campaign had begun directed towards 'winning to our ranks the majority of the factory sports clubs away from the influence of the bosses'.[49] The campaign however, quickly spread much wider than that. In the early editions the *Daily Worker* carried racing tips and F.A. football results and commentary — by the end of January both had vanished. F.A. football was 'staged by the bosses for the dual purpose of providing profit and doping the masses',[50] and racing tips went because 'we cannot possibly assist capitalists in the carrying on of a gigantic swindle and money making concern'.[51]

It was not only capitalist sport that was declared beyond the pale. The history of the BWSF demonstrated according to George Sinfield quite how dangerous the social fascist could be. In 1927 a 'sham' workers' football team, selected by 'right wing' and 'reformist elements' in the BWSF leadership and led by 'an unscrupulous clique of reformists' went to Austria, only to disgrace itself in the eyes of the Austrian proletariat by fouling its way through the tour.[52] In similar vein when the Labour Party and the TUC set up the National Workers Sports Association in August 1930, to keep workers out of the BWSF, Sinfield wrote that 'It was an attempt to saddle the workers with an insidious piece of Social Fascist machinery'.[53]

However, to characterize the BWSF by its sectarianism alone is too easy. It was certainly a successful organization both in political and sporting terms. By mid-1930 it had sections covering most sports (except cricket as far as I can tell). Football, cycling and rambling were the most popular. In cycling, the section was called the Red Wheelers and had a number of regional branches and ran a national twenty-five-mile time trial championship[54] as well as publishing its own paper *The Red Wheeler* (the BWSF paper was called *Red Sport*). It was the Red Wheelers, one imagines, who were the 'worker cyclists' singing 'revolutionary songs' whom Edward Upward pictures in his short story 'The Island'.[55] In football the BWSF organized a challenge cup which was played for annually in London; but it was in rambling that the BWSF was most influential. Every weekend BWSF rambles left the major cities. In the summer there were camps which combined walking with political activity, like the ones at New Brighton in August 1932 where the campers were selling the *Daily Worker* to trippers or at Carbeth, in the same month where a motion to 'fight against the warmongers' was passed'.[56]

The other thing about rambling was that it brought participants into conflict with the ruling class, as at Canvey Island in 1932 where a group of BWSF campers were evicted from their site, which they claimed was common land.[57] The most significant clash, though, was around the mass tresspasses in the Peak District in the summer of 1932, organized largely by the Ramblers' Rights Movement, a BWSF organization. These mass invasions of private grouse moors won an enormous amount of support and publicity for the BWSF, and led directly to the creation of the National Parks. They also politicized many of the young workers who took part in them.[58]

By 1934 the BWSF seems to have had sections for boxing, road running, athletics and gymnastics as well as cycling, rambling and football. There is barely a week of the *Daily Worker* without some BWSF activities, which seem to have been well attended; and now they began to work closely with the WTM, with the latter putting on shows at sports days as well as doing gymnastic displays.[59] Coincidentally, the fate of the BWSF was identical to that of the WTM. Born in the period of sectarianism, it was unable formally to adjust to the change of line. In January 1936 the *Daily Worker* carried the Central Committee report on the paper's future. It ended:

'We have to change completely the whole character of the *Daily Worker* from a narrow Party organ into the fighting daily newspaper of the United Front, the mouthpiece of unity'.[60] The BWSF was a victim. Sometime the previous Autumn it liquidated itself into that 'insidious piece of social fascist machinery' the NWSA, and the NWSA now got the *Daily Worker* coverage. Racing tips were also back in, and there was the unlikely and slightly pathetic sight of George Sinfield's writing on the F.A. cup's early rounds.[61]

But it was not only the WTM and BWSF, but the whole of the *Daily Worker* that had changed following the Seventh Congress of the International and the victory of the Popular Front in France. As the editorial of 31 January 1936 said: 'We have a paper which we must think of not merely as a political organ but as a popular workers' paper'.[62] More pictures appeared, the articles got shorter, and the lessons of Harmsworth were learned. This shows most clearly in the women's page. In place of building the movement, we see patterns for serviettes with a hammer and sickle design; in place of reports on women's strikes, 'Alice O'Neal's Home Beauty Parlor'.

The 'third period' stands universally condemned by history. There can be little doubt, for instance, that the analysis split the German working-class movement, creating a fundamental weakness which helped Nazism to power. This cannot be ignored in the historiography of communism. Yet the very sectarianism that divided the movement produced, in Britain as well as on the Continent, a remarkable revolutionary culture. This culture was revolutionary because the politics of the Party, no matter how misguided, were also revolutionary. The political break with social democracy forced a cultural break — the party now had to differentiate itself artistically, intellectually and socially from its former allies. It also had to embrace its members into the differentiation. The organizational forms produced by this moment bear the stamp of the moment. They were sectarian and often puritanical. Yet they presented a challenge, formally and organizationally, at least both to social democracy and capitalism.

The blame for the failure is easy to assign — the change of line. Yet it is difficult to know if they could have continued and made a greater impact. At most they involved a few thousand people and their sectarianism automatically excluded many. But we should not forget the mass tresspasses which involved 30,000 to 40,000 that the WTM could draw 700 to a week night open air performance in Greenwich, or 50,000 during the Lancashire strikes of 1931–2. Also the influence worked through in other ways. Joan Littlewood served her time with the WTM, and *Oh, What a Lovely War*, shows very strong WTM influence, even down to its troupe of pierrots. Nor is it romanticism to admire the honesty of many of the positions taken up. Uncompromising they may have been, even if only too easily changed, but there is something enormously refreshing in the culture of the early 1930s, which is so lacking from 1936 onwards when socialism was handed over the liberal Anglicans, Red Duchesses and all the parasites of an ill-conceived and worse practised 'popular front of all progressive forces'. This honesty comes through in the poems of John Cornford, who joined the party in the third period, and seems to have been one of its most uncompromising supporters. In *Keep Culture out of Cambridge*, he surveys the undergraduate fashions in literature and art and ends:

> There's none of these fashions have come to stay,
> And there's nobody here got time to play.
> All we've brought are our party cards
> Which are no bloody good for your bloody charades.[63]

Notes

1 *Daily Worker* (hereafter cited as, *D.W.*) 1 January 1930.
2 D.W. *ibid.*
3 J. Degras (1956), *The Communist International: 1919–43 Documents Vol II*, Oxford University Press, 485.
4 *D.W. op. cit.*
5 *D.W. IBID.*
6 J. Degras, *op cit*, 455–7.
7 Losovsky, quoted in R. Martin (1969), *Communism and the British Trade Unions*, Oxford University Press, 109.
8 *D.W.*, 20 June 1931.
9 R. Martin, *op cit*, 113–21 *passim.*
10 R. Martin, *ibid*, 121.
11 H. Dewar (1976), *Communist Politics in Britain: The CPGB from its Origins to the Second World War*, London (1976), 102.
12 See for example, M. Johnson (1976), 'Trotsky and World Revolution', *Cognito*, 9 'Trotsky's criticisms of the line of the International were essentially correct'.
13 R. Martin, *op cit.* 102.
14 Membership figures from *Communist Review*, August 1932.
15 Quoted in H. Dewar, *op cit*, 26.
16 J. Cornford 'Full Moon at Tierz; Before the Storming of Huesca' in R. Skelton (ed) *Poetry of the 1930s*, Penguin, Harmondsworth, 137–9.
17 B. Dark (1952), *The Communist Technique in Britain*, Penguin, Harmondsworth, 87.
18 E. Trory (1974), *Between the Wars*, Brighton 50.
19 P. Nettl, (1965), 'The German Social Democratic Party 1890–1914 as a Political Model', *Past and Present* Vol.30, 94.

20 J. Degras *op cit*, 432.
21 *World News and Views*, 6 April 1939.
22 *D.W.* 1 January 1930.
23 *D.W.* 4 January 1930.
24 *D.W.* 7 January 1930.
25 D.W. *ibid.*
26 *D.W.* 24 January 1930.
27 *D.W.* 28 April 1930.
28 *D.W.* 15 April 1930.
29 *D.W.* 24 April 1930.
30 *D.W.* 15 April 1930.
31 *D.W.* 12 April 1930.
32 *D.W.* 2 January 1930.
33 P. Stansky and W. Abrahams (1966), *Journey to the Frontier, Julian Bell and John Cornford: their lives and the 1930s*, London, 197.
34 E. Upward (1977), *The Rotten Elements: Part 2 The Spiral Ascent*, London 306–7.
35 B. Hogenkampf (1976), 'Film and the Workers Movement in Britain, 1929–39' *Sight and Sound*, Spring 1976, 69–76; *D.W.* 8 April 1936.
36 Quoted in P. Stansky and W. Abrahams, *op cit*, 191.
37 'RES: Eva Reckitt', *History Workshop Journal* No.2, 238–9; D. Goodway (1977), 'Charles Lahr: Anarchist, Bookseller, Publisher', *London Magazine*, June/July 1977, 46–55.
38 I. Montague (1970), *The Younger Son: Autobiographical Sketches*, London, 126.
39 P. Stasky and W. Abrahams, *op cit.* 188–200, *passim.*
40 *D.W.*, 5 January 1934.
41 R. Samuels (1977), 'Documents and Texts from the Workers Theatre Movement 1928–36', *History Workshop Journal*, No.4, 103–110.
42 R. Samuels, *ibid.*
43 *D.W.* 4 January 1930.
44 *D.W.*, 20 January 1930.
45 R. Samuel, *op cit.* 130.
46 *D.W.* 24 January 1936.
47 R. Samuel, *op cit,* 125.
48 *Discussion*, March 1938.
49 *D.W.*, 1 January 1930.
50 *D.W.* 11 January 1930.
51 *D.W.*, 28 January 1930.
52 *D.W.*, 8 January 1930.
53 *D.W.*, 6 August 1930.
54 *D.W.* 30 April 1930.
55 E. Upward (1972), 'The Island', in *The Railway Accident and Other Stories*, Penguin, Harmondsworth, 228.
56 *D.W.*, 4 August 1932.
57 *D.W.*, 30 August 1932.
58 A.W. Gillett (1932), *The Student Vanguard*, Vol. I, No.1.
59 *D.W. op. cit.* 30 August 1932.

60 *D.W.* 7 January 1936.
61 *D.W.* 11 January 1936.
62 *D.W.* 31 January 1936.
63 P. Stansky and W. Abrahams, *op cit*. 218.

10 BATTLES FOR THE COUNTRYSIDE
John Lowerson

The idea that rural England was primarily an urban playspace was not new in the 1930s, but the growth of pressure during the decade from a variety of towndwellers' recreations was unparalleled. It has become a truism that nudism and hiking, although rarely practised together, represented the more crankish sidelines of a mass desire for the 'Open Air', whilst suburbia and motor transport were the serious threats to a vaguely defined 'national heritage'. Nudism can be largely discounted, for despite the propaganda of the Gymnic Association and the prestige of the German 'Strength Through Joy' movement, the English climate, atmospheric and moral, kept it as the pursuit of an esoteric and, one suspects, frequently cold minority. But the other leisure developments and their associated controversies brought into relief the strength of continued social inequalities, the subtle ramifications of a sophisticated class society, and sharpened both regional differences and a deep sense of division about the direction and speed of social change. The use of the countryside became a focus for these because it faced an overlapping series of mass incursions for the first time, both in terms of space and use.

A German observation that 'The only great achievement of the English people since the war has been their housebuilding'[1] brought home the scale of the first assault; between the wars the urban area of England and Wales increased by about 26 per cent although the town population only rose by some 15 per cent. New factories, sewage farms and municipal airports contributed to some of this, but the largest single factor was housing; four million dwellings in two decades, a quarter of them as local authority replacements for slums. The impetus for the latter had come from World War I: 'Homes for Heroes' had developed into massive suburban housing estates round most of the large cities, Wythenshawe in Manchester, Kirby in Liverpool, Moulescoomb in Brighton and so on. Internal urban building to replace the cleared slums followed in the 1930s with classic estates like Leeds' Quarry Hill, but the inevitable pattern of local authority building was internal dereliction and 'exurban' sprawl. Becontree, planned for 100,000, spread into Essex: 'Streets of small, sometimes minute, houses monstrously alike stretch for miles, crossing and recrossing at right angles . . . . It is a social experiment on a most prodigious scale. It amounts to the creation of large and medium-sized towns inhabited wholly by the proletariat'.[2]

This working-class migration to the 'country' was rarely

voluntary since higher-cost housing and the planners' notions of desirable residences, not to mention distances from work and relatives, actually made it difficult to attract many established urban families out to live in what could be, even on the largest estates, a frightening isolation, the unnerving quiet of night. The major pressure, the cheerful exodus into a new suburbia, was a dream realized by large numbers of the middle classes, with a wide variety of patterns.

The totality implied in the 'Garden City' produced Welwyn and a number of lesser imitators, breaking with much of the late Victorian and Edwardian experience, but these were far less typical than the agglomeration of smaller private speculations in which reforming purpose was a distinct second to immediate profit. A carefully delimited and controlled 'rural' environment was a much less common 1930s suburban experience than the job-lot of semi-detached building, 'a tangled monotony of ill-planned villadom'.[3] Cheap transport and cheaper finance, as well as 'Romantic' influences produced in many areas a lowest common denominator of design, eating up the countryside at the rate of 60,000 acres a year. Wollaton Park in Nottingham was little different, superficially, from Saltdean or the dreamy streets of Whyteleaf, south of Croydon. Yet even the apparent monotony, the cheap mimicry of the grander Edwardian examples of a revived vernacular, could produce a grudging respect. Osbert Lancaster preferred 'Wimbledon Transitional' to 'By-pass Variegated', 'that insures that the largest possible area of countryside is ruined with the minimum of expense'.[4] But it was a matter of subtleties within class, the latter paling-down of the Wimbledon model could become the white-collar workers' hope. Although this wholesale devastation has become a crime in retrospect, its purchasers were rarely vocal in its defence, a silent army of proud obstinacy, happy in their mediocrity of *rus in urbe*, a mediocrity raised to the level of a positive virtue: 'There may be five thousand suicides a year in Great Britain, but they do not largely occur, as our lugubrious Chelsea authors would suggest, amid the residents of Fauntleroy Park'.[5] The happiness of tennis club and herbaceous border stretched even further with the more prosperous able to escape from suburban dreariness, as they saw it, into the 'real' country: 'Sometimes the word 'weekender' is used in a reproachful sense. But really the man living a simple life in the country will be healthier and happier than the town-stayer. And as he can bring up children superior in every respect to the town child, besides carrying mental activity into what are often uncivilized districts, he is of great social use'.[6]

Fresh air, weekend walks and that most carefully contrived of all rural environments, the golf course, gave the Home Counties' commuter the illusion of minor gentility; for his wife there were the carefully contrived social meetings that Richmal Cromptom pilloried in the *William* books. It was, after all, only a slight downwards extension of a pattern well established before 1914. The mass suburb of half-timbered 'semis' was a threat in terms of size, although it often obliterated land of only marginal agricultural value. More glaring was the clash between the rural and urban posed by one-off ventures and the ambitions of the retired and the 'weekender'. South from Liverpool into the Welsh hills, and along the Sussex and Yorkshire coasts spread shanty towns of bungalows very different from their Victorian models. Converted railway carriages, redundant trams and pink-roofed asbestos shacks (the most hated of all by aesthetes) popped up like excrescences, their cheap incongruity masking the hundreds of individual hopes and patiently saved-for ambitions that made them possible. The archetypical example was Peacehaven on the Sussex Downs, whose population had increased from 400 to over 3, 000 in the first four years of the 1920s during a brilliant but unprincipled speculation; with over seventy-five different types of bungalow available, and its own 'Peacehaven Song', it marked the steady growth of an English 'Costa Geriatrica'.[7] As the caravan camps, the 'Dunrobins' and 'Kia Oras' (the word is Maori for 'Good Health') spread, they represented far more than cheap housing and an urge for a healthy retirement. The social chord which they hit was a nostalgia for a resurrected past, a rediscovery of yeoman roots, a search for a half-remembered countryside, what Raymond Williams so perceptively called '. . . this strange formation in which observation, myth, record and half-history are so deeply entwined'.[8]

Paradoxically, for many people this was the 'real' England and the urge to locate oneself within it was strengthened in the 1930s as never before by a powerful current of 'countryside' literature. By no means uniform in direction, structure or quality it was often submerged in a lowest common denominator of popular books. In many ways the problems of some 1930s' rural novelists such as Adrian Bell were similar to those of Hardy before them: he had found the serious intent of his later fiction distorted by readers' expectations of stories about quaint country folk, expectations which his earlier writing had fostered. That Bell was also a chronicler of deeper tragedies probably went largely unnoticed by many readers except insofar as the implanted notion of rural decline acted as a stimulant both to nostalgia and to an anxiety to overcome alienation from natural roots. Those writers who broke away from the strong tradition of yokel caricature only served to deepen expectations of, and affection for, a countryside seen and smelled through train, bus and car window. Stella Gibbons' *Cold Comfort Farm* of 1932 may have drowned the vogue for the 'drearier back to the land school'[9] and the whimsy custumals of Mary Webb's *Precious Bane* in a welter of ridicule, but did little to stop the wholesale production of works in the 'Beautiful England' (i.e. the non-industrial, non-urban) mould, or even to prevent the widespread misreading of such balanced works as Flora Thompson's *Lark Rise*.[10]

Cheap photogravure brought to many local newspapers and magazines the fruits of a debased school of photographic landscape pictorialism as contrived as many later Victorian sub-'Merrie England' steel engravings. These, and the style of some publications, fostered a bitty and soft-centred approach to rural life, as distinct from living. Whereas *Country Life* and *The Field* continued to treat both sport and housing with seriousness, the newer journals often produced a hotch-potch in which some sharp observations on contemporary agricultural problems were lost in a crowd of articles on topics such as 'Bird-watching by car and telescope'[11] and 'Disappearing Crafts'. The best-known of these, the quarterly *Countryman*, was produced from Idbury in Oxfordshire by J. Robertson Scott, beginning in 1927. Scott occupied an important place in the rural defensive tradition to be discussed below, after the publication in 1925 of his *England's Green and Pleasant Land*. As the anonymous *Times Literary Supplement* reviewer pointed out, the loudest praise for this caricature of new middle-class country dwellers had come from urban middle-class sources; yet Scott's points about the preservation of an alternative culture were driven home sharply: 'There is no particular virtue in leaving London to live in a cottage, a farmhouse or a manor. Those who make the mistake of doing so, when outer suburbia, or a garden suburb, or one of those remoter be-villaed villages within an hour's season ticket ride out of town, would have served them much better are seldom at their most virtuous'.[12]

How sharp had become the notion that the townsman, the weekender, was not necessarily the angel of culture. But the 'something for everyone' nature of the *Countryman*'s articles, and those of its late 1930s' contemporary *The Yorkshire Dalesman*, undermined the serious intent of its founder and played on the distorted urban vision in such a way as to spread the process of spoliation it had emerged to resist. Complaints about the lack of adequate protection against urban intrusion appeared side by side with the indefatigable Master of Sempill's series on the 'Country House Aeroplane', advertisements for the speculative developments at East Dean, Sussex: 'Retire to the South Downs for leisured living

. . . a beautiful rural settlement surrounded by twenty-three square miles of permanently preserved country',[13] and paeans of praise for the life that really mattered:

> In the country, recreation is recreation. You make up your spiritual losses whenever you have time to 'stand and stare'. Half the tragedy of unemployment is due to the urbanised minds of the unemployed. The establishment of 'recreational centres' — which is recognised as an outstanding need — is far more elaborate and costly than it should be because the happy countryman's means of recreation are not understood and can with difficulty be brought home to the urban dweller.[14]

The fact that the average country dweller did not enjoy urban leisure patterns because he was too isolated and poorly paid to be able to reach them, was glossed over in this paternalistic distortion of the vision of William Morris. In the flood of writings that turned the countryside into an extra-urban service centre, the hardness of agricultural economics was replaced with a series of surface images that distanced the viewer by their very selectivity as he came closer to the landscape itself.

Publishers, latching on to a booming market, reinforced this with the surge of guidebooks and topographies which poured out in the 1930s. Even Tom Stephenson, the Ramblers' Rights campaigner, produced an encylopaedic *Countryside Companion* in 1939 for Odhams, the most prolific publisher of cheap, heavily illustrated books:

> To become a wayfaring man on a July day, when the air is fragrant with the scents of summer, is no difficult task. In the valley the pale green-gold of the freshly mowed fields makes a mosaic pattern against the pasture land and the grain fields. At the noonday hour the brown men who have toiled on the land since early morning rest in the shade of the elms.
>
> Down the ancient pack-horse track blackberry flowers give promise to fruit in autumn and convolvulus loops white bells over the hedges.[15]

Paul Beard's *English Byways*, Roland Wild's *Southshire Pilgrimage*, Clare Cameron's *Green Fields of England*[16] and the cheap reprints of the older *Highways and Byways* series were only a few of the massive output of the decade. Within the same tradition, but distinctly superior in quality and expectation were John Betjeman's *Shell Guides*, the first of which appeared in 1934, Dent's new *Open Air Library* series of 1932, and the Batsford books in the *British Heritage* and *Face of England* series. The latter found distinguished writers such as H.J. Massingham and were plentifully illustrated with superb photographs, but even they distorted in much the same way as their poorer relations.[17] The end product was to increase pressure on the countryside they wrote so vigorously to protect; the ideal photographs, well-lit by spring and summer sun, were a tourist's picture. Despite the real concern of editors and writers to provide an instructed appreciation of the countryside, many of the warts were missing from the final composite portrait.

There were two particularly strong examples of the treatment of rural society as an untidy museum of the quaint, in which the rigorous appreciation of the Batsford volumes was replaced with a ragbag of the arcane, the antiquarian and the picturesque. Arthur Mee's 'didactic and longwinded' *The King's England*, a many-volumed survey of 10, 000 towns and villages, appeared in 1936 and 1937, a boon to the nostalgic wanderer. But even this was outshone, or rather outweighed, by the outpourings of S.P.B. Mais, a middle-brow and very prolific writer and broadcaster of the 'commonsense' school. Apart from his other works Mais produced twenty-three 'guidebooks' between 1930 and 1940: *England of the Windmills, Southern Rambles for Londoners, This Unknown Island* and *England's Character* reflect the names and subject types. *The Times Literary Supplement* review of the latter probably encapsulates the nature of Mais's achievement:

> The author has talked to bus conductors, auctioneers, countrymen and townsmen and has recorded their conversation, which is not very illuminating. Indeed, the chief significance of these contacts is possibly the emphasis that they lay on the fact that the Englishman does not readily reveal himself to strangers . . . very little insight into the subject as a whole can be gained in the course of hurried journeys by omnibus and train and short visits to ancient buildings.[18]

Yet it was these 'hurried journeys' that the consumers of guidebooks wanted, a rural England of hurried glimpses with actual contact usually limited to visiting churches and patronizing a growing cream-tea industry. The writers formed part of a widespread supportive network for the rapid growth of automobile production: with motorists' maps and pre-packaged route cards they created a sense of exploring the 'byways', which was in itself a growing exercise in collective self-delusion, a countryside which was a succession of interesting views.

Car ownership was a socially limited phenomenon, but its sharp rise accompanying the 50 per cent fall in nominal prices between 1924 and 1936 saw a 500 per cent increase in vehicle production over the same period, most of which was fed into the domestic market. Ownership and pride in a marque identity was provided by 'one brand' magazines which turned increasingly to the delights of the leisure use of cars after instructing owners in the problems of simple maintenance; for the owner of the 'modern magic carpet': 'The pretty villages, the old farmsteads, besides numberless quaint features to be found in our old towns, all reach out from those bygone centuries and captivate us with their reminiscences of ancient peace.'.[19]

The very banality of the appeal, the erection of a cardboard rural façade for urban consumption were best represented in the *Morris Owner*, the glossiest and longest-running of this new breed. Coupled with a growing nationalism in the 1930s, aiming to boost the home-holiday industry, it linked up with free cinema shows ('See Our Beautiful England') to create a sense of heritage where only a hazy perception had previously existed; in many ways, the whole genre of this writing was a watered-down and distinctly liberal version of the much stronger rediscovery of folk vernaculars elsewhere in contemporary Europe. With organizations like Trust Houses Ltd, formed in the 1920s to convert old country pubs into tasteful roadhouses, the motoring press combined to produce a sense of an unchanging and accessible, but nonetheless distant, English countryside that would provide refreshment for the retired suburbanite, with an underlying 'folk' appeal linked to a growing chauvinism. The car and bus became devices for travel in time as well as space. Paradoxically, the descent on the countryside produced another, very defensive urban response.

'Everything slick and streamlined, everything made out of something else. Celluloid, rubber, chromium-steel everywhere, arc-lamps blazing all night, glass roofs over your head, radios all playing the same tune, no vegetation left, everything cemented over, mock turtles grazing under neutral fruit trees'[20] In fact, the nightmare landscape of many 1930s writers was not Orwell's, with the hateful modernism of the International Style of architecture, and Le Corbusier's *Ville Radieuse* turned into Lang's *Metropolis* or Korda's *The Shape of Things to Come*, but the new suburbanized countryside of the jerry-builder and the filling-station proprietor; the vernacular and the organic crushed beneath a mass of bungalows and choked arterial roads, with electricity pylons marching across beauty spots in the service of a clean domesticity. It would be easy to caricature the self-important and vague aestheticism implicit in Betjeman's 1938 poem, 'Slough', but the growing horror at the rape of the landscape revealed an essential dichotomy about the uses of the countryside by an urban society. It was much easier for many of the critics to decry what was wrong than to formulate an adequate response for development; for many 'preservation' of a newly-realized amenity was easier than an understanding of the individual and economic forces which produced the blights in their lines of vision. The attack on unsightly village garages and mock-Tudor tea shoppes often concealed a contempt for the economic opportunism which had prompted their owners. Few rural people were, or could afford to be, as concerned with trimness and neatness as those to whom their villages had become a solace.

The protection of this 'disappearing heritage' was already well established by 1930. The Society for Checking the Abuses of Public Advertising (SCAPA) was founded in 1863; the Commons and Footpaths Preservation Society (CFPS) in 1865; William Morris's 'Anti-Scrape', the Society for the Protection of Ancient Buildings in 1877; and Octavia Hill, Canon Barnett and others had formed the National Trust in 1895. But the devastation of the early 1920s revealed their limits; the next decade produced a number of *ad hoc* groups, but also a number of attempts to provide both an overall co-ordination of amenity bodies along with a regeneration and re-education of rural people, which would bring them more closely into line with an urban conception of how they should behave. Prime amongst them was the Council for the Preservation of Rural England, founded in 1925, and followed closely by local associations and the spread of the Rural Community Council movement. The latter had a chequered history, trying with the Women's Institutes and Workers' Educational Association to regenerate enough 'community spirit' through a village hall movement to halt a continued drift into the towns. Some of the attempts were bizarre; in Sussex, one of the first tasks suggested for the new Rural Community Council was the preparation of a gourmet map of the area. The key figure in the CPRE was Patrick Abercrombie, England's first Professor of Town Planning, from the University of Liverpool. As was the case with many of his associates, Abercrombie's vision was primarily architectural, strongly influenced by the idea of an evolving but controlled vernacular, not too distant from the school of 'Progressive Historicism' which was sweeping through Germany as the reaction to post-Bauhaus theories of environmental engineering.[21] The English movement was rarely distorted with the racialism that developed abroad as Nazism took control of it; but it contained, nevertheless, a powerful component of folk-myth, largely composed of an extended model of the Cotswold-Jurassic yeoman village. Abercrombie and his leading disciple, Thomas Sharp, were imbued with the idea of an overall rural/urban balance, but many of their followers lacked the breadth of vision that this required, and became mere preservationists. Abercrombie was particularly impressed with the new 'garden suburb' mining towns being built in South Yorkshire and Nottinghamshire (he should see them now!), when opposed to the horrors of the speculator: 'A single bungalow roof with pink, artificial tiles, a factory chimney at a focal point, or a glaring advertisement is able at a stroke to destroy the composed beauty of such a landscape'.[22]

The balance of much of the English countryside, which was the accidental product of centuries of speculation and individualism, was submerged in the idea of organic and gradually developing relationships between buildings and environment. Abercrombie and a number of others were greatly influenced by the doctrine of *Feng Shui*, a Chinese code of aesthetics and the balance of elements that was more flexible than the rigid classicalism of the Golden Mean, but still imbued with the necessity of each vista's providing a satisfactory and harmonious composition. His pamphlet, *The Preservation of Rural England*, was the first of many. In 1928 appeared *England and the Octopus* by Abercrombie's eccentric friend, Clough Williams-Ellis; in two portions, it combined a powerful diatribe on the destruction of England with a 'Devil's Dictionary. Containing some specific Complaints, Warnings and Proposals'. Apart from a timely warning about archaeologists, 'These, like elephants, are generally useful, but sometimes extremely dangerous',[23] Ellis's alphabet was an indictment of most new features of the 1920s' countryside: aerodromes, petrol pumps, golf courses and the universities were each guilty of rape. The major difficulty with this style of argument was that, although it undoubtedly brought home many of the problems to readers, and with amusement, it was easier to attack the new developments than to be precise about the desired aesthetic alternative. By instructing people in existing horrors and pointing them to the beauties of the past, it was hoped that a spiritual revival could be started. Inevitably, this could only appear as the studied poses of an effete minority anxious to clamp down on hard-earned pleasures of 'ordinary' people.

The movement's pattern of Fabian permeation had predictably limited results in the legislation of the 1930s. The Town Planning Act of 1932 and the Ribbon Act of 1935 were gestures in the direction of this new balance, but lacked teeth, and were more expressive of a Victorian conception of permissive restriction than of the emergent doctrine of progressive control.[24] In terms of saving pieces of the countryside from wholesale spoilage, some individual local authorities proved far more effective. Eastbourne Town Council bought Beachy Head in 1926 to prevent the erection of a coastal chain of bungalows; but the best known was the creation of a Green Belt of 35, 500 acres in the London and Home Counties Act of 1938. Faced with widespread indifference, rather than concerted hostility, and the vital need for urban growth implicit in much piecemeal development when the regional economic emphasis shifted to the

Midlands and the South, the reforming groups turned to preserving pieces of countryside more visually rewarding than most. In the growing demand for National Parks, many of the tensions between established landed property rights, individual exploitation of leisure time, and the discordant voices of the amenity bodies became most apparent. CPRE pressure had led the government to establish a National Parks Committee in 1929, but its report had been lost in the financial and ministerial crises of 1931. One major problem that did not face the models on which the English proposals were based, such as Yellowstone in the USA, was that there were practically no absolute wilderness areas in the United Kingdom, where even the most desolate moorland was normally used for intensively capitalized leisure. The English tourist had to fit in with sport and farming as well as the wild country; control and designation would be necessary if 'a rapid extension among the mass of the people of a, love of wild nature and a desire to visit and take exercise in beautiful and unspoilt country'[25] was not to be counter-productive. A National Park would go beyond meeting local needs and so a central policy would be inevitable. Three obvious areas presented themselves: Snowdonia, Lakeland and the Peak District, the last by far the most controversial as we shall see. Parts of the coastline might follow. When successive governments failed to implement the 1931 report, the CPRE set up a Standing Committee for National Parks as a watchdog and mouthpiece. What it demanded repeatedly was a central policy and the co-ordination of local authorities, demands which met major stumbling blocks in a decade when Westminster and Whitehall staggered repeatedly from policy to half-implementation. Persistently though the case was put, it ran aground on the implications of a national policy, which was linked inevitably with possibilities of the nationalization of land. Attacks came from other directions as well, not least from landowners worried about forest fires, damage to game and to indigenous wildlife: 'There is only one reason that I can think of in favour of the Park. It might become an attraction for holidaymakers and keep some of them away from the grouse moors and deer forests in August and September. But I doubt if this plea is one which a Park advocate would rate very highly'.[26] It was left to the Forestry Commission to make a first hesitant step in 1938, with a Forest Park at Ardgarten in Scotland; a much more substantial demand and favourable political environment was needed before England got National Parks.

The strong voices and fissiparous weaknesses of the amenity movement became obvious in 1937 with the publication of *Britain and the Beast*, edited by Clough Williams-Ellis. Cast within a liberal mode of informing public opinion it showed the preoccupation of many of its twenty-six contributors with minority attitudes and manifested a strong sense of paternalism. Some were pro-nationalization, others cried for the awakened public responsibility of landowners, almost all were élitist: 'There are still some of us with a little pride who would sooner be dead in Bath than in Bognor Regis!'[27] C.E.M. Joad, the author of a *Ramblers' Charter*, wanted educated townsmen, while Sheila Kaye-Smith deplored the mercenary attitudes of many landowners and farmers who saw building bungalows as one way out of their problems. Only A.G. Street put up a significant defence of the right of the countryman to his own, the harmless native misled and abused by rude townspeople; in the company in which he was writing, it was a hopeless plea. As one reviewer pointed out, the contributors were an unlikely collection, so that their coming together was all the more remarkable.[28] But whilst the CPRE demonstrated its indignation and the aesthetes puffed out their jeremiads, there were more urgent pressures. It was the basic question of access to the countryside on foot that produced the sharpest dichotomies.

I'm Happy When I'm Hiking, a popular group song of the early 1930s, represented a significant shift away from the older, more socially exclusive use of open spaces; the cliquish respectability of the Victorian gentleman's passion for mountaineering. 'Hiking' and 'Rambling' became a mass activity during the decade, often with few of the overtones of the pre-war model of the German *Wandervogel* movement. Some estimates put the number of regular country walkers in the 1930s at over 500,000 with some 10,000 in the Derbyshire Peak of a summer weekend. A mass working-class activity, it resulted in a series of open clashes between the defenders of 'traditional' rights of property on the one hand, and the assertive proponents of a different tradition on the other. It produced a conflict over the use of land unmatched since some of the protests against the alienation of common rights by eighteenth-century Parliamentary enclosures, although the beginnings were muted enough.

Walking in the countryside became easier in the later 1920s with cheap rail and bus fares and a small rise in real wages, at least among skilled and white-collar workers. But the outpouring to the hills hardly justifies taking it as a sign of prosperity, despite the recent claims of some historians who appear to have treated it as entirely outside the grim urban context from which it sprang. Paradoxically, one of the cheapest of all recreations did acquire equipment and facilities provided by a new leisure industry: tents, rucksacks, shorts and boots; but these only heightened the contrasts between different social groups pursuing the sport. Camping, an accompaniment of the more prosperous new nomads, remained largely a pursuit of road-users anxious to cut hotel bills and to meet 'real' country people, although often as quaint specimens: 'Do not put on superior airs when talking with farm or other country folk. They are far from being "simple". Don't be annoyed if they show natural curiosity as to your camping arrangements. There is often little else for them to be interested in'.[29]

The internal contradictions of such counsel should be obvious. Few of the new countryside users were actually so well equipped as to arouse rural curiosity, but they often caused considerable antagonism, particularly as hikers took increasingly to the fields and woods to avoid the lethal traffic on the roads which had once served many Edwardian walking tours. What emerged was a distinct regional pattern of walking activities — and of reaction to them — which favoured the prosperous of the South. It had long been relatively easy for the suburbanite to get out into the country for a weekend ramble. The Chilterns, like the North and South Downs, were criss-crossed with a network of ancient tracks and footpaths easily accessible from railway stations, and, more importantly, of little economic value to local landowners. Rambling (purists tended to use 'hiking' for more purposeful trips) posed little real threat to the sheep pastures of the south and its practitioners evinced a respect for established codes of property, which made them generally acceptable. Linked with churches and chapels or respectable political groups, the small parties posed little threat to marginal land, and even the wholesale exploitation of rambling by the Great Western and Southern Railways produced little adverse response. When a midnight excursion was organized (by the ubiquitous S.P.B. Mais) to see the sun rise over Sussex's Chanctonbury Ring in 1932 the response was staggering; 16,000 people turned out, and four special trains were necessary, although the sun was hidden by clouds in the event. Groups of 800 were typical on similar ventures for the rest of the decade. At odds though such pilgrimages were with the notion of an individual communion with Nature, they struck powerful chords and possibly removed some of the frightening isolation of the countryside for some of the participants.

By contrast the experience of many Northerners was restrictive and painful. What had become a relatively gentle, often externally-organized weekend activity in the South, became a popular crusade in Lancashire and Yorkshire, upheld by a fierce local spirit of co-operation and a sense of a desperate need to escape from urban prisons that the much-vaunted prosperity of the 1930s was doing little to open. For the suburbanite, a ramble was the logical extension of his rural-dream fulfilment; but for many inhabitants of Manchester and Sheffield it offered virtually the only hope of some form of self-discovery. Many industrial towns sat within a tantalus of moorland, easily visible from their centres, yet often unreachable because of a concerted refusal by landowners to allow access. Notions of older patterns of rural escape remained strong within the urban oral culture and were re-inforced in many instances by a sense of wrongly alienated traditional rights. The railway boom which had fostered the continued Victorian growth of many Northern towns had contributed also to the erection of a *cordon sanitaire* of increasingly restrictive property rights around them as the moorlands became the playground of the *nouveaux riches*, and the *battue* replaced the occasional gentleman with a shotgun. The opening of the season, 12 August, was also the peak time for urban recreation, since the moors were unusable by all but the most hardy and well-equipped for much of the year. The poverty of the Victorian legacy of urban parkland and its very formal restrictiveness made bigger urban lungs a vital necessity; many Northern working-class children were still rickety, pigeon-chested and stunted; they compared very badly with their richer contemporaries and, equally importantly, with the carefully fostered images of a radiantly healthy Nordic youth abroad. The sharpness of social and physical contrasts was rarely more clearly expressed than in the annual photographs of one great act of philanthropy, the Duke of York's Summer Camp for boys. Surrounding the Duke, later George VI, and his public school helpers, there stood boys of the same age as the latter, but four or five inches shorter, with large gaps in their front teeth, generally looking a good ten years older.[30] Despite the value of outdoor recreation as an antidote to this, surprisingly none of the critics of urban squalor — such as Hutt and Rowntree — gave it any mention.[31] Some commentators undoubtedly saw middle-class organized sport and excursions as a half-gesture, a refusal to take problems seriously to their roots. Such views had considerable substance, but pointed also to a split in supporting access, to strong reservations protracted until after World War II.

A strong initial impetus to the movement came from organized bodies; but their very patterns of organization imposed major restrictions on their effectiveness. Possibly the greatest achievement of the outdoors associations during the 1930s was their creation of a sense of institutionalized respectability for activities all too readily seen as subversive. The Holiday Fellowship and the Co-operative Holidays Association were the oldest and most restrained, dating from before World War I. With non-conformist and co-operative roots, their main aim was to provide cheap and wholesome accommodation on the edge of the wilder Welsh and English areas, to attract young men and families away from the cheap and lurid commercialism of Blackpool and Morecambe during Wakes Week.[32] By the late 1920s they offered nearly thirty guest houses in England, and a growing number abroad. Users of these rose from 12, 000 in 1926 to 41, 000 a decade later; for around £2 a week, they provided a rather more spartan and purposeful version of the all-in escapism Butlins began to offer in 1937.[33] The links with older, artisan, secular mutuality groups such as the Workers' Educational Association was strong, most obviously in the annual series of weekend schools at some of the centres, including in 1933 G.D.H. Cole on 'Economics', Arthur Greenwood on 'The Use of Leisure in the New Age', and, inevitably, C.E.M. Joad on a large number of issues. One steady component of the annual pattern was the provision through a special fund of free holidays for 'the distressed areas', although the criteria of eligibility and selection were left unstated.

Helping the deserving unfortunate was a minor feature of another 1930s organization with similar roots in working-class improvements, the Youth Hostels Association (YHA). Based loosely upon the idea of a teacher in pre-war Germany, Richard Shurrman, it came into being in 1929; the Liverpool and District Ramblers' Federation founded a Merseyside Youth Hostels Association which was soon submerged in a national body. By 1931 it had established seven hostels in North Wales for a few hundred members; a year later it had 150 hostels for over 20, 000. From the first, it attracted powerful support from established authorities, with substantial financial aid from the Carnegie Trust. Almost in the same category came the £100 gift from the Workers' Travel Association, the Labour Party's answer to the non-political Holiday Fellowship. The Archbishop of York and successive Prime Ministers sent messages of support; G.M. Trevelyan became the first president. The overlap of officers with other bodies such as the National Trust and the CPRE meant that the YHA would take a controlled and cautious view of the implications of mass rambling, seeing it as yet another in the long series aimed at the channelling of the energies of a potentially troublesome urban proletariat.

For 1/- a night basic accommodation was provided at the hostels, bunk beds avoiding the promiscuous overtones of the continental *matratzenlager*. It remained a regional federation, strongest in the North, but nationally established from 1932 by a quarterly journal, *YHA Rucksack*. From early 1933 it was making attempts to break into the limbo of unemployment, although with a paternalism that reduced its appeal. Four parties were organized for the Pilgrim Way, hardly a strenuous route, with free accommodation; but the expectation was that the participants would give 1/7d a day out of their dole money towards food, apparently to avoid the stigma of charity. Recruits were drawn from the Occupation Centres, Wal Hannington's 'Slave Camps'[34]: 'All the men who enrol for these trips will undergo a special training to fit them for this unaccustomed exertion'.[35] Takers were, not surprisingly, few. The YHA provided, nonetheless, a substantial service for those willing to be regimented, and able to afford the cumulative costs of equipment ('good walking shoes' at 17/6), transport and accommodation. It also provided a modest official voice in the controversy over access to moorland: but its role was invariably constitutional. The location of its early hostels in Snowdonia and the Lake District reiterated the fact that its facilities could only attract those who could afford the time and money to make the longer trips in the wake of Edwardian plutocrats seeking country repose.[36] To reach the areas immediately surrounding the industrial cities the day rambler needed another voice.

It came in 1932 with the National Council of Ramblers' Federations, later called the Ramblers' Association; overlapping with the YHA, the National League of Hikers and the Pedestrians' Association, its voice was more sharply militant and it provided an umbrella for a range of smaller groups which preferred direct action to committee voices. The early issues of its journal, *Rambling*, spoke in the modest tones of Patrick Abercrombie and Sir Lawrence Chubb, the secretary of CFPS; but when Edwin Royce, the President of the Manchester and District Ramblers' Association, became editor in 1935, a much more forthright attack on what he regarded as half-hearted deferent gestures in the direction of landowners emerged: 'There is something wantonly perverse and profane in a society in which the rights of property can be used to defeat the emotions in which mankind had found its chief inspiration and comfort — the right to climb the mountains, the right to dream beside the sea'.[37]

Royce poured out a series of attacks on 'the modern Forsytes', 'plutocrats' and 'molochs', and the half-hearted attempts of the YHA, Sir Lawrence Chubb and the élitist Fell and Rock Climbing Club, for their refusals to face up to basic problems. He dismissed their concern with the tidy footpaths of the Southern counties and their vague dreams of National Parks in areas too distant for them to be of any value to those who needed them most. The real goals of a spiritual communion with the wilderness were blocked by class property rights: the hills outside Sheffield and Manchester should be more than mirages. The whole range of issues came to focus on one area, Kinder Scout in Derbyshire, and on one piece of legislation, the

Access to Mountains Bill.

Much of the land on the high plateau of Kinder belonged to the Duke of Devonshire whose keepers jealously guarded the grouse. In addition the land around Bleaklow was owned by Sheffield Corporation, which barred its own ratepayers on the grounds that they would disturb the grouse for which the moor was let profitably, and possibly contaminate the reservoirs into which the bogs drained. Although there were paths around both areas, the stark beauties of the High Peak were closed to those who arguably needed them most. A National Trust estate at Longshaw had been opened for the public with no sign of damage, but the example failed to persuade other landowners; the 1930s saw the stepping-up of a struggle which had already raged for over half a century: much of the debate centred on interpretations of the law of trespass and of rights of common. There was a long history of individual trespass on to the shooting preserves, often with little interference from keepers; but the question assumed a new significance with the onset of mass hiking and the emergence of a number of ramblers' organizations increasingly disaffected from what was regarded as the pussyfooting of bodies like the YHA. Manchester and Sheffield had a number of groups linked with labour organizations, the *Sheffield Clarion*, ILP Guild of Youth and the *Onward*, as well as bodies such as the Woodcraft Folk with its overtones of Teutonic nature mysticism; though small individually, they claimed to speak for some 10, 000 walkers who wanted to use the local hills on summer weekends.[38] Their individual power was limited to a war of skirmishes with keepers, but took on new direction in 1932 under the aegis of the Communist-inspired British Workers' Sports Federation (BWSF) which had fifteen branches in Lancashire and two in Sheffield.[39] A foray onto Bleaklow from one of their camps in 1931 had been turned back by keepers: so the response was to organize the first of the 'mass trespasses' in the following year. Whilst a number of non-political clubs associated themselves with the projects, some dropped out when the apparent illegality of the new stage became apparent. The subsequent events dramatized the circumscribed plight of urban walkers, but revealed within the movement a dichotomy over what was regarded as suitable behaviour; they also produced myths and martyrs with reputations barely justified by the scale of what took place, but which paradoxically re-inforced the determination to seek constitutional settlements among the more conservative leaders.

On the morning of Sunday, 24 April 1932 Benny Rothman, the secretary of the Lancashire BWSF, led a group of between 150 and 600 ramblers (accounts vary) up to Kinder Scout from the village of Hayfield. It was brilliantly stage-managed; he had contacted the

'The landowners have met in a friendly and accommodating spirit the proposal for freer access to mountains and moorlands, but they have naturally wished to make sure that this is combined with a reasonable safeguarding of the interests of property'.[42] The key was 'freer' rather than 'free' access, but it was a valuable means of defusing the potential bomb of the aggrieved and desperate Northern unemployed (not that they ever were). But there were even more pressing reasons for the reluctant grace with which landowners changed their policies. The image of the strong-limbed, suntanned hiker contrasted sharply with the pasty faces of most townsmen in a society limbering up for a major war. When the government put £2 million aside for a Physical Fitness Programme in 1938, the way to an Access Bill lay open.

It was still not popular with the government, nor with *The Times*: 'Nothing is easier than to paint a picture of the glorious open spaces of moorland and forest being denied to the youth of the nation in the selfish interests of sport, of hostile landlords with their vigilant minions, of locked gates and barbed wire fences. Yet normally nothing could be further from the truth . . . . Exceptional cases are easily magnified into a general grievance'.[43]

Throughout its pages and those of other journals stalked two contrasting spectres: 'A mob of young men and women — hatless, raucous, yellow-jerseyed, slung with concertinas,'[44] contrasted with the 'genuine' rambler, cast in the mould of the solitary late Victorian artisan naturalist, studious, interested in birds and flowers, deferent and, most importantly, sticking to well-marked footpaths rather than wandering into the midst of a *battue*.

The Field ('shooting is jolly good fun'[45]) was in a quandary. It had come to recognise the need to escape from a 'brickbound existence' and the functional values of hiking; a widespread ability to read maps for instance, would have undoubted wartime use. But it saw a gloomy price as the result: widespread unemployment in the shooting industry, a sharp drop in rural rateable values, the destruction of indigenous wild life, and a massive spread of moorland fires. Yet it gave a grudging support to the Bill on its introduction in November 1938 by the Labour MP for Shipley, Creech Jones. It was a moderate measure — much weaker than its predecessors — yet still strong enough to be toned down considerably during the Committee stage where substantial modification of the trespass clauses, rather than open destruction, was used to remove the sting. The only openly expressed Parliamentary opposition came from a member who deplored the likelihood of hapless Prime Ministers being pursued across the moors by hordes of photographers during every grouse season; it

actually became the fate of the unfortunate Harold Macmillan. The Home Office's attempt to effect its rejection on the grounds that it would prejudice existing negotiations on footpath rights was ignored.[46] Amended, it passed the Lords on the grounds that it would both provide teeth against the trespasser, and heal social divisions: 'When I see those who champion the rights of health-seeking pedestrians, and those who represent the landowning community, clasping hands in your Lordship's House with a view to a happy arrangement between both those classes of the community, the sight brings joy to my heart'.[47] The peers' mutual congratulation hid the fact that the measure was largely emasculated. Access could only be declared at the behest of the Ministry of Agriculture, which was more concerned with impending war; it took post-war exertion to reach an acceptable solution, without, however, the need for militant action. However disappointed the pioneers of 1932 felt with their immediate result, they could congratulate themselves on bringing the extent of the deprivation into the open, and on making some reversal of the separation from a real, rather than an imagined, countryside which industralization had begun.

On to a hazy folk memory, the decade had grafted a strange and florid growth reflecting a thirst for the rural. Whether in the products of whimsical antiquarians, or in the much more studied, and biting works of authors like Adrian Bell, the inherited sense of removal and decay was poignantly re-inforced. Only a few could work out the full significance of this, for most writers, and even more for their readers, the countryside had become a symbol of some vague mirage of 'real' life. The growing political uncertainty and the grind of depression made the search for hazily imagined roots even stronger, and the desperation at its destruction or annexation even more intense. The peak of this was the terrible journey into bleakness of George Orwell's George Bowling, the sedentary hero of *Coming Up For Air*, blocked repeatedly by the sprawl of the Thames valley and the sense that the waste of human society was overwhelming it. For the tormented Orwell, there was no escape, not even into the countryside; it was no accidental whim that the suburban's favourite retreat, Burnham Beeches, should be bugged by the secret police in *Nineteen Eighty-four*. But more revealing than the author's own despair was the feeling that had driven George Bowling on his quest in the first place. For many similarly frustrated in the 1930s, the drive was equally intense, but their nostalgia could, with an effort and some imagination, be gratified both in their reading and travels.

Manchester Evening News beforehand and reporters and photographers were on hand. After a 'mass rally' in the village at which they were exhorted to demand open access, low fares, non-militarism in rambling groups, cheap catering, and the removal of restrictions on open-air singing, they marched to the top, to be met there by a group of eight keepers, backed up by temporary wardens. The pushing and shoving that followed saw only a few open fights; then they left. As they returned to Hayfield singing revolutionary songs, five of the 'ringleaders' were arrested and charged with violence and causing grievous bodily harm to one of the keepers. One of these, a Manchester University student called A.W. Gillett, admitted later to a 'tactical mistake' in confronting the keepers. All five were subsequently imprisoned at the assizes for from two to six months. What the demonstration outlined was a clear distinction between rambling Radicals, committed to activity within the law, and rambling Revolutionaries, bent on an extension of the class war. The Radicals, in the shape of the Ramblers' Association, were as quick as their Victorian political predecessors to use the threats of such activity, whilst deploring its necessity and outcome.

The Kinder episodes revealed a growing ambivalence amongst previous supporters of the conservative response: the initial shock and horror gave way to an approach that was at least reflective, if not enthusiastic: ' "Hiking" in moorland country at certain seasons of the year may be harmless and even to be encouraged, but what would be the effect of fifty hikers in open order searching a moor, say, for white heather on the Twelfth of August?'[40] The source was that bastion of shooting rights, *The Field*, which took to printing pictures of occasional bands of cheerful walkers, 'The England that is', as if to reassure its readers that they were not really harmful; they certainly appeared a great deal happier than *The Field*'s more common run of pictures, of the wealthy performing their prescribed social rituals.

The 'Wild Scenes on Kinder' were the first in a series of 'mass' attempts to break through cordons onto the moorland, although no subsequent incident attracted either such violence or such an adverse reaction. On 18 September 1932, 200 Sheffield ramblers began a march from the Middlewood tram terminus to the Duke of Norfolk's road, an ancient trackway claimed as a traditional right of way, though closed by the Howards a century earlier. Despite a skirmish with keepers and perspiring policemen, the ramblers withdrew in good order, and the police refrained from arrests, mindful of the risk of creating more martyrs to such an unlikely cause. Plans for similar demonstrations on Stanage and Froggatt Edge were called off, possibly because the more orderly majority doubted the value of being used by BWSF activists as well as the risk of police action. But group and individual trespass went on, to produce eloquent demands for access. The best of these, and the most poignant, was a 1/6d pamphlet by Phil Barnes of Sheffield, *Trespassers Will be Prosecuted; Views of the Forbidden Moorlands of the Peak District*. Superbly illustrated with photographs snatched whilst trespassing, it revealed a barren beauty that might as well have been as far away as Tibet, itself a growing interest in 1930s exploration writing; it revealed also the extent of deprivation, in that only 764 of the 84, 000 acres of the Peakland were open to the public.[41]

Barnes was quick to point out that, even given the opportunity, few would venture on to the higher ground; what was needed was a safe access for the majority and freedom for a very small minority. After the demonstrations and open confrontation, there came a return to the central issue of legalized access; but it can be fairly claimed that the events of 1932 brought the issues into an arena of public debate in a way in which the subdued deference of the established organizations never had. An Access to Mountains Bill had been first introduced privately in 1888 by James Bryce of Aberdeen, as an attack on American millionaires in Scotland, but it had been thrown out by successive governments. In 1931 Ellen Wilkinson made the fourth attempt since 1924 to re-introduce it, only to be defeated at the hands of Ramsay MacDonald; it was thrown out again in 1932 as a vicious and bolshevik attack on the rights of private property. 10, 000 ramblers demonstrated at Winnats Pass, near Castleton, over the 1932 measure, to be interrupted by a red banner-waving contingent calling for mass invasion rather than legislation; even C.E.M. Joad, whose reaction to ramblers was not entirely consistent, called for taking the law into their own hands. But legalism and respectability won, since the constitutional Federations invariably saw the problem in terms of the individual and small groups rather than as a question of mass proletarian liberation. The response of either faction was that of an élitist minority.

The incensed Left used the Access Bill as a stick to beat both the renegade Ramsay Macdonald and to harass the sleepy Baldwin. A successful Footpaths Act in 1934 had more effect on Southern commons than in the North. But events were to overtake the demand. With their long tradition of careful adaptation to changing pressures, and the prompting of an awakening social conscience, many landowners came to agreements with local walkers to allow limited and controlled access, preserving both paternalism and the rentable values of their moors. In 1936 Sheffield Corporation finally gave way and allowed its citizens onto the land owned in their name:

Notes

1 K. Silex (1931), *John Bull at Home*, 39.
2 K. Silex, *ibid*, 42–3.
3 I. Brown (1935), *The Heart of England*, 67. There is a growing appreciative, indeed almost nostalgic, literature of suburbia reflected in recent works such as D. Thorns (1972), *Suburbia*. A.A. Jackson (1973), *Semi-detached London*, and G. Darley (1975), *Villages of Vision*.
4 O. Lancaster (1938), *Pillar to Post*, 81.
5 I. Brown (1935), *The Heart of England*, 72.
6 G. Allen (1919), *The Cheap Cottage and Small House*, 6–8.
7 For a splendid description of this, see P. Dickens (1975), 'A Disgusting Blot on the Landscape', *New Society*, 17 July 1975.
8 R. Williams (1973), *The Country and the City*, 261.
9 See the review of Stella Gibbons' work in *The Times Literary Supplement*, 8 September 1932, 622.
10 Arguably one of the most important 'country books' written in this century, Flora Thompson's *Lark Rise*, (1939) is one of those widest open to being glossed with the quaint.
11 The title of an article by Dr F.S. Crowther Smith, in *The Countryman*, (Idbury), January 1936, 499–500.
12 J. Robertson Scott (1925), *England's Green and Pleasant Land*, 47 and the review in *The Times Literary Supplement*, 19 November 1925, 771.
13 *The Countryman*, July 1937, 698.
14 W. Beech Thomas (1938), 'Why I Live in the Country', *The Countryman*, Vol.XI, no.I, 88–90.
15 H. Read, 'A Countryman's Diary', in Tom Stephenson (1939), *The Countryside Companion*, 292 ff.
16 P. Beard (1936), *English Byways*; R. Wild (1939), *Southshire Pilgrimage*; C. Cameron (1930), *Green Fields of England* constitute a tiny handful of the decade's outpourings. *The Times Literary Supplement* 'Summer Reading Supplement', 15 July 1939 named seventeen similar works alone and it is clearly apparent to any browser in a secondhand bookshop that the number of similar works was legion.
17 See, for example, H.J. Massingham (1936), *English Downland* or Edmund Vale (1937), *North Country*. There is a discussion of Massingham in W.J. Keith (1975), *The Rural Tradition*, Harvester Press, Hassocks, chapter 12, which puts him in a line leading back to Cobbett and Izaak Walton but isolated him effectively from his contemporaries. It should be compared with the different approach to a similar theme in G. Cavaliero (1977), *The Rural Tradition in the English Novel*, 1900–1939, especially 10ff.
18 *The Times Literary Supplement*, 30 January 1937, 79. The list of Mais' writings is based on a straight count of his publications listed in the British Library's *Catalogue of Printed Books*.
19 Morris Motors Ltd (1926), *The Morris Owner's Road Book*, Oxford, 8.

20 G. Orwell (1939), *Coming Up for Air*, Secker & Warburg, London, 27.
21 See the discussion of this in B. Miller Lane (1968), *Architecture and Politics in Germany, 1918–1945*, Harvard University Press, particularly Chapter 5.
22 P. Abercrombie (1926), *The Preservation of Rural England*, 16.
23 C. Williams-Ellis, *England and the Octopus*, 131.
24 See P. Hall (1974), *Urban and Regional Planning*, Chapter 2. For a few of the contemporary reactions in a largely one-sided pamphlet war, see V. Cornish (1932), *The Scenery of England* CPRE, London, CPRE (1932), *The Threat to the Peak*, CPRE Sheffield and CPRE Lancashire Branch, (n.d.) *Posters and the Public.*
25 The Standing Committee on National Parks (1938), *The Case for National Parks*, 3.
26 An article by Lord Latymer in *The Countryman*, July 1939, 581 ff.
27 C. Williams-Ellis (ed) (1937), *Britain and The Beast*, xviii.
28 *The Times Literary Supplement*, 12 June 1937, 433.
29 C.F. Carr (1931), *The Complete Hiker and Camper*, 119.
30 *The Field*, 13 August 1932.
31 See, for example, A. Hutt (1933) *The Condition of the Working Class in Britain* and B.S. Rowntree (1937), *The Human Needs of Labour.* Presumably, any concentration on open air activities might have reduced the power of such attacks on the slums, giving a superficial appearance of growing prosperity. Certainly in J. Stevens and C. Cook (1977) *The Slump*, 26, the authors have written of hiking as if it were this rather than a desperate attampt to escape from urban depression; to simplify the complex gradations within a mass activity is not a convincing form of argument.
32 The moving spirit in the Holiday Fellowship had been a young Congregationalist Minister, T.A. Leonard. See Ramblers' Association (1948), *In Memory of T. Arthur Leonard, 1864–1948*, 3.
33 The figures in the following paragraph are based on the *Annual Reports* of the Holiday Fellowship, held by the British Library.
34 See W. Hannington (1937), *The Problem of the Depressed Areas*, Chapter 7.
35 *Y.H.A. Rucksack*, Vol.2, Spring 1933.
36 See O. Westall (ed.) (1976), *Windermere in the Nineteenth Century*, Lancaster, for a discussion of the earlier trends.
37 *Rambling*: *The Journal of the National Council of Ramblers' Federations*, Vol.1, June 1933: Royce was apparently quoting from the *Manchester Guardian*.
38 There is a considerable pamphlet literature on this, much of it held in the unique collection of the Frows of Manchester. I am particularly grateful to Helen Walker for drawing my attention to this and for her advice on the significance of the Kinder demonstrations.
39 Based on a claim in the *Manchester Evening News*, 18 April 1932. The events of Kinder and their sequel were very well covered in both the national and local press, with predictable variations. Gillett's account appeared in *The Student Vanguard*, Vol.1, No.1, November 1932, 15

ff. A recent account, D. Cook (1977), 'The Battle for Kinder Scout', *Marxism Today*, August 1977, 241–243, gives a reasonably detailed outline of the campaign and a refreshing contribution to the movement's hagiography. See Howard Hill (1980), *Freedom to Roam*, Moorland Publishing: this book appeared after the present study was in the press. Its interesting (if disjointed) account of a whole century's struggle for access to moor and mountain is accompanied by fine and original photographs.

40 *The Field*, 7 May 1932, 689.

41 P. Barnes (1934), *Trespassers Will be Prosecuted: Views of the Forbidden Moorlands of the Peak District*, Sheffield.

42 *The Times*, 21 February 1939.

43 *The Times*, 7 March 1939.

44 *The Times, ibid.*

45 *The Field*, 21 January 1939, 128.

46 Hansard's *Parliamentary Debates, (Commons)*, Vol. 342, col. 817ff.

47 Hansard's *Parliamentary Debates (Lords)*, Vol.112, col.989.

Index

Index

Acknowledgements:

May I thank the many individuals and institutions for the ready assistance and graceful permission to use their resources and to reproduce their material:
Edmund Frow, Working Class Movement Library, Manchester; Mrs Phil Barnes ('Trespassers Will Be Prosecuted' picture); Batsford Books ('Old Village, New Suburb'); British Library (Colindale Newspaper Library); The Field ('Happy Hikers' picture); H.M.S.O. (Southampton); Manchester City Library; Sheffield Central Library; South Yorkshire Times (Kinder Scout photograph); Tom Harrisson Mass Observation Archive, University of Sussex.

Cover pictures:
H.M.S.O. Ordnance Survey map, early 1930s; advertisement for *The Shape of Things to Come* (Alexander Korda, 1935); and Erich Salomon's picture of Stanley Baldwin and J. Ramsay MacDonald, September 1931, printed in *The Graphic*. (Caption: 'Pool their Brains and also their Popularity'.)

Frank Gloversmith